COLUMBIA PICTURES

COLUMBIA PICTURES

Portrait of a Studio

BERNARD F. DICK
Editor

THE UNIVERSITY PRESS OF KENTUCKY

Copyright © 1992 by The University Press of Kentucky

Scholarly publisher for the Commonwealth,
serving Bellarmine College, Berea College, Centre
College of Kentucky, Eastern Kentucky University,
The Filson Club, Georgetown College, Kentucky
Historical Society, Kentucky State University,
Morehead State University, Murray State University,
Northern Kentucky University, Transylvania University,
University of Kentucky, University of Louisville,
and Western Kentucky University.

Editorial and Sales Offices: Lexington, Kentucky 40508-4008

Library of Congress Cataloging-in-Publication Data

Columbia Pictures : portrait of a studio / Bernard F. Dick, editor.
    p.   cm.
    Filmography: p.
    Includes bibliographical references (p.) and index.
    ISBN 0-8131-1769-0
    1. Columbia Pictures—History. I. Dick, Bernard F.
PN1999.C57C64   1991
384'.8'06579497—dc20   91-13459

For Peter Kells and Lynne Larsen

CONTENTS

Illustrations follow page 86

PREFACE

If one were writing the history of a publishing house, it would be a chronicle of founders and successors, personalities and policies, takeovers and mergers, and finally survival or extinction. Naturally, writers would be included, but only as part of the history, not for themselves or their art. One could easily write a critical study of Hemingway's fiction without mentioning Scribner's except, perhaps, for purposes of citation. Yet no history of Scribner's would be complete without mention of Hemingway, who would appear as one of its authors but not as the center of attention. In fact, Hemingway would even be eclipsed by Scribner's editors, particularly Maxwell Perkins and John Hall Wheelock.

A movie studio is similar to a publishing house in the sense that its films can be, and generally are, studied independently of the company that made them. The analogy, however, is imperfect. While films are to a studio what books are to a publishing house, the "product," to use a favorite Hollywood expression that only appears in the singular, is different in each case. Hemingway's *To Have and Have Not* (1937) can stand by itself without anyone's invoking the name of Scribner's; it would still be *To Have and Have Not* if it were published elsewhere. Yet no two studios would film Hemingway's novel the same way; and even if the same studio made the film twice, each version would be different. Warners made *To Have and Have Not* twice, once in 1944 under the original title, and again in 1950 as *The Breaking Point*. Each is unlike the other because each had different writers, stars, directors, and cinematographers. If MGM had attempted to film the novel in 1944 and 1950, the results would have been different still, since MGM had its own writers, stars, directors, and cinematographers. Many more factors, decisions, and, above all, people are involved in the making of a movie than in the production of a book. For one thing, a book is authored. But who is the author of a film? Those accustomed to thinking in terms of the print media would say, "the screenwriter." The screenplay, however, is only one aspect of the complex process known as moviemaking; another is the film's relation to the studio or production company that made it. While studio history cannot explain a film's artistic merit, it can explain the circumstances that made such art possible.

Traditionally, histories of the studios fall into three categories: the foundation-to-extinction (or transformation) type, the studio head biography, and the coffee table book, lavishly illustrated with a still and a synopsis of each film. The last kind, represented by Crown's "story" series (*The MGM Story*, *The Universal Story*, and so on), at least acknowledges the dual nature of studio history. There is the studio and there are its films; each has its "story," but the studio's is "history."

Hence, the dual format of *Columbia Pictures: Portrait of a Studio*: a history of the studio followed by previously unpublished essays by film scholars representing a variety of fields (literature, American studies, communications, film, foreign languages) and applying different methodologies to Columbia's stars, directors, writers, genres, and, of course, films.

Like Columbia's history, its art is best understood in chronological form. Therefore, to complement the first part of the book, the second continues the chronological approach so that, read in sequence, the essays provide an overview of the studio from the late 1920's, when Frank Capra arrived there and gave it a status it previously lacked, to the late 1980s, when *The Last Emperor* won nine Oscars, one in each of the categories in which it had been nominated.

On a technical note, for the sake of consistency, "Warners" refers to Warner Bros., the studio, while "Warner" refers to Warner Communications, whose filmed entertainment division includes Warner Bros. The semantic problem has been complicated by the Time-Warner Communications merger of 1989.

If films need interpreters, so do their studios. This is the rationale of this book.

In addition to the authors whose contributions appear in Part II, I have also drawn on the knowledge, good will, and friendship of Robert Blees; Mary Corliss, of the Museum of Modern Art's Film Stills Archive; Sam Gill, archivist, the Margaret Herrick Library of the Academy of Motion Picture Arts and Sciences; Kristine Krueger, National Film Information Service; Mary Ann La Falce, media technician, Fairleigh Dickinson University (Teaneck Campus); Mary MacMahon, periodicals librarian, Fairleigh Dickinson University (Teaneck Campus); Alan Press, manager of product research, Columbia Pictures Entertainment Film and Tape Facility; my wife, Katherine M. Restaino, dean of St. Peter's College at Englewood Cliffs; Irwin Rosenfeld, associate director of Negative Control and Archival Services, Columbia Pictures Entertainment Film and Tape Facility; and Daniel Taradash.

PART I

The History of Columbia
1920-1991

FROM THE BROTHERS COHN TO SONY CORP.

BERNARD F. DICK

Film historians distinguish between the Big Five (MGM, Warners, Paramount, Twentieth Century-Fox, and RKO) and the Little Three (Universal, Columbia, and United Artists), the eight motion picture companies that provided the bulk of the movies made during Hollywood's heyday—the "studio years," which ran roughly from the mid-1920's through the 1950s. Certainly Columbia was not on a par with MGM; it could neither boast, as MGM did, of "more stars than there are in the heavens," nor lay claim to MGM's title, "The Tiffany of Studios." Columbia also had no theater chain; although the absence of one proved a blessing in the late 1940s, when studios with theater circuits were ordered to divest themselves of them, it also meant that Columbia had no guaranteed outlet for its films. In this respect, Columbia was like Universal; neither was vertically integrated.

Columbia and Universal are similar in another sense. Although each made its share of classics, each evokes less than classic associations. Universal will always be remembered as the studio that gave the world Abbott and Costello, Frankenstein's monster, the Mummy, Dracula, and the Wolf Man, rather than *All Quiet on the Western Front* (1930), *My Man Godfrey* (1936), and *Shadow of a Doubt* (1943). Columbia also made films that were as important as those of any studio—Frank Capra's best movies, *His Girl Friday* (1940), *The Lady from Shanghai* (1948), *On the Waterfront* (1954), to name only a few—yet it will always be identified with two names that have become synonymous with uncouthness: the Three Stooges and Harry Cohn, dubbed "His Crudeness" by none other than Frank Capra.

Columbia was created in the image of Harry Cohn (1891-1958), its cofounder, who was also the studio's president from 1932 until his death. While Cohn is numbered among the movie czars who "invented" Hollywood,[1] it might be more accurate to say that he invented himself and imposed that self on his studio. The inventor was an anomaly: obscene and well-spoken, anti-intellectual and uncannily perceptive, heartless and compassionate. Columbia is equally bipolar.

The other studios of Hollywood's Golden Age are easy to characterize. Warners was the proletarian studio that made viewers socially conscious, whether they were watching films about chain gangs, upwardly mobile gangsters, or gum-chewing hoofers. MGM flattered its audiences by ennobling the bourgeois lifestyle; if Emma Bovary had seen MGM movies, she would never have taken her life. While MGM was high gloss, Fox was highbrow; its screen versions of *The Grapes of Wrath* (1940), *How Green Was My Valley* (1941), and *Jane Eyre* (1944) were literature tailored for the screen, designed for the discerning—or at least those aspiring to be.

But what was Columbia's specialty? Three Stooges shorts? Blondie movies? Rita Hayworth musicals? Or perhaps *It Happened One Night* (1934), *Mr. Smith Goes to Washington* (1939), *All the King's Men* (1949), *From Here to Eternity* (1953)? Confronted with a studio matching test, film students would have no difficulty pairing MGM with "home of the stars," Universal with "horror and low comedy," Republic with "westerns and serials," and Warners with "social consciousness and gangster movies." But if a student were debating whether to match Monogram with "Poverty Row," and Columbia with "series films," or vice versa, and decided Monogram belonged with "series films" and Columbia with "Poverty Row," only a pedant would mark the student wrong. Monogram was a Poverty Row studio that was known for its series (Charlie Chan, the Bowery Boys). Columbia, which had several popular series (Blondie, Boston Blackie, Crime Doctor, the Whistler), originated on Poverty Row.

Columbia, in fact, originated in the center of Poverty Row, a section of Sunset Boulevard between Beachwood Drive and Gower Street in West Los Angeles. Poverty Row was the home of the storefront studios that ground out the movies shown in the theaters of side-street America or on the lower half of double bills. The corner of Gower and Sunset, "Gower Gulch," was a favorite meeting place for cowboy actors looking for jobs in Poverty Row productions. Since "Poverty Row" was a label slapped on other studios (for example, Republic) that were not even near Gower Gulch, it really designates a style of moviemaking that ceased with the coming of television when the "B" movie tradition left the screen for the tube, depriving Poverty Row of its raison d'être. Thus it is unfair to include Columbia under the Poverty Row rubric, yet film historians have done so. Clearly it is a case of guilt by location.

Although Columbia was within walking distance of Marathon Street, where Paramount was (and still is) located, there was a significant difference between the two studios. Paramount may not have had MGM's heaven of stars, but it did have an impressive constellation.

During the 1930s Paramount's roster included directors such as Josef von Sternberg, Rouben Mamoulian, and Ernst Lubitsch (famed for his touch), and performers on the order of Marlene Dietrich, Ruth Chatterton, Fredric March, Mae West, and W.C. Fields. Columbia had Frank Capra and, at the beginning, three cramped soundstages. While Bette Davis, Spencer Tracy, and Clark Gable each made a movie at Columbia in the 1930s, they eventually became associated with other studios: Davis with Warners, Tracy and Gable with MGM. While Columbia did not repudiate the contract policy (Rita Hayworth, Glenn Ford, Evelyn Keyes, and Larry Parks, among others, were Columbia contract players), it preferred loan-outs, freelancers, defectors from the majors who were dissatisfied with their material and hoping for a change of image, and onetime "names" whose marquee value had not completely vanished. Columbia may not have had a stock company à la Warners, but it did score a coup in 1933 that gave the scoffers, who referred to the studio as the "germ of the ocean" and the "gem of commotion," pause: Columbia's *The Bitter Tea of General Yen*, directed by Frank Capra, was the first movie to be shown at Radio City Music Hall.

Columbia did not leave Gower Street until 1972, but before it did, it had produced some of the world's most honored films; it also, of course, made its share of schlock—but then, so did all the studios, including the Tiffany of Culver City.

The move from Poverty Row to world class was not a direct one; it was circuitous, and the journey lacks a final destination because the trip began with an open ticket. Columbia has lasted while Monogram, Republic, and RKO have not;[2] it could easily have stayed Poverty Row in spirit and product, going the way of Monogram and Republic. That Columbia remained on Poverty Row for half a century but was not "Poverty Row" is a tribute to Jack and Harry Cohn.

While the Cohns knew privation, they did not know poverty. William Fox, whose studio merged with Twentieth Century Pictures to form Twentieth Century-Fox, could point to his useless right arm and attribute it to his parents' inability to pay for surgery when he broke it. Louis Mayer could admit to having been a junk dealer; Sam Goldwyn, to having walked from Warsaw to Hamburg. If the Cohns had at least been born on the Lower East Side, it would have compensated for their not coming from a *shtetl*. But the Cohns came from Manhattan's Upper East Side, the home of assimilated Jews and German Jewish barons who spoke German, not Yiddish.

Harry's initiation into moviemaking did not come from an early realization of film's importance or a magical afternoon at the nickelodeon. He did not buy a theater, unlike Louis Mayer, whose initial purchase led to a second and eventually from exhibition to production. It was Jack Cohn who introduced his younger brother to the new medium. Jack recognized film's potential long before Harry. In 1902, when Jack was working for the Hampton Advertising Agency, he met Joe Brandt, later to become one of the trio that brought Columbia into existence. Although Jack tried to persuade Brandt to enter the fledgling movie business with him, Brandt was more interested in pursuing a law degree at New York University—an institution that would provide Columbia with many of its top executives. Jack, who never even completed high school, had less lofty aspirations. In 1908, he left Hampton for Carl Laemmle's IMP (the Independent Moving Picture Company), shortly to be known as Universal, where he started as an assistant to the lab manager, C.A. "Doc" Willat. Around the same time, Brandt became disenchanted with law and also joined IMP, as Laemmle's secretary.

Soon Jack became a cutter and, in 1912, was instrumental in creating Universal's newsreel, *The Animated Weekly*. As a cutter, Jack reached a conclusion that all filmmakers eventually reach: while films may not be made in the cutting room, they can be improved there. Jack excelled at editing films, especially in reducing them from ten reels to six, as he did with *Traffic in Souls* (1913), Universal's first feature-length movie.

Initially, Harry was uninterested in the "flickers"—"show biz" was more to his taste. Accordingly, in 1912 Harry teamed up with composer Harry Ruby in an act called "Edwards and Ruby" (Harry being "Edwards") that played nickelodeons. In his own way Harry was making history, since there is a connection between vaudeville and film.[3] Between 1896 and 1906, films were shown mainly in vaudeville theaters; movies were considered "chasers," designed to clear the auditorium between the acts. Soon the opposite occurred—vaudeville waned and movies captured the public's fancy. When the demand for movies exceeded the supply, vaudeville acts were added to stretch out the bill. Sing-alongs were common, with song lyrics written on slides projected onto the screen. It was in this type of venue that Edwards and Ruby performed, Ruby playing the piano, and Edwards singing from the slides.

In 1912 the age of the nickelodeon, barely a decade (1905-1914), was ending, along with Harry Cohn's contribution to its twilight. Thus Harry switched from singer to song-plugger. In 1912 song-pluggers were expected to ply their trade not just in the usual places—theaters, restaurants, ratskellers—but on the street, at bike races and parades, and in dance halls and five-and-ten-cent stores. Harry's experience in leading sing-alongs in nickelodeons stood him in good stead; in his new job he was expected to do the same.

Harry's song-plugging career was almost as brief as his vaudeville stint. Impressed by the success of *Traffic in Souls* (and no doubt envious of his brother's growing reputation in the industry), Harry took a job with IMP as a "travelling exhib," supplying movie houses throughout the country with prints of the film his brother had edited (which was really an exploitation film). Harry was meant to be more than the movies' Willy Loman. Gradually, he was moving closer to his brother's world. Just as Jack conceived the idea of news-on-film for *The Animated Weekly*, Harry was inspired to do the same for popular song. Harry managed to sell Laemmle on the idea of making a musical series with lyrics on film instead of on slides. He was so successful that Laemmle made him his secretary, or, to be more accurate, his administrative assistant. In the movie business, as elsewhere, there are secretaries and secretaries. Laemmle's executive secretary was Joe Brandt; his confidential secretary, Irving Thalberg. That Laemmle should have had three secretaries two of whom cofounded a studio and another of whom determined a studio's style (as Thalberg did at MGM) is a mark not so much of Laemmle's perceptiveness as of the nature of an industry where what seems to be chance is often the result of connections— who knows whom: Jack Cohn's association with Laemmle landed Harry a job at Universal; Henrietta Thalberg's childhood friendship with Laemmle's wife started her son on a career that ended, far too soon, with his becoming one of the greatest production heads in Hollywood history.

Harry Cohn would also become a legend, as would Jack to a lesser degree. After more than a decade at Universal, Jack became restless; he was eager to form his own company. So too was Brandt, who had advanced from executive secretary to the head of Universal's serial department. Meanwhile, Harry had a plan of his own. Because of the popularity of two-reel comedies, Harry conceived the idea of a two-reeler based on the Hall Room Boys, a vaudeville act that derived from a comic strip. In 1919, the Cohns formed Hall Room Boys Photoplays, Inc., produced by the National Film Corporation of America, of which Joe Brandt was general representative. The next stage of Columbia's evolution was inevitable: in 1920 the Cohns and Brandt formed the CBC Film Sales Company. "CBC" was both ironic and prophetic: one Brandt flanked by two Cohns. Within little more than a decade, there would be no Brandt and two Cohns at opposite ends of the country in a business relationship as polarized as their personal one.

At first CBC was a distributor of shorts such as the Hall Room Boys; the one-reel Screen Snapshots, which lasted until 1956 and showed audiences another side of Hollywood—the stars at home and at play; and the two-reel Star Ranch Westerns. When CBC started producing features it was another matter: the studio had to go forward or fold. Shorts would still be important when CBC was reconstituted as Columbia, but they could never be the sole product. Nor could a studio afford a name that lent itself to parody; within the industry CBC was considered an acronym for "corned beef and cabbage."

When the "Short Subjects Kings," as the Cohns were dubbed, decided to found a real studio, they had to find another means of distributing their films as well as a name for the new company. As it happened, one led to another. CBC distributed through states' rights: independent distributors bought territorial rights to films for which they charged exhibitors a flat fee or a percentage. States' rights distribution was hardly the ideal, since it meant sharing profits with the film exchanges. Thus in 1924, CBC began establishing its own exchanges, the first of which was called Columbia. Apparently Columbia also seemed a catchy name for a studio; it was certainly as high-sounding as Peerless, Tiffany, and Eclair. And so in 1924 CBC ceased to exist and Columbia Pictures was born.[4]

Changing distribution procedures was simple compared to changing an image. While CBC could rent space, Columbia had to own it. Yet Columbia's home was literally around the block—on Gower Street, close to CBC's Poverty Row roots. Originally the home was "a dreadful . . . stucco affair consisting of offices along Gower with stages behind, all the structures being pressed together along a couple narrow private streets within the overall maze."[5]

A home needs a head. While a studio has a head, the head is rarely the president but the vice president in charge of production. While Louis Mayer's name will always be synonymous with MGM, he was never president. MGM had no president, since it was a subsidiary of Loew's, Inc. At the beginning, Columbia conformed to the industry model. Joe Brandt was president, Jack Cohn was vice president, sales, and Harry was "Vice President and Director General of Production"— more grandiose than "vice president, production." Harry was thinking big. If he had the chance, he would be something Louis Mayer never was: president *and* head of production.

The opportunity came in 1932 when Jack, disturbed by what he considered extravagance, tried to depose Harry, who proved immovable. As a result, Brandt, tired of being caught in the brothers' crossfire, relinquished his position, which Harry quickly assumed in addition to purchasing Brandt's share of the studio. Jack then became executive vice president, a position he would hold for the rest of his life. Although Harry was now president and production head, he could not act unilaterally. Jack, as head of the New York office, controlled the purse strings, and all studio heads, even those who were presidents, had to contend with New York.

Despite Harry's consolidation of power, Columbia remained a corporate family that was partly natural (the Cohn brothers) and partly created (executives and their kin). Together, they formed a macrocosm/

microcosm, the latter working within the former, to make Columbia Hollywood's gem rather than germ. The Cohn macrocosm parodied the usual West Coast (production)/East Coast (distribution) paradigm. The distance separating Harry and Jack was not merely geographical. While the moviemaking West Coast had always been at loggerheads with the money-minded East, in Columbia's case, the bicoastal tension was rooted in something deeper: fraternal rivalry and radically opposite viewpoints. Jack could no more understand Harry's temperament than Harry could understand his brother's. To Harry, New York was something to be tyrannized, especially since its head had tried to topple him. Since Harry had to defer to New York in matters of marketing, distribution, and in many instances, casting (New York had the ear of the exhibitors, who had the ear of the public), he could only vent his anger at Jack, whose office prevented Harry's having total control of Columbia.

It was impossible to bridge the abyss between the brothers or change their ways; they functioned on energy generated by tension and friction that, happily for Columbia, proved to be creative, although it was emotionally draining for Jack. What finally mattered was not whether the West or the East coast won on such matters as movie titles, advertising, or budget, but whether the studio was thriving. Harry Cohn's Columbia was a patriarchy comprised of fathers and sons, brothers and brothers-in-law; it may not have been a happy patriarchy, but at least it never had to worry about extinction as long as the principle of succession operated, as it did during the Briskin-Schneider-Jaffe years.

Samuel Briskin's association with the Cohns began when Columbia was still CBC. Although Briskin left the studio periodically to take other jobs, he always returned to his roots. Between 1920 and 1968, when he died, Briskin progressed from accountant to vice president in charge of West Coast operations (1958), a post he relinquished three years later to become board member and vice president of the newly formed Columbia Pictures Industries.

Abraham Schneider, Briskin's brother-in-law, began at Columbia two years later—in 1922, retiring three weeks short of his seventieth birthday. Schneider, who also started as an accountant, assumed the presidency of Columbia after Harry Cohn's death in 1958. All three of Schneider's sons worked at Columbia in various capacities: Harold as an executive, Bert as an independent producer, and Stanley as president (1970-73) of Columbia Pictures, then a division of Columbia Pictures Industries and a different Columbia from the one his father had known.[6]

Abe Schneider's brother-in-law was Leo Jaffe, who would also spend half a century at Columbia. Jaffe, who began at Columbia as an accountant, too, would also be president of the Columbia that was a division of Columbia Pictures Industries. Before Jaffe's son, Stanley, teamed up with Sherry Lansing to form the profitable Jaffe-Lansing Productions, he was production chief at Columbia in 1976.

While "ruling families" is a recurring phrase in history books, it was more than a phrase at Columbia; it was a fact.

THE 1930s & 1940s

Although the 1930s are synonymous with the Great Depression, Columbia was less affected by it than most studios for two reasons: the lack of a theater chain and Harry Cohn's frugality. While Warners had to worry about a drop in attendance at its theaters, Columbia's main concern was upgrading its product as inexpensively as possible. Harry Cohn's policy of short-term contracts, tight budgets, and limiting directors to one take of a scene for printing and viewing (regardless of how many takes had been shot) proved it was possible to produce art on the cheap.[7] The beginning of the decade saw Columbia moving toward the recognition that would come within five years; films such as *Platinum Blonde* (1931), *American Madness* (1932), and *Man's Castle* (1933) made it evident that Columbia was only on but not of Poverty Row.

As Columbia's films improved, so did its finances. For fiscal 1931 Columbia reported a net profit of $560,292; for fiscal 1932 it was $574,292. In fact, Columbia and MGM were the only studios showing a profit in the early 1930s.

While Harry Cohn could take credit for Columbia's financial health, it was Frank Capra, to a great extent, who gave Columbia stature. Capra, who came to the studio in 1927 and remained there until 1939, became a name that both exhibitors and moviegoers recognized. By 1932, the same year Harry Cohn assumed the presidency of Columbia, exhibitors ranked the studio sixth in consistency of product. Three years later, Columbia was vindicated: at the 1935 Academy Awards presentations, Columbia won a total of seven Oscars: five for *It Happened One Night* and two for *One Night of Love*.

Throughout the decade, Columbia continued to gain in prestige; *You Can't Take It With You* (1938) won Oscars for both Columbia and Capra as Best Picture and Best Director, respectively. *Mr. Smith Goes to Washington* (1939), Columbia's contribution to an *annus mirabilis* that included *Stagecoach*, *Dark Victory*, *Gone with the Wind*, *Beau Geste*, and *The Wizard of Oz*, made film history. To release a movie the year World War II erupted in Europe that admitted there were Americans capable of subverting the democratic process took courage. *Mr. Smith* was not the usual case of Hollywood's balancing the pros and cons to achieve an innocuous neutrality. Perhaps the highest compliment that can be paid to Capra's last film for Columbia is that the French chose it as the final English-language motion picture to be shown before the Nazis imposed a ban on British and American movies.

In 1940, knowing that a world war would diminish foreign grosses, Harry Cohn established certain priorities for Columbia, the result of which was a hierarchy with the "quality film" at the apex and the "series film" at the base. Like any ideal model, Columbia's underwent various changes during the decade. It was fine to push excellence, but there were exhibitors wanting movies to fill out their bills or play separately, depending on the theaters; and no studio, least of all Columbia, could turn out a steady stream of what Cohn termed "AA" movies.

Cohn understood that quality and big budget were not identical; quality could be achieved for as little as $750,000 or as much as $2 million. *Penny Serenade* (1941) cost around $800,000; *A Song to Remember* (1944), over $1.5 million. Of the two, the former was better received; it also had bigger stars—Cary Grant and Irene Dunne—and a major director, George Stevens. The latter had Cornel Wilde and Merle Oberon as Fredric Chopin and George Sand; the director was Charles Vidor. Yet each film represented quality in its own way: *Penny Serenade* in terms of performance and direction, *A Song to Remember* in terms of production.

The Talk of the Town (1942), Stevens's second Columbia film and one of the great social comedies of the period, is an excellent example of the way quality can be achieved without excessive spending. With Capra's departure, Cohn was eager to find a replacement who could make both sentimental comedies and screwball. He managed to lure Stevens to the studio with a three-picture deal and the promise that the director would encounter no interference.

The Talk of the Town was originally budgeted at $750,000, too low for an AA movie with stars of the caliber of Cary Grant, Jean Arthur, and Ronald Colman.[8] It ended up costing $1 million, which was not excessive for a film that runs almost two hours and has more sets (including one of the Supreme Court) than Warners' *Casablanca* (1942), which was budgeted at $878,000, cost around $950,000, runs 102 minutes, and has a less-than-lavish look. The cost of *The Talk of the Town* was minor compared to the $2.5 million RKO spent on *Sinbad the Sailor* (1947) with its pseudo-Arabian Nights decor, or the $2 million Universal wasted on the forgettable *This Love of Ours* (1945). Columbia could afford to spend $1 million on *The Talk of the Town* since, in the early 1940s, only one-tenth of its movies in a given year (four to five films) cost over $500,000. Similarly, two or three could even be made for $100,000 a picture. Most Columbia movies at the time averaged about $250,000. By contrast, the average MGM B movie cost more than $400,000 in 1942.

One reason *The Talk of the Town* cost less than it might have at, say, MGM was the female star's salary. While Grant and Colman received $106,250 and $100,000, respectively, Arthur got $50,000—the same amount Claudette Colbert had been given almost a decade earlier when she agreed to make *It Happened One Night* for Columbia if she got double her Paramount salary (which was then $25,000). Stevens's last Columbia film, *The More the Merrier* (1943), is also a classic and cost even less (about $878,000); yet Arthur again received the same $50,000—along with an Oscar nomination, which implies worth of a different sort. On the other hand, at the same time Arthur was getting Colbert's 1934 salary, Colbert was getting $265,000 for *Since You Went Away* (1944), which cost well over $3 million.

Another reason was the director's salary. While Alfred Hitchcock went from $130,000 for *Saboteur* (1942) at Universal to $300,000 for *Lifeboat* (1944) at Fox, Stevens got Frank Capra's 1935 salary—$100,000 per picture—for each of his three Columbia films.

A quality film at Columbia was not necessarily a star vehicle. Of the *Talk of the Town* trio, Cary Grant was the biggest name, yet he did not dominate the film; the roles were evenly distributed. Since Harry Cohn frowned on long-term contracts, there were relatively few big names at the studio for extended periods of time. There were, however, stars like Grant, Rosalind Russell, and Loretta Young who freelanced and who could be contracted for one or several films. There was also another kind of star, less luminous than the performer but still capable of influencing a moviegoer: the director. Capra made Columbia director-conscious. Thus throughout the 1940s directors such as Wesley Ruggles, John Stahl, Alexander Hall, Charles Vidor, and S. Sylvan Simon were singled out for recognition. For *The Talk of the Town*, George Stevens's name appeared in the same size lettering as the title. In fan magazine ads, the directors' names began to be featured in boldface and large print; this was true even of directors who were not exactly household names. The May 1945 *Screen Romances* contained only one ad for a Columbia movie: *Counter-Attack*, but the director's name, Zoltan Korda, loomed large. By contrast, the ad for RKO's *The Enchanted Cottage* had John Cromwell's name in lightface, which placed him, typographically, in the same category as the supporting cast. Korda's name was even bigger than Vincente Minnelli's in the ad for MGM's *The Clock*.

In Columbia's 1940 hierarchy, the western followed the quality film. If this seems odd, one should remember that Columbia's cowboys included Tim McCoy, Ken Maynard, "Wild Bill" Elliott, and Charles Starrett (who spent almost twenty years at the studio, 1935-1952). Columbia was so aware of the western's popularity that it decided to make its first Technicolor film a western—*The Desperadoes* (1943).

The serial ranked below the western but above the series film. The reason, perhaps, is that Columbia entered the serial market late—in 1937—and was never known for cliffhangers, as Republic and Universal were. Yet the serial market was one Columbia wanted to crack and did so successfully with *The Shadow* (1940), *Batman* (1942), and *Superman* (1948), among others.

The order of the serial and the series was soon reversed; not only did the series films prove popular but some of them—a few Boston Blackies and Whistlers—are recognized as model "B" movies (*Confessions of Boston Blackie* [1941] and *One Mysterious Night* [1944]; *Secret of the Whistler* [1946] and *Mysterious Intruder* [1946]). Series films had the advantage of originating elsewhere. Blondie, the most durable of the series films (1939-1951), started as a Chic Young comic strip. Boston Blackie, the eponymous hero of another long-lived series (1941-49), was a character in Jack Boyle's stories, then the hero of a few silent films, and finally a vehicle for Chester Morris. The Lone Wolf also originated in fiction and then appeared in some early films until Columbia made Louis Joseph Vance's reformed jewel thief, Michael Lanyard, a series character. The Lone Wolf movies had great longevity—1926-1949—although there were frequent gaps, sometimes as much as four years, as new Lanyards came and went (Melvyn Douglas, Francis Lederer, Warren William, Gerald Mohr, and finally Ron Randell). Surprisingly, the Ellery Queens lasted only two years—1940-1942—although the detective was no stranger to the public. There had been earlier Ellery Queen movies, and *The Adventures of Ellery Queen* was a popular radio show. The Whistler and Crime Doctor series also derived from similarly named radio programs.

The 1940s ended with an addition to the Columbia family. While Columbia could boast of having made the first film to play Radio City Music Hall in 1933, it could make an even more impressive, and historically more significant, claim in 1948: it became the first studio to enter the medium of television.

In 1948, Jack Cohn's son, Ralph, wrote a fifty-page rationale that convinced Columbia to gain a foothold in television by creating a subsidiary, Screen Gems, originally the name under which Columbia's short subjects were produced. And so the old Screen Gems became Screen Gems, Inc.[9] For the first two years Screen Gems, Inc. avoided film programming, concentrating instead on commercials. But a movie studio's offspring could not ignore requests for filmed entertainment, particularly in 1951, when more than five million Americans owned television sets. Thus, when Du Pont decided to recreate its radio program *Cavalcade of America* on television, Screen Gems was the logical producer. Then came *Ford Theatre*; series such as *Wild Bill Hickok*, *The Adventures of Rin Tin Tin*, *Father Knows Best*, and *Dennis the Menace* followed. In 1956, Screen Gems proved itself a true scion of Columbia when it started releasing Columbia films to television; around the same time the subsidiary began acquiring television and radio stations. It was expanding so rapidly that shareholders wondered if the child was more successful than the parent.

THE 1950s

1948 was significant for another reason: it was the year the Supreme Court ruled that the vertically integrated studios (Paramount, MGM, Fox, RKO, and Warners) must relinquish their theaters, thereby separating production and distribution from exhibition. This decision, known as the "consent decrees," had far-reaching consequences; in combination with other factors (inflation, the blacklist, television, the erosion of the studio system), it hastened the decline of the industry after World War II.

Although Columbia had no theater chain, it was still affected by the conditions prevailing in postwar America, one of which was the diminution of interest in the movies. Once a powerful symbol of wartime unity, the movies began to play a less dominant role in the lives of Americans. The GI Bill gave education priority over film; recreation became more varied, with competition coming from bowling and miniature golf; and a down payment on a house, even a prefabricated one, took precedence over entertainment. And for families who were still moviegoers, drive-ins, where admission was frequently by the carful, proved cheaper than theaters, many of which were being converted into supermarkets and chain stores.

Then there was television, which irrevocably changed the public's perception of film. Once filmed entertainment (as distinct from "live TV") became available on television, the distinction between theatrical films released to television, filmed television series, filmed television drama, and made-for-TV movies began to blur in the public's mind, so that "movie" no longer meant what it had in previous decades. While the star system was dying out in Hollywood, it was revived on television, where "name" actresses like Loretta Young and Jane Wyman played leads in their own shows. Had these actresses remained in the movies, even assuming they could get parts (Wyman did but they were forgettable), they would be playing parents or grandparents. Even performers who were only moderately successful in Hollywood (Ann Sothern, Lucille Ball, Joan Davis, Jane Wyatt, Robert Young) found their niche in television. Screen Gems was particularly helpful in giving stars past their cinematic prime a second chance on the tube, especially in the *Ford Theatre* dramas. Many of them—Marguerite

Chapman, Janet Blair, George Macready, Gloria Henry—had worked at Columbia.

Screen Gems went beyond providing television with filmed entertainment in the form of series and dramatic shows; it also released Columbia films to television. Although Monogram and Republic had released some of their films to television in 1951, the other studios steadfastly refused. Columbia might have been the first important studio to yield if RKO had not beat it to the punch. Just before 1955 came to an end, RKO announced it had released 740 features and 1,000 short subjects to television. Early in 1956, Columbia issued a similar announcement: it would be releasing 104 pre-1948 films to television through Screen Gems.

Licensing its own films to television was not enough. Two years later Columbia arranged with Universal for a seven-year lease of Universal's pre-1948 backlog (about 600 features) to television, also through Screen Gems. Since the arrangement would make Screen Gems the largest distributor of theatrical films to television, the Justice Department balked, charging a violation of the Sherman Anti-Trust Act. The deal, however, went through: the limited lease and MCA's recent acquisition of about 750 pre-1948 Paramount films weakened the conspiracy charge.

While Screen Gems was thriving, Columbia was going through its usual cycle of peaks and slumps. Buoyed up perhaps by the thought that the "consent decrees" would not affect production, Columbia announced it would release sixty-seven films in 1949, the largest number in its history. Actually, sixty were released, twenty-five of which were outside productions.

The number of such films increased in the 1950s. Columbia always had about ten salaried producers whose job was to find properties for the approval of Cohn and vice president Ben Kahane, who played prime minister to Cohn's king. Beginning in 1950 the situation began to change as more independent producers started coming to the studio. During that decade three major producers arrived at Gower Street: Jerry Wald, Stanley Kramer, and Sam Spiegel. In 1950, when Wald was in his eighteenth year at Warners, Howard Hughes enticed him to RKO. There he and Norman Krasna headed a production company, Wald-Krasna Productions, that was supposed to produce sixty films for Hughes. Only four were ever made. By 1952, Wald, who had had enough of Hughes, received the proverbial unrefusable offer—head of production at Columbia. The offer was not without a hitch; while Sidney Buchman had been assistant head of production between 1942 and 1944, Cohn reserved the title of production head for himself. And as Wald soon discovered, Cohn had no intention of bequeathing it.

Wald would simply be a Columbia producer: hence, his stay at the studio was brief, 1952-1956.

Cohn's deal with Wald included the absorption of Wald-Krasna. His arrangement with Stanley Kramer was more complex: a $25-million contract requiring the Stanley Kramer Company to produce thirty films—six a year— that Columbia would finance and release and whose profits Columbia would share. The arrangement did not prove lucrative, and in the fall of 1954 Columbia terminated its agreement with Kramer. That Kramer's production of *The Caine Mutiny* (1954) was a hit did not matter; it did not compensate for the ten that were not. Still, Columbia had no intention of relinquishing control of these films. When Columbia settled with Kramer, it also acquired the rights to the flops, a few of which (including *The Sniper* [1952] and *Member of the Wedding* [1952]) have claimed the attention of film scholars.

Sam Spiegel, who gave Columbia three of its most prestigious films (*On the Waterfront*, *The Bridge on the River Kwai*, and *Lawrence of Arabia*), had actually come to the studio in 1948 but under a different name, "S.P. Eagle," which had become so transparent that when he finally dropped it at the time of *On the Waterfront*, *Variety* commemorated his rebirth with the classic headline "The Eagle Folds Its Wings." Since everyone in the industry knew "S.P. Eagle's" identity, the headline was an announcement, not a revelation.

Spiegel had reason for adopting a pseudonym. Like most of the moguls, he had Eastern European origins.[10] Born a Galician Jew, he had the most diverse career of any of the movie tycoons; Mayer's junk-dealing and Harry Cohn's song-plugging pale in comparison. Spiegel had been, among other things, a ditch digger, cotton broker, stock promoter, talent scout, translator, felon, and deportee. He was incredibly resilient; after his first deportation in 1930, he returned to the United States via Mexico. This time he could not afford to be deported again, much less to Poland. The year was, after all, 1939. So he assumed the name of "S.P. Eagle" and by 1945 had made enough influential friends so that he could apply for American citizenship as a Polish immigrant.

In 1948, Spiegel and John Huston formed Horizon Pictures, whose first feature, a Columbia release, was distinctly left-wing at a time when the country had moved to the right. *We Were Strangers* (1949) dealt with the 1933 Cuban revolution that brought about the overthrow of the Machado regime. Despite the opening title, Jefferson's "Resistance to tyranny is obedience to God," the film was attacked as Communist propaganda: "a shameful handbook of Marxian dialectics," fumed the *Hollywood Reporter* (22 April 1949). Although the *Daily Worker* took the opposite view, accusing *We Were Strangers* of espousing capitalist values, the movie found favor neither with critics nor with audiences, and Columbia withdrew it after a few months.

Throughout his career, Spiegel was associated with left-wing writers, such as Dalton Trumbo, Carl Foreman, Michael Wilson, and Lillian Hellman, for reasons that had to do more with expediency than with politics. Essentially, Spiegel was as apolitical as Harry Cohn, yet neither quaked as visibly as Jack Warner when the House Committee on Un-American Activities began its investigation of Communist subversion of the movie industry in 1947. To his credit, Harry Cohn never volunteered information, nor was he loose-tongued like Warner, who implicated one of his best writers, Howard Koch. That Koch was not even a Communist mattered little to Warner, although Koch suffered because of Warner's recklessness. One suspects it would have mattered a great deal to Harry Cohn for one reason—Sidney Buchman, whom Cohn regarded as a son and an alter ego, although Buchman was little more than ten years younger than Cohn.

Buchman never denied having been a Communist. Although he left the party in 1945, he was still subpoenaed to appear before HUAC in 1951. His position—that he would talk about himself but would not name names—may well have influenced Lillian Hellman to take a similar stand in 1952. HUAC, however, wanted names, and by a combination of a procedural gaffe on HUAC's part and extraordinary courage on Buchman's, a jail sentence was averted, although a career was damaged.

The witchhunt that began in 1947 and continued throughout the next decade made it impossible for Buchman to remain at Columbia. Cohn, who ignored his writers' politics for the most part, found himself in a bind. In 1952 HUAC accused Columbia of being lax in hiring "persons of questionable loyalty," noting that of the 930 writers who had been on the payroll since 1945, 38 were Communists or fellow travellers. Columbia denied the charge, claiming that the writers had been employed before the blacklist took effect in 1947. Columbia was right; of the Hollywood Ten, five—Herbert Biberman, Edward Dymtryk, John Howard Lawson, Samuel Ornitz, and Dalton Trumbo—had worked at Columbia between 1935 and 1945. But before there were the Hollywood Ten, there were the Hollywood Nineteen, the nineteen unfriendly witnesses that HUAC subpoenaed in 1947. Of these, one had been a Columbia star, Larry Parks, who had appeared in several Columbia films but was best known for his impersonation of Al Jolson in *The Jolson Story* (1946) and *Jolson Sings Again* (1949).

In 1952, when the *Los Angeles Daily News* (4 April 1952) reported that "Columbia has voluntarily and firmly dedicated itself to fighting Communism and those who support or sympathize with it," it was clear that the maverick in Harry Cohn had galloped off.

Harry would not live out the decade. Buchman's departure was the beginning of the inevitable end. In 1954 a thyroid operation on Harry revealed a malignancy; two years later Jack Cohn died. Despite their estrangement, Harry was deeply affected by his brother's death. Unlike most of the moguls, who exceeded their three score and ten, Harry died of heart failure on Thursday, 27 February 1958, at sixty-seven.

To insure continuity, Abe Schneider assumed the presidency, with Leo Jaffe moving up to first vice president and treasurer and Abe Montague becoming executive vice president. Since Columbia would not be Columbia without a Cohn, Ralph became a vice president as well as remaining president of Screen Gems. But the Cohn presence at Columbia would not last much longer: Ralph died suddenly in 1959 at forty-five. While Ralph's brother Robert had joined Columbia's "B" unit after World War II, he was really interested in independent production, forming his own production company in 1960. Thus, for all practical purposes, the Cohn era ended in 1958.

THE 1960s

The 1960s witnessed Columbia's transformation from a studio to a corporation in the true sense of the word: it lived up to its name— Columbia Pictures Corporation. Until Harry Cohn's death the studio took precedence over the corporation; now it was the reverse. Diversification was the key. It was not enough to create a television subsidiary; diversification was not limited to the entertainment sector but extended to real estate—its acquisition and resale. Real estate was a factor when lack of space led to Columbia's purchase of the Burbank ranch in 1935; it was also a factor in 1960 when the property became too large or at least too large for the post-studio era. By 1960 Burbank had five soundstages and many standing sets. Accordingly Columbia sold off thirty-four and a half acres behind the Burbank facility to apartment house developments. The sale was another testimonial to the magic of California real estate: the property, originally purchased at $2,500 an acre, was sold at $50,000 an acre.

Columbia may no longer have been a studio, but it was a survivor. As a new decade began, it could look back at its Poverty Row origins and boast of having outlived PRC and Republic, which ceased to exist in 1946 and 1958, respectively. Columbia also held on to its name, which is more than Monogram did in 1953 when it metamorphosed into Allied Artists, whose films bore little resemblance to the Monogram product. Moreover, Columbia could take pleasure in knowing that RKO, one of the Big Five, had ceased production in 1957, and that Universal, which merged with International Pictures in 1946 to become Universal-International, had been absorbed by Decca Records in 1952 (and would soon become a subsidiary of MCA). It would be two more decades before Columbia became a spoke in Coca-Cola's umbrella.

Nevertheless, Columbia was ripe for a takeover. Wall Street had been keeping tabs on the studio, often despairing of understanding its financial reports. Columbia had always been tight-lipped, so much so that, according to *Daily Variety* (23 August 1966), a story began circulating around Hollywood that Columbia's secretaries would answer the phone by saying "Hello, but don't quote me." The story may have been apocryphal, but it did suggest that the studio had become byzantine as well as secretive.

1966 was a crucial year. Columbia stockholders had never been a passive lot, but this time there were enough dissidents to call for radical change. In the fall of 1966 a takeover scenario began to evolve; the leading players were the Geneva branch of the Banque de Paris et des Pays-Bas and a group of American stockholders, the best known of whom was corporate raider Maurice Clairmont. Whether they were acting in concert or whether theirs was a fortuitous alliance based on mutual dissatisfaction is problematical. On the other hand, few alliances are fortuitous.

For a year, the dissidents had been complaining about Columbia's practice of combining its earnings with those of Screen Gems. There could be only one explanation: Screen Gems' profits offset Columbia's losses. In fact, at the 15 December 1965 meeting, an angry stockholder introduced a resolution that Columbia, which owned about 89 percent of Screen Gems, acquire the rest and merge it with the studio, thus doing away with Columbia Pictures Corporation. Although the resolution was voted down, within three years that is exactly what happened.

The dissidents also noted that Columbia's net earnings for fiscal 1965 had fallen to $2,024,000 (or $1.02 a share) as opposed to $3,154,000 (or $1.62 a share) for the comparable 1964 period. Screen Gems *seemed* to be in the black, however, with twenty programs in prime time in 1965—a 50 percent increase over the previous year; "seemed" because it is difficult to ascertain the truth from consolidated figures. It was fairly evident, though, that the child was supporting the parent. As *Forbes* (15 October 1966) implied, Columbia could go on making flops and still stay afloat because of Screen Gems; whenever the situation became desperate, Columbia could license another movie package to television and thus give the impression of a profit.

Although Wall Street criticized Columbia's "sale" of movies to television, Columbia was not selling them but leasing or licensing them. Leasing was a form of profit and longevity. There is nothing more repellent to a studio head than a studio's liquidation; and if Maurice Clairmont's practices were indicative, the takeover of Columbia would have resulted in liquidation. To a takeover artist, liquidation means profit; to a studio head, liquidation is annihilation. It would be better for the studio to merge with another, change its name, or become a subsidiary of a conglomerate.

If leasing films to television can prevent the demise of a studio, it can also extend the life of its product. With a limited number of revival houses, television was a godsend—a museum for old movies as well as a source of revenue for making new ones. In Columbia's case the parent-offspring relationship was genuine; while the offspring contributed to the parent's support, the parent made the offspring's life easier: Columbia provided Screen Gems with studio space and a pool of talent, including technicians as well as performers and directors. The offspring reciprocated by publicizing the parent: in July 1964 Screen Gems leased sixty pre-1948 Columbia films to fifteen stations—its third such package.

Columbia had discovered that the moviegoer is not a monolith. There is no longer just the moviegoer who pays admission at a theater; there is also the moviewatcher who sees it free on network television. And with the rise of pay-TV, cable, and homevideo, there would be additional kinds of viewers. For each of them Columbia would have something.

In October 1966 the rationale for packaging movies for TV would have been lost on Banque de Paris which, encouraged by the general feeling on Wall Street that Columbia was due for its comeuppance, surprised the American contingent by behaving more audaciously than Maurice Clairmont: Banque de Paris obtained 680,000 shares of Columbia stock, spinning off 100,000 and 190,000 shares to the Madison and Dreyfus funds, respectively. But Banque de Paris failed to realize that, according to an FCC regulation (Title 47, section 310), aliens are prohibited from obtaining control of any corporation holding broadcasting licenses and/or owning more than 25 percent of the corporation. Banque de Paris already owned 20.03 percent of Columbia, which owned about 89 percent of Screen Gems, which had radio and television interests.

Columbia had triumphed and indicated as much in a bluntly worded joint statement that appeared in *Daily Variety* (15 November 1966) to the effect that Columbia and Banque de Paris "have resolved all issues between them so as to maintain control of the company in the present management." As if to punish the aggressor, Columbia extracted a promise from Banque de Paris that it would remain a 20 percent minority investor, engage in no attempt to gain control of Columbia, and "take such action as may be required to safeguard the radio and television licenses held by the subsidiaries of Columbia Pictures Corporation."[11]

Although the takeover threat had passed, Columbia was still apprehensive. Since it was the first studio to create a television subsidiary, it realized Screen Gems could no longer be a separate entity whose earnings were combined with its own. And so the disgruntled stockholder's resolution that Columbia Pictures Corporation be dissolved in favor of a Columbia-Screen Gems merger came to pass in September 1968. The reason was not capitulation to dissent, which had been momentarily silenced; rather it was to prevent dissent from reaching the stage of another takeover bid. Thus in the fall of 1968 Columbia Pictures Corporation (CPC) faded out and Columbia Pictures Industries (CPI), an "integrated entertainment complex," faded in. The extent of that integration would become clearer in the next decade.

In the tradition of in-house realignments, Leo Jaffe succeeded Abe Schneider as president of CPI, while Schneider became chairman of the new company. Stanley Schneider, Abe's son, who had joined Columbia in 1946, was made president of the film division, Columbia Pictures. Had Sam Briskin not died on 14 November 1968, he would have been a CPI board member and a vice president.

Continuity had been maintained, especially in the cases of Jaffe and Schneider, who had spent their frequently intersecting careers at Columbia. Schneider started as a bookkeeper in 1922; Jaffe, as Schneider's assistant, in 1930. Between 1929 and 1942, Schneider had advanced from assistant secretary (1929) to assistant treasurer (1930), then to treasurer (1935), and finally treasurer and vice president (1942). In 1956, Schneider became first vice president, and a year later Jaffe moved up to treasurer. When Harry Cohn died, Schneider became president and Jaffe assumed Schneider's title of first vice president and treasurer, becoming executive vice president in 1962. In 1967 Jaffe succeeded Schneider as president when Schneider became chairman of the board and CEO. The following year, when CPI was formed, Jaffe naturally became president; in 1973 when Schneider became honorary chairman of CPI, Jaffe became chairman. The tribe of Harry was at least represented in Columbia's third incarnation, although its role was greatly reduced.

CPI was more than a union of parent and offspring; it was a restructuring so that the offspring's progeny (consumer research, music publishing, and records—all part of Screen Gems) became separate divisions of CPI. There are casualties in any reorganization; in this instance the casualty was Mike Frankovich, one of Columbia's—and the industry's—most humane producers. Frankovich, UCLA football star and a former child actor, came to Columbia in 1951 as an independent producer. From 1955 to 1964 he was Columbia's European production chief. In 1964 he left London, where he had been based for nine years, and returned to Los Angeles as Columbia's head of production.

Frankovich, who once incurred Harry Cohn's wrath when he

refused to give him tips on football games, nonetheless continued Cohn's practice of offering important actors a percentage of the film to compensate for a lower salary. Since percentage deals ease tax burdens on the actors as well as reap profits for the studio, Frankovich, while in London, negotiated a contract for William Holden to costar in *The Bridge on the River Kwai* for $50,000 in cash and a 7½ percent share of the profits, to be paid in annual installments of $50,000. He worked out a similar arrangement with Sidney Poitier for *To Sir, with Love* (1967). Both films were huge successes, and *Bridge* won seven Oscars.

When it became impossible for Frankovich to get insurance for Spencer Tracy, then seriously ill, for *Guess Who's Coming to Dinner* (1967), he pursuaded Katharine Hepburn and director Stanley Kramer to work for less than their usual salaries, and Tracy to work on deferment. *Guess Who's Coming to Dinner* was the second highest grossing film of 1968.

There is no doubt that Columbia's succession of hits in the 1960s—*Lawrence of Arabia* (1962), *Dr. Strangelove* (1964), *Cat Ballou* (1965), *The Professionals* (1966), *The Silencers* (1966), and *Casino Royale* (which sent Columbia's stock soaring in 1967)—resulted, in great part, from Frankovich's ability to harmonize the talents of stars, directors, and writers. It is also not accidental that, during Frankovich's tenure, Columbia films won thirty-five Oscars.

With the formation of CPI, Frankovich's relationship with Columbia changed from head of production to independent producer. The head of production at CPI's Columbia would not wield the same authority as he did at CPC, as Frankovich's successor, Peter Guber (who would eventually head a new Columbia two decades later), discovered. Moving into independent production, Frankovich released through Columbia until 1973, using the Columbia approach of offering stars a percentage deal when he could not meet their salary demands. Unable to pay Natalie Wood her usual $750,000 for *Bob & Carol & Ted & Alice* (1969), he offered her a percentage, which she reluctantly accepted. Both Wood and Columbia benefited: by the time Natalie Wood died in 1985, she had made more than $3 million, and Columbia about $14 million.

When Frankovich left film entirely in 1977, the industry was not even what it had been when he went independent a decade earlier. "Someday I'll write a book about it all—if I can find a way not to hurt people," he mused in 1984.[12] The book was never written, and even if it had been it would have been more of a reflection of the author's decency than of an industry in which decency barely exists. What Frankovich could do that many producers could not is inspire loyalty and confidence from colleagues unable to find those qualities elsewhere. When the board of governors of the Academy of Motion Picture

Arts and Sciences voted him the Jean Hersholt Humanitarian Award in 1984, it was not just for helping underprivileged children and serving on boards of hospitals, but for making moviemaking humane.

THE 1970s

The 1970s have become synonymous with the Begelman scandal, which began with Cliff Robertson's discovery that David Begelman, president of Columbia Pictures (and also president of Columbia Pictures Television as well as senior vice president of Columbia Pictures Industries), had forged his signature on a $10,000 check in September 1976. The forgery was the tip of the iceberg; more accurately, it was the rim of a conical hell that David McClintick traversed on his Dantean journey, the results of which are recounted in a masterpiece of investigative reporting, *Indecent Exposure*.[13] The book's subtitle, *A True Story of Hollywood and Wall Street*, is even more revealing than the double entendre title. The scandal lay at the juncture of two worlds whose styles are antithetical but whose goals are identical—money and its concomitant, power.

While Hollywood scandals have always attracted attention, the Begelman affair could only have done so in an ethically minded America. Had the incident occurred a decade earlier during the height of the Vietnam War, it would have remained local news, eclipsed by the draft resistance, the Tet Offensive, and the My Lai massacre. Watergate made righteousness fashionable, and while the evidence McClintick marshaled was not so demoralizing as Watergate or so numbing as Iran-Contra, it had the same effect: it confirmed the public's suspicion that there was as much chicanery in Hollywood as there was in Washington.

In 1970, however, David Begelman was still an agent, Richard Nixon's paranoia had not yet surfaced, and "freedom fighter" was a phrase associated with the World War II resistance. What was considered newsworthy in Hollywood was not the killing of the Kent State students but *Midnight Cowboy's* winning the Oscar for best picture of 1969 despite its X rating. As far as Columbia was concerned, the 1970s looked promising. While there had been an anticipated decline in earnings for fiscal 1969, Leo Jaffe could report in 1970 that 1967-1968 and 1968-1969 had been the most profitable years in the studio's history. For the pattern to continue, certain changes would have to be made, one of which involved independent production. Columbia had been a home to independent producers since the mid 1930s, but now it began to see itself as home for both independents who released through the studio and those who did not. In July 1969 Columbia decided to abandon its policy of an overhead charge for independents, probably influenced by Warner Bros.–Seven Arts' creation of a separate facility rental division for independents.[14]

Under Columbia's new policy, independents would pay only for what they used instead of paying an overhead charge of 20 percent of the budget. The change was intended to make Columbia even more attractive to independents. At Paramount, for example, there were overhead charges for films financed by the studio but flat rental deals for others. Fox rented only to independents releasing through the studio, charging them a percentage of the budget; MGM charged a flat daily rate except for studio-financed productions, for which there was an overhead charge. Columbia started building mobile units for in-house and independent producers, and by 1970 about twenty production companies were releasing through the studio and twenty-five independents were filming there but releasing elsewhere.

The decade began auspiciously, but decades are misleading. Historians may think in decades and eras, but Hollywood thinks in weekly grosses and fiscal years. Depending on the grosses, one year can be a boom, another a bust; if that irregularity persists, the end of a decade may see the end of an era—or the end of a studio.

While Columbia was apparently thriving at the close of the 1960s, in 1971 it was reporting the greatest net loss in its history, more than $28 million. No doubt its 1970 films contributed to that loss; rarely had so many unmemorable films—especially by major directors such as William Wyler (*The Liberation of L.B. Jones*), Anatole Litvak (*The Lady in the Car with Glasses and a Gun*), and Stanley Kramer (*R.P.M.*)—appeared in one year. Then, too, there was the decline in movie attendance (from forty-nine million in 1955 to eighteen million in 1970) that caught up with Columbia at a time when the studio was most vulnerable.

If there was a decline in attendance, there was also a decline in the quality of the product. Oldtimers had become disaffected by the screen's new permissiveness and resented the glorification of youth at the expense of age. A *quo vadis?* mentality prevailed in the industry. "Who are the moviegoers?" executives asked. At one time Columbia knew—when it created Screen Gems, which, ironically, began by offering the TV equivalent of the B movie. But once television usurped that function, there was no need for studios like Republic and Monogram, which specialized in B's, to make them; soon there was no need for Republic and Monogram. While Columbia made more B movies than any of the Big Five, it began shedding its B movie image at the end of the 1940s as its series films were ending and as it embarked upon a succession of films (*All the King's Men, Born Yesterday, From Here to Eternity, On the Waterfront, The Caine Mutiny, The Bridge on the River Kwai*) that brought it international recognition.

A television subsidiary made Columbia realize there was a major difference between television and film, or at least there was in 1948. In 1970, the difference between A and B movies, or B movies and B television, was academic; more important was the distinction between big screen and small screen and what was suited to each. *Bob & Carol & Ted & Alice* (1969) and *The Last Picture Show* (1971) would not turn up on network in their original form; at the time it was doubtful they would turn up there at all. But the longevity of theatrical films is not limited to their theater life. The classic distinction between moviegoing in the 1940s and the present—that in the 1940s people went to the movies while today people go to *a* movie—is undeniably true; but it is also true that more people would go to the movies if more movies came to the people. In 1971 Leo Jaffe correctly predicted the age of cable and homevideo. In preparation, Columbia entered the pay-TV field, with operations limited to closed-circuit television in hotels.

Expanded facilities for independents and closed-circuit TV, however, would not put Columbia in the black. Reversing Cohn's policy of expansion, Jaffe started retrenching. In 1971 there were 300 dismissals, and both Jaffe and Schneider took pay cuts. That same year Columbia announced it would sell the fourteen-acre Gower Street studio and move to Burbank, forming with Warners what became the Burbank Studios. Although each studio would operate independently, each would also rent facilities to the other. This was the first time two studios had shared space while being autonomous and competitive at the same time. At least Columbia would not be treated as a tenant; besides, Warners had twenty-three soundstages as opposed to the fourteen at Gower Street. The move, which was completed by 1972, cut production costs by 20 percent. Thus the net loss for fiscal 1972 was $3,397,000 as compared to $28 million-plus the previous year. *Variety* noted the turnaround, as did the rumor mongers, who observed that since Warners, the joint owner of the Burbank Studios, had registered a net profit of $23 million in 1972, a Warners-Columbia merger was not unthinkable. Hollywood rumors are never consistent; one spawns another that is often more bizarre than the first. Soon, the scuttlebutt was that Tandem Productions, the Norman Lear–Bud Yorkin company that produced *All in the Family*, *Maude*, and *Sanford and Son*, was a potenial buyer. In Hollywood, irony is not a literary device but a fact of life. In 1985, Columbia acquired Embassy Communications and Tandem Productions, along with Tandem's TV library for syndication.

It was not by accident that Columbia and Warners ended up as neighbors. In corporate Hollywood there are no missing links. What appear to be gaps are information that, for various reasons, cannot or will not be shared. Columbia's becoming part of the Burbank Studios was not purely a matter of expediency; it was the outgrowth of a sequence of events and a convergence of personalities that shaped the futures of both studios.

The story of Columbia in the 1970s is a convoluted tale resembling a multiplot film with crosscut and interlocking narratives. When the story is pieced together, there is no doubt that the regime that took over Columbia in 1973 had been moving steadily toward that goal since the 1950s. 1973 was merely the culmination of a series of maneuvers and transactions that had begun almost two decades earlier, linking the lives and the destinies of David Begelman and his boss, Alan Hirschfield, president and CEO of Columbia Pictures Industries; investment banker Charles Allen and his nephew Herbert Allen, Jr.; and a producer whose power only a Hollywood tyro would underestimate—Ray Stark.

Understanding this interweaving of personalities requires a comprehension, if not an appreciation, of Hollywood's allure, which affects the financier as well as the fan. There are two Hollywoods: the myth and the business. While moviegoers invest their time and money in the myth, financiers invest theirs in the business. Ever since the industry began, banks have been important to its survival. It was through a $100,000 loan from Attilio Henry Giannini—the California banker who, by 1931, could boast of having loaned $10 million to movie companies—that Columbia was founded. The growing number of bankers at the Cannes film market and the increasing number of banks with film divisions occasioned the *Variety* headline (14-20 June 1989): "There's no business like show business, more banks say; investments lucrative." As an investment, Hollywood offers financiers more than the vicarious pleasure and intangible profit the fans derive; it offers real pleasure and real profit. The real pleasure comes from the opportunity to consort with the fantasy makers; the profit is the money to be made from the fantasies.

As Hollywood became more dependent on investment capital, a new breed of film executive emerged: one who could straddle the stock market and the studio, make deals with bankers and agents, and feel as much at home on Wall Street as in Beverly Hills. The new moguls, often CPAs and MBAs, brought a masculine aggressiveness to the art of the deal. Perhaps the best portrait of the new mogul appears in David Mamet's play *Speed-the-Plow* (1988), in which Hollywood is an extension of the locker room, where the typical insult is not a belittling of one's intelligence but of one's masculinity; where joy is expressed in a mock homoerotic embrace; and where a woman is a box on a sexual score card. *Speed-the-Plow* is essentially about power, whose root is a sexual energy that is neutralized in relationships between men, leaving only the trappings of affection (the arm around the shoulder, the

bearhug). The energy that is not expended in the workplace is chan-
neled into women, who provide a release from the tensions of a
"mannist" society (to use the phrase George Stade coined as an an-
tonym of feminist).

Columbia in 1973 was very much a mannist society—of fathers
looking for surrogate sons and sons looking for surrogate fathers; of
insiders and outsiders, social inferiors and intellectual superiors, de-
gree-flaunters and degree-fakers. To a sociologist Columbia was a
microcosm of corporate America: a dynasty/fraternity/country club.

This was the microcosm that Herbert Allen, Jr., entered when he
joined Columbia's board in the summer of 1973; it was not, however,
his uncle's. When Charles Allen founded the investment firm of Allen
and Company in 1922, he could hardly have thought he would be on
the periphery of the entertainment world, much less at its center.
When Charles married his first wife, Rita, he was unknowingly becoming part of that world. First it was the theatre, when Rita coproduced
The Grass Harp and *My Three Angels* on Broadway in the early 1950s. But
theatre and film impinge on each other, and Charles's circle expanded
to include Jack Warner and Ray Stark. The expansion was due primarily
to Charles's meeting Serge Semenenko of the First National Bank of
Boston, which became Columbia's principal bankroller in the 1960s.
Semenenko's financial wizardry (which had its dark side) was legendary in Hollywood; it was Semenenko who worked quietly behind the
scenes during the negotiations between Columbia and Banque de Paris
at the time of the abortive takeover attempt. To know Serge Semenenko
was to know Columbia's biggest shareholder, Matthew ("Matty")
Rosenhaus. When Banque de Paris's shares were up for sale, Semenenko encouraged Rosenhaus, head of the pharmaceutical firm J.B.
Williams, to buy.

In 1956 Charles Allen and Serge Semenenko came on the board of
Warners, whose net profit was down $2 million from 1955. Their
joining the board constituted a bailout; it also left them with majority
control of the studio. Another, and not unrelated, event occurred in
1956 that brought Ray Stark into this ever widening gyre: the sale of the
pre-1948 Warners film library to Associated Artists (AA) for $21 mil-
lion—the same library that United Artists would purchase the following year and that Turner Broadcasting would eventually acquire.

AA was headed by Eliot Hyman. In 1957, Ray Stark, then an agent
whose clients included Ben Hecht, Lana Turner, Ava Gardner, and Kirk
Douglas, joined AA's board. Within a year Stark and Hyman formed
Seven Arts which, like AA (of which it was really an offshoot), licensed
films to television; however, unlike AA, Seven Arts moved into production and then became Seven Arts Productions, Inc.

With the creation of Seven Arts Productions, one would have

thought Ray Stark's first producing credit would have come from his own company; instead, it came from Paramount, which in 1958 reported its highest annual profit in a decade: $12.5 million. Stark was taking no chances; his first producing credit was Paramount's hit *The World of Suzie Wong* (1960).

Stark had not abandoned Seven Arts; it was simply that Seven Arts supported Ray Stark, not the other way around. Seven Arts was the means to an end—the end being a Ray Stark production. But the first Ray Stark–Seven Arts production was for Broadway, not Hollywood: *Funny Girl* (1964), "A Ray Stark Production in Conjunction with Seven Arts." The musical was an idealized version of the life of Stark's mother-in-law, Fanny Brice, indelibly played by Barbra Streisand, who would repeat her role in the film version produced by Stark and released by Columbia.

At about the time *Funny Girl* opened on Broadway, Alan Hirschfield graduated from the Harvard Business School and immediately joined Allen and Company. It was a foregone conclusion that he would become part of the firm. Norman Hirschfield, Alan's father, and Charles Allen were contemporaries and had been close friends since the 1920s. Working at Allen and Company not only brought Alan in contact with Herbert Allen, Jr., who had graduated from Williams in 1962, but also with Ray Stark. The same year Hirschfield joined Allen and Company (1964), he became a member of the Seven Arts board. Two years later Hirschfield engineered Seven Arts' purchase of Jack Warner's Warner Bros. stock for $32 million, resulting in the formation of Warner Bros.–Seven Arts in 1967. Stark and Allen and Company profited from the deal; they profited again when Warner Bros. became part of Warner Communications in 1971.

Just as Stark and the Allens were involved in the affairs of Warner Bros., so too was Hirschfield, who spent 1967 as vice president for finance at the newly formed Warner Bros.–Seven Arts. 1967 was also the year Ray Stark moved to Columbia, where he would form his own production company; and as Stark moved, so did Allen and Company and Alan Hirschfield. The movie version of *Funny Girl* was inevitable; so was Barbra Streisand's recreation of the role she had originated. Less certain was the studio. Apparently, Mike Frankovich was instrumental in Columbia's buying *Funny Girl*, which, like the Broadway musical, became a Ray Stark production. Stark's association with Columbia, then, started in 1967—the year Columbia's spirits were revived after the Banque de Paris affair; the year "Matty" Rosenhaus became Columbia's largest shareholder and came on the board; the year before Columbia changed its corporate name to Columbia Pictures Industries, with Columbia Pictures and Screen Gems as divisions.

Stark knew Columbia had potential but was appalled that its stock was trading at $4 a share. Thus he encouraged Allen and Company to buy into Columbia. It was a repeat of the Warners bailout of 1956. Again Allen and Company came to the aid of a studio. This time the Allen in question was not Charles but his nephew Herbert. Nevertheless it was an Allen, and if an Allen would be involved with Columbia, so would Hirschfield and, of course, Ray Stark.

Stark wanted a new management team but also something similar to the family model that had kept Columbia in business since the 1920s. Since a real family was impossible, a quasi-family would have to do. Stark had a habit of developing paternal and filial relationships with colleagues; he regarded Charles Allen as a surrogate father and Herbert Allen, Jr., as a surrogate son. Herbert went from a surrogate to a substitute son, when, in 1970, Stark's own son fell fourteen stories to his death in what was presumably a suicide. It was inevitable, then, that Herbert would become part of the new regime—specifically, a board member. With Herbert would come Hirschfield, whose ties with Allen and Company and whose role in the creation of Warner Bros.–Seven Arts made him the logical head of Columbia Pictures Industries but not of the film division, Columbia Pictures. For that, someone was needed who could deal with stars and agents; someone, in fact, who had been an agent. Enter David Begelman.

In 1961, Ray Stark, eager to have Judy Garland star in the Fanny Brice project that eventually became *Funny Girl*, approached her agent, David Begelman. Garland was not interested. When *Funny Girl* became a reality and was about to be cast, Stark found himself again negotiating with Begelman, who was now Barbra Streisand's agent. Begelman had the ability to find the right star for the right project; he was the obvious choice to head Columbia Pictures.

And so in July 1973 Abe Schneider vacated the board chairmanship, becoming honorary chairman; Jaffe vacated the CPI presidency, replacing Schneider as board chairman; Alan Hirschfield succeeded Jaffe as CPI president (and CEO, to boot); and David Begelman moved into the film division of CPI, replacing Stanley Schneider as president of Columbia Pictures. A corporate family had emerged at whose head stood a paterfamilias who was not an officer of the studio but who had put together its new management as if it were a deal: Ray Stark.

Since Stark preferred to maintain a low profile, it was up to Hirschfield and Begelman to promote the new Columbia. Taking a position that, ironically, David Puttnam would adopt a decade later, Hirschfield decried inflated salaries, complaining that the times are out of joint when minor actors could collect six-digit paychecks. Begelman was less outspoken but still insisted on realistic budgets in accordance with the nature of the movie; thus he allowed *Close Encounters of the*

Third Kind to go well over the original $2.8 million budget; had he not, the film would never have been the classic it is.

Hirschfield also had to defend tax shelters. He admitted that 54 percent of Columbia's 1975 productions were financed by outside investments. He even went so far as to state that if there had been no tax shelters, Columbia would have been bankrupt. Since tax shelters were coming increasingly under attack, Columbia continued to diversify—acquiring and divesting, and divesting to acquire. In 1976 Columbia sold the Screen Gems music publishing division to the London-based entertainment conglomerate EMI and acquired D. Gottlieb, the pinball machine company, for $50 million. Columbia had discovered that pinball machines were not limited to bars and diners; they had even begun to appear in dens and game rooms.

By the end of fiscal 1975 Columbia was in the black, with a $5.3 million profit, although with Columbia one could never tell; a debt could become a profit through write-offs, tax losses, and changes in accounting procedures. At any rate, Columbia was on a roll; *Shampoo, Funny Lady*, and *Tommy*—all 1975 releases—were hits. As if to celebrate, Columbia modified its logo: "We Thought The Moment Was Right To Let The 'Lady' Relax," a full-page ad in the 1 October 1975 *Hollywood Reporter* read. The lady now dissolved into a semicircular sunburst, leaving only the laser-like points of her torch. By the 1980s, the dissolve had been dropped, leaving the lady intact and no less resplendent.

Hirschfield could boast that Columbia was worth $8 million when he came on board in 1973 and almost four times as much in 1976. Hirschfield naturally deserves some credit, but so do Begelman and particularly Ray Stark, whose role was not merely that of shareholder and *éminence gris*. Among Columbia's acquisitions were Rastar Productions and its subsidiary, Rastar Pictures, whose purchase at the end of 1974 gave Columbia the rights to the films made under those trademarks.[15]

Stark's association with Columbia continued after the acquisition. "Rastar" became a quadripartite organization consisting of Rastar Productions (wholly owned by Columbia), Rastar Films, Inc. (Rastar Pictures' replacement), Rastar Features, and Rastar Television. In 1980 Columbia bought Rastar Films; the sale gave Stark more Columbia stock in the event of a takeover attempt. It was a shrewd move; Kirk Kerkorian had designs on Columbia and would make them known the following year.

Stark, then, would be loath to see Columbia's new image tarnished by scandal; thus he would not sanction the dismissal of David Begelman, whom he credited to a great extent with Columbia's renascence. But Stark, although calculating, was not clairvoyant. Although the industry has always tried to keep the unpredictable from undermining the prearranged, no one could have anticipated that an actor's discovery that his signature had been forged would result in a new coinage: Hollywoodgate. Nor was it a lone forgery; there were others. And it was not just forgery but forgery and embezzlement. The full amount was not $10,000 but closer to $75,000, reduced through rationalization to $61,008, which the press reported as $60,000.

Generally, forgery and embezzlement mean termination—at the minimum. But corporate Hollywood is neither Madison Avenue nor Wall Street; in Hollywood, when one closet gets too small for its skeletons, another is made ready. A case of embezzlement will not bring down a studio, but executives, fearing for their undeserved six-digit salaries and unreported perks, quake at the thought of scandal. Watergate ushered in the age of accountability, and by post-Watergate criteria, David Begelman was accountable.

Columbia—or, more specifically, Herbert Allen, Jr., Ray Stark, and Matty Rosenhaus—did not want to see Begelman go. He had been a successful studio head and, more important, he and Ray Stark were not in competition. As former agents, Stark and Begelman knew that deals are highly individual: Stark had his successes; Begelman, his. And whomever or whatever Ray Stark wanted, so did Herbert Allen, Jr.; and Stark wanted Begelman. The problem was not with Begelman and Allen/Stark, but with Begelman and Hirschfield. While Hirschfield was right in wanting Begelman fired, he did not understand the loyalty that Begelman inspired.

Ultimately, it was not even a matter of money; Begelman could pay Columbia back. It was a question of intransigence on Hirschfield's part—not moral intransigence, for the morality of the affair only mattered to the outside; rather it was an intransigence rooted in pride that briefly yielded to expediency and finally hardened into adamancy. At the end of September 1977, when it became obvious that Begelman could not remain at the studio, he was suspended; in December he was reinstated; two months later he resigned—involuntarily.

That initially Begelman was suspended instead of fired speaks volumes. The board had waffled. But motives are never pure, nor are they simple. The Begelman affair became a split screen on which were projected the actors' images along with their murky psyches. Hirschfield wanted Begelman out for reasons both valid and specious. As CEO, Hirschfield had the right—some would argue the obligation—to recommend termination; as an outsider, Hirschfield could not appreciate the extent of Begelman's reputation. It is one thing to know that the new Hollywood is an agents' market; it is something else to come up against an agent's—or even an ex-agent's—power. As a man in early middle age, Hirschfield believed someone fifteen years his senior had little to contribute: "Hirschfield, at age forty-one, was coming to the conclusion by the summer of 1977 that Begelman, at age fifty-six, would soon be too old—if he wasn't already—to possess all of the vision required to guide the studio in the new era of video cassettes and discs, and cable and satellite television. . . . Hirschfield felt that it would take men like himself—men whose careers encompassed Hollywood but were not enveloped by it—to lead Columbia and the industry at large into the new age."[16]

The age factor was only one facet of this dark mosaic. Intellectual arrogance was another. Hirschfield and Begelman were the antitheses of each other: Wall Street vs. Hollywood, Scarsdale vs. Beverly Hills, Quo Vadis vs. Chasen's, soccer vs. baseball, bridge vs. poker. Having acquired his degrees in the usual way, Hirschfield must have found it irritating to hear about Begelman's "Yale degree," which was nonexistent; Begelman's only association with Yale was a few months in a training program. In the Cohn era, academic credentials were meaningless; a high school diploma was the norm, and many (including the Cohn brothers) never had even that. The degree-holders were usually writers. With the advent of sound, the industry wooed writers shamelessly, and many who trekked west realized their importance and were contemptuous of the new medium. Writing to Ben Hecht, Herman J. Mankiewicz encouraged his friend to try screenwriting because "your only competition is idiots."[17] If writers could look with disdain on an industry that paid them far more than they would have received elsewhere, it is only natural that, as the educational level of the studio executive rose, the degreed would look down on the degreeless and even more on the degreeless purporting to have degrees.

Hirschfield found himself in a situation where, as Begelman's boss, he was really in Begelman's shadow, a shadow that in turn, was adumbrated by Ray Stark's, over which hovered a monolithic board. It is small wonder that Hirschfield's vision was obscured; he failed to understand the men's club mentality that prevailed at Columbia, with its unsworn loyalty oath requiring members to close ranks and defend their own—until, of course, their own became indefensible. It was the club's parochialism that led to the curtailment of Hirschfield's power; since Hirschfield had never been a member, he would have to be initiated in its ways if he was to serve it. It was the club's misguided compassion for Begelman that led to his reinstatement, much against Hirschfield's better judgment; but good judgment can weaken from the psychological pressure of a war waged on two fronts. This was not just Hollywood vs. New York but the herd vs. the maverick.

Eventually Hirschfield won, but it was a Pyrrhic victory. The press's reaction to Begelman's reinstatement was so strong that Begelman could not possibly remain at Columbia. The entire affair was described in the imagery of metastasis, the Begelman scandal being seen as an aberrant cell in a none too healthy system. If Begelman would be sacrificed, so would Hirschfield. This was the opportunity to expel the outsider who could never play by the rules of the club because he had no respect for the club. Hirschfield would never give Ray Stark the obeisance he wanted; clearly there could be no father-son relationship between them as there was between Stark and Allen.

Between Allen and Hirschfield there was more a clash of worlds than personalities. Herbert Allen, Jr., came from a world of privilege; Hirschfield spent much of his youth in Oklahoma, another planet compared to the Hotel Carlyle. While Allen went to Williams College and Hirschfield to the University of Oklahoma, Hirschfield could at least claim Harvard as an alma mater of sorts, but even a Harvard degree did not give him the authority he thought he should have as CEO. While Stark wondered why Hirschfield would not leave Begelman alone, Hirschfield wondered why Stark would not leave *him* alone. Stark did not understand that Hirschfield's approach was totally in keeping with his title of CEO; Hirschfield did not understand that, in view of Stark's power at the studio, "CEO" was an honorific.

Compared with insider traders, junk bond kings, and influence peddlers, Begelman was a petty thief; compared to the $300,000 that Screen Gems employee Audrey Lisner embezzled between 1974 and 1978, Begelman's take was pocket money. Even his punishment was a vindication of Hollywood morality: a $5,000 fine, three years' probation (revoked after a year), community service in the form of producing *Angel Death*, a documentary about the evils of the drug "angel dust," and the reduction of his offense from a felony to a misdemeanor.

Nevertheless, David Begelman had become a symbol of greed-driven Hollywood, whose corruption, like its imminent demise, has been greatly exaggerated. Even if the affair had never become public, the polarization at the studio was too extreme for the current management to continue. Bipolar personalities are one thing; but when polarization extends to class, education, and lifestyle, the abyss is unbridgeable.

If Begelman had to leave, so would Hirschfield. Although each discovered there was life after Columbia—Begelman first at MGM and then at Gladden Entertainment, Hirschfield in investment banking—neither would achieve the same celebrity again.[18]

THE 1980s

With the departures of Begelman and Hirschfield, it was time for another chorus of "Change Partners and Dance." Since their exits were not concurrent, Begelman's job was filled before Hirschfield's. It was the usual case of the second-in-command's taking over. Thus, Daniel Melnick slipped into Begelman's shoes, but so briefly that his presidency was barely acknowledged. Hirschfield's replacement lasted longer. Since there was no one within the company to assume Hirschfield's title and duties, Herbert Allen, Jr., went to the outside—to a Williams College alumnus who was a year behind him and whom he knew casually. But, unlike Allen, Francis (Fay) Vincent, Jr., was *cum laude* and Phi Beta Kappa. It was not his academic credentials, which also included a Yale law degree, that made Vincent desirable; he had also been an associate director of the Division of Corporate Finance of the Securities and Exchange Commission. Since the SEC had been investigating Columbia because of the Begelman episode, Vincent could restore the studio's credibility. There was one problem: Vincent knew nothing about movies. Hirschfield knew more, but not that much. Hirschfield was interested in money making, not moviemaking—unless moviemaking led to money making. Vincent's interests were similar; while he improved internal auditing controls and accounting procedures at Columbia and reduced the bank debt, he was not a movie lover. That was apparent when he made a career change in September 1989 that had nothing to do with film: Vincent succeeded the late Bart Giamatti as baseball commissioner.

Where there is no love of film, there is only a film company, and a film company is what Columbia had become. Anyone smitten with moviemaking had gone elsewhere, except the omnipresent Ray Stark. Daniel Melnick loved movies; his replacing Begelman was one of those ironies endemic to the business. It was Begelman who had been responsible for Melnick's coming to Columbia in 1977 as head of production. Previously, Melnick had been production chief at MGM; and, of course, it was to MGM that Begelman went after leaving Columbia.

Melnick was never meant to be a studio head. Instead of continuing in a job that lay under a corporate curse, he formed his own company, IndieProductions (later, Indieprod). Melnick was an indie at heart; he "did not want the administrative burdens [but] only to 'make pictures.'"[19] Since Melnick could not avoid administrative responsibilities at Columbia, he vacated the presidency, with his second-in-command, Frank Price, taking charge. In 1978, Price inherited Melnick's job when Melnick replaced Begelman; with Melnick's departure, he inherited Melnick's job again when he became president of Columbia Pictures in March 1979.

Price's career is paradigmatic of a Hollywood whose pool of creative personnel has shrunk so dramatically that one can complete an executive's resumé almost on the basis of job changes alone. If A leaves studio Y for studio Z, B and C will follow A to Z. But if A leaves Z, it does not follow that A has burned his or her bridges; A may return to Z in a different capacity. In 1978 Price left Universal for Columbia; in 1983 he returned to Universal before dropping anchor in the port of independent production; in 1990 he was back at Columbia in a radically different role—as chairman of Columbia Pictures, now a division of the Sony-owned Columbia Pictures Entertainment.

Price began in the industry in the mid-1950s, starting as a reader at Columbia before moving to Universal in 1959, where he remained for the next two decades. His experience at Universal was in its television division. As president of Universal Television, Price was responsible for such TV movies as *Duel* (1971), *That Certain Summer* (1972), *A Case of Rape* (1974), *The Execution of Private Slovik* (1974), and *Tail Gunner Joe* (1977), and for such series as *Kojak*, *Baretta*, *Columbo*, and *The Rockford Files*. Under Price, Universal Television became the world's foremost independent producer of television programming, although it lost that distinction in the late 1980s. Since Price had been at Universal even before it became part of MCA, it seemed odd that, after two decades there, he would depart for Columbia. Quite simply, television is not the movies, and Frank Price wanted to make movies.

No sooner had Price come on board than it was takeover time again at Columbia. Anticipating a takeover attempt by Kirk Kerkorian, who then owned 47 percent of MGM and 25.5 percent of Columbia Pictures Industries, Columbia acquired Rastar Films, Inc., the reincarnation of Rastar Pictures, which Columbia had bought earlier. Stark, as Columbia's principal shareholder after Matty Rosenhaus's death, was Columbia's buffer against Kerkorian.

When Kerkorian purchased his Columbia stock in 1978, he agreed to refrain from attempting to gain control of the company for three years. Columbia tried to buy Kerkorian's stock, valued at $76.4 million, but Kerkorian would not sell. Previously an antitrust investigation had caused him to waver; but when the Justice Department, which had ordered him to sell, lost the case, Kerkorian was encouraged to proceed with his plan to merge Columbia with MGM. To do so, he would have to purchase 1.25 million additional Columbia shares, which would violate his agreement not to buy more Columbia stock until 1982. Kerkorian argued that the agreement should be terminated because of breach of contract on Columbia's part: Columbia had failed to consult with him prior to engaging in "material financial actions," meaning Columbia's issuance of 300,000 shares of its stock to Ray Stark as a result of the Rastar Films acquisition. Kerkorian interpreted the Rastar purchase as an attempt to block his takeover bid—which was precisely the case.

A lawsuit developed, with Columbia charging Kerkorian with using the assets of MGM Hotels and MGM Films for personal gain. The fire that ravaged the Las Vegas MGM Grand in November 1980 did not help Kerkorian; Columbia, which only owned ten shares in MGM Grand, maintained that the hotel had been unsafe even before the fire. Kerkorian was forced to back off, although by no means did he suffer a loss; he sold his interest back to Columbia at a profit. The Columbia stock that Kerkorian picked up in 1978 when it averaged $24 a share was repurchased by Columbia at $37.50 a share.

The litigation was expensive, costing Columbia around $6 million. The expense, however, was offset by such hits as *Kramer vs. Kramer* (1979) and *The Electric Horseman* (1979), which were begun under Begelman and completed under Price. *The Blue Lagoon* and *Seems Like Old Times* were both 1980 successes. Frank Price was clearly due for a promotion.

In May 1981 Price was elevated to chairman and president of Columbia Pictures in acknowledgment of the "great accomplishments [he] had made in building Columbia Pictures to its leadership position in the motion picture industry."[20] Price immediately made Victor A. Kaufman, then senior vice president and general counsel of CPI, vice chairman. Kaufman, Price's protégé, was destined to move even higher, for a time eclipsing his mentor.

The Price years were busy ones. Anxious to move into homevideo, Columbia joined with the RCA Corporation to establish, first, a worldwide division (RCA/Columbia International Video) and then a domestic one (RCA/Columbia Home Video). Equally interested in pay-TV, Columbia signed a licensing agreement with Home Box Office calling for HBO to pay approximately 20 percent of Columbia's production expenses in return for equity ownership in the films and exclusive pay-TV rights.

Price approved both the RCA and the HBO deals. One of the reasons for his being made chairman as well as president of Columbia was the studio's expansion in the areas of television and home entertainment. Price, who had built Universal Television into a programming giant, had similar plans for Columbia Pictures Television, which in 1981 had acquired the television assets of Time-Life Films: seventy made-for-TV movies (and a number of theatrical films as well) to which Columbia would have distribution rights.

Price had became Columbia's golden boy. But a golden boy must think of a golden parachute. Although Price had signed a new four-year $10 million (plus) contract with Columbia in September 1981, he would not finish it out. An old beverage and a new studio led to his leaving Columbia in October 1983. The new studio was Tri-Star; the beverage was the soft drink whose fame had become so widespread that in *Sail Away* (1961), Noel Coward could write, without exaggeration, that "there isn't a rock / Between Bangkok / And the beaches of Hispaniola / That does not recoil / From suntan oil / And the gurgle of

Coca-Cola." As the commercial insisted, "Things go better with Coca-Cola." Columbia had become one of those things.

In January 1982, Coca-Cola, seeking an entrée into the movie business, decided upon Columbia. Coke's $750 million offer struck some financial analysts as inordinately high, especially after Marvin Davis paid $725 million for Fox. On the other hand, any company interested in buying a studio, particularly one whose roots lay deep in Hollywood's past, had little choice. With the formation of MGM/UA, Davis's purchase of Fox, and the reduction of Universal, Paramount, and Warners to satellite status, Columbia was the last frontier. It also had some attractive assets: a film library, a television division, five TV stations, and twelve radio stations.

The success of The Blue Lagoon, Stir Crazy (1980), and Stripes (1981) further enhanced Columbia's appeal. From Columbia's point of view, being a subsidiary could be an advantage: there would no longer be the worry of takeovers, hostile or otherwise. It would also be to the shareholders' advantage, since Coca-Cola was purchasing Columbia's stock at $75 a share—almost twice the market value. Standing to gain the most was Allen and Co., which at the time of the purchase had 495,800 shares.

Price did not feel threatened by Coke's acquisition of Columbia; rather, he took it as a compliment, since one of the reasons Coke gave, according to the Wall Street Journal (8 February 1983), was the "business-like demeanor of Mr. Price and other top officials." But Price's demeanor changed when Columbia embarked on a joint venture with HBO and CBS to form a new studio, Tri-Star. Columbia's licensing arrangement with HBO was only the prelude to something far more elaborate: the creation of a studio that would reap benefits from both network and pay-TV by giving HBO exclusive rights to even more films but limited rights to CBS.[21] HBO would pay up to 25 percent of each film's cost, and CBS would be given TV rights to fifteen films at $2 million per film.

The creation of Tri-Star went completely against Price's philosophy of less, not more. But Price's philosophy was not Coca-Cola's. While Coke promised not to infringe on Columbia's authority (a promise impossible to keep), it issued a clear mandate: more, not less. Movies, then, were no different from soft drinks bottled in mass quantities for mass consumption. What distressed Price even more than the formation of Tri-Star was the recruitment of Columbia personnel for Tri-Star positions, particularly for the position of chairman and CEO, which went to his protégé Victor Kaufman. In fact, Kaufman waited until Coca-Cola had bought Columbia to sell the company on the idea of Tri-Star, thereby making Coca-Cola the parent of two offspring—one too many as far as Price was concerned.

It soon became evident that Price had no place in the new Columbia. In July 1982 he lost half of his title to Guy MacElwaine, who became president of Columbia Pictures while Price continued as chairman and CEO. But even before then it was clear that Coca-Cola wanted neither Price nor his close friend, Marvin Antonowsky, president of marketing and research for the film division. Coca-Cola's own Peter Sealey, a former vice president and manager of Coke's marketing operations, was installed at CPI to apply the company's marketing techniques to film; the result was streamlining and the general unhappiness that goes with it.

Other factors were also involved in Price's leaving. *Annie* (1982) was a failure that *Time* compared to a corpse awaiting burial. Price, however, should not have been blamed for *Annie*; it had been initiated under Begelman and ended up a Ray Stark production directed by John Huston, who loathed the material and gave it a nasty, mean-spirited edge. There were other failures, too: *Hanky Panky*, *Things Are Tough All Over*, and *Wrong Is Right*, all 1982 releases. Throughout 1983 there were rumors that Price would be leaving Columbia and going into—what else?—independent production. By the fall he did, but first there was a stopover at his old stand, MCA, where he was named chairman of the motion picture group as well as vice president of MCA. But repeat performances, like repeat performers, tend to lose their magic. While Price was responsible for several Universal successes during his tenure at MCA (1983-1986)—*Out of Africa*, *Mask*, and *The Secret of My Success*—he also greenlighted *Howard the Duck*. A *Daily Variety* headline (17 September 1986) summed it up: "DUCK COOKS PRICE'S GOOSE." It was not quite that simple; Price also ran afoul of MCA president Sidney Sheinberg and alienated Steven Spielberg to the point that neither spoke to the other.

Price's career is typical of the circular journey known to most Hollywood executives. In the movie business, the corporate ladder is more of a corporate turnstile. The paucity of major studios makes it difficult for former studio heads to move up, down, or laterally without at some point returning to their old stomping grounds or to former associates. In 1987, Price formed Frank Price Entertainment, Inc., with Tri-Star, the studio whose formation he had once fought, as distributor. In 1987, Tri-Star and Columbia were both under the banner of Columbia Pictures Entertainment (CPE), headed by Victor Kaufman. Supposedly one cannot go home again, but Frank Price did—three times, in fact; literally, to MCA; geographically, to Columbia (Price Entertainment was located at the North end of Columbia Plaza in the building where Price had had his office as president and CEO); and literally, again, to Columbia in 1990 as chairman of Columbia Pictures. Price could say he had worked at Universal when it was still Universal-

International and twice when it was a subsidiary of MCA; he could also claim to have been at Columbia under Harry Cohn, Coca-Cola, and Sony Corp.

While Price had fond memories of Cohn's Columbia, he had nothing good to say about Coca-Cola's when he left in 1983. With his departure, CPI's organizational chart changed significantly. Fay Vincent became CPI Chairman and CEO; Richard Gallop, formerly executive vice president of CPI, was elevated to CPI president and COO. Vincent's authority was increased when Coca-Cola's board of directors made him senior vice president of Coca-Cola as well as president of the new entertainment sector. For all practical purposes Vincent ran Columbia, and whoever replaced Price would be serving two masters: Vincent (and therefore Herbert Allen) and Coca-Cola.

The servant—short-lived, as one might expect—was Guy MacElwaine, who was already president of the film division; all that remained was for him to become CEO as well. Then he would have Price's old title and old job but not his production schedule. Coca-Cola expected earnings growth; accordingly, production had to be increased from Price's conservative eight films a year to MacElwaine's adventuresome eighteen. It was not so much the difference between quality and quantity as between "less is more" and "more is better." The larger the number of films, the larger the number of theaters that could play them; the larger the number of films, the easier to replace an obvious dud with a potential hit. The hitch was Columbia's lack of theaters. Since Columbia had never been vertically integrated, it was unaffected by the 1948 "consent decrees." But the situation had changed in the 1980s: having made inroads into homevideo, pay-TV, and network television, Columbia bought 81 percent of the Walter Reade Organization in 1981 and the rest in 1985. Even though it would sell the Reade chain (eleven screens in eight locations) to Cineplex Odeon two years later, it was evident that Columbia was eager to enter exhibition. That finally happened the following year with the acquisition of Loews Theater Management, consisting of about 850 screens.[22]

That same year, MacElwaine—who had been told in 1983 by Donald Keough, president and COO of Coca-Cola, that he "had docked [his] boat with Coca-Cola for the rest of [his] life"[23]—discovered that it was adrift. By April 1986 the captain was off "to pursue other interests."

MacElwaine's fall was the result of a few flops and a few miscalculations, the latter being the more serious. While MacElwaine turned down Ray Stark's film versions of Neil Simon's *Brighton Beach Memoirs* (1986) and *Biloxi Blues* (1988) (which Stark then took to Universal, where Frank Price greenlighted them), he also closed deals on certain films on which he had been instructed to pass. Yet as president and CEO, he supposedly could do so. On the one hand, Coca-Cola chairman Roberto Goizueta told him, "There is only one head of the studio, and you are the head of the studio."[24] Words, however, are winged, especially those uttered over the telephone, as Goizueta's were. They lost much of their force en route from Coca-Cola in Atlanta to Columbia Plaza in Burbank. MacElwaine was never sure about the nature of his autonomy: "Autonomy . . . is a strange word. Everyone likes to use it. I can remember a lot of studio heads going around [saying] 'I have complete autonomy.' Nobody has complete autonomy."[25]

MacElwaine was right; no studio head, much less one of a Coca-Cola subsidiary, can be autonomous. Even the old moguls never were. For one thing, they were not presidents, except for Harry Cohn, yet even he had to accede to New York. What the new breed of studio head coveted was creative autonomy—the freedom to make movies that were right for the studio and that in some way reflected personal tastes, values, or beliefs. This was auteurism of a new sort. The old moguls never craved that kind of authority because they had it; they may not have been autonomous but they were able to get the kinds of films they wanted made. New York may have curtailed their budgets or saddled them with titles they deplored, but New York could not interfere with production; in that area studio heads and those to whom they would delegate authority had as much creative control as one could get in an industry founded on the principle of division and specialization of labor.

With the breakup of the studio system and the imposition of a corporate mentality on what remained of it, the idea of control became stronger. Control meant the authority to greenlight a movie. Unfortunately, that light can also flash red, and the new studio heads had to learn to read ambiguous signals.

MacElwaine did not understand that flashing red meant "stop," not "proceed with caution." As his authority began to ebb, an air of *déjà vu* hung over the studio. 1985 became a playback of 1983. Again Coca-Cola was unhappy with the way Columbia was marketing its films; again Columbia's marketing head left; again Peter Sealey called the shots. When Ashley Boone, Columbia's marketing and distribution president, departed for MGM, Sealey replaced him. It was Sealey's presence that had been partly responsible for Price's departure; it would also play a role in MacElwaine's. Sealey's background made him indifferent to such matters as promotional tours (which should be curtailed), production costs (which should be reduced), and charity premieres (for which prints would be provided but not theater rentals or receptions). On the other hand, the production schedule was doubled, resulting in a glut of films that could not be marketed properly because the ad budgets had been cut.

It was a vicious circle, with MacElwaine in the center. In the summer of 1985 he experienced Price's fate: he was "promoted" to chairman but lost the title of president. As usual a replacement was waiting in the wings: Steve Sohmer, the former executive vice president of NBC Entertainment, who virtually ran the studio from the time McElwaine stepped down in April 1986 to the arrival of David Puttnam that September. Not wanting to lose Sohmer, Columbia made him president and COO of Columbia Pictures, but only briefly. Puttnam had other plans for that position.

MacElwaine was off to that great face-saver, independent produc-tion, becoming chairman of the motion picture division of Jerry Wein-traub's Weintraub Entertainment Group (WEG), which was formed in 1987 thanks to securities, loans, and advances from, among other sources, Columbia Pictures and RCA/Columbia Homevideo, which advanced Weintraub $156 million.[26] MacElwaine may not have gone home, but he was not far from it: Columbia distributed WEG films until Warners took over that function in August 1989. MacElwaine, a former agent, quickly realized that WEG was no more secure than Coca-Cola's ship of false hope. Thus he really went home—back to International Creative Management (ICM) as vice chairman.

MacElwaine's successor was not an American but a Briton whose successes had made him attractive to Columbia even earlier. At that time he did not want Columbia. But with Coca-Cola in the picture, Columbia was a better prospect—or so David Puttnam thought.

THE SHORT UNHAPPY REIGN OF DAVID PUTTNAM

While studio heads have never enjoyed the same popularity as their stars, the Golden Age moguls were at least a colorful lot whose indis-cretions, aphorisms, and malapropisms, real or fictitious, have become part of film lore. As they died—Louis Mayer in 1957, Harry Cohn in 1958, Jack Warner in 1978, Darryl Zanuck in 1979—their replacements were mostly colorless. In 1948, Howard Hughes had the opportunity to provide RKO with a legendary presence; instead, he facilitated its destruction, making RKO the first of the majors to cease production. Even if the epigones had had the moguls' style, they would have lacked their impact. The studios were not what they had been, nor, for that matter, was the industry.

The history of the studios is inseparable from the history of the American film, which is easily periodized until the end of the 1950s; from that point on, diffusion and fragmentation replace cohesion and order. The studios, many of which were once associated with a single name, witnessed a succession of replacements, none of whom could perpetuate the myth of the studio-as-family with a patriarchal head and a household of stars. There would be no more group portraits like the famous 1949 photo of the MGM family, a last-ditch attempt to convince the public that there was still a dynasty at Culver City. The studio households were growing smaller, less stable, and more individualistic.

Thus, it was startling to hear David Puttnam, Columbia's new chairman and CEO, say that he intended to run Columbia as a 1940s kind of studio by following the division of labor principle and setting up specialized units à la Arthur Freed's musical unit at MGM, Bryan Foy's B unit at Warners, or Val Lewton's horror unit at RKO. Puttnam may have admired Irving Thalberg, but Thalberg's MGM could not be recreated at Coca-Cola's Columbia.

Equally startling was the amount of publicity Puttnam's appointment generated during the summer of 1986; the hoopla had less to do with Puttnam's reputation as a filmmaker than with several unrelated factors that became interconnected by procrustean logic. While Puttnam had coproduced the successful thriller *Midnight Express* (1978), a Columbia release, and had produced the Oscar-winning *Chariots of Fire* (1981), he was British, and not even an American citizen. Thus his arrival occasioned extremes of suspicion and anticipation, Anglophobia and Anglophilia, despair and hope. Columbia needed a savior, particularly after a string of 1986 failures—*A Fine Mess*, *Violets Are Blue*, *Armed and Dangerous*, *Jo-Jo Dancer*, *Your Life Is Calling*—led some analysts to wonder how long Coca-Cola would retain the entertainment business sector. Anyone promising a turnaround would be welcome, so a British Shane was called to the aid of a beleaguered American studio to remind the Hollywood prodigals of the inheritance they had squandered. Shane, however, always left after he completed his mission; Puttnam only had time to preach his gospel, which proved so alien that he was out of a job in little more than a year. Even Hirschfield, Price, and MacElwaine had lasted longer.

MacElwaine was chairman and CEO when he left Columbia, and Puttnam inherited that dual title. He deliberately did not want the title of president, although Columbia had proposed it. "I'm not the head of production," Puttnam insisted. "I'm chairman and chief executive of the company, which—as I see it—means that my role is to put together the structures and policies that dictate the manner and direction in which the company moves forward, not to select individual projects. I hope to have a huge input into at least six of our films a year. But my job is really to hire the people who would make them best."[27]

A president, however, was necessary, and Puttnam chose David Picker, whom Puttnam preferred to call his "partner." They were definitely a team. Picker, whose varied background included high positions at United Artists, Paramount, and Lorimar, shared Puttnam's views on cutting costs, reducing the number of films in development, and adhering to a fifteen-pictures-a-year schedule, slightly lower than MacElwaine's goal.

This was to be a new Columbia, a studio with its own identity and an international character. Since the first movies Puttnam saw as a child were those of the 1950s, they would be the paradigm: "I was brought up on and by the movies. They formed, far and away, the most powerful cultural, social, and ethical impact on my formative years. These were the movies of the '50s, and for the most part, they were American movies."[28]

When Puttnam made those remarks to the Coca-Cola executives in Atlanta, he was not appealing to their patriotism; he was utterly sincere. Yet what he envisioned—movies reflecting the values of the 1950s, produced under the conditions of the studio system—was impossible. It was, of course, still possible to make the kinds of movies Puttnam had seen in his youth; he had already done so with *Chariots of Fire*, *Local Hero*, (1983) and *The Killing Fields* (1984). But it was the system responsible for such movies—movies with "the positive and powerful aura of post–Marshall Plan, concerned and responsible America"[29]—that Puttnam wanted to revive, with some modifications and concessions to modernity.

"To my mind there haven't been studios for years. I'd like to turn Columbia back into a studio."[30] Even a partial realization of such a goal would require radical restructuring. The number of independent producers would have to be reduced in favor of executive or in-house producers whose films would define the studio's image, as Thalberg defined MGM's and Hal B. Wallis defined Warners'. Although Puttnam never had the chance to put together such a team, he knew exactly how to go about it: he would surround himself with those who shared his enthusiasm for films high in values and moderate in budget, and who were young and therefore inexpensive, but whose worth would be measured in terms not of experience and reputation but rather of competence and commitment. Their movies, while diverse, would have social and moral concerns in common. A typical budget would be $10.7 million, $4 million less than usual. What mattered was quality; the profits would come, but not exclusively from the United States. Puttnam's motto was quite different from MGM's *Ars Gratia Artis*; it was "smaller films, smaller risks, smaller profits—but regular profits." What was important was not domestic grosses but international ones; domestic grosses fluctuate, while international ones are steady.

A global approach would mean that a film might not be a smash in America but would do well internationally. Puttnam planned to abolish domestic marketing, substituting a worldwide marketing division headed by Gregory Coote, whom he had lured from an Australian production company and who, until Puttnam's departure in the fall of

1987, remained part of his team—a team that was becoming so British that Ray Stark referred to the studio as "British Columbia."

Puttnam was not averse to Americans who thought along his lines, especially if they were young, intelligent, and inexpensive. He therefore invited Catherine Wyler, daughter of director William Wyler, to join Columbia as a senior vice president of production, where her chief responsibility would be to develop the kind of factual film that Puttnam favored. He was especially eager to remake her father's Academy Award–winning documentary *Memphis Belle* (1944) as a feature film. (Ironically, the movie was made only *after* Puttnam's departure from Columbia.)

Puttnam was interested in films about events of international significance such as the 1986 Chernobyl nuclear disaster. Determined to make a movie about it, he devised a plan for a joint production between the United States and the Soviet Union, whose cooperation would be easy to get because of Puttnam's close relationship with the head of the Soviet filmmakers union, Elem Klimov.

Rarely had a newcomer generated so much excitement and, in certain quarters, fear as David Puttnam. It was as if Capra's Jefferson Smith had been reborn as a studio head. Encouraged by what he thought was Coca-Cola's sympathy for his moral manifesto, Puttnam, whenever the opportunity arose, inveighed against inflated salaries and bemoaned the tyranny of the box office. Given Columbia's relationship with Coke, Puttnam's cavalier attitude toward box office receipts was naive, to say the least. Yet he insisted that in his negotiations with Coca-Cola, domestic profits were never an issue: "Although I didn't necessarily feel that I could deliver dramatically high domestic grosses, I was absolutely confident I could deliver increased foreign grosses."[31] Coke's alleged reply—that 60 percent of its profits came from abroad and 40 percent from the United States—was more a statement of fact than a matter of policy: Coke could charge more for its product abroad than it could at home. What Puttnam chose to hear in his discussions with Coke may have been the voice of his own conscience, which never learned to be silent. In reality, it made no difference in Atlanta whether or not Columbia was internationalized. The bottom line was box office—domestic *and* foreign.

While Atlanta favored smaller budgets, it also favored bigger profits. Puttnam's appeal to the mores of yesterday may have struck a responsive chord in Roberto Goizueta and Donald Keough, but their nodding approbation was not Puttnam's cue to preach the good news to the entire industry. There is no doubt that Puttnam was sincere in his unpopular views, yet he could never have believed that his attacks on undeserved salaries for undeserving stars for overbudgeted and overproduced films would endear him to Hollywood or Atlanta. His tirades fostered the image not so much of a frugal filmmaker as of a frugal filmmaker who is self-destructive. Puttnam was candid, but candor is often tinged with self-righteousness—a quality that was not alien to Puttnam.

As a Hollywood outsider, Puttnam could be more forthright than his colleagues, some of whom felt as he did but could not admit it. Puttnam not only assailed big-budget productions, remakes, cronyism, numerically designated sequels, and similar ills; he also cited examples and named names. He deplored deals allowing Warren Beatty and Dustin Hoffman to get $5.5 million each for *Ishtar* (1987), a $43 million fiasco; he always boasted that *Chariots of Fire*, which he produced for $17 million, won the Best Picture Oscar over Warren Beatty's *Reds* (1981), which cost over $40 million—a figure Puttnam considered obscene.

A Hollywood where agents, lawyers, and accountants dictate what reaches the screen was anathema to Puttnam. Agents were particular *bêtes noires*. Asked to address Michael Ovitz's Creative Artists Agency (CAA) in October 1986, Puttnam used the occasion to launch a three-front attack: "No more big agency packages. No more big stars. No more big salaries."[32]

During his brief stay at Columbia, Puttnam tried to implement his program. Convinced that films form values, he showed no interest in a sequel to *Jagged Edge* (1985), which he considered valueless. If there would be no sequel, there would be no Martin Ransohoff, who produced the successful original. If there would be no big-budget movies, there would be no need for Rastar Productions, known for big budgets and big stars. In keeping with his goal of giving Columbia its own signature, Puttnam advocated in-house productions instead of independent ones. As a result, he lost Daniel Melnick, whose *Roxanne* (1987) gave Columbia a moderate success. Puttnam also saw no need for Norman Jewison, whose seven-picture deal with the studio was permitted to "expire" in March 1987 even though two of Jewison's productions, *A Soldier's Story* (1984) and *Agnes of God* (1985), were the kind of conscience-prodding movies Puttnam was touting. One of those seven films would have been MGM's *Moonstruck* (1987), an earlier draft of which Puttnam had read but without any enthusiasm. If Puttnam had had his way, there would never have been a *Ghostbusters II* (1989), which is far more humane than the original. Bill Murray was not one of Puttnam's favorite people; speaking at a British American Chamber of Commerce luncheon in February 1987, Puttnam criticized actors like Murray for demanding upfront money instead of a share in the movie's profits; to Puttnam, such types take from a studio but give nothing in return.

Although Puttnam had alienated stars, agents, and producers, he at least had the respect of the Los Angeles film teachers, who honored him with the Jean Renoir Humanitarian Award, claiming Puttnam was "the best last hope we have." The reason was obvious. Puttnam was proposing for Hollywood what educators were proposing for the classroom: back to basics—back to the studio system, back to values, back to lower budgets. But the situation was irreversible; while one could still make flag-wavers, the flag no longer sported forty-eight stars.

If Puttnam had lasted at Columbia and had succeeded in making his kind of film, the studio would have developed a reputation for value-oriented movies, just as Louis Mayer's MGM was known for family fare and Jack L. Warner's Warner Bros. for social consciousness. In 1986, however, it was impossible for a studio to acquire a signature. Paramount came close with its Eddie Murphy movies, but even there it was the case of a studio's having a star under contract with enough clout to dictate his terms. Thus what in the past might have been called "Eddie Murphy's Paramount films" are just Eddie Murphy's films that happened to have been made at Paramount.

Puttnam was more than an anachronism; he was an anachronism from Britain. His criticism might have been bearable if it had come from an American, since there were many in Hollywood who would have welcomed a return to the palmy days of Harry Cohn. Unfortunately, British-accented criticism can sound condescending and moralistic, particularly if delivered in a low-key manner. While Puttnam was not patronizing, he sounded it. He had a quality common to moralists: a humorless passion. There was wisdom in his words, but no wit; even Ray Stark was more skillful at phrase-making.

Puttnam played out the classic scenario of the savior who believes in his salvific power which, even if it brings salvation, leaves the bringer a scapegoat. He himself provided the plot points: hybris, obsession, ambition. Fortune took care of the irony; *Ishtar*, featuring two actors, Warren Beatty and Dustin Hoffman, who had been victims of Puttnam's barbs, was about to be released when he came on board. While *Ishtar*'s failure cannot be attributed to Puttnam, it was also not attributed to the stars, who emerged unscathed, since each had enough of a reputation, or persona, to withstand failure. Yet *Ishtar* represented everything Puttnam loathed: a project that went wildly overbudget because the stars and director Elaine May were indulged in matters where indulgence should never have been tolerated. Although the script involved a running gag about a blind camel, for example, there was no reason to search for a camel that was really blind.

"Death wish" is a phrase that comes to mind as one reviews Puttnam's brief hour at Burbank. Had he been convinced he could effect a turnaround at Columbia, he would not have limited himself to a three-year contract. Such an arrangement made firing difficult, but it did not prevent sacrificial lambs from being placed on the corporate altar. Furthermore, Puttnam had been in the business too long not to realize that his remarks would backfire. It was as if he could curb neither his heart nor his tongue. He was no more capable of genial chiding than he was of changing Columbia back to a Golden Age studio. The only explanation for his behavior was that he viewed the three years as an opportunity to leave his mark on the industry—not in terms of films (since he could not have made that many in so short a time) but in terms of his philosophy. Otherwise, it is hard to explain his wholesale alienation of the most important people in Hollywood. To criticize agents is to criticize film's movers and shakers; to criticize the stars represented by Michael Ovitz's Creative Artists Agency is to bring down the wrath of one of the most powerful men in the business: "In today's Hollywood, if you want your career to thrive, you do not cross Michael Ovitz." [33]

Not only did Puttnam cross Ovitz, but he also crossed Bill Cosby, who had starred in Coca-Cola commercials and was regarded as a company spokesperson. Columbia's decision to film *Leonard Part 6* (1987) with Cosby had been made before Puttnam's arrival. But Puttnam's antipathy to the big-budget ($24 million), big-star film prompted him to turn *Leonard* over to a young, inexpensive, and British team— Paul Weiland and Alan Marshall—when he could have transferred the film to Tri-Star, where it might have become the moneymaker Cosby insisted it could be instead of the disaster it became.

Puttnam's short reign ended on 1 September 1987, when Coca-Cola announced it would separate its entertainment business sector from its soft drink operations—or, as *Variety* put it, sever show biz from fizz biz, by merging it with Tri-Star. This was not a typical Hollywood merger but rather a sale. Coca-Cola *sold* its entertainment sector to Tri-Star. Before the sale, Coke owned 100 percent of the entertainment business sector (which comprised film entertainment, television programming, and music publication) and 36.9 percent of Tri-Star. After the sale Coke would own 80 percent of Tri-Star's stock, 31 percent of which would be distributed to the stockholders as a dividend. A new entity would be born—Columbia Pictures Entertainment (CPE), 49 percent of which would be owned by Coca-Cola, 31 percent by Coca-Cola shareholders, and 20 percent by Tri-Star shareholders. The entertainment business was too costly for Coca-Cola. Coke had spun off its bottling companies into Coca-Cola Enterprises in 1986; it did the same with the entertainment sector a year later. Coke was no longer an owner but an investor.

Although supposedly Puttnam was given assurance on 3 September that the formation of CPE would not affect his position, he would have had to be a naif to believe it. While the sale/merger was not intended to unseat Puttnam, it had that effect. CPE, which would consist of Columbia, Tri-Star, Columbia Pictures Television, and other units, would need a head. When Victor Kaufman was named president and CEO of CPE, the fact that Puttnam had been bypassed should have convinced him he had no place in the new operation. Although Columbia and Tri-Star would be separate in terms of production and marketing, Puttnam, even if he swallowed his pride, could not remain as chairman and CEO of Columbia Pictures. When Dawn Steel was appointed Puttnam's successor, her title was president, and she was to report to the president and CEO of CPE, Victor Kaufman—a situation Puttnam would have found intolerable.

Kaufman embodied everything Puttnam disliked about the new Hollywood: he was a Wall Street lawyer who had not been bred on the movies as Puttnam had. Puttnam belonged to the tradition of the studio head as mediocre student with, at best, a high school diploma. Kaufman, a graduate of Queens College (CUNY) and New York University's law school, joined Columbia in 1974 as assistant general counsel; having survived the Begelman scandal and the Coke purchase, he moved up to vice chairman of Columbia Pictures. It was Kaufman's idea to form Tri-Star; it was also Kaufman who convinced Coca-Cola, HBO, and CBS of its feasibility.

Coke wanted a corporate type, not a filmmaker, to head CPE, and Kaufman emphasized money over values: "Clearly my judgment is based on a perception of the commerical potential of a film."[34] His philosophy was in line with the new and, to be honest, with the old Hollywood, too. While Mayer believed in glorifying home and family, and Warner in evoking pity for the downtrodden, they expected their humanitarianism to pay off at home and abroad. Puttnam expected his to pay off eventually—first abroad, then (perhaps) at home.

Although Puttnam had no golden parachute, he had one with a silver lining. He could claim that he had not been fired but had resigned, that he was not unemployed but would be returning to his own production company, Enigma, from which he had taken a leave, and that he was not leaving empty-handed but with a $3 million settlement.

David Puttnam's place in Columbia's history is difficult to assess.[35] Not only was his tenure brief, but, as *Variety* has also pointed out, there is a difference between the films Puttnam inherited and approved and those he personally brought in.[36] In an era when a handful of worthwhile films is expected to vindicate an entire industry, Puttnam can at least claim to have enriched the human spirit with *The Last Emperor* (1987) and *Hope and Glory* (1987), the latter an Oscar nominee but not a winner. It is hard to imagine too many studios being attracted to *Hope and Glory*, a World War II movie without big-name stars that was set in

London and told from a child's point of view. While the American films of the 1940s portrayed youths who were so patriotic that they apologized for being 4-F, *Hope and Glory*'s boy-narrator is oblivious to everything except the excitement the war has brought; he hunts for unexploded bombs and plays Allies-Axis with his friends. While *Hope and Glory* may have been the antithesis of *Mrs. Miniver* (1942), in its own way it was as much a tribute to the invincible British, whose talent for survival lay in knowing how to cope with adversity and at the same time enjoy the diversion it creates.

The Last Emperor was a pickup from Hemdale, but it was still a coup: it is one of the most honored films in the history of the Academy Awards. Apart from its nine Oscars and despite its Marxist bent (as one would expect from director Bernardo Bertolucci), *The Last Emperor* is deeply moral. The rehabilitation of China's last emperor, Pu Yi, at the hands of his North Korean captors results in his transformation from god-on-earth to human being; thus the viewer does not witness the fall of an emperor but the metamorphosis of a wastrel. *Hope and Glory* and *The Last Emperor* represent the twin boundaries of Puttnam's vision: the small-scaled film and the exemplary epic. What lay in between was a fascinating mix of styles, genres, and stars. *The Adventures of Baron Munchausen* (1989) may have gone over budget, but it possessed a lunatic charm that was more appealing to adults than to children, since it argued that adults must always remain children at heart if they do not wish to grow old. A trio of "little films"—*Housekeeping* (1987) *Rocket Gibraltar* (1988), and *Things Change* (1988)—showed that Puttnam was still taken with eccentrics, loners, and isolatos: character types that had appeared in some of his earlier productions (*Midnight Express*, *The Mission*, *The Killing Fields*, and even *Chariots of Fire*). Moreover, Puttnam's trio enabled three actors to give performances that will be ranked among their best: Christine Lahti (*Housekeeping*), Burt Lancaster (*Rocket Gilbraltar*), and Don Ameche (*Things Change*).

Although some of Puttnam's films have been miscalculations (such as *Pulse* [1986], *A Time of Destiny* [1989], and *Me and Him* [1989]), no apologies are necessary for *White Mischief* (1988), *Eat a Bowl of Tea* (1989), and *Time of the Gypsies* (1989). Nor should Puttnam regret imposing the Columbia logo on *School Daze* (1988) and *The Adventures of Milo and Otis* (1989). As Spike Lee's second film, *School Daze* will prove invaluable to anyone studying the role of the black filmmaker in contemporary American cinema. And even though *Milo and Otis* was an animal story, it won over the critics. Puttnam had done what he claimed he would do: he had brought in an international slate of films representing the work of American, British, German, Italian, Scandinavian, Yugoslav, Chinese, and Japanese talent.

Puttnam's reign lasted little more than a year—from late summer

1986 to December 1987. Although he insisted that his team would not be affected by his leaving, almost everyone was. This time the second-in-command, David Picker, did not move up because he was too closely allied with Puttnam. Coke would go to the outside, and Puttnam's replacement would have Picker's title of president, not Puttnam's title of chairman.

DAWN STEEL

Her name and background forged her mythology. She was the dawn of a new day and as strong as her cognomen. Puttnam would have respected her (their middle-class origins were not very different), although he would have found her as formidable as her adversaries, who dubbed her the Queen of Mean. If her hair was more like a mane, it also went with her image: she was Boss Lady who came up from the ranks and would let no one forget it. The ranks were merchandising, first at *Penthouse* magazine, then at Paramount, where she found her métier. Although movies were never as much a part of her youth as they were of Puttnam's, she at least knew how to sell a product; and once she became Paramount's head of production, she sold movies.

It was not easy. The press made headline fodder of her name ("Dawn's Rise," "Steely Dawn" and, when she left Columbia, "Dawn with the Wind") and delighted in reminding readers that between *Penthouse* and Paramount, she had had her own company, Oh, Dawn!, whose specialty was designer toilet paper. But once Steel was confirmed as Columbia's president, she shed her past. She became a champion of film preservation; authorizing the restoration of *Lawrence of Arabia* won her the respect of David Lean, who rarely said anything laudatory about studio heads. When Paramount rejected *Casualties of War* (1989) because some executives balked at Michael J. Fox's appearing in a movie about the rape and murder of a Vietnamese girl, Steel approved it for Columbia. That is how *Casualties of War* became Steel's first greenlighted film.

The press had assumed that Steel had left Paramount to accept the presidency of Columbia, but at the thirteenth annual Crystal Awards Luncheon of Women in Film (9 June 1989), Steel admitted that Paramount had fired her shortly before she gave birth to her first child; that alone strengthened her resolve to succeed. But circumstances intervened that would have made success at Columbia impossible for anyone. Early in 1989, rumors began circulating that Coca-Cola had become increasingly disenchanted with Columbia and planned to rid itself of the entertainment business sector. Equally strong were reports that Sony was studio-hunting and that Columbia was a likely prospect. Sony's attraction to Columbia was more than speculation; the electronics conglomerate was looking for a studio with television interests—and Columbia Television had become a major force in network programming. In addition to producing two popular soaps, *The Young and the Restless* (CBS) and *Days of Our Lives* (NBC), Columbia also claimed such series as *Who's The Boss?* (ABC), *Designing Women* (CBS), and *Married . . . With Children.* (Fox)

Concomitant with stories of Sony's overtures to Columbia were predictions of Steel's imminent departure. Eventually, she would leave Columbia, but it seemed otherwise in March 1989, when Columbia and Tri-Star were merged into CPE's motion picture group. The restructuring left Steel even more powerful—but only for six months. With restructuring goes retrenchment. Thus the possibility that Coke would sell CPE remained strong during the spring and summer of 1989.

THE GOLDEN YEAR

1989 was the year Warners and Columbia received new parents and MGM just missed out on adoption. MGM, which attracted a new buyer (Pathé) the following year, had been coveted, bought, sold, deserted, and transformed so often that it began to resemble Lithuania on the eve of World War II.[37] And so, when Qintex, the Australian resorts, real estate, and television company, and Rupert Murdoch's News Corporation vied with each other for control of MGM/UA Communications (under whose umbrella MGM shivered), a longtime Hollywood observer might have asked which of the two was the lesser evil.

The era of Louis Mayer had passed. While it may have been autocratic, it was an autocracy tempered by paternalism; it was also an autocracy that produced classic movies—something the latter-day MGM did not. But those classic movies were not part of the sale; they belonged to Turner Broadcasting and were showing up regularly on Turner Network Television (TNT). What Qintex would be getting was a recent vintage lacking bouquet and taste. But the deal was not just MGM but MGM/UA. UA, at least, was choice: well over 1,000 titles. Whether the package was worth $1.5 billion was irrelevant; Qintex could not afford it, and by October 1989 the deal was off.

While the Qintex-News Corporation struggle for MGM/UA was a battle, Paramount's attempt to sabotage the Time-Warner Communication merger was a war.[38] The stakes were higher, the drama more intense, and the players more Machiavellian. Early in 1987, Time and Warner began discussing a friendly merger in the form of an exchange of stock; the result would be the world's largest communications company. Martin S. Davis, who transformed Gulf + Western into Paramount Communications, Inc., made a $10.7 billion (or $175-a-share) cash offer for Time, Inc., which would have rivaled the Time-Warner merger as the ultimate wedding of entertainment and publishing.

Determined to get Time, Paramount raised its bid to $12.2 billion (or $200 a share). Time then proposed to acquire Warner for $14 billion, a transaction that would not require shareholders' approval. When Paramount tried to block the deal, arguing that the shareholders would be getting more for their stock if Paramount acquired Time, the matter ended up in the Delaware Court of Chancery in Wilmington. In a decision predicted on Wall Street because of Delaware's tendency to favor management over shareholders, Paramount's request for an injunction was denied and the Time-Warner merger was upheld. Whether Paramount bought Time, or Time and Warner merged, there would be vertical integration, which has always made certain lawmakers uneasy because it spells monopoly. Certainly Sony's bid for Columbia was another attempt at vertical integration, which, forty years earlier, had resulted in the severance of exhibition from production and distribution. But what had been a cause of the industry's decline in the late 1940s became, in the Reaganistic 1980s (when the Sherman Anti-Trust Act was mainly invoked in price-fixing cases), a means of offsetting a decline.

Since Hollywood knew Sony was studio-shopping, Sony's $3.4 billion bid for Columbia in September 1989 was no surprise. Sony had been coveting Columbia for over a year, during which time it had also courted MCA. Sony's interest in either was understandable. MCA, Universal's parent, had a 13,000-film library, including both the Universal library and the pre-1950 Paramount sound films. Then, too, there was Universal Television. Sony apparently preferred MCA, but MCA chairman Lew R. Wasserman, who had rejected buyouts in the past, was not interested, although in 1990 he was considerably more amenable to selling when Sony's rival, the Matsushita Electric Industrial Company, made an even more attractive offer—$6.6 billion.

Even though Columbia may not have been Sony's first choice, it was still an attractive prospect. Columbia meant software for Sony's hardware, movies for the Sony Watchman. This was the same principle that had motivated Sony's $2 billion purchase of CBS Records in 1987. From Columbia's point of view, Sony's offer meant deliverance. 1989 was not Columbia's best year even though some of its box office disappointments were more interesting than other studios' hits. *The Adventures of Baron Munchausen* may have bored children, but it fascinated adults with enough of the child in them to recall a time when the imagination was not darkened by memory or fettered by reason. *Ghostbusters II* featured a more subdued Bill Murray and a plot both humane and touching—qualities the original had lacked. *Ghostbusters II* came too close on the wings of *Batman* to generate the kind of box office Columbia envisioned; hence, the studio wrote the film off as a failure, since it did not live up to its expectations. *Casualties of War* was not merely another Vietnam psychodrama but a probing study of guilt and responsibility against the background of a war that still haunts even those who never lived through it.

Since *Casualties* was Dawn Steel's first greenlighted film, she was all the more vulnerable. While Pauline Kael interrupted her summer hiatus to review *Casualties* favorably for the *New Yorker*, her enthusiasm has never spelled the difference between success and failure, only the difference between her readers' acceptance or rejection of her endorsement. The real Columbia hit of 1989 was *When Harry Met Sally . . .* , a tiresome cross between screwball and romantic comedy produced by Castle Rock Entertainment, of which Columbia owned one-third.

In addition to coming at the right time, Sony's offer made sense. It was not just one giant's lust for another's gold, but an electronics giant's desire for an earthling's software. The real battle of the giants took place the following year, in fall 1990, with the largest acquisition of an American company by a Japanese concern: Matsushita Electric Industrial Company's $6.6 billion corporate buyout of MCA, which gave the owner—the world's largest manufacturer of consumer electronic goods—proprietorship of a Hollywood studio, Universal. The package included not only Universal Pictures but also Universal Television, MCA Home Video and Pay Television, MCA Records and MCA Music, the Putnam publishing group, Universal Studio tours in Los Angeles and Orlando, Florida, a retail and mail order division, 49 percent of Cineplex Odeon theaters, and food and lodging concessions at Yosemite National Park (which MCA agreed to sell to the National Park Foundation for $49.5 million after objections were raised to a foreign company's owning concession rights at a national park). Sony, by contrast, acquired Columbia's 3,000-film library (Universal's was about 13,000), 25,000 episodes from 270 television shows, a theater chain (Loews Theatre Management) with 850 screens in sixteen states; homevideo (RCA/Columbia); Tri-Star; and Triumph, a distributing arm of Columbia that had begun releasing films under its own logo.

Since the Sony purchase occurred first, it generated more controversy. For one thing, Columbia became the second studio sold to a foreign owner, the first being Twentieth-Century Fox, now part of Rupert Murdoch's Australian-based News Corporation. For another, Pathé's bid to acquire MGM/UA preceded Matsushita's negotiations with MCA. Thus, when the deal finally closed, Universal became the fourth foreign-owned studio.

In the case of both Columbia and Universal, however, it was not just foreign ownership; it was Japanese ownership. The American public did not perceive the Sony purchase as simply an intelligent business move but as another example of Japan's quest for economic supremacy. Of those surveyed in a *Newsweek* poll, 43 percent believed it was a "bad thing"—bad for the United States.[39] Whether or not it benefited Columbia was irrelevant. In Hollywood, Sony's offer was seen as the clearest indication yet of Japan's desire for a stake in the American film industry. Earlier signs included CST Communications' partial financing of *Bright Lights, Big City, Fatal Beauty*, and *Betrayed* (all 1988 failures), Fuji-Sankei Communications' $50 million coproduction deal with David Puttnam, and JVC's (Victor Company of Japan) $100 million arrangement with Larry Gordon's Largo Entertainment for three movies a year for five years.[40]

The Sony purchase seemed to have all the earmarks of the JVC-Largo Entertainment setup (in which JVC would put up the money and Largo would make the movies), although skeptics wondered how Columbia's new owners would react to a Pearl Harbor movie, since *The Bridge on the River Kwai* is banned in Japan and "rape of Nanking" footage was excised from *The Last Emperor* when it opened in Japan in 1988. Sony, however, was thinking not about the future but about the present: having bought an entertainment complex, Sony had to hire someone to run it.

At least ten days before its 25 September bid, Sony approached Peter Guber and Jon Peters about heading Columbia Pictures Entertainment. There is some disagreement as to whether they or Mike Ovitz was the first to be asked. (Insiders claim it was Ovitz, whose Creative Artists Agency received a handsome consulting fee from Sony for its role in the Columbia acquisition.) If it was Ovitz, he was not interested at the time, although in 1990, after acting as go-between for Matsushita and MCA, the story was that he was angling for some position at MCA—perhaps head. At any rate, Sony wanted either Hollywood's most influential agent or its most successful producers; it was simply a question of getting the best.

The Guber-Peters decision was ingenious regardless of who made it; since one can safely assume it was not Sony chairman Akita Morita, two possibilities remain: Walter R. Yetnikoff, then president of CBS Records (a recent Sony acquisition that Yetnikoff reportedly arranged), who had known Peters from the 1970s, when Peters was managing Barbra Streisand; and Sony's president and chief executive, Norio Ohga, who made the cover of the *New York Times Magazine*, his picture juxtaposed with Columbia's logo.[41]

Although Guber and Peters were a duo, Guber was the filmmaker and Peters was the hustler.[42] Each man's story is fascinating, Guber's particularly so, since he is paradigmatic of the new breed. In 1968, Guber, then a twenty-five-year-old Syracuse University alumnus, joined Columbia's creative affairs department while studying at the same time for an MBA and a law degree at New York University. At twenty-six he was a Columbia vice president. Of the seven years

(1968-1975) he spent at the studio, the last three were as executive vice president for worldwide production.

Guber aspired to be an old-style production head, delegating authority rather than being involved in the studio's day-to-day activities. Thus a year after leaving Columbia, he formed FilmWorks. Thinking in more corporate terms, he teamed up with Neil Bogart of Casablanca Records to create Casablanca Records/FilmWorks, whose purpose was to feature Casablanca recording artists in movies, such as Donna Summer in *Thank God, It's Friday* (1978). Initially, Guber was both chairman of the board and president of the company. Soon he became restless, and within two years he withdrew from the presidency, which David Puttnam assumed—thence the beginning of a relationship that reached its ironic apex within less than a decade, when Guber assumed the leadership of the studio that Puttnam was unable to head. Before irony intervened, PolyGram, one of the world's biggest music companies (and an independent subsidiary of the Netherlands-based electronics conglomerate N.V. Philips), bought half of Casablanca/FilmWorks in 1980 and then acquired a controlling interesting in it. Bogart resigned and shortly thereafter died. Casablanca/FilmWorks—beset by turnover, unable to attract important filmmakers, and reduced to a production schedule consisting of *Foxes* and *Hollywood Knights* (both 1980)— was near collapse. Yet the entire experience had a salutary effect on Guber: it resulted in a new alliance, this time between himself and former hair dresser Jon Peters, supposedly the model for the Warren Beatty character in *Shampoo* (1975). Peters's blow-dry cut attracted Barbra Streisand, whose manager he became and whose remake of *A Star Is Born* (1976) he coproduced. Peters was struck from the mogul mold; minimally educated, he was a shaker in need of a mover, a Dionysus awaiting an Apollo. Had he been born at the turn of the century, he would have gone straight from grade school to Hollywood, not even wasting time in junior high school as the brothers Cohn did. To use the classic distinction, Peters would have been Los Angeles; Guber, New York.

Guber abandoned Casablanca/FilmWorks and, with Peters, formed PolyGram Pictures. Again, it was interference from the parent company, PolyGram Corporation, that a few years later led to the demise of PolyGram Pictures and the birth of the Guber-Peters Company. In December 1987, Guber-Peters went public, merging with Barris Industries; with that merger came the rights to the game shows Chuck Barris had developed (*The Newlywed Game, The Gong Show, Dating Game*). When the merger proved unsatisfactory, the company became Guber-Peters Entertainment (GPE). Guber really wanted a studio and made no bones about it. It was common knowledge that GPE failed in its attempt to buy 40 percent of MGM in 1988 and that

Guber has second thoughts about settling for 25 percent of a studio controlled by Kirk Kerkorian. Thus he and Peters were anxious to accept Sony's offer to run Columbia. Sony was equally anxious to get Guber and Peters because of such hits as *The Color Purple* (1985), *The Witches of Eastwick* (1987), *Gorillas in the Mist* (1988), *Rain Man* (1988), and *Batman* (1989). Sony, in fact, was so eager to get the team that it paid $200 million to acquire GPE. Yet there was a problem: GPE had a five-year exclusive arrangement with Warners, for which it had already produced *Batman* and where it had some fifty projects in development. Warners had also provided GPE with a separate building for its employees at the Burbank Studios. While Sony wanted Guber and Peters, so did Warners with whom GPE had a contract running through 1994.

Since it had been the men's dream to have their own studio, they accepted Sony's offer on 14 September 1989. It was an extraordinary deal: in addition to buying CPE, which it planned to merge with Columbia Pictures Entertainment, Sony also agreed to make both men cochairmen of the newly formed company, with Guber as CEO, senior executive officer, and member of the board's executive committee; Peters would hold the same titles except for CEO—an indication of which one Sony considered the real head of the company. Financially, they would at least be equal: their salaries would be $2.75 million a year for the first 30 months, and $2.9 million thereafter.

Sony, perhaps affecting naïveté, assumed it could buy GPE as it had bought CPE, despite GPE's commitment to Warners. On 26 September, Guber informed Warners president Terry Semel that his dream had come true; he would be running a studio. According to Guber, Semel "hugged and congratulated" him.[43] Semel's version is quite different; denying that he had "orally agreed" that Guber and Peters could opt out of their contract if a studio came their way, Semel maintained that if they "were under any misapprehension about my intentions (I don't believe they were), such a misapprehension certainly ends on September 25 when they asked Warners to release them in writing so they could work for Sony/Columbia."[44]

Guber and Peters knew Warners had the upper hand; if they were ever to go to Columbia, Warners would have to be compensated for their departure, which had overtones of seduction and defection. If Guber, who holds a law degree, actually believed in his "oral" agreement, he may have recalled the saying attributed (perhaps erroneously) to Sam Goldwyn: "A verbal agreement isn't worth the paper it's written on."[45] Guber waited over a week to inform Semel of Sony's 15 September offer; that he did so suggests that he was concerned the deal might fall through if Sony learned Warners would not release himself and Peters from their contract.

Warners sued Sony, Guber, and Peters for $1 billion for breach of contract. Sony, Guber, and Peters countersued for $100 million, again citing the oral agreement, which Warner dismissed as "a piece of fiction."[46] On 19 October, Warners filed for an injunction to prevent the producers from assuming their duties at Columbia. Guber and Peters were valuable to Warners (which claimed to have invested $13 million in fifty GPE projects, including a *Batman* sequel).

Having become a communications giant, Time Warner, of which Warners was now part, would not tolerate a rival's raiding a subsidiary to acquire talent for its own. Sony cried prejudice—"racist" having replaced "fascist" in the postmodern lexicon of slurs. While there may have been an element of truth in Sony's charge, there was none at all in Guber's and Peters's countercharge that they would "suffer a devastating injury to their careers" if an injunction were granted, and "would be put out of work with their goals shattered, or put in a position with nowhere to go rather than to Warners, which has said that it does not want them."[47]

While it is hard to imagine Warners' dropping anyone with Guber's and Peters's track record, it must have been evident that if the men finished out their contract, Warners would be getting a disillusioned, embittered, and perhaps ineffectual team. If the two really wanted to run Columbia, Warners could profit from their ambition. Sony was not about to get involved in a breach-of-contract suit, especially if Sony's claims could be proved to be "reckless and irresponsible," as Warners insisted they were. Besides, Warners had made some strong allegations: "improper conduct," statements "both unfounded and cynical," and "hands [that] are unclean."[48]

Still, Time Warner had to save face, for it was not so much a contest between Warners and Columbia as between Time Warner and Sony, both of which were first-time parents of studios that shared the same location at Burbank. Thus Sony would pay for the raid. To release Guber and Peters from their contract, Time Warner wanted—and got—half ownership of CBS Records/Columbia House, the world's largest mail-order record club; ten-year distribution rights to Columbia's theatrical and TV movies, including the Columbia library (except for 1,000 titles that had been licensed to Turner Broadcasting) for its pay-cable service; the Guber-Peters Entertainment projects in development at Warners; Columbia's 15 percent of Jerry Weintraub's Entertainment Group, which was not exactly choice (it filed for bankruptcy in 1990) but was still another piece of booty; and an unusual and historic studio swap: Columbia would yield its 35 percent stake in the Burbank Studios to Warners and move to the former MGM lot in Culver City that Warners had purchased from Lorimar. As if that were not enough, Sony would pay for the cost of the litigation.

Since Harry Cohn was always jealous of MGM, he would have felt vindicated by Columbia's relocation at the Tiffany of Studios. In the old days, a *Variety* headline might have read: "Gower Gulch Moves to Culver City." Actually, it was not the best of arrangements, since the MGM lot was in need of repair, but in some cases the symbolism of an event surpasses the event itself.

The other producers at Warners (Puttnam, Clint Eastwood, Richard Donner, Steven Spielberg) were not unhappy about the departure of Guber and Peters; it would mean less competition for themselves. Besides, the attention the team received, including a profile in the *New York Times Magazine*, gave the impression that their leaving constituted a permanent void. Some even wondered whether Sony would have courted them so royally if *Batman* had not been so obscenely successful (some $250 million by November 1989).

Since there could be no sympathy in Hollywood for Guber and Peters, whatever feelings that were remotely human were directed toward Dawn Steel, more in the form of inquisitiveness than of concern. (Hollywood is rarely concerned with people, only with rumors about them.) When Sony hired Guber and Peters to run CPE, it was evident there would be no room for Steel, who had taken the job initially because she had been promised autonomy. With a team like Guber and Peters, whose resumé outstripped hers (which, admittedly, had little time to expand), autonomy would be impossible because autonomy, by its nature, cannot be shared. Hence, Columbia's insistence that Steel would stay on was never taken seriously; it was the kind of statement company spokespersons make, hoping someone out there will believe it. On 8 January it was official: Dawn Steel would be leaving Columbia and going into, naturally, independent production. To Steel, departure was deliverance: "I feel like I've been let out of a cage," she exclaimed, beaming despite a leg brace—the result of a skiing accident.[49]

While David Puttnam's legacy is at least debatable, Steel's is not because there is none; there was no time. One can commend her for authorizing *Casualties of War* and *Ghostbusters II* (the latter vetoed by Puttnam); but there were also *The Karate Kid III* (1989) and *Immediate Family* (1989), which were miscalculations. The 1990 films she had put into production (*Postcards from the Edge*, *Awakenings*, and *Flatliners*) came out under a new regime, and only those whose memories have not unravelled will give her some credit for them.

Like her predecessors, Steel eventually went home—home being not Paramount, where she had been senior vice president for production, but the Walt Disney Company, where her former Paramount colleagues Michael Eisner and Jeffrey Katzenberg were now CEO and Walt Disney Studios chairman, respectively. And, like her predecessors, she left Columbia richer than when she arrived—$7 million richer after selling her CPE stock to Sony. If Steel finds at Disney the autonomy she sought at Columbia, it will be because her goals coincide with Katzenberg's. All Steel really did in spring 1990 was to move her fledgling production company, Steel Pictures (with a slate of 0 films), to Disney for a three-year period. At any rate, she found a niche—for the time being.

Unlike Steel, Victor Kaufman knew he would not be staying on at CPE after the Sony purchase and said as much. His was a different situation, however: Steel was Los Angeles; Kaufman, New York. Kaufman's position had become extraneous; Steel's, irrelevant. Moreover, with Jeff Sagansky's leaving the Tri-Star presidency to return to television (as president of CBS Entertainment), Tri-Star needed a replacement, whose title would be chairman rather than president. The rumors that the Tri-Star chairman would be Mike Medavoy of Orion were confirmed early in 1990. It was an interesting choice, since it reflected the tendency to place former agents in key positions. Medavoy had advanced from Universal's mailroom to casting director, then to agent, first at General Artists and later at the Creative Management Agency. In 1971 he became vice president of International Famous Agency's movie division. Three years later he was production head at United Artists, and in 1978, along with Arthur Krim, Robert Benjamin, Bill Bernstein, and Eric Pleskow, created Orion Pictures Corporation.

By spring 1990, all but one of the key positions at CPE had been filled. It was a formidable roster. In addition to Guber, Peters, and Medavoy, there was Alan J. Levine, whose specialty was entertainment law, as president and COO of the filmed entertainment group. But Columbia did not have a chairman, while Tri-Star did. Tri-Star was a novice in the industry, but Columbia, which had a venerable past, required someone experienced but able to fit into the new regime. At one time Columbia had had such a person: Frank Price, who agreed to return as chairman—a position he vacated in 1983 after Coca-Cola acquired Columbia. At that time the issue was autonomy; in 1990 autonomy was a given, Price claimed. Whether it is or not remains to be seen; one can at least understand Price's confidence because he had a bargaining chip in 1990 that he did not have in 1983: his own production company, Price Entertainment, which would be assimilated into CPE. With that assimilation would come fifty Price Entertainment projects, including original screenplays by Barry Morrow (of *Rain Man*) and Nancy Dowd (of *Slap Shot*).

When Price left Columbia for Universal in 1983, his marketing genius, Marvin Antonowsky, followed him; if Price would be returning to Columbia, so would Antonowsky—not as president of marketing but as executive vice president and Price's assistant.

The team was in place—at least as of mid-1990. Whether that team could make Columbia a true studio, as opposed to a movie bank that handled the deposits of others (as David Puttnam characterized the Columbia he briefly headed), is another matter. The old studio system was primarily the creation of production heads and producers (and directors like John Ford, Frank Capra, Alfred Hitchcock, and Billy Wilder, who wielded the authority of producers). It was such men as Thalberg, Arthur Freed, and Dore Schary at MGM, Hal B. Wallis, Henry Blanke, and Jerry Wald at Warners, and Darryl F. Zanuck at Fox who helped forge their studios' hallmark. As Thomas Schatz has put it, "The chief architects of a studio's style were its executives."[50] A producer's efforts were not necessarily reflected in the actual making of a film but in its planning and supervision; the legendary producers— Goldwyn, Thalberg, Wallis, Selznick, Zanuck—could elicit the best efforts from each person associated with the project. Thus, a signature began to evolve, a collective signature whose strokes, alternately broad and tentative, calligraphic and undecipherable, blended like a dissolve into uniform penmanship.

In this respect, Columbia was not very different from the Big Five. While Harry Cohn kept tabs on his personnel to the point of knowing where they would be dining on a given evening, he did not nurse every film through to completion; no studio head did. The Columbia signature was created by diverse hands. If Columbia is associated with certain series, such as Ellery Queen, the Whistler, and Crime Doctor, it is not because they were Harry Cohn's brain children. The Ellery Queens were produced by Larry Darmour; the Crime Doctors, except for the first, were produced by Rudolph Flothow, who also produced all but one of the Whistlers. If Columbia's Randolph Scott westerns, from *Desperadoes* (1943) to *Commanche Station* (1960), have a consistency of style, it is due, in great part, to their being Harry Joe Brown productions first, later Scott-Brown productions.

The progressive phase Columbia went through between 1949 and 1954 cannot be credited entirely to Harry Cohn; liberals like Robert Rossen and Stanley Kramer helped Columbia acquire that image through such films as Rossen's *All the King's Men* and Kramer's productions of *Death of a Salesman* (1952), *The Sniper* (1952), *The Juggler* (1953), and *Member of the Wedding* (1952).

Columbia was accustomed to producers and production companies; had Puttnam not made so many enemies, he could easily have imposed the signature of his own company, Enigma, on Columbia, and his Enigma films, released by Warners, would have been Columbia movies. Puttnam's signature was small but legible; Guber-Peters's was felt-tipped and flamboyant. Puttnam believed in modestly budgeted movies with talented but not necessarily "name" actors; Guber-Peters, big-budget productions with bankable stars. Puttnam would look for properties with social or humanitarian appeal; Guber-Peters, those with an air of familiarity (bestsellers, fashionable subjects, popular genres). There is little likelihood that Guber-Peters's taste will change. The team did, after all, shock the industry by paying an unprecedented $1.25 million for a script, *Radio Flyer*, by a neophyte screenwriter.

Since predictions about Hollywood tend to be either uncanny or embarrassing, one should avoid waxing oracular about Columbia's new management—whatever or whoever it may be. Columbia Pictures Corporation has long been defunct, and Sony's Columbia is part of a corporation more powerful than anything the brothers Cohn could have imagined. The standard metaphors for the post-Cohn Columbia have been "bank" and "pipeline": Columbia has been a place of transactions and the conduit through which movies arrive at theaters, appear on television, or are sold in video stores. Columbia offers "output," a term that vies in popularity with "product," with which it is virtually synonymous. That product can be wholly or partially financed by Columbia; it can also be financed by an independent and only distributed by Columbia. While it may be an exaggeration to say that there are as many ways of financing a film as there are films, it is certainly true that one way is to take as little risk as possible by working out deals with outside investors and television networks.

Thus, *Stir Crazy*, whose negative cost was $10 million, cost Columbia only $1 million; the rest came from West German investors ($3 million) and the sale of the television rights to ABC ($6 million).[51] Columbia only distributed *That's Life*; it was totally financed by Blake Edwards's own company and cost about $8 million, yet it opens with the Columbia logo.[52] Also sporting the Columbia logo is *Bloodhounds of Broadway*, whose credits speak for themselves: "An American Playhouse Theatrical Film, produced in association with American Playhouse, with funds from public television stations, the Corporation for Public Broadcasting, the National Endowment for the Arts and the Chubb Group of Insurance Companies." *My Stepmother Is an Alien* (1988), on the other hand, does not bear the Columbia logo, yet the credits identify it as a Columbia release; the copyright is not Columbia Pictures but Weintraub Entertainment Group. Still, it is not just a WEG movie but a "Franklin R. Levy/Ronald Parker Production in association with Catalina Production Group, Ltd." The movie may have been "output" for Columbia, but Columbia's "input" seems to have been negligible.

It was somewhat different in the 1940s and early 1950s; then, what Columbia considered "outside productions" (not to be confused with independently produced films released by Columbia) were really studio financed, made for and usually at Columbia. As veteran screenwriter Robert Blees (*Magnificent Obsession, Autumn Leaves, Slightly Scarlet, Screaming Mimi,* and others) describes it, "A typical deal would be to advance an agreed sum for space and services, plus a salary for the producer, plus an amount to 'develop' properties—all of which had to be approved. Ben Kahane took care of the financial details with Cohn's approval obviously necessary. Thus total sums were deducted if and when the picture was made. Nobody I ever heard of put any monies of his own into the pot."[53]

There still are—and always will be—production companies that are based at studios and whose films are studio-financed, although one suspects the financing is limited to the film per se, with advance funding for optioning, purchasing, and developing properties coming from outside sources (a bank or, to use a term beloved in the industry and elsewhere, "abroad"). Yet studios need more product than what such companies can generate; hence, they must resort to "pickups," independently made films that are produced for release only and that can range from minor masterpieces to mindless dreck.

Anyone seeking to change Columbia from a vault or a supply route to a studio must achieve some consistency in the sort of movies to be made, the signature they bear, the genres they represent, and the actors they feature. Only then will there be a studio—not a Golden Age studio, for that kind will never return—but one for the corporate age. Otherwise it will be the Bank of Columbia or the Columbia Pipeline, not Columbia Pictures.

NOTES

1. The reference is to the misleading subtitle of Neal Gabler, *An Empire of Their Own: How the Jews Invented Hollywood* (New York: Crown, 1988). Jack and Harry Cohn owe more to their abilities than to their parents' origins.
2. "Republic" was resurrected in the 1980s as the name of a TV program distribution and home video company; it has the old Republic eagle-in-the-clouds logo but is not a studio. Similarly there is an "RKO," the film development and production division of RKO/Pavilion, formed in 1989 and not to be confused with RKO, the studio that stopped filming in 1957.
3. This point is cogently made by Robert C. Allen, "The Movies in Vaudeville: Historical Context of the Movies as Popular Entertainment," in *The American Film Industry,* rev. ed., ed. Tino Balio (Madison: Univ. of Wisconsin Press, 1985), 57-82.
4. On the early history of Columbia, see Joel W. Finler, *The Hollywood Story* (New York: Crown, 1988), 68-69; Douglas Gomery, *The Hollywood Studio System* (New York: St. Martin's, 1986), 161-72; Clive Hirschhorn, *The Columbia Story* (New York: Crown, 1989), 7-15,; Bob Thomas, *King Cohn: The Life and Times of Harry Cohn* (New York: Bantam, 1968), 27-60. But the best way to understand

Columbia's creation is to read the trades—*Motion Picture News, Exhibitors Daily, Variety*, etc., from 1919 to 1924.

5. Gene Fernett, "The Historic Film Studios," *Classic Images* 145 (1988): 5.

6. On the Schneider and Jaffe clans, see Stephen Farber and Marc Green, *Hollywood Dynasties* (New York: Putnam, 1984), 267-84.

7. Cohn's one printed take policy could be circumvented, as Frank Capra illustrates in his autobiography, *The Name above the Title* (New York: Vintage, 1985), 105, 108.

8. Production information about *The Talk of the Town* is taken from the George Stevens Collection in the Margaret Herrick Library of the Academy of Motion Picture Arts and Sciences in Los Angeles.

9. *Columbia Pictures Television: The Studio and the Creative Process* (New York: Museum of Broadcasting, 1987) contains several articles and interviews on the formation and importance of Screen Gems.

10. Spiegel's fascinating career is chronicled in Andrew Sinclair, *Spiegel: The Man behind the Pictures* (Boston: Little, Brown, 1987).

11. In 1967 Banque de Paris was out of the picture entirely when its stock was sold to "five well-known industrialists friendly to management," as *Daily Variety* (1 Sept. 1967) phrased it—namely, the pharmaceutical firm J.B. Williams, shipping magnate Stavros Niarchos, two mutual funds, and two employee stock retirement funds at Screen Gems and Columbia.

12. Roderick Mann, "An Award for the Man Who Said 'Yes,'" *Los Angeles Times*, 8 April 1984, Calendar, 5.

13. References are to David McClintick, *Indecent Exposure* (New York: Dell, 1983).

14. Because Warner Bros. merged with Seven Arts in 1967, the corporate title became Warner Bros.-Seven Arts until 1970.

15. At the time neither the press nor the SEC knew of the purchase, which was disclosed in 1978; see *Variety*, 8 Feb. 1978, 5, 33.

16. McClintick, *Indecent Exposure*, 53.

17. As quoted in Thomas Schatz, *The Genius of the System: Hollywood Filmmaking in the Studio Era* (New York: Pantheon, 1988), 71.

18. In 1980 MGM split into the Metro-Goldwyn-Mayer Film Company and MGM Grand Hotels, Inc.; Begelman became president and COO of the former—hardly a comedown and slightly better than a lateral move. In 1981 MGM acquired UA, becoming MGM/UA; Begelman became CEO and chairman of UA. After slightly more than seven months on the job, Begelman was fired in July 1982 because he authorized so many unsuccessful projects at MGM. In 1984 he formed his own company, Gladden Entertainment, which, except for *The Fabulous Baker Boys* (1989), has provided little in the way of entertainment (e.g., *The Sicilian* [1987], *Millennium* [1989], *Weekend at Bernie's* [1989].) Hirschfield spent 1979 as consultant for Warner Communications. He joined Fox in 1980, first as vice chairman and then as chairman and CEO. He lasted four years at Fox and then went back to investment banking. In 1991 he was part of a team that arranged the sale of the Financial News Network to CNBC, General Electric's cable division.

19. McClintick, *Indecent Exposure*, 270.

20. News release, Columbia Pictures, in Frank Price file, Margaret Herrick Library.

21. In 1985 CBS sold its 6.2 million Tri-Star shares in a public offering for about $50 million.

22. It was Tri-Star that acquired Loews in 1986. With the formation of CPE, Loews belonged to neither Columbia nor Tri-Star but to CPE.

23. *Variety*, 30 Oct. 1984, 94.

24. Ibid., 92.

25. Ibid.

26. Kim Masters, "Lonely at the Top: A Mogul's Woes," *Premiere*, Aug. 1989, 27.

27. Colin McCabe, "Puttnam's New Mission," *American Film*, Oct. 1986, 40.

28. David Robb, "U.S. Drifting from Its Ideals, Assesses Puttnam on His Exit," *Variety*, 27 April 1988, 26.

29. Ibid.

30. McCabe, "Puttnam's New Mission," 40.

31. Ibid., 44.

32. Charles Kipps, "The Rise and Fall of the Coca-Cola Kid," *Variety,* 18 May 1988, 9.

33. L.J. Davis, "Hollywood's Most Secret Agent," *New York Times Magazine*, 9 July 1989, 26.

34. Geraldine Fabrikant, "Hollywood's Newest Heavyweight: Victor A. Kaufman," *New York Times*, 6 Sept. 1987, D 8.

35. Puttnam has already been the subject of two books: Andrew Yule, *Fast Fade: David Puttnam, Columbia Pictures, and the Battle for Hollywood* (New York: Delacorte, 1989), and Charles Kipps, *Out of Focus: Power, Price, and Prejudice: David Puttnam in Hollywood* (New York: Morrow, 1989). Kipps's is the more substantial.

36. *Variety*, 25 May 1988, 8, lists eight "inherited and approved" films (*Leonard Part 6, Little Nikita, Vice Versa, The Beast, Old Gringo, The New Adventures of Pippi Longstocking, True Believer,* and *Vibes*); and twenty-four films "brought to Columbia" (*Pulse, School Daze, The Big Easy, Hope and Glory, Housekeeping, The Last Emperor, Someone to Watch over Me, Stars and Bars, A Time of Destiny, White Mischief, Zelly and Me, The Adventures of Baron Munchausen, The Big Picture, Bloodhounds of Broadway, Earth Girls Are Easy, Eat a Bowl of Tea, Flying Blind, Gypsy Caravan, Hanussen, Me & Him, The Adventures of Milo and Otis, Rocket Gibraltar, Things Change,* and *To Kill a Priest*). *Gypsy Caravan* became *Time of the Gypsies*. Dawn Steel vetoed a theatrical release of *Flying Blind*, a joint venture of Columbia and NBC, which was finally aired on NBC (30 July 1990). To the Inherited and Approved category should be added *Punchline* and *Physical Evidence* (see Kipps, *Out of Focus*, 155). *Earth Girls Are Easy* left Columbia to become a Vestron film, and, to amend Kipps's slate (324-25), *Bloodhounds of Broadway* had been sold to Vestron; when Vestron ceased film production in 1989, it became a Columbia release.

37. The twenty-year despoliation of MGM (1970-1990) is well told in Peter Bart, *Fade Out: The Calamitous Final Days of MGM* (New York: Morrow, 1990). The Qintex scenario was repeated in 1990 when another buyer for MGM/UA emerged, Pathé Communications' Giancarlo Parretti, who, desperate to raise the necessary $1.31 billion, wheeled and dealed—stalling, postponing, missing deadlines, and finally coming up with $600 million from various European sources while planning to get the remainder by licensing rights to the Pathé and MGM/UA libraries to Time Warner, which offered Parretti a $650 million loan. When Time Warner discovered Pathé was selling the same rights twice, it reneged and sued Pathé for $100 million. Pathé then turned to Turner Broadcasting, to which it sold rights to the MGM/UA library for $200 million. Time Warner and Pathé settled, with Time Warner giving Pathé $125 million for domestic and foreign homevideo rights to 1,700 titles. See *Hollywood Reporter*, 2 Nov. 1990, 6; *Variety*, 5 Nov. 1990, 101. Parretti revised the figures in 1991, but

there are still discrepancies according to *Variety*, 21 Jan. 1991, 6.

38. The most readable account of the affair is Connie Bruck, "The World of Business: The Deal of the Year," *New Yorker*, 8 Jan. 1990, 66-89. For the remainder of the discussion, one should remember that "Warner" refers to Warner Communications, whose filmed entertainment division includes Warner Bros. Films, referred to as "Warners."

39. "Japan Goes Hollywood," *Newsweek*, 9 Oct. 1989, 62.

40. On Japanese investments in American films, see Charlotte Wolter, "Going Hollywood: The Japanese Financial Invasion," *Hollywood Reporter*, Weekly International Edition, 26 Sept. 1989, S20-S58; also *Hollywood Reporter*, 2 July 1990, 1, 21 and *Variety*, 18 Feb. 1991, 3, 20.

41. David E. Sanger, in "Sony's Norio Ohga: Building Smaller, Buying Bigger," *New York Times Magazine*, 18 Feb. 1990, 24, believes Ohga not only managed to "secure the services of Guber and Peters" but also "led Sony's $3.4 billion buyout of Columbia Pictures Entertainment, Inc." In Hollywood the story was that Mike Ovitz, or Walter R. Yetnikoff or both were responsible for the installation of Guber and Peters. Most favored Yetnikoff, who had engineered the purchase of CBS Records and who fell out of favor when Sony concluded that the team cost too much. Other factors (an inability to deal with Michael Jackson and Bruce Springsteen) resulted in his abrupt resignation as president and CEO of CBS Records (now Sony Music Entertainment) in summer 1990.

42. Biographical material on the team has been taken from a variety of news sources, the most detailed of which are Nancy Griffin and Kim Masters, "Columbia's New King Pins," *Premiere*, March 1990, 89-101; Diane K. Shah, "The Producers," *New York Times Magazine*, 22 Oct. 1989, 27.

43. *Hollywood Reporter*, 27 Oct. 1989, 8.

44. Ibid., 31 Oct. 1989, 6.

45. On this alleged Goldwynism, see A. Scott Berg, *Goldwyn: A Biography* (New York: Ballantine, 1990), 396.

46. *Hollywood Reporter*, 20 Oct. 1989, 56.

47. Ibid., 27 Oct. 1989, 8.

48. Ibid., 31 Oct. 1989, 1.

49. Aljean Harmetz, "Dawn Steel Quits Columbia Post," *New York Times*, 9 Jan. 1990, C 15.

50. Schatz, *Genius of the System*, 7.

51. Lisa Gubernick, "Walter Yetnikoff's $300 Million Mistake," *Forbes*, 11 Dec. 1989, 108, 109.

52. Samir Hachem, "Case Study: *Switch*," *Hollywood Reporter*, Weekly International Edition, 7 Aug. 1990, S28.

53. Letter to author, 28 Aug. 1990.

CHRONOLOGY

1882   Joe Brandt is born in Troy, New York

1889   Jack Cohn is born to Joseph and Bella Cohn, 355 East 88th St., New York City, the second of five children

1891   Harry is born, the Cohns' third child

1908   Jack joins IMP (soon to be Universal), followed by Brandt

1912   Harry enters vaudeville briefly, then tries song-plugging

1913   Jack reedits *Traffic in Souls*, making it Universal's first full-length feature

       Harry becomes a "travelling exhib" for Universal; conceives the idea for musical shorts

1918   Harry becomes Carl Laemmle's administrative assistant at Universal

1919   The Cohns and Brandt leave Universal; the Cohns go into two-reelers with *Hall Room Boys*

1920   The Cohns and Brandt form CBC Film Sales Company, distributing through states' rights

       Sam Briskin joins CBC as accountant, beginning a forty-eight year relationship with Columbia

1922   Briskin's brother-in-law, Abe Schneider, arrives at CBC, beginning a lifelong association with Columbia

1924   CBC starts to create its own exchanges, the first of which is Columbia

       CBC Film Sales Company is transformed into Columbia Pictures Corporation, with Joe Brandt as president, Jack Cohn as vice president for sales, and Harry as vice president for production

1927   Frank Capra joins Columbia

1929   Columbia issues its first stock

1930   Schneider's brother-in-law, Leo Jaffe, comes on board

1932   Columbia wins its first Oscar nomination, for *The Criminal Code* (1931) screenplay

       A power struggle results in Harry's buying out Brandt and becoming both president and production chief

1933   Capra's *The Bitter Tea of General Yen* is the first movie to play Radio City Music Hall

1934   Capra's *Lady for a Day* (1933) wins four Oscar nominations

1935   Columbia purchases the Burbank ranch

    Columbia wins its first Oscars—five for Capra's *It Happened One Night*; two for *One Night of Love*

1937   Columbia releases its first serial, *Jungle Menace*

1939   Capra's *You Can't Take It with You* (1938) is voted Oscars for Best Picture and Best Director

    Capra leaves Columbia

    Joe Brandt dies

1943   Columbia releases its first technicolor movie, *The Desperadoes*

1948   The formation of Screen Gems, Columbia's TV subsidiary, marks the studio's entrance into television

1949   Producer Sam Spiegel (then "S.P. Eagle") begins his long association with Columbia

1951-54   Stanley Kramer makes eleven films for Columbia, one of which—*The Caine Mutiny*—is a hit

1956   Columbia begins licensing films to television through Screen Gems

    Jack Cohn dies

1958   Harry Cohn dies

    Abe Schneider becomes president of Columbia

1967   Ray Stark becomes part of Columbia

1968   Screen Gems is merged with Columbia Pictures Corporation to form Columbia Pictures Industries (CPI), with Leo Jaffe as president

    Sam Briskin dies

1971   Columbia records it greatest net loss—more than $28 million

    Columbia decides to sell its West Hollywood studio

1972   Columbia moves to Burbank, forming with Warners the Burbank Studios; losses decrease

1973   Herbert Allen, Jr., joins the Columbia board

    Alan Hirschfield becomes president of CPI; David Begelman becomes president of Columbia Pictures

1974   "Screen Gems" is renamed "Columbia Pictures Television"

1976   The Begelman scandal begins

1978   Begelman leaves Columbia, followed by Hirschfield

    Fay Vincent replaces Hirschfield as president of CPI

    Dan Melnick briefly replaces Begelman as president of Columbia Pictures

1979   Frank Price replaces Melnick as president of Columbia Pictures

1981   Columbia enters exhibition, buying 81 percent of the Walter Reade Organization (eleven screens) and the rest in 1985

1982   Coca-Cola buys Columbia Pictures Industries

Tri-Star is formed as a joint venture of Columbia, Home Box Office, and CBS

1985   Guy MacElwaine becomes president of Columbia Pictures, replacing Price

1986   Columbia acquires Loews Theater Management (850 screens)

MacElwaine is out and David Puttnam becomes chairman and CEO of Columbia Pictures

1987   Dawn Steel replaces Puttnam but with the title of president, Columbia Pictures

Coke merges Columbia and Tri-Star to create Columbia Pictures Entertainment (CPE), with Victor Kaufman as president

Columbia sells Walter Reade Organization to Cineplex Odeon

1988   *The Last Emperor* wins nine Oscars

1989   Sony buys CPE for $3.4 billion, also buying Guber-Peters Entertainment; Peter Guber and Jon Peters are named cochairmen of CPE, with Guber also as CEO

1990   Dawn Steel leaves, succeeded by Frank Price with the title of chairman, Columbia Pictures

Columbia moves from Burbank to the old MGM lot in Culver City

1991   Sony plans to buy Orion with management drawn from Castle Rock Entertainment, of which Columbia owns one-third, but talks prove fruitless

Stanley R. Jaffe, Leo Jaffe's son, becomes president and COO of Paramount Communications

Jon Peters resigns as co-chairman of Columbia Pictures

PART II

The Art of Columbia

1

FRANK CAPRA AT COLUMBIA
Necessity and Invention

CHARLES MALAND

It all started, Frank Capra tells us, by accident. Late in 1927 Harry Cohn ran down a list of unemployed directors, looking for one to hire. At the top of the list was Frank Capra, a Sicilian-American immigrant who had worked his way through Throop Polytechnic Institute (soon to be known as "Caltech") and had already achieved modest success as gag writer for Mack Sennett and director of two Harry Langdon silents, *The Strong Man* (1926) and *Long Pants* (1927). Fired by Langdon and then unable to find a directing job after the failure of *For the Love of Mike* (1927), Capra reluctantly returned to Sennett and even considered studying for a doctorate. But after talking with Sam Briskin at Columbia and boldly asking for independence in exchange for $1,000 a picture, Capra had the job. At the time, neither Capra nor Cohn realized the significance of the occasion. Yet when Capra left Columbia in 1939, Columbia had graduated from a Poverty Row studio to one of the eight majors, and Frank Capra had become one of the most celebrated directors in America.

Capra needed boldness to survive at his new studio. As he put it in his autobiography, "Columbia was not a place for the weak or the meek. Here they would measure you not by what you could do, but by how you did it under Cohn's bullying." Despite their many differences, Cohn and Capra shared intractable natures: "Both had been street hustlers, both were iron-willed and uncompromising. And if they were often like two immovable objects, it was this very obduracy that created a grudging mutual respect."[1] From their first meeting to Capra's departure over a decade later, these dynamic personalities pressured one another in mutually productive ways.

When Capra arrived at Columbia he joined a small but growing independent company that was releasing about thirty features a year, most of which were low-budget. A 1927 exception was the studio's most expensive film to that time, *The Blood Ship,* directed by George Seitz and the first Columbia movie to play at New York's Roxy Theater.[2]

Although Capra was brash enough to stand up to Harry Cohn, he was not a seasoned director when he arrived at Columbia. One of the benefits the studio offered him was a chance to learn by doing, as long as he kept within Columbia's stringent budget and his films did well in rentals. This was a rich opportunity for a young moviemaker; in an expensive medium like film, few can find patrons willing to pay for one's training. And Capra took full advantage of the situation; in his first year at the studio he directed seven films, typical Columbia fare: *That Certain Thing, So This Is Love, The Matinee Idol, The Way of the Strong, Say It with Sables, Submarine,* and *The Power of the Press* (all 1928). Of these, all but one were B pictures, running between 60 and 70 minutes. The exception, *Submarine* (103 minutes), was a more expensive ($150,000) action-adventure with Jack Holt and Ralph Graves that Capra was called upon to direct three weeks into shooting when the original director was fired.[3] By the end of his first year, Capra was already beginning to graduate to more substantial pictures, as is evident when one looks at his working pace after 1928. He directed three films in 1929, *The Younger Generation, The Donovan Affair,* and *Flight;* two in 1930, *Ladies of Leisure* and *Rain or Shine;* then three again in 1931, *Dirigible, The Miracle Woman,* and *Platinum Blonde.* Thereafter, two Capra-directed films appeared in 1932, 1933, and 1934, and, following a lapse in 1935, one came out each year between 1936 and 1939.

Capra's increasing importance to Cohn after his first year is also suggested by the length of his subsequent films and his successful transition to talkies. Capra's 1929 films became increasingly longer: *The Younger Generation* ran 75 minutes; *The Donovan Affair,* 83; *Flight,* 110. Furthermore, Capra was quickly adapting to the technology of sound. *Submarine* and *The Younger Generation* were both "part talkies"—films with only some scenes using synchronized dialogue—made while Columbia, like other studios, was in the process of converting to sound.[4] *The Donovan Affair,* his first all-talking film (although a silent version with titles was also released to theaters not yet equipped for sound[5]), was significant for two other reasons. "It was," Capra wrote, "the beginning of a true understanding of my craft: how to make the mechanics—lighting, microphone, camera—serve and be subject to the actors" (NATT 105). The film also marked the start of an obsession that was finally realized in 1935: Capra's determination to win an Oscar for Best Director.

In March 1929, about the time Capra was directing *The Donovan Affair,* Columbia issued its first stock option.[6] From then on, Capra's stock and Columbia's rose together. Capra's reputation was growing, and *Flight* showed how Cohn's confidence in Capra had grown. Like *Submarine*, it was, by Columbia's standards, a big-budget film which the studio treated as a major release, charging $2.00 admission at its New York opening and giving it a well-publicized advertising campaign to enable it to compete with A films from the major studios.[7]

Between 1930 and 1934, Capra, driven by his desire for an Oscar, solidified his position at the studio and began to discover the aesthetic voice for which he is remembered. The sharper focus of Capra's vision stemmed in part from the fact that he was working increasingly with a regular group of collaborators. Cinematographer Joseph Walker, who worked sporadically with Capra in 1928 and 1929, shot all Capra's Columbia films from *Flight* on. Beginning with *American Madness* (1932), Stephen Goosson was Capra's art director for all films through 1938. Beginning with *Lady for a Day* (1933), Gene Havlick became Capra's editor; until then, Maurice Wright edited most of Capra's films. Finally, with one exception, *The Bitter Tea of General Yen* (1933, written by Edward Paramore), Capra worked regularly with two principal screenwriters between 1930 and 1938: Jo Swerling (*Ladies of Leisure, Rain or Shine, Dirigible, The Miracle Woman*, and *Platinum Blonde* [all 1931]),[8] and Robert Riskin, the screenwriter most closely associated with Capra. Riskin co-wrote, with John Meehan, the play on which *The Miracle Woman* was based and shared screen credit with Swerling on *Platinum Blonde*, in which Swerling was credited for "adaptation" and Riskin for "dialogue." Riskin then collaborated with Capra on *American Madness*, *Lady for a Day, It Happened One Night* (1934), *Broadway Bill* (1934), and the rest of the director's Columbia films except for his last, *Mr. Smith Goes to Washington* (1939), written by Sidney Buchman. There is clearly a connection between Capra's growing self-confidence as a filmmaker and the stable work environment and group of collaborators that Cohn and Columbia offered him from 1930 on.

Cohn did not provide Capra with this largesse from the goodness of his heart. The films were doing well enough at the box office to suit Cohn, and even more important—for both Cohn and Capra—they were getting better bookings. This was absolutely central to Columbia's growth and health, since the studio owned no theater chain. Thus Columbia had to expend enormous energy to convince the Big Five to book its films in first-run theaters.[9] *Dirigible* became the first Columbia picture to play the famed Grauman's Chinese Theatre in Hollywood; *The Bitter Tea of General Yen* was the first film shown at Radio City Music Hall after it had been converted to a continuous-run movie theater. Except for *Lost Horizon* (1937), all of Capra's subsequent Columbia films premiered at Radio City. Even *Lost Horizon*'s opening proves Capra's value to Columbia: when it premiered at New York's Globe Theater on

3 March 1937 and at the Four Star theater a week later, *Lost Horizon* became Columbia's first film to be shown on a reserved-seat basis.[10]

Capra's self-confessed desire to win an Academy Award also served Cohn's purposes, chief of which was to turn Columbia into a major studio. It was difficult for a studio like Columbia to get an Oscar nomination, much less win one. The reason was, in part, because only major studios could afford to make the kind of movie that defined the industry's sense of quality. But even more important, membership in the Academy in the early 1930s was by invitation only, based on "meritorious achievements." As one might expect, Academy membership was made up primarily of employees from the Big Five, whose films won most of the awards.

In a typically brash move, Capra decided to attack the problem head on. When *Ladies of Leisure*, with Barbara Stanwyck in her first Capra film, received no Oscar nominations in 1931, Capra protested the general injustice of the way the Academy treated films of independent studios. By attacking the Academy himself and getting Cohn to complain about the narrow representation on the Academy's board of governors, Capra received an invitation to become an Academy member in May 1931. Then on 8 September, the Academy's executive secretary, Lester Cowan, asked Capra to serve on a nominating committee to put up a candidate for the board. By 18 September, Capra learned he had been selected to serve.[11] Within five months he went from a frustrated outsider beating on the doors to an insider helping to call the shots.

Capra and Columbia now had a foot in the door of the industry mansion. Although by this time the country was moving into an economic depression, Columbia weathered the difficult years of 1930-1934 quite well, raising the number of releases from twenty-one features in 1929 to forty-seven in 1934 and seeing corporate assets grow from $5.8 to $7.9 million.[12] This comparatively strong performance came at a time when some of the majors were in dire economic straits.

Capra's films surely contributed to the studio's economic strength and growing prestige. Although Capra was disappointed that the "arty" *Bitter Tea of General Yen* received no Oscar nominations, his next film, *Lady for a Day*, received four (Best Film, Director, Adapted Screenplay, and Actress). Although it won in none of the categories, it set the stage for the film that, more than any other, moved Columbia into the ranks of the majors: *It Happened One Night*.

Much has been written about this film. The leads were Clark Gable, on loan from MGM as punishment for having upset studio head Louis B. Mayer, and Claudette Colbert, who tried to avoid the project by making what she thought were unreasonable schedule and salary demands. To her surprise, they weren't unreasonable enough. In their adaptation, Riskin and Capra changed the hero of the story on which the film was based from a bohemian artist to a fast-talking reporter, and the heroine from a spoiled heiress to a bored but searching one. Though the studio did not have great expectations for the film when it opened in February 1934, it became a box-office bonanza, the fifth highest grossing movie of the year.[13] And it was still playing in some theaters when, at the 1935 Academy Awards ceremony, it won five Oscars: Best Film, Director, Actor, Actress, and Adapted Screenplay— as yet the only film in Hollywood history besides *One Flew over the Cuckoo's Nest* (1974) to sweep all five categories.

This was the turning point in Capra's career. By 6 June 1935 Capra had signed a new four-picture contract with Columbia that called for him "to produce and direct four (4) feature length motion picture photoplays and to cooperate in the selection, writing and preparation of the stories, treatments, adaptations and screenplays therefor, and to supervise the cutting and editing thereof." For this work Capra would receive a "fixed salary of One Hundred Thousand Dollars ($100,000.00) per photoplay," 25 percent of the profits generated by the films, a separate card for his director's credit, and an announcement that the film was a Frank Capra production.[14]

The contract was not the only indication of Capra's rising status in the industry. As if to validate it, the Academy's board of governors elected Capra president at the end of 1935; it was a position he held through 1939. That, combined with Capra's presidency of the Screen Directors Guild (to which he was elected in 1938) and his appearance on the cover of *Time* that same year, made it apparent how important a Hollywood figure he had become.

After *It Happened One Night*, Capra pretty much had his way at Columbia. Initially the movie's success led to a kind of immobility as Capra began to worry how he could match or surpass it.[15] In his autobiography, Capra describes an undiagnosed ailment that laid him low for some months in 1935. If the autobiographer can be trusted, he was able to conquer the illness only after a kind of conversion experience. As his health continued to fail, Capra was visited by song publisher Max Winslow, who brought along an anonymous friend who berated Capra for his lassitude and waste of talent during so crucial a time for America and the world. Deeply affected, Capra gradually recovered, resolving to make films that "had to say something. . . . . From then on my scripts would take from six months to a year to write and rewrite; to carefully—and subtly—integrate ideals and entertainment into a meaningful tale" (NATT 185).

Before leaving Columbia, Capra went on to direct *Mr. Deeds Goes to Town* (1936), *Lost Horizon* (1937), *You Can't Take It with You* (1938), and *Mr.*

Smith Goes to Washington (1939). Clearly, it was the success of *It Happened One Night* that led to his making these films. Until then, Capra was a relatively anonymous figure in the press. In the early 1930s he was often not even mentioned when his films were reviewed. Gradually he began receiving positive, albeit brief, notices; yet these were frequently in newspapers outside of California and rarely in the more important ones. The *New York Times Index* does not include a single reference to Capra before December 1934. *Reader's Guide to Periodical Literature* lists nothing on Capra through June 1935. By the late 1930s, however, features about Capra appeared regularly—among others, the 1938 *Time* cover story "Columbia's Gem" and the 1938 *Saturday Evening Post* piece "Capra Shoots as He Pleases."[16]

All this attention may have helped Capra more than it did Columbia. Still, Capra's films were being reviewed more widely than before and, in general, positively. While there are only two *American Madness* reviews in *Reader's Guide*, there are seven for *Mr. Deeds* and nine for *Mr. Smith*. If one counts the reviews in American newspapers and magazines, there are eight for *American Madness*, thirty-eight for *Mr. Deeds*, and forty for *Mr. Smith*.[17]

Such publicity also translated into more Oscar nominations for Capra films. The four movies Capra directed from *Mr. Deeds* to *Mr. Smith* received thirty-one nominations and won six Oscars, including Best Director (*Mr. Deeds*, *You Can't Take It with You*) and Best Film (*You Can't Take It with You*). More revealing is the fact that, of the thirteen Oscars Columbia won in the 1930s, eleven went to Capra movies. A similar disproportion held with Oscar nominations: for the entire decade of the 1930s, Columbia received sixty-five Oscar nominations in various categories: forty nominations went to films Capra had directed.[18]

Thus, by the time he was making *Mr. Deeds Goes to Town*, Capra had probably become more important to Columbia than Columbia was to him. *It Happened One Night*, budgeted at less than $300,000, proved a bonanza.[19] Cohn responded by providing Capra with bigger budgets. He authorized $500,000 for *Mr. Deeds*, which earned over $1.1 million in North American rentals alone, thereby justifying Cohn's confidence in Capra.The cost of Capra's last three Columbia films, however, made them less profitable to the studio. All were budgeted at between $1.5 and $2 million, and while they brought the studio prestige, received Oscar nominations, and won generally positive reviews, they were not especially profitable. (*Lost Horizon* was probably least successful. It was budgeted at $1.66 million, but the combined U.S. and Canadian gross was only $1.683 million, thus barely covering production costs. Columbia was then forced to rely on foreign rentals to generate profit.) The declining profits from Capra's films were reflected in Columbia's corporate records. From peak profits of $1.8 million in 1935 (due, in part, to the strong performance of *It Happened One Night* in 1934 and 1935), Columbia's profits fell to $1.5 million in 1936, $1.3 million in 1937, $200,000 in 1938, and no profits in 1939.[20]

It was no major surprise, then, that Capra and Columbia would experience disagreements in the late 1930s. The declining profit margin of the Capra films, combined with Capra's own sense of his importance to the company, made it almost inevitable that Cohn and his star director would clash. And clash they did when, in September 1937, Capra filed suit against Cohn, charging that Cohn owed him $100,000 and that he (Capra) considered his contract terminated as of mid February 1937, the month before *Lost Horizon* opened. Evidence suggests that both an advertising disagreement and a salary dispute motivated the suit. In his autobiography Capra describes how Cohn, in England in 1937, advertised a Columbia B movie, *If Only You Could Cook* (1935), as a Capra film (NATT, 217-35). Although this unauthorized use of his name galled Capra, the suit in September also stemmed from a problem over salary. Cohn's biographer notes that Cohn also angered Capra by refusing to pay him any salary after he finished *Lost Horizon* because Capra had taken far too long to make the film and was slow in beginning another one. Both this salary dispute and the disagreement about the unauthorized billing in England helped create the rift.[21]

The dispute was a serious one, given the pride and intensity of purpose that characterized both men. Capra refused to continue working while the suit was in the courts. Cohn stonewalled, too. When Capra's suit was thrown out in Los Angeles, he filed another in New York. When that was dismissed because the disputed action had taken place in England, Capra filed in England. After staying away from the studio for the summer and most of the fall of 1937, Capra was at wit's end. But then in November, Cohn visited Capra to work out a deal. Playing on Capra's sympathies, Cohn begged him to desist, adding that, were it up to him, he would free Capra from his contract if he would drop the suit; but the New York office insisted, Cohn claimed, that if Capra didn't return, he (Cohn) would be fired. "I built Columbia into a major studio," he told Capra. "Yes, you helped, but I picked you out of the gutter and backed you. Now you wanna leave Columbia. It's dreck to you. Poverty Row. But to me, goddamn you, Columbia is— is—not just my love. It's my baby, my life. I'd die without Columbia" (NATT 233). Capra, whether moved by Cohn's performance or motivated by a compulsion to return to work, relented. Cohn countered by buying Capra the rights to the hit stage play *You Can't Take It with You* for $200,000—more than the entire budget for an average Columbia feature only five years earlier.

Capra responded by fulfilling his contract in high style. *You Can't*

Take It with You won Oscars for Best Picture and Best Director. *Mr. Smith Goes to Washington* generated considerable publicity and controversy when it premiered in Washington in October 1939.[22] *Variety* named Capra Hollywood's second highest grossing director that year, behind Victor Fleming, who was credited with both *The Wizard of Oz* and *Gone with the Wind*. And Capra's final two films appeared to have strong box office appeal, with *Variety* predicting "an easy $5,000,000 return" in domestic rentals.[23] The prediction was inaccurate since neither film lived up to the studio's expectations; still, by the time Capra had fulfilled his contract, he had clearly established himself as one of Hollywood's most important filmmakers.

He had also developed a kind of personal genre that was recognizable to audiences and critics. The positive reviews of *Mr. Smith* from critics of vastly different political persuasions suggest just how widely Capra was admired. The conservative *Time* magazine called *Mr. Smith* more than just another excellent film; rather, it explored what Lincoln asked about the American democratic experiment: "whether this nation or any nation so conceived can long endure." The industry bellwether, *Daily Variety*, judged it "the most vital and stirring drama of contemporary American life yet told in film." The liberal *Nation* felt that Capra expressed "the spirit of true democracy" in *Mr. Smith*, at times approaching the "poetic realism" of the best French cinema. Even the Communist *Daily Worker* was enthusiastic, claiming it "has all the Capra genius and all the instruments by which fine films are made."[24] By 1939 Capra had clearly established a rapport with American moviegoers. In fact, it is no exaggeration to suggest, as Raymond Carney does, that "the power of Capra's work, especially for American audiences, is a result of the fact that he was—unconsciously, no doubt—making films that explore certain prototypical imaginative situations that are deeply ingrained in the American experience."[25]

Although it is impossible to give a full account of Capra's achievements in his Columbia films and the social vision that emerged from his movies as he grew more confident as a filmmaker, four films—*American Madness* (1932), *It Happened One Night* (1934), *Mr. Deeds Goes to Town* (1936), and *Mr. Smith Goes to Washington* (1939)—resonate with the distinctive voice Capra discovered at Columbia.[26]

Before concentrating on these films, we can make at least four generalizations about Capra's Columbia films. First, Capra moved from low-budget B films to more costly AA ones after the tremendous success of *It Happened One Night*. As the 1930s wore on, Cohn relied on Capra more and more to provide the studio with its most prestigious movies. It is equally safe to say that in his early years at the studio Capra found Columbia a congenial training ground that enabled him to achieve full mastery of a style that became distinctive in the mid-1930s and continued to the end of his career a quarter of a century later. Because Columbia risked less financially with Capra's early films than with his last four, it was easier for him to experiment with different genres or fresh stylistic devices.

Third, Capra's Columbia films were very often topical in the broad sense of incorporating matters of public discussion and interest. In *That Certain Thing*, his first Columbia film, Capra worked box lunches, a frequently discussed novelty at the time, into the plot. The main character in *The Miracle Woman* was a female evangelist resembling Aimee Semple McPherson; *It Happened One Night* showed the auto camps that had become popular in 1933. Sometimes the topicality was social or political, particularly in the middle and late 1930s. *American Madness*, made early in the Great Depression, featured a beleaguered banker and a run on his bank. The central figure in *Lady for a Day*, victimized by the economy, sells apples on street corners. In *It Happened One Night*, a mother and son go without food as they travel east on a bus. A crucial scene in *Mr. Deeds Goes to Town* shows a starving farmer bursting into Deeds's mansion and berating him for his selfishness; as a result, Deeds develops a plan for distributing his money among the poor.[27] Capra's ability to connect with audiences was partly because of the topicality of his films.

Finally, Capra's Columbia films were also, like most Hollywood movies, related to genres or popular cycles of the day. For example, his three films with Jack Holt and Ralph Graves—*Submarine*, *Flight*, and *Dirigible*—owe something to the popularity of *Wings*, which celebrated male camaraderie and won the first Academy Award for Best Picture in 1928. While *Submarine* changed the mode of transport, it borrowed from the narrative of *Wings*.

Similarly, Capra's *Forbidden* (1932) is one of the "fallen woman" films of the period, along with MGM's *Susan Lenox, Her Rise and Fall* and Warners' *Safe in Hell* (both 1931); Paramount's *Blonde Venus*, and MGM's *Faithless* and *Letty Lynton* (all in 1932). And, of course, the genre most associated with Capra is screwball comedy, which was especially popular from 1934 through the 1940s. *It Happened One Night* is considered vintage screwball, and many commentators would also include *Mr. Deeds* and *You Can't Take It with You* in that category.[28]

As Capra became more assured and successful, he began to develop a widely recognized artistic voice, defined largely by the way he blended genres. By the time he left Columbia, he had become identified with movies that combined elements of screwball with aspects of the social problem film. Like screwball, a Capra film involves a romantic relationship between a man and a woman who, at the start, exhibit different sensibilities. Their differences and unpredictable behavior generate comedy, but by the end the apparently incompatible duo becomes a couple. The relationship between Ellie Andrews (Claudette Colbert) and Peter Warne (Clark Gable) in *It Happened One Night* provides the model; Longfellow Deeds (Gary Cooper) and Babe Bennett (Jean Arthur) in *Mr. Deeds*, and Jefferson Smith (James Stewart) and Saunders (Jean Arthur) in *Mr. Smith* evolve along similar lines.

Like the social problem film, the Capra "personal genre" also treats a social problem as a central narrative conflict. While the Capra brand of screwball centers on the relationship between hero and heroine, the Capra social problem film emphasizes the conflict between hero and villain. Of the four films under discussion, *American Madness* is most closely related to the social problem film. Made in 1932, it focuses on two bank-related problems of the Great Depression: the mob psychology that leads to bank runs and the financial conservatism of banks and the wealthy that contributes to economic stagnation.[29]

Although *American Madness* prefigures themes in later Capra movies, the social dimension of his Columbia films becomes prominent only after his 1935 "conversion," which resulted in his vow to make movies that were both significant and entertaining; this he accomplished, to a great extent, by widening the perimeters of screwball comedy. *It Happened One Night*, whose popularity led to Capra's crisis and conversion, is the screwball antithesis of the social problem thesis of *American Madness*. *Mr. Deeds*, the first film after his conversion, is a blend of screwball and the social problem film, spreading its villains among various cynical and pseudo-sophisticated city types and touching on the economic dislocations confronting farmers during the Depression. *You Can't Take It with You* (1938), based on Kaufman and Hart's 1936 Pulitzer Prize play, emphasizes an aspect of Anthony J. Kirby that was unimportant in the original: Mr. Kirby is a war-obsessed munitions manufacturer. (Munitions magnates were, of course, considered villains during the isolationist 1930s.) Edward Arnold, who played Kirby, was also the villain in *Mr. Smith* and in Capra's first independent production after leaving Columbia, *Meet John Doe*. The former explores the gap between American political ideals and American political realities; the latter, the way the wealthy and powerful manipulate patriotic sloganeering for their own ends. By the time of *Meet John Doe*, social problem elements were threatening to eclipse the screwball motifs; indeed, a recent book on screwball comedy doesn't even list *Meet John Doe* in the filmography; the references to Capra stop with *Mr. Smith*.[30] Yet the fact remains that Capra reached the height of his fame at Columbia when he was making films set in contemporary America that blended screwball and the social problem film.[31]

Besides amalgamating genres, the mature Columbia films exhibit a relatively stable set of narrative conventions in terms of both character types and plot development. The character types include a hero, a heroine, an individual or collective villain, a benevolent authority figure, and a community that, after some reluctance, rallies around the hero. The plot development includes a conflict between hero and villain(s) that is, at its most effective, rooted in the broader cultural conflicts of values and belief. As the conflict plays itself out, the Capra hero undergoes a ritual humiliation that often leads to self-doubt. He may even consider withdrawing from society and refusing to continue struggling against the obstacles erected by the villain.

Then the Capra heroine becomes the key to the narrative. Overcoming her initial skepticism about the hero's idealism, she moves closer to his ideological perspective and, at a crucial moment, urges the hero to continue his battle. Restored and energized, the hero returns to fight the antagonist at a public forum and, thanks to the support of a benevolent authority figure (a judge or a vice president, for example) and a larger community that shares or comes to share his perspective, he emerges with at least a partial victory over the villain and a romantic integration with the heroine.[32]

As an early film, *American Madness* exhibits only some of these conventions. The hero function is split between Tom Dixon (Walter Huston), the president of the Union National Bank, and his prized employee, Matt (Pat O'Brien). Because Dixon is married, the romantic relationship is relegated to a subplot involving Matt and Dixon's secretary, Helen, who plan to marry when they can afford it. Three villains create problems for Dixon: his board of directors, who are trying to force him to merge the bank with a larger institution; Cluett, a bank employee, who helps some gangsters break into the bank because he owes them money from gambling debts; and a mob of depositors making a run on the bank after rumors circulate following the robbery. Dixon experiences a kind of ritual humiliation when, during the bank run, the board refuses him additional cash to stem the run; then he learns that his wife, Phyllis, was with Cluett the night before, thus unwittingly giving Cluett an alibi. Instead of the heroine's providing support at the crucial moment, Matt and Helen telephone small businessmen to whom Dixon loaned money over the years. When they arrive to deposit money, Dixon, now revitalized, shames the board into doing the same to save the bank. *American Madness* ends with the bank back to normal and with two romantic reconciliations: Matt and Helen, and the Dixons.

It Happened One Night follows the pattern more closely, although the social problem elements are largely absent. Here, the Capra hero is Peter Warne (Clark Gable), a maverick newspaper reporter who stumbles across the heroine, Ellie Andrews (Claudette Colbert), an heiress on the run from her father. The antagonists are Ellie's father, Alexander Andrews, who seeks to have Ellie's marriage to King Westley annulled.

Westley, the other antagonist, is an effete man of leisure whom Ellie has married to spite her father. Initially Peter sees Ellie as a scoop, while Ellie sees him as an inconvenience who might enable her to elude her father. As the couple travel from Miami to New York, they grow fond of each other. One reversal makes Peter believe that Ellie has rejected his attentions, leading to a scene of romantic dejection (and, one might argue, a kind of public humiliation when newspapers report Ellie's return to Westley). But when Alexander Andrews and Peter meet, Andrews realizes that Peter really loves his daughter. Thus Ellie leaves Westley at the altar, and, in the prototypical screwball reconciliation, the "Walls of Jericho" come tumbling down.

Mr. Deeds offers perhaps the purest and most typical Capra narrative. Longfellow Deeds, a small-town denizen, inherits a million dollars and goes to the city, where he is accosted by a variety of antagonists, from poets to greedy members of a symphony board to shyster lawyers. Their conflicts pit a variety of assumptions associated with small-town life against contrasting city values. At first, reporter Babe Bennett seems like another antagonist as she uses her wiles to get a story about Deeds, but she becomes more sympathetic as she begins to know him better. Deeds's ritual humiliation comes after lawyers block his plan to distribute his wealth among farmers suffering from the Great Depression. Jailed as mentally unstable, he lapses into silence, refusing even to speak at a hearing to determine his mental competence. At a crucial moment during the proceedings, Babe comes to his aid, defending his sanity and declaring her love. Thanks to a sympathetic judge and a courtroom full of farmers who would have benefited from his plan, Deeds achieves his ritual victory and is reconciled with Babe.

The title of *Mr. Smith* mirrors that of *Mr. Deeds*; their narrative structures are also nearly identical. In *Mr. Smith*, a young political idealist, Jefferson Smith, goes to Washington to serve out the remaining months of the term of a U.S. senator who has died in office. He is assisted by Saunders, a secretary who, through her experience in Washington, has become cynical about national politics. Saunders initially views the patriotic Smith as a "Don Quixote." The villain is James Taylor, a wealthy magnate from Smith's state who manipulates the other state senator, Joseph Paine, for his own economic ends. When Smith accidentally stumbles on Taylor's plan to enrich himself by selling land he owns to the government for a dam project—a plan supported by Paine—he tries to expose the plan, Taylor, and Paine. His ritual humiliation takes place in the U.S. Senate chambers, where Paine counters with a false charge that Smith is corrupt. When Smith, on the steps of the Lincoln Memorial, considers leaving Washington and casting off his political idealism, Saunders challenges him to stand up to Taylor and resume his fight. Aided by Saunders's knowledge of Senate protocol, Smith filibusters, eventually achieving a ritual victory when a broken and shamed Paine confesses his guilt and admits the truth of Smith's allegations.

At the core of these narrative conventions is the Capra hero, who increasingly in the late 1930s was depicted as a representative American type. Perhaps the best way to characterize the Capra hero is to connect him to what Robert Ray has called the "official hero" in American movie mythology. Ray has suggested that two hero types have developed in American movies: the outlaw hero and the official hero. Rooted in a tension in American culture between individual and community, the two contrast in their attitudes toward aging, women and civilization, and politics and the law. The outlaw hero, embodied throughout American cultural history by the mountain man, the explorer, the gunslinger, and the loner, represents a flight from maturity and often acts impulsively. He distrusts women and marriage, considering them as representing the constricting values of civilization. Finally, and related to this uneasiness with civilization, the outlaw hero is ambivalent about politics and the law, often posing his own private sense of right and wrong against society's. On the other hand, the official hero, often portrayed by a lawyer, a teacher, a family man, a politician, or a farmer, accepts adult responsibility and exhibits sound judgment. Very often married, the official hero accepts society, even embraces it. Instead of rejecting society's laws and politics, he is willing to sacrifice personal desires for the public good: the official hero is a man of civic virtue. If the motto of the outlaw hero is "Be sure you're right, then go ahead," the official hero would counter with, "We are a nation of laws and not of individuals" and "No one stands above the law." In contrast to the outlaw heroism of Davy Crockett stands the official heroism of George Washington.[33]

Ray argues that there has been an imbalance in the American mythology over these two hero types. As he puts it, "The national ideology clearly preferred the outlaw" (66). That may be understandable, given the celebration of youth and freedom so central to the dominant American culture. Yet one of Capra's chief contributions to the mythology of American film, firmly established in the Columbia years, is his ability to create and celebrate the official hero. Tom Dixon, Longfellow Deeds, and Jefferson Smith all function comfortably as official heroes; all are firmly rooted in society and exhibit a strong sense of social responsibility. Dixon, a veteran of twenty-five years with the bank he has built up, continually voices his support for loans to people whose character he can trust. He is friendly and democratic with his employees, loyal to his depositors. A product of a small town, Longfellow Deeds maintains his integrity when confronted by city types who mock or try to take advantage of him. Jefferson Smith, a boy scout leader steeped in the American political tradition, accepts his appointment to the Senate with reverence, measuring what he experiences in Washington against the principles of the Founding Fathers. Although Capra makes both Deeds and Smith butts of humor, particularly in the early parts of the films (in keeping with his peculiar brand of screwball comedy), he clearly directs the viewer to identify with the idealism and innocence of both characters while rejecting the worldliness and cynicism of those who deride them. One of the keys to Capra's vision in his later Columbia films lies in his depiction of these official heroes.

Capra's success and popularity in those years surely owes something to the blend of comedy and drama fostered by this narrative pattern. But they also rest on two other factors: cinematic style and the appropriateness of the films' ideology for audiences of the Great Depression.

Though Capra has sometimes been underrated as a stylist, a careful look at his Columbia films demonstrates that he became increasingly adept at communicating ideas and evoking emotion through cinematic style. Mise-en-scène is carefully manipulated to create an air of authenticity: the locking and unlocking of the bank vault in *American Madness*, the meticulous reconstruction of the Senate chamber in *Mr. Smith*. Costumes subtly contrast the homespun hero with the well-heeled villain. Expressionistic, low-key lighting appears at pivotal moments: when the bank is robbed in *American Madness*, when Peter and Ellie go to sleep by the haystacks in *It Happened One Night*, when Deeds stands, discouraged and silent, by a window after being jailed, when a disillusioned Jeff Smith sits on the steps of the Lincoln Memorial. Acting is also an important feature of the Capra style. After the success of *It Happened One Night*, Capra was fortunate to work with gifted actors, including not only those in central roles like James Stewart, Jean Arthur, Gary Cooper, and Edward Arnold, but also dozens of actors cast in lesser roles (for example, Thomas Mitchell, Donald Meek, Eugene Pallette, Beulah Bondi).

Capra and his Columbia collaborators employed framing, editing, and sound track in effective ways. Dialogue scenes offer textbook examples of how framing and editing function within the classical Hollywood continuity style. At other times, Capra uses framing and editing more dramatically and expressively. In *American Madness*, for example, he uses thirty-five consecutive closeups of people on the telephone with various camera angles and lighting techniques to show how a rumor spreads, leading to a bank run. After the run is in progress, he uses a long-take dolly shot of Tom Dixon as he hurries along a row of bank tellers, stopping briefly at each teller to issue instructions while depositors clamor in the background. The rapid cutting during the climaxes of *It Happened One Night*, *Mr. Deeds*, and *Mr. Smith* also illustrates the importance of editing in Capra's films, as do the low-angle closeups and medium closeups at crucial moments during Jeff Smith's filibuster.

Another device Capra employed as social problem elements became increasingly more important to his films was documentary montage—the Washington tour montage in *Mr. Smith* and, in the same film, the "Stop Smith!" campaign, as Taylor's thugs sabotage attempts to clear Jeff's name. These documentary montages emphasize the public importance of the official hero's actions. The fact that they are accompanied by commentative music—patriotic tunes in the Washington tour montage, and low threatening strains in the "Stop Smith!" one—only intensifies their impact. Besides underlining emotional tone, music in Capra is sometimes associated with particular characters—Deeds, for example, plays the tuba—or helps create a sense of community and forge personal bonds; thus Ellie and Peter seem to grow closer together when they join in the singing of "The Man on the Flying Trapeze" in *It Happened One Night*. Music blends with sound effects and dialogue, as well as with the other elements of cinematic style, to enable Capra to achieve his aims.

Besides their narrative patterns and stylistic effectiveness, Capra's mature Columbia films were also successful because of their ideological thrust, expressed most clearly in the hero-villain conflict and the heroine-hero relationship, which spoke to vast numbers of Americans as the nation was experiencing and then emerging from the turmoil of the Great Depression. In contrasting the cultural values of his official hero with those of the villain, Capra affirmed a sense of social responsibility and community and challenged the villain's lust for inordinate wealth, power, or prestige. Capra consistently defended his official heroes—men of integrity, warmth, and civic virtue—against the ruthlessness, heartlessness, and greed of the villains. In general, the polarization of hero and villain was, to a large extent, a class conflict between the middle and upper classes (with the middle-class official hero sometimes acting as spokesman for the besieged lower classes as well, as in *Mr. Deeds*), and it is no surprise that depression audiences would respond to such vivid portrayals.[34] Although they did not have to (and not all did), depression audiences *could* understand the conflict between the official hero and the villain as metaphorical support for Roosevelt and the New Deal and opposition to what he called "economic royalists" in his 1936 reelection campaign. More broadly, however, the mature Columbia films affirm an ideological perspective rooted in the ethic of Christian community and self-sacrifice, and those aspects of American political tradition that emphasize nationalism, democratic equality and fraternity, and a tem-

pering of liberty.[35] To audiences living through the economic dislocations of the depression and the rising threat to democratic values posed
by European fascism later in the decade, this ideological blend was
compelling indeed.

Capra's personal correspondence in the Wesleyan Cinema Archives clearly indicates that audiences of the 1930s, particularly from
Mr. Deeds on, associated the director's films with an affirmation of
American ideals. For example, to a moviegoer who praised *Mr. Deeds*,
noting that the character "typifies the wholesome personality . . . each
one of us would have if we could" and that "America has need of Mr.
Deeds," Capra replied: "Thank you for your understanding letter. . . .
I quite agree with you that if Mr. Deeds became a fashion it would be a
great help to American life. I'll admit we were somewhat hopeful that
would happen when we were making the picture." To another
moviegoer who commended Capra for *Mr. Smith* because he "opened
the road of inspiration to millions of people . . . who want desperately
to cling to American ideals," Capra wrote in response: "Expressions
like yours inspire us to tackle real problems in pictures in the face of
some decidedly powerful opposition to try to say something important
on the screen." Both the viewers' sentiments and Capra's replies suggest a shared understanding of the ideological thrust of his films.[36]

The Capra heroine and her relationship with the hero also spoke to
audiences. Like many heroines in American movies after the Production Code began being enforced more stringently in 1934, the Capra
women were most often working women—intelligent, witty, and
competent at their job. Their "conversions" to the hero's perspective
may seem patronizing to contemporary viewers, but the mature Capra
films stress that the heroines are less converted to a new perspective
than returned to a set of cultural values they had grown up with and
strayed from (Saunders in *Mr. Smith*, for example, is the daughter of an
idealistic and humanitarian doctor). Furthermore, their actions are vital
in sustaining the hero during his moments of trial. The romantic
integration at the end of *Mr. Deeds* and *Mr. Smith* provides occasions for
the celebration of values *mutually* shared by the heroine, the hero, and
the community that comes to support them. The 1930s audience,
through the ritual of watching the film, participated in that celebration.

Thus, by the time the lights went up in depression theaters after a
Capra film, viewers had gone through an intellectual-emotional-psy-
chological experience that included the depiction of very real cultural
conflicts and the affirmation of an ideological perspective compelling to
large numbers of Americans in the 1930s. Of all the relationships
between directors and studios during Hollywood's classic era, the one
between Frank Capra and Harry Cohn's Columbia was one of the most
fruitful and curiously symbiotic. There is no doubt that when Capra

arrived on the scene and began to establish himself as a director, he needed Columbia. Yet, increasingly as the 1930s wore on, Columbia also needed Capra. Between 1927 and 1939, this mutual necessity yielded unforgettable invention.

NOTES

1. Frank Capra, *The Name above the Title* (New York: Macmillan, 1971), 82 (hereafter cited in the text as NATT). Neal Gabler, *An Empire of Their Own: How the Jews Invented Hollywood* (New York: Crown, 1988), 164.
2. Joel Finler, *The Hollywood Story* (New York: Crown, 1988), 68. Finler includes a number of useful charts on the history of the studio's releases, financial condition, personnel, and Oscars. See also Ed Buscombe, "Notes on Columbia Pictures Corporation, 1926-1941," *Screen* 15 (Autumn 1975): 65-82; Douglas Gomery, *The Hollywood Studio System* (New York: St. Martin's Press, 1986), ch. 8.
3. Synopses of all Capra's films, along with credits and notes, are available in Charles Wolfe, *Frank Capra: A Guide to References and Resources* (Boston: G.K. Hall, 1987).
4. Columbia announced (*New York Times*, 2 Feb. 1929) that it had made arrangements with the Victor Talking Machine Co. to produce jointly sound motion picture shorts and feature films.
5. Wolfe, *Frank Capra*, 68.
6. Gomery, *Hollywood Studio System*, 163.
7. Wolfe, *Frank Capra*, 71.
8. Swerling, an immigrant like Capra, came to the United States from Russia as a child. Although *Ladies of Leisure* was only his second screen credit, he went on to write many screenplays, including some for a number of distinguished directors: Frank Borzage (*No Greater Glory*), John Ford (*The Whole Town's Talking*), Rouben Mamoulian (*Blood and Sand*), William Wyler (*The Westerner*), and Alfred Hitchcock (*Lifeboat*). He also served as script doctor on *It's a Wonderful Life* and is credited with having contributed "additional scenes" to that film.
9. Gomery, *Hollywood Studio System*, 163.
10. Wolfe, *Frank Capra*, 79, 96; Wolfe notes that Radio City had opened "as a showcase for live entertainment two weeks before [the opening of *Bitter Tea*]."
11. See *The Name above the Title*, 116, and three letters to Capra—from Fred Niblo, secretary of the Academy (8 May 1931); Lester Cowan (8 Sept. 1931); and Niblo again (18 Sept. 1931), in Frank Capra Archive, box 40, folder 2, Wesleyan Cinema Archives, Wesleyan University (hereafter cited as FCA).
12. Gomery, *Hollywood Studio System*, 162; Finler, *Hollywood Story*, 280.
13. *Daily Variety*, 1 Jan. 1935, 36.
14. A copy of the contract can be found in FCA, box 2, folder 8.
15. *Broadway Bill* was made and released after *It Happened One Night* but before the 1935 Academy Awards ceremony. It is very much a Capra-Riskin film, and although it was positively reviewed and did well at the box office, it was obscured by the popularity of *It Happened One Night*. Capra helped foster its obscurity by failing to mention it in his autobiography.
16. "Columbia's Gem," *Time*, 8 Aug. 1938, 35-38; *Saturday Evening Post*, 4 May 1938, 1-9, 67, 69, 71-72. Wolfe, *Frank Capra*, 189-245, gives one a sense of how Capra's reputation grew during his Columbia years. Similarly, the volume

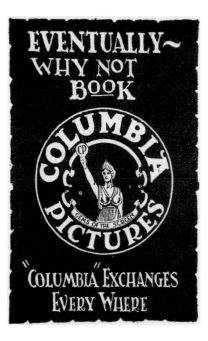

An ad in *Motion Picture News*, 1 May 1926, shows an early version of the Columbia logo that evolved into the familiar lady-with-the-torch. Courtesy of the Academy of Motion Picture Arts and Sciences.

Below, Harry Cohn (1891-1958), president of Columbia Pictures from 1932 until his death, at a 1942 Hollywood premier flanked by two "promising young players," Shirley Patterson (left) and Alma Carroll. Courtesy of the Academy of Motion Picture Arts and Sciences.

Unless otherwise indicated, all photos are courtesy of the Museum of Modern Art Film Stills Archive.

Frank Capra (1897-1991), whose twelve years at Columbia (1927-1939) resulted in a distinctive kind of film now called "Capresque," at his Palm Springs home in the 1980s. Courtesy of Frank Capra.

George Stevens (1904-1975), who directed three of Columbia's best remembered films, *Penny Serenade* (1941), *The Talk of the Town* (1942), and *The More the Merrier* (1943).

Oscar-winning screenwriter Daniel Taradash, whose Columbia credits include *Golden Boy* (1939), *From Here to Eternity* (1953), *Picnic* (1955), and *Bell, Book and Candle* (1958). Courtesy of Daniel Taradash.

Frank Price, who began as a reader under Harry Cohn and in 1990 became chairman of Sony's Columbia. Courtesy of the Academy of Motion Picture Arts and Sciences.

David Puttnam, Columbia's short-lived head (1986-1987), who antagonized the industry by criticizing its extravagant budgets and overpaid stars.

The team—Jon Peters (left) and Peter Guber—that Sony hired to head Columbia Pictures Entertainment in 1989, now reduced to one with Peters's resignation in 1991.

Columbia's first home on Gower Street as it looked in 1935, the year the studio won its first Oscars for *It Happened One Night* and *One Night of Love*. Courtesy of Bruce Torrence Historical Collection. Below, Columbia's new home—the former MGM lot in Culver city (circa 1945, with Peter Lawford in the foreground), where Columbia relocated in 1990.

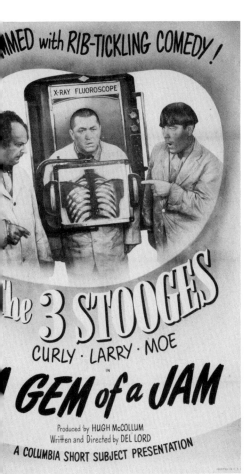

The Three Stooges, stars of Columbia's best known short, appeared in theaters for a quarter of a century (1934-1958) and continue on television indefinitely. Courtesy of Archival Photography.

A lobby card for *The Power of the Whistler* (1945), a film in Columbia's popular mystery series based on "The Whistler" radio program.

Two Frank Capra-Robert Riskin collaborations. Above, the reporter (Clark Cable) and the heiress (Claudette Colbert) in *It Happened One Night* (1934). Below, the reporter (Jean Arthur) and the heir (Gary Cooper) in *Mr. Deeds Goes to Town* (1936).

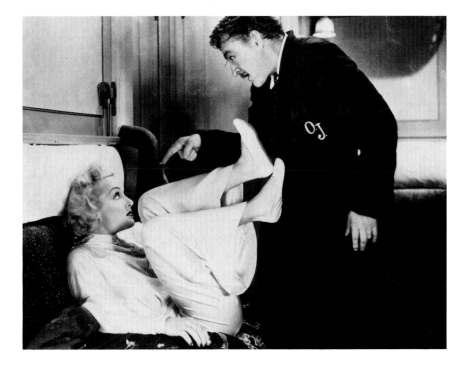

Two of Columbia's vintage screwball comedies. Above, Carole Lombard wards off John Barrymore in *Twentieth Century* (1934). Below, Irene Dunne tugs at Melvyn Douglas in *Theodora Goes Wild* (1936).

Film noir was a genre in which Columbia excelled in the 1940s. Above, in *Dead Reckoning* (1947), Humphrey Bogart and Lizabeth Scott reenact the Sam Spade-Brigid O'Shaughnessy relationship of *The Maltese Falcon* (1941). Below, Orson Welles and a blonde Rita Hayworth as the *femme fatale* in *The Lady from Shanghai* (1948).

Scenes from two more Columbia *films noirs*. Above, William Holden, as an escaped convict, threatens the psychiatrist (Lee J. Cobb) who eventually reveals the source of his neurosis in *The Dark Past* (1949), Columbia's remake of 1939's *Blind Alley*.

Gloria Grahame as one of *film noir's* few dark ladies who is not a *femme fatale* and Humphrey Bogart as the troubled writer whose uncontrollable rage destroys their relationship in *In a Lonely Place* (1950).

Judy Holliday (1922-1965), who spent most of her film career at Columbia, where she demonstrated her ability to blend comedy and pathos. Below, in one of Holliday's greatest successes, *Born Yesterday* (1950), Paul Verall (William Holden) tries to make Billie Dawn an informed citizen.

Rita Hayworth (1918-1987), Columbia's biggest star of the 1940s, in *Cover Girl* (1944). Below, Hayworth and Fred Astaire in *You Were Never Lovelier* (1942) with music by Jerome Kern and lyrics by Johnny Mercer.

Marlon Brando as Terry Malloy in *On the Water-front* (1954), a key film of the Cold War that justifies informing.

Paul Biegler (James Stewart) makes the fishing fly that may affect the outcome of a trial in *Anatomy of a Murder* (1959).

Robert DeNiro in one of his greatest characterizations, Travis Bickle in *Taxi Driver* (1976).

Peter O'Toole perpetuates the enigma of T.E. Lawrence in *Lawrence of Arabia* (1962). Courtesy of Columbia Pictures.

Casualties of the sexual revolution are, left to right, Bob (Robert Culp), Carol (Natalie Wood), Alice (Dyan Cannon), and Ted (Elliott Gould) in *Bob & Carol & Ted & Alice* (1969). Below, Harold and Sarah (Kevin Kline and Glenn Close) are a successful couple playing host to college friends for a sobering weekend in *The Big Chill* (1983).

Howard E. Rollins, Jr., as Captain Davenport, sent to investigate a 1944 murder in a *Soldier's Story* (1984). Courtesy of Columbia Pictures. Below, Wyatt (Peter Fonda) bikes toward America—and death—in *Easy Rider* (1969).

Richard Vuu as the young Pu Yi in Bernardo Bertolucci's nine-Oscar winner, *The Last Emperor* (1987). Courtesy of Columbia Pictures. Below, Sean Penn (left) and Michael J. Fox in Columbia's searing drama of the Vietnam War, *Casualties of War* (1989). Courtesy of Columbia Pictures.

of correspondence Capra received from fans, friends, and acquaintances became significant with *It Happened One Night* and grew steadily through the release of *Mr. Smith*; see FCA, boxes 2-4, passim.

17. See Wolfe, *Frank Capra*, 198-201, 211-19, 237-46.

18. See Richard Shale, *Academy Awards*, 2nd ed. (New York: Ungar, 1982), 311-38.

19. Even this budget was high by Columbia's standards. *Variety*, 3 Jan. 1933, 4, reported that Columbia's average budget per feature at $175,000, was the lowest among important studios. Warners' was second ($200,000), and MGM's was highest ($450,000).

20. The figures on domestic rentals for *Mr. Deeds* and *Lost Horizon* are available in FCA, box 3, folder 23; the itemized budget for *Lost Horizon* is in box 3, folder 21. See also Finler, *Hollywood Story*, 75; Gomery, *Hollywood Studio System*, 162.

21. See Bob Thomas, *King Cohn* (New York: Putnam's, 1967), 124; *Variety*, 1 Sept. 1937, 3; *Motion Picture Herald*, 14 Sept. 1937, 34.

22. *Variety* (29 Oct. 1941) worried that the unflattering depiction of U.S. senators had helped generate ill feeling toward the movie industry, speculating also that the film increased the likelihood that Congress would pass anti–block booking legislation.

23. *Variety*, 3 Jan. 1940, 28.

24. *Time*, 23 Oct. 1939, 51-52; *Daily Variety*, 4 Oct. 1939, quoted in Wolfe, *Frank Capra*, 239. *Nation*, 28 Oct. 1939, 55; *Daily Worker*, n.d., Lincoln Center Library for the Performing Arts.

25. Raymond Carney, *American Vision: The Films of Frank Capra* (New York: Cambridge Univ. Press, 1986), xi.

26. In addition to his renown in Hollywood, Capra continues to attract film scholars and critics; cf. Wolfe, *Frank Capra*, Carney, *American Vision*, and Wolfe's edition of the *Meet John Doe* screenplay (New Brunswick, N.J.: Rutgers Univ. Press, 1989), which also includes an introduction about the making of the film, reviews, and three recent essays by Richard Glatzer, Dudley Andrew, and Nick Browne.

27. Capra's penchant for topicality through social and political allusions was somewhat unusual for Columbia. Warners was the more likely studio; it also distributed Capra's first film after leaving Columbia, *Meet John Doe*.

28. On Capra and screwball comedy, see Andrew Bergman, *We're in the Money* (New York: New York Univ. Press, 1971) and the standard works cited in notes 2 and 3 of Joy Gould Boyum, "Columbia's Screwball Comedies" (p. 104, below).

29. For an interesting reading of *American Madness*, see John Raeburn, "*American Madness* and American Values," in Richard Glatzer and John Raeburn, eds., *Frank Capra: The Man and His Films* (Ann Arbor: Univ. of Michigan Press, 1975).

30. See Ed Sikov, *Screwball: Hollywood's Madcap Romantic Comedies* (New York: Crown, 1989), 218. Although Sikov lists *Mr. Smith* as one of Capra's screwballs, it isn't even mentioned in the text. *It Happened One Night* is the only Capra film discussed in detail; *Mr. Deeds* is mentioned four times, and *You Can't Take It with You*, five.

31. *Lost Horizon* is the obvious exception. Capra appears to have been attracted to the novel's Asian setting (a similar attraction is evident in *Bitter Tea*) and the depiction of a utopian society. Expensive to make, it did not do well financially, and Capra returned to contemporary American settings except for his last film, *A Pocketful of Miracles* (1961), a remake of *Lady for a Day*. Yet even in

the 1930s, critics could associate *Lost Horizon* with other Capra films (for example, Otis Ferguson, *New Republic*, 21 Sept. 1938, called *Lost Horizon* "Shangri-La in a frame house").

32. For more detail on Capra's middle and late 1930s films, see Robert Sklar, *Movie-Made America* (New York: Random House, 1975), and Charles Maland, *Frank Capra* (Boston: Twayne, 1980), 92-94.

33. See Robert Ray, *A Certain Tendency of the Hollywood Cinema, 1930-1980* (Princeton: Princeton Univ. Press, 1985), 59-69. Subsequent references are placed in the text.

34. Carney, *American Vision*, suggests that Capra could dramatize the hero-villain struggle so effectively because he found himself in a similar position as he sought to make films of integrity within the studio system. This suggestion would make Cohn and Columbia even more important to Capra as he developed as an artist. They not only provided him with a place to work but also with the personal experience of tension and conflict that helped feed and intensify the narrative conflicts in his films.

35. For a more detailed discussion of Capra's blend of Christian-American mythology, see Maland, *Frank Capra*, 91-93.

36. See FCA, box 2, folder 13, and box 4, folder 8.

2
COLUMBIA'S SCREWBALL COMEDIES
Wine, Women, and Wisecracks
JOY GOULD BOYUM

The golden age of American movie comedy is traditionally held to be the 1910s and 1920s, the time before pictures learned to talk. It was then that such artists as Chaplin, Keaton, Lloyd, and Langdon dominated the screen, swathed by the silence that has always been a *sine qua non* for clowns and that comic theorists and movie historians tend to take as requisite for great film comedy as well. Unencumbered by speech, the argument goes, funnymen were able to give play to their anarchic energies, to the pratfalls and bumbles, the chases and double-takes that are not only the heart of slapstick but grist for the movie mill. The result was over-the-top visual burlesque, the runaway physical gags that gave rise in turn to the titters, the yowls, the belly and boffo laughs celebrated by James Agee in his famous *Life* paean to the silent clowns.[1] It was Agee's view that after the 1920s, movies never again could elicit "laughs that kill."

Still, America, as we know, is the land of second chances, and although Agee (writing in 1949) may have been too close to perceive it, American movie comedy had a second chance, too. For if the coming of sound put an end to side-splitting silent farce, it created a new kind of comedy in its place—a species of dialogue farce that may not have had quite the hilarity of its predecessor but still ended up a much beloved form. Born in the Great Depression and running its course somewhere toward the end of World War II, its heyday lasted for about a decade. Its name was "screwball comedy."

Defined by neither geography like the western nor occupation like the gangster and the detective film, screwball comedy tends to be distinguished by those more difficult-to-pin-down qualities of theme and style—in particular, as Thomas Schatz suggests, by a "style of behavior."[2] Consequently, it emerges an incredibly elusive genre. It has, in fact, been so diversely described and comes in so many variations (the newspaper comedy, the remarriage comedy, the screwball mystery, and so forth) that commentators have not even managed to generate a consistent list of films.[3] Nonetheless, a few unarguable classics remain, as do certain prevailing characteristics.

One constant, for example, is romance, which tends to be at the forefront of the action. (Thus screwball comedies are distinct from such near relatives as Marx Brothers farces, where romance is strictly part of the backdrop.) Romance, here, is also of a particular kind. Molly Haskell, in her Foreword to Ed Sikov's book on screwball comedy, defines screwball romance as "a sort of existential American version of the French *l'amour fou.*"[4] Sikov himself underscores, rather than madness, the notion of battle, particularly, of course, of the sexes. "In the world of screwball comedy, there is one primary axiom: Hatred is no reason to give up on a relationship. Just because two people seem to despise each other doesn't mean they're not in love. It could, on the contrary, provide the final proof of a couple's delight in one another, their passion, devotion, and joy."[5] It also tends to be proof of the spirit and spunk of the women involved. Characteristically, in screwball romance, either because they are wealthy or because they make their own living, women are strong, determined, and strikingly independent. These women (with nary a housewife or a mother among them) are also delightfully sexy. Indeed, reminding us that screwball comedies thrived precisely when censorship was reemerging, Andrew Sarris points to sex itself as key to the form. What gives screwball comedies their peculiar distinction, he contends, is that they are sex comedies without the sex.[6]

There are other constants in these movies, too, among them a prevalent narrative pattern in which an heiress marries down (or a Cinderfella marries up) with the characteristic setting—an urban world of wealth and glamour. Thus Depression audiences were given a glimpse into the lives of the filthy rich while being assured that if money could buy duplexes, furs, and automobiles, it still could not buy happiness. It did, however, allow for considerable nuttiness. Heiresses in these films were invariably "madcap," and if their riches were suspect, their craziness was not. Screwball comedy affirmed screwballism; stuffy sanity and small-minded conventionality, whether upper or middle class, were portrayed negatively.

Setting, subject, and theme aside, perhaps the most striking characteristic of screwball comedies is that they were writers' films which, for all their fine direction and appealing performances, were most fully controlled by their scripts. And it was not only that wisecracks, wordplay, and in-references were so important in these films, or that the narrative structure unmistakably revealed a writer's touch. It was that, by and large, screwball comedy grew out of a literary rather than a cinematic tradition.

Arguing for screenwriter Herman Mankiewicz's contribution to *Citizen Kane* (1941), Pauline Kael makes the case that much of "the new spirit of the talkies was the twenties moved West in the thirties."[7] The spirit was that embodied by Mankiewicz's New York pals who, back in the flapper decade, exchanged wisecracks at the Algonquin Round Table and wrote wry critiques for magazines and fast-talking comedies for Broadway. Sound made it possible to bring such plays to the screen, and many of the screwballs were, in fact, stage adaptations—*Twentieth Century, Design for Living, Holiday, His Girl Friday, The Philadelphia Story.* Sound also created a desperate need for writers, especially those who could supply snappy dialogue. Mankiewicz, among the first of the New York set to arrive, invited his pals to seize the opportunity, his famous 1925 telegram to Ben Hecht making the point even before the sound film underscored it: "Millions to be grabbed out here, and your only competition is idiots."[8] And Hecht was not the only one who came to grab the millions. So did Marc Connelly, Edna Ferber, Ring Lardner, Morrie Ryskind, Moss Hart, Robert Benchley, Dorothy Parker, and Nunnally Johnson. Some commuted, some simply moved, earning their gold but tarnishing their reputations and separating themselves from the literary mainstream of their time. It was in the movies alone that their sophistication, cynicism, and unerring feel for the gag found a home. And because as writers they took second place to directors, producers, and studio heads, they were pretty much forgotten. "Hollywood," says Kael, "destroyed them, but they did wonders for the movies."[9]

But clear as the link to New York of the 1920s is, the literary roots of screwball comedies run even deeper. They are in form not simply romantic comedies but comedies of manners. Writing about the form as it flourished in Restoration England, Allardyce Nicoll notes: "The invariable elements of the comedy of manners are the presence of at least one pair of witty lovers, the woman as emancipated as the man, their dialogue free and graceful, an air of refined cynicism over the whole production, the plot of less consequence than the wit, an absence of crude realism, a total lack of any emotion whatsoever."[10] This last point does not quite apply: with a few notable exceptions (*His Girl Friday* and *Twentieth Century*), warmth rather than coolness characterized screwball comedy. But otherwise, Nicoll has managed, while talking about the stage form, to describe its celluloid descendants with startling accuracy.

In his extensive survey of screwball comedy, Ed Sikov lists some forty-four writers and thirty-eight directors who contributed to the form. Among the latter is Alfred Hitchcock, who early in his American career directed the little-known screwball movie *Mr. and Mrs. Smith* (1941). There is also Michael Curtiz, who in 1934 made *Jimmy the Gent* but who lives in most of our memories as the director of *Casablanca* (1942) and *Mildred Pierce* (1945). Screwball comedy is a form, in other words, in which many have dabbled. Still, as with most genres, certain writers and directors are inseparable from it.

Among directors, Frank Capra, Howard Hawks, Gregory La Cava, Leo McCarey, George Cukor, and William Wellman immediately come to mind; as for the writers they worked with, one thinks of Robert Riskin, Ben Hecht and his long-time collaborator Charles MacArthur, Charles Lederer, Sidney Buchman, Donald Ogden Stewart, and Dudley Nichols—many of them near-legendary wits, several, at one time or another, part of the Broadway/Algonquin crowd. There were also key screwball stars, though with the possible exceptions of Cary Grant, Katharine Hepburn, and Carole Lombard, none were as strongly or exclusively associated with the form as, say, John Wayne was with the western or James Cagney with the gangster film. Screwball stars were, by and large, dramatic actors who may have found their most distinctive personas in these comedies, as did Cary Grant, the most elegant of screwball performers, but who also went on to develop strong ties with other types of films, as Grant did with the Hitchcock thriller.

Genres, however, are not only linked with their practitioners. Embedded in the Hollywood studio system (screwball comedy, in fact, thrived at its height), genres tend to be associated with particular studios, serving as key elements of a given studio's style. Horror, for instance, had its chief home at Universal; the gangster film at Warners; expensive epics and glossy adaptations at MGM.

Screwball comedies, in contrast, were not associated with any single studio. Like other wide-ranging genres—family melodramas and musicals—they were movies every studio made in one form or another. MGM produced, among others, the screwball mystery *The Thin Man* (1934) and its sequels. Paramount gave us Ernst Lubitsch comedies in the early 1930s, Preston Sturges's movies in the late 1930s and 1940s. (Purists, by the way, have argued that both Lubitsch and Sturges films fall outside the screwball range, the former because they are too early and too continental in tone and values to qualify, the latter because they were produced too late and have a flavor of their own.[11]) Goldwyn, Warners, and Fox also made screwball comedies. Two studios, however, did make more than any others: RKO and Columbia. Long as RKO's list of screwball comedies may be, only two rank as classics, *My Favorite Wife* (1940) and *Bringing up Baby* (1939), admittedly the form's acknowledged masterpiece. Columbia's list, however, is a veritable screwball treasury. The studio lent its logo to *It Happened One Night, Twentieth Century, The Awful Truth, You Can't Take It with You, His Girl Friday, Theodora Goes Wild,* and *The More the Merrier,* not to mention

Here Comes Mr. Jordan, Holiday, and *The Talk of the Town.* If screwball comedy had any studio association, then, it was with Columbia, whose style in turn was in large part created by it. As Bob Thomas puts it, the studio's "features seemed to be peopled by beauties in long gowns and handsome men in dinner jackets. They thrust themselves into outrageous situations, always maintaining their *savoir faire.* Columbia became the home of the sophisticated film, an eventuality that astounded the many people in Hollywood who considered Harry Cohn the compleat vulgarian." [12]

It is not easy to explain Columbia's penchant for screwball comedy. The more than decade-long union between the studio and Frank Capra, however, certainly had a good deal to do with it. Capra became Harry Cohn's golden boy almost immediately on joining Columbia late in 1927 and confirmed his boss's nose for talent most forcefully when, in 1935, he won the studio its first Academy Awards and in this way won Cohn himself the "big-time status" he had always hungered for. [13] The picture, of course, was *It Happened One Night,* written by Robert Riskin, with whom Capra collaborated so nearly exclusively in his Columbia years that their style has been dubbed the "Capriskin touch," [14] and starring two borrowed stars, Claudette Colbert from Paramount and Clark Gable from MGM. Emerging not only as Columbia's most prestigious film, *It Happened One Night* was also a box office phenomenon. Audiences adored it, and its madcap love/hate romance between a runaway, spoilt heiress and a down-and-out, hot-headed newspaperman established the pattern of screwball comedy for the remainder of the genre's brief life. The golden rule in Hollywood is, in any case, when you first succeed, do it again and again. And Columbia was naturally determined to repeat the movie's feat if it could, which meant making more screwball comedies.

Yet, what is missing from this picture is that in 1934 Columbia also released *Twentieth Century.* And though nowhere so successful with audiences as *It Happened One Night* (perhaps because this adaptation of the Hecht/MacArthur play about two egomaniacal Broadway types was simply too sophisticated for the provinces), the movie established another towering screwball director, Howard Hawks, as well as the great screwball star, Carole Lombard. What's more, Hecht and MacArthur (who adapted their play for the screen) had supplied nonstop patter, which Hawks directed with bullet-speed pace. And so, if Capra had fixed the dominant plot pattern for screwball comedy, Hawks set its classic style.

Quite simply, the two films generally acknowledged to have started the screwball cycle were both Columbia products. Could it have been mere coincidence? Or, was it, as commentators such as Richard Schickel have suggested, a crass matter of money that just happened to pay off in art as well?[15] Harry Cohn was notorious for running the tightest ship in Hollywood: it was one of the ways he managed to steer Columbia up from Poverty Row. Comedies, generally filmed on weather-free, delay-proof interior sets with small, often low-paid casts, were relatively cheap and tended to turn substantial profits, especially in Depression America. These comedies were also emphatically contemporary in content—a quality that not only contributed to keeping costs down but also jibed with Cohn's outlook and sensibility, since Cohn "felt insecure when he ventured away from modern subjects."[16]

All of these factors probably played some role in making Columbia the special home of screwball comedy. But more important yet was Cohn's particular responsiveness to writers. He recognized early on how crucial good writing was to the sound film and filled his studio with the best, the brightest, the funniest writers he could woo to Hollywood. "Oddly," notes Bob Thomas, "Cohn had an affinity for writers." Perhaps this was because "the writing process was something Cohn could not comprehend. He secretly viewed it with awe and wonder, although he never betrayed those feelings to writers."[17] Cohn, in fact, battled with his writers, many of whom detested him: Ben Hecht's epithet for Cohn was "White Fang."[18] But whether writers hated Cohn or not, they did great work for him, and it was their wit together with his instinct for the solid, well-honed script that helped explain Columbia's success with the screwball form. The point is that, though Cohn may indeed have been "the compleat vulgarian," like the other moguls he had the gift of knowing what would work on screen. And so, with typical Hollywood irony, it was this "vulgarian" who had the extraordinary good taste to produce some of Hollywood's most sophisticated and literate comedies.

Except for It Happened One Night and You Can't Take It with You, the Capriskin collaborations aren't easy to accept as screwball comedies. The Deeds-Smith-Doe trilogy may show up on various screwball lists, but these tales of naive and idealistic ordinary Joes battling corruption and power are essentially social-message movies that just happen to be spiced with screwball elements. Some purists, such as Robert Sklar, will not admit any Capra films to the genre: they lack the "wacky style" characteristic of screwball. Moreover, Sklar argues, "in screwball comedies, the screwballs are the rich. . . . In Capra's comic fantasies, imagination comes from below and requires recognition and participation by the rich or powerful to make one's dreams come true."[19] Sklar's criteria seem a bit stringent and overly sociological; still, somewhere in his claim there is a point. For even if taken as screwball in form, Capra's comedies are run through with a sentimentality that in many ways is antithetical to the screwball sensibility, though in its last gasp in the 1940s, screwball comedy totally succumbed to "Capracorn." Still, more characteristic of the form, at least in its classic stage, were a cynicism, a biting wit, an irresponsible pleasure in sheer foolishness, and an urban sophistication that made mockery of Capra's small-town America. (In *The Awful Truth* and *His Girl Friday*, part of what makes Ralph Bellamy such a dullard is that he's from the American heartland and embodies its values.) Such a vision, of course, derives from the transplanted Broadway/Algonquin wits. But to discover that sensibility on screen one has to look elsewhere than Capra in the Columbia canon and nowhere so fruitfully as in the savage comic confrontations and verbal sparring of the Ben Hecht/Charles MacArthur/Howard Hawks collaborations: *Twentieth Century* and *His Girl Friday*.

Though centered on battling couples working out love/hate relationships and even classified as comedies of remarriage[20] (inaccurately in the case of *Twentieth Century*, where the couple never were man and wife[21]), *Twentieth Century* and *His Girl Friday* are as much about vocation as they are about love. Or, as Gerald Mast puts it in his study of Howard Hawks, they are curious and complex romantic comedies in which "love is expressed through work and work is expressed through love."[22] One may be a backstage story, the other a newspaper yarn, but as adapted from Hecht/MacArthur stage plays, they have similar plots, center on similar conflicts, and even feature characters who are in many ways dead ringers for one another. In both, a Machiavellian Svengali—Broadway producer Oscar Jaffe (John Barrymore) and newspaper editor Walter Burns (Cary Grant)—wishes to woo a lost Trilby back, less to his bed, however, than to his place of work. In Jaffe's case, she is Lily Garland (Carole Lombard), a brilliant actress he has created out of bit player Mildred Plotka and without whom his own career is floundering. In Burns's case, she is Hildy Johnson (Rosalind Russell), the ex-wife and great reporter he now needs to help pull off a scoop.

Significantly, in both cases, the dramatic conflict is the woman's. She must choose between an old love and a new one, between independence and submitting to a bullying male ("I want to be an actress," Lily has announced early on, "but I won't crawl on my stomach for any man"), between career and home. Hildy puts the choice this way: to be a "woman" or a "newspaperman." In both films, too, the resolution goes without saying: the Svengali isn't simply the woman's creator, he is her mirror image. And much of the comedy springs from this recognition. Lily may hate Oscar's theatrics, but her behavior ends up identical to his. Hildy may not want to be a newspaperman like Walter, but it is the only way she can be fulfilled. Much of the comedy, too, derives from the fact that at their core both men are thoroughly detestable. Oscar is a monster of vanity and self-absorption; Walter is the epitome of callousness and sleaze; and both are liars and cheats who, through such tricks as stealing, kidnapping, and false suicide, win their women back. Their worlds, moreover, are of appropriately similar texture. The theatre is a place where everything is pretense, while in yellow journalism things are not much more real. In short, though these films may be screwball comedies, they are also satires.

And fairly cynical ones, at that. For as exposed as these worlds and characters are in their chaos and amorality, we nonetheless end up accepting, even affirming them, somehow finding ourselves persuaded to go along with the notion that getting by in the world requires a little larceny. Put another way, Walter's pragmatism and Oscar's theatrics not only win the day and the women but ultimately win us as well. It helps, of course, that both are played by extraordinarily handsome, marvelously self-mocking actors: Barrymore hams it up outrageously, and we adore him for daring to do so; Grant clearly delights in Walter's brashness, and we share that pleasure with him. And the women are no slouches either, though their roles are less showy than the men's. Thus we are put in the same relationship with these characters as they are with each other: we hate them and love them at the same time.

Though Howard Hawks clearly deserves substantial credit, it is difficult to grant him too much for these *tour de force* performances. Whatever directors Grant and Barrymore, Lombard and Russell worked with, they invariably came up with clever, energetic, effortlessly sexy performances. Nor in watching these movies is one particularly struck by Hawks's visual style. Hawks was a straightforward director, relying on the accepted studio conventions of his day: he rarely used a fancy angle or a tricky shot, he tended toward medium-distance, eye-level compositions, and he opted for functional, invisible editing. He did have special gifts, however, which Mast rightly pinpoints when he subtitles his Hawks study "storyteller." Hawks had a strong feeling for narrative and invariably worked with the writers of all his films.

In the case of *Twentieth Century* and *His Girl Friday*, Hawks's contributions were substantial and helped make both movies more effective than their sources. (It was Hawks who insisted on adding the marvelous rehearsal sequences to *Twentieth Century*; it was Hawks's idea to transform *The Front Page*'s Hildy into a woman.[23]) And though Hawks had a propensity for slapstick, as in the scene in which Barrymore plays with his putty nose, elongating it Pinocchio style and then blatantly picking it), physical action is far from the key to his work here. Both these movies are, in any case, largely confined to a single set that would inhibit it: to the speeding train where Oscar and Lily accidentally meet; to the newsmen's room at the courthouse. What Hawks appreciated even more than action was language, with nearly every-thing in these two movies tending to serve it. Indeed, the classic Hawks innovations have everything to do with language: the rapid-fire line deliveries, the overlapping dialogue. Hawks's characters never stop talking, shouting, screaming; it is this of all qualities that he lent to the screwball comedy. (And he made what are widely considered the best.) He also helped purge the form of sentimentality, substituting, with the help of Hecht and MacArthur, a healthy dose of irony in its place. Consider that both of these romantic comedies end without so much as a kiss. In *Twentieth Century*, Oscar is once more directing Lily in a play; in *His Girl Friday*, Hildy and Walter are rushing off to cover a story in, of all places, Albany. Conventional romance be damned: these four battling lovers are off to work.

If *Twentieth Century* and *His Girl Friday* reflect the characteristic screw-ball rhythm and style, *The Awful Truth*, *Holiday*, and *Theodora Goes Wild* best exemplify screwball atmosphere and values. All may share with *His Girl Friday* the notion that normalcy is stifling and urban life is more fulfilling than its small-town counterpart. But *The Awful Truth*, in particular, has a good deal more in common with that Hawks/Hecht/ MacArthur film yet. It too is based on a successful Broadway play; it too is a remarriage comedy; most important, it also features Cary Grant and Ralph Bellamy in their respective and now-classic charming ex-husband, drip-of-an-other man roles. (Made three years earlier than *His Girl Friday*, *The Awful Truth* actually set the pattern.) Still, there are considerable differences between these two movies. *The Awful Truth* is set among the super-rich, none of whom ever even go to an office, much less reflect a sense of vocation. Its characters are husbands, wives, and lovers; its story is unadulterated romance with the kind of sheer nuttiness and suggestive overtones that make it the epitome not only of Sarris's "sex comedy without the sex" but, along with *Bringing up Baby*, of screwballism itself.

The director was Leo McCarey, in whom Harry Cohn apparently invested a good deal of hope. Capra had defected from the studio (briefly, it turned out) and Cohn wanted to prove Columbia was not dependent on a single director. McCarey (who in the manner of Hawks habitually collaborated on his scripts, this time with Viña Delmar) was reportedly at odds with Cohn throughout the production[24] and never worked for Columbia again. The film was, however, a great success and won the Academy Award for Best Direction. McCarey, on the other hand, went on to direct "maudlin pearls" like *Going My Way* (1944).[25] But aside from its controlling vision of marriage as of necessity based on faith—"when that's gone, you've lost everything," remarks our hero—and the accompanying notion that you've got to retain that faith even in the face of "the awful [that is, illogical] truth," this deliciously airy movie doesn't have a serious notion in its celluloid head or a sentimental bone in its body.

Jerry and Lucy Warriner (Cary Grant and Irene Dunne), who on the thinnest of misunderstandings (a mutual momentary loss of faith) end up impetuously taking their marriage to the divorce court, are the very prototypes of the feckless rich. They live in a world of exclusive clubs, elegant apartments, and charming country get-a-ways. They haven't a single care or responsibility—no jobs, no children, only a dog named Mr. Smith who ends up central to a farcical custody battle in which the court leaves the decision to the dog as to whom he will live with.

As this legal absurdity suggests, much of the movie is inescapably silly. Indeed, as Andrew Sarris notes, Dunne and Grant "romp through a series of slapstick situations that would have given pause to Laurel and Hardy."[26] Jerry tickles his wife as she is being wooed with love poems by suitor Bellamy and gets entangled in a chair at a concert; Lucy pretends to be Jerry's racy sister at a party being held at the home of his new bride-to-be; Mr. Smith crashes down mirrors and mixes up bowler hats. In short, there is as much physical comedy here as there is verbal, with the former given a rare quality first by the striking lightness of McCarey's touch and even more, perhaps, in being performed not by a couple of clowns but by an overwhelmingly glamorous pair. (This, by the way, became a distinctive feature of screwball—romantic leads playing out slapstick—and was part of why one-time acrobat Grant emerged as such a great screwball star.)

What's more, in romping and rolling about, these debonair types seem to be having the time of their lives. Reproducing a still of Grant from the scene in which Grant watches Bellamy put Dunne through some embarrassing paces on a dance floor, Stanley Cavell remarks, "This man, in words of Emerson's, carries the holiday in his eye."[27] And if less so, so did Dunne in her smile, with that incredible sense of pleasure and delight the very point. For in *The Awful Truth*, as in screwball comedy in general, marriage is not the end of youthful adventure after which you settle down and get serious; it is a variety of fun-filled adventure itself. When Lucy admits to her confidant Aunt Patsy that she is still in love with Jerry, she explains why: "We had great laughs." And such laughs simply are not possible with the other mates they have chosen, nor are the whimsical battles either: neither Lucy's mother-dominated beau nor Jerry's snobby heiress has even a touch of irony or a smattering of unconventionality about them. With Lucy and Jerry, though, it is all amusement and affection, the former being key to the latter. Screwball comedies, Pauline Kael writes, "made love and marriage into vaudeville acts and changed the movie heroine from a clinging vine into vaudeville partner."[28] Nowhere was this truer than in *The Awful Truth*, where even sex is a matter of playfulness, as we discover in the reconciliation scene. Here, Jerry and Lucy find themselves in a pair of adjoining bedrooms in Aunt Patsy's weekend get-a-way, connected by a door with a faulty lock. One can hardly imagine a lovelier bit of sex farce, a more appealing vision of marriage, or a more appetizing vision of life as unadulterated fun.

Holiday, made a year later, was also set in the world of the super-rich and shared much of *The Awful Truth*'s vision and values. But its tone could not have been more different. Indeed, it is only in the broadest sense that one can accept it as a comedy at all, much less a screwball one. Not that it lacks many of the standard elements (explaining to some extent its presence on screwball lists). Among other things, its source is a play by Philip Barry, its director is George Cukor, and its stars are Cary Grant and Katharine Hepburn, all of whom were to rejoin forces shortly to create that screwball masterwork *The Philadelphia Story*. (Not for Columbia, however. Cukor did not return to the studio until 1950, when he directed *Born Yesterday*, Hepburn, not until she made *Suddenly, Last Summer* in 1959. But she was never one of Cohn's favorites.[29]) There is an earnestness to the spirit and performances of *Holiday* that is antithetical to these other zany comedies, and the script by Donald Ogden Stewart and Sidney Buchman contains neither a gag line nor cues for slapstick. The closest one gets to physical comedy is a couple of back flip-flops, but they are meant less to make us laugh than to illustrate the free-wheeling nature of Grant's character.

Still, there are charm and elegance here that help account for the film's classic status. Some, like Richard Schickel, even prefer it to *The Philadelphia Story*, finding it "less convoluted and less sententious."[30] Others, like Pauline Kael, speak of the film's rare "grace" and grant it particular interest as the work that first provided the young Hepburn with her archetypal role, that of the heiress tomboy, the elegant "angular beauty."[31] And Hepburn *is* immensely appealing here, as is Grant, with the chief delight being what so many of these 1930s films offered: the opportunity to spend time with truly likable people.

Grant plays Johnny Case, a young man from a working-class background who has made some money and now wants to take a holiday in pursuit of self-discovery. His wealthy fiancée, however, is not at all sympathetic; Johnny's true soulmate turns out to be her older sister, Linda. Not simply a tomboy but an authentic individualist, Linda detests the materialism, snobbery, and conventionality of her father and sister, which have turned her brother into an alcoholic (Lew Ayres in a quite touching performance). Perceiving Johnny's specialness almost immediately—"Life walked into this house this morning," she enthuses—she invites him to share the intimacy of her former playroom, the only human room in the cold, repressive mansion and the place where she spends most of her time. (As in *His Girl Friday* and *Twentieth Century*, the action in *Holiday* is pretty much confined to a single locale, the mansion that Cukor makes appropriately claustrophobic.) It is in the playroom that Linda and Johnny fall in love—their romance played out, significantly enough, in rich language alone. The atmosphere contributes substantially, however. There is the fireplace suggesting warmth; the toys and gym bars, childhood innocence and imagination. Decent and good people that they are, however, they do nothing about their feelings. Johnny, in fact, does not even seem to recognize them until the sister herself backs off, at which point Linda races to join Johnny on board the ship that will take them on what we have no doubt will be a lifelong holiday. What else could it be, given the purity, nonconformity, and goodness of this pair to whom money and class mean nothing? Like the people, the values are irresistible.

More authentically screwball in spirit than *Holiday* is an earlier Columbia romp, *Theodora Goes Wild*, a little-seen but delightful 1936 comedy that, set in small-town America rather than the world of heirs and heiresses, also has a distinctly Capraesque feel, or what Kael calls "a corny vitality." [32] The Capra connection hardly seems a coincidence: the producer was Everett Riskin, brother of Robert, the other half of Capriskin. Riskin bought the original story from Mary McCarthy and then assigned Cohn's favorite writer, Sidney Buchman (later to serve as co-writer of *Holiday*), to do the script. [33] The movie made Buchman's reputation. But witty (and relentlessly verbal) as the script is, this is one of those rare screwball comedies equally noteworthy for the play of the camera. You do not simply recall the images, or the performances, or the lines; you also remember the shots. The director was Richard Boleslawski, who had been trained in Russia and had worked with Carl Dreyer in Germany.

Irene Dunne, who here comes into her own as comedian, stars as New England spinster Theodora Lynn, who has secretly written a risqué bestseller banned in her own small-minded town. Out with her publisher in New York, she meets up with illustrator Michael Grant (the urbane Melvyn Douglas), who invites himself along for dinner, gets Theodora drunk, wheedles her true identity out of her, and follows her to her home town. Pretending to be a folksy stranger, he causes considerable brouhaha, the result of which is, quite naturally, that the two find they are meant for each other. There is a complication, however: Michael is married and, though unhappily, his politician father will not permit a divorce. So the guilty Michael returns to the big city. But Theodora has been liberated; turning the tables on him, she now follows *him* home, embarrassing him to the point where he can not escape divorce. She moves into his apartment, makes her real name and current whereabouts known to the press, and, garbed in feathers, boas, and satins, takes on a false identity of her own—the madcap woman-of-the-world. She also pulls a terrific trick on the town gossip, Mrs. Perry (Spring Byington) when she returns home unmarried with a baby in her arms, a baby who is actually the gossip's grandchild.

Filled with nuttiness, both visual and verbal, *Theodora* is great fun. Buchman tosses in all kinds of digs at small-mindedness, and Boleslawski too rakes over the hypocritical and stodgily conventional. In one montage he intercuts images of a cat with the buzzing phone calls of the gossips; in another, when Theodora gets off the train, baby in arms, he has glasses falling off the townspeople's noses, hats off their heads, even the band's mouthpieces breaking away. But perhaps the film's most appealing quality is its vision of a woman coming alive, finding her spirit and self-esteem and helping a man to do the same—a process that no actress—screwball or otherwise—seemed quite so gifted at dramatizing as Irene Dunne.

By the 1940s, the screwball era was pretty much over. Here and there one comes across a film made at the time whose screwball flavor is sufficiently strong that at least one film historian or another has admitted it to the canon. Three Columbia movies are among these: *Here Comes Mr. Jordan* (1941), *The Talk of the Town* (1942), and *The More the Merrier* (1943). All, whether strictly screwball or not, reflect the influence of Capra; and all, in their time, were enormously popular.

Here Comes Mr. Jordan is probably the most beloved of the lot. In the *Topper* (1937) vein, it is an otherworldly comedy; this time the focus is not on a rich couple but a prizefighter, Joe Pendleton (Robert Montgomery). Because of a mix-up caused by a novice Angel-Messenger (Edward Everett Horton), Pendleton is taken to heaven fifty years before his time. The task of returning his spirit to earth is complicated by the fact that Joe's remains have been cremated. And so a search ensues, headed by a heavenly higher-up, Mr. Jordan (Claude Rains), to find Joe's spirit another habitation. The first is the body of a millionaire who has been murdered by his faithless wife and scheming male secretary and whom Joe's kindly spirit transforms into a benefactor, winning the love of Bette Logan (Evelyn Keyes) in the process; the second is the more appropriate body of a boxer, allowing Joe to become the champ he was always meant to be.

As even this brief summary suggests, there are few screwball elements in *Mr. Jordan*: romance, an upper-class atmosphere, some wild mix-ups, absurd situations, and a playful celebration of vaguely off-the-wall behavior by Joe and his kindly manager, Max Corkle (James Gleason). Another Everett Riskin production, again co-written by Sidney Buchman (this time together with Seton I. Miller) and directed by Alexander Hall, the movie also has its Capracorn touches. For example, immediately on inhabiting the millionaire's body, Joe gives away a small fortune to investors who have been taken in a fraudulent stock deal; there is also much talk about human kindness and inner selves shining through. Still, Joe comes across as a truly lovable dope, and there is something in the ingratiating heavenly atmosphere that gets to the viewer, who is left in a Capracorn glow.

As for *The Talk of the Town* and *The More the Merrier*, they are both the work of a single director, George Stevens, and feature Columbia's then reigning screwball star, Jean Arthur, one of whose qualities was her distinctive voice; the other was that, as Andrew Bergman puts it, "she was the one movie star men could actually visualize marrying."[34] And both films are, at least in part, about precisely that process. *The Talk of the Town*, though, has other things on its mind. Written by Irwin Shaw and Sidney Buchman, it too reminds one of Capra, especially the late Capra of *Meet John Doe*. For this is a message picture with a vengeance, and one that, like *Meet John Doe*, only qualifies as a comedy by the skin of its teeth.

Leopold Dilg (Cary Grant in one of his rare journeyman performances), a small-town individualist with political and moral principles, is falsely accused of arson and murder. Escaping from prison, he makes his way to the home of a local schoolteacher, Nora Shelley (Jean Arthur), who, believing him innocent, agrees to hide him. (The film, which begins darkly, only declares itself a comedy at the moment the two meet: as the rain-soaked Leopold faints and Nora pours water over him.)

The hitch is that Nora has rented her house to Michael Lightcap (Ronald Colman), a law professor, who, to make matters worse, arrives only moments after Dilg. Nora's solution is to introduce Dilg as the gardener and drop an egg on his picture in the morning paper. Dilg and Lightcap hit it off famously and have endless discussions about the law, with the intention of getting Lightcap, currently a Supreme Court nominee, to bend his hard-line principles in the name of humanity and to do some good. Predictably he does, managing not only to help clear Dilg and put the wrongdoers away but also to insure his own prestigious appointment. Dilg, for his part, gets his freedom—and Nora.

Again, there isn't much here for the film to qualify as screwball. The relationship between the two men is more central than that between either of them and the woman, leaving the film more a buddy movie than a romance. But Arthur does supply some authentic zaniness, and more screwball yet is the film's ideology: its celebration of emotion over reason, its view of conventions (even legal ones) as making for lifelessness and inhumanity, its suspicion of those with power and position, and its distrust of the mob. Admittedly, it is all rather simplistic and a bit melodramatic. But the sentiments cannot help but appeal, and the characters are not only intelligent, funny, good-natured people you would like to spend time with; they are also strikingly credible, particularly Ronald Colman as a Supreme Court judge.

The lesser of the two Stevens movies, *The More the Merrier*, is also the funnier. And though it lacks the glamorous atmosphere and debonair upper-crust characters, it does, in contrast to these other 1940s movies, incorporate many screwball motifs. Our chief screwball character, however, is a distinctive type: Charles Coburn in an Oscar-winning performance as a cuddly old nut with a penchant for playing a cupid named Dingle. The setting is wartime Washington, where, desperate for a room, the wealthy Dingle rents half the apartment of Connie Milligan (Jean Arthur). Attractive Connie may be, but she is also prissy, punctual, and engaged to a stuffy petty official. Dingle, deciding to effect a screwball-like awakening, rents half of his half to handsome inventor/soldier Joe Carter (Joel McCrea), who, though fairly laid-back, is basically a free spirit given to making Tarzan-like noises in the shower and dancing the rhumba alone in his room. After a squabble or two, Cupid's arrows of course find their mark.

Although it has witty lines and classic screwball bits (double takes, mix-ups, even a running slapstick gag about a pair of pants with a mind of its own), the film, written by Arthur's husband, Frank Ross, and an uncredited Garson Kanin, among others,[35] often strains for effect. This is especially true at the end, where the plot seems preposterous even by screwball standards and where Connie never seems to stop crying and whining. (Having been rushed into an unlikely shot-gun type marriage with Joe to save her reputation, she now believes he does not love her.) There is also a final bit involving the tearing down of the wall between their bedrooms that owes too much to the Walls of Jericho scene in *It Happened One Night*. But Arthur and McCrea really click as lovers; the upshot is screwball farce that is more romantic than funny, and dreamily romantic, at that. The giveaway is what is generally taken to be the movie's most memorable scene[36]—a quietly amusing and sweetly sexy one in which, sitting on her stoop on a summer night, Connie is awakened to her desires by Joe's gentle caresses. The sequence climaxes in the kind of glowingly lit, close-up clinch one simply does not find in classic screwball. Like the image, the genre itself has somehow gone soft.

Can Columbia, or any studio, for that matter, ever give us screwball comedy again? Despite intermittent efforts to revive the form (*What's Up, Doc?* [1975] or the *Mr. Jordan* remake, *Heaven Can Wait* [1978]), it seems unlikely. Screwball comedy may not have been precisely embedded in the *facts* of the Great Depression; notwithstanding the claims of those like Arthur Knight that these comedies had "as their points of departure the terrible realities of that period—unemployment, hunger and fear,"[37] they rarely addressed anything resembling the real world. But the form certainly reflects something of the 1930s spirit. There is a sexual innocence, a political idealism, a charmingly simplistic concept of unconventionality, and an old-fashioned romanticism running through these films that would be hard to duplicate. There is also something peculiarly American about the values at work in these films: Emerson's affirmation of self-reliance and rugged individualism, Thoreau's commitment to living fully and deliberately, Thomas Paine's suspicion of wealth and the celebration of common sense. And as an age of conformism, materialism, and practicality plays itself out, who knows what types of nonconformity and out-and-out wackiness may not arise in reaction? For such renewed screwballism to reach the screen, however, something else must be renewed first: a sense of the importance of language to movies and a recognition that, at their very best, talking pictures are not only pictures but also talk.

NOTES

1. Reprinted in James Agee, *Agee on Film: Reviews and Comments by James Agee* (New York: McDowell Obolensky, 1958), 1-19.

2. Thomas Schatz, *Hollywood Genres: Formulas, Filmmaking, and the Studio System* (New York: Random House, 1981), 151.

3. For example, Schatz includes among "notable" screwball comedies *In Name Only* (1939), *The Great McGinty* (1940), *Christmas in July* (1940), *Meet John Doe* (1941), and *Here Comes Mr. Jordan* (1941). None of these, interestingly enough, appears on the more exhaustive list provided by Ed Sikov in *Screwball: Hollywood's Romantic Comedies* (New York: Crown, 1989). Sikov, however, lists *Design for Living* as a screwball comedy, a 1933 film Schatz considers a precursor to the form. A seminal list of screwball comedies appears in Lewis Jacobs, *The Rise of the American Film: A Critical History* (New York: Teachers College Press, 1968), 535-36. Andrew Sarris, however, in "The Sex Comedy without Sex," *American Film*, March 1978, 8-15, takes issue with some of Jacobs's claims and choices (chiefly *Friends of Mr. Sweeney* and *Hired Wife*).

4. Sikov, *Screwball*, 10.

5. Ibid., 15-16.

6. See Sarris, "Sex Comedy," n.3.

7. Pauline Kael, "Raising Kane," *The Citizen Kane Book* (New York: Bantam, 1971), 24.

8. As quoted in Ben Hecht, *A Child of the Century* (New York: Simon & Schuster, 1954), 466.

9. Kael, "Raising Kane," 26.

10. Allardyce Nicoll, *A History of Restoration Drama* (New York: Cambridge Univ. Press, 1923), 185.

11. See, among others, Sarris, "Sex Comedy," n.3.

12. Bob Thomas, *King Cohn: The Life and Times of Harry Cohn* (New York: Putnam, 1967), 73.

13. Clive Hirschhorn, *The Columbia Story: The Complete History of the Studio and All Its Films* (New York: Crown, 1989), 50.

14. Schatz, *Hollywood Genres*, 173.

15. See Richard Schickel, *Cary Grant: A Celebration* (Boston: Little, Brown, 1983), 64.

16. Thomas, *King Cohn*, 72-73.

17. Ibid., 84.

18. Ibid., 85.

19. Robert Sklar, *Movie-Made America: A Social History of American Movies* (New York: Random House, 1975), 207.

20. See Stanley Cavell, *Pursuits of Happiness: The Hollywood Comedy of Remarriage* (Cambridge: Harvard Univ. Press, 1981).

21. Schatz, for example, refers to Lombard as an ex-wife (*Hollywood Genres*, 151).

22. Gerald Mast, *Howard Hawks, Storyteller* (New York: Oxford Univ. Press, 1982), 209.

23. Thomas, *King Cohn*, 175-76.

24. Ibid., 125-30.

25. Ephraim Katz, *The Film Encyclopedia* (New York: Perigee Books, 1982), 748.

26. Sarris, "Sex Comedy," 13.

27. Cavell, *Pursuits of Happiness*, frontispiece; also 235.

28. Pauline Kael, *When the Lights Go Down* (New York: Holt, 1980), 15.

29. Hirschhorn, *The Columbia Story*, 95.

30. Schickel, *Cary Grant*, 86.

31. Pauline Kael, *5001 Nights at the Movies: A Guide from A to Z* (New York: Holt, 1982), 253.

32. Ibid., 586.

33. Hirschhorn, *The Columbia Story*, 69.

34. Andrew Bergman, *We're in the Money* (New York: New York Univ. Press, 1971), 133.

35. See Thomas, *King Cohn*, 178-80.

36. See, among others, Kael, *5001 Nights*, 390.

37. Arthur Knight, *The Liveliest Art: A Panoramic History of the Movies* (New York: Mentor, 1957), 241.

3

FILM NOIR AT COLUMBIA
Fashion and Innovation
J. P. TELOTTE

In the immediate post–World War II era, one of the most popular kinds of film was *film noir*. This genre,[1] with its tales of urban crime and corruption, typically shot with low-key lighting and an expressionist concern for shadows, strange camera angles, and irregular compositions, differed from mainstream Hollywood in both subject and style. Yet Columbia, known for its conservative production policies and conventional narrative practices, became in this period one of the leading producers of such films. The studio's embracing of *film noir* may, however, have been less noteworthy than the sort of *noir* it turned out. Columbia produced a number of movies that out*noired*, in subject matter, style, and narrative, standard *noir*; in the process it also helped to open up conventional cinematic practice.

During the war, Columbia, like other studios, prospered partly because of the general expansion of domestic movie audiences in the 1940s but also because of Harry Cohn's determination to run a cost-conscious operation by keeping few stars and directors on long-term contracts, keeping executive salaries lower than industry standards, maintaining "a tight rein on book-keeping practices," looking to independent producers to supply films, and carefully choosing which trends to exploit.[2] One of those trends was *film noir*.

In the 1930s, Columbia had effectively exploited one of *noir*'s roots, the crime genre, although largely after it was shown to be profitable by major studios like Warners. A few of these earlier titles even point toward motifs that would come to dominate *film noir* as it emerged in the 1940s. Consider, for example, *Women in Prison* (1938), which anticipates the dangerous female figures of *noir*; *Convicted* (1938), remade in the *noir* vein in 1950, with its suggestion of the trapped and alienated individual; *I Am the Law* (1938), with its intensely subjective emphasis; or *Blind Alley* (1939), with its focus on the criminal psyche. For the most part, though, Columbia entered the 1940s taking a more formulaic and conservative approach to the issues of crime, corruption, and destructive desire that would characterize *film noir*. To serve the audience for such fare, it relied mainly upon staple series such as the Lone Wolf, Ellery Queen, or Boston Blackie, with their predictable plots and far from disturbing themes.

With customary caution, then, Columbia edged into *film noir* only after the larger studios had established both the form and an audience for it. RKO had already produced *Stranger on the Third Floor* (1940) and *Murder, My Sweet* (1944); Warners, *High Sierra* and *The Maltese Falcon* (both 1941); Paramount, *This Gun for Hire* (1942) and *Double Indemnity* (1944); and Twentieth Century-Fox, *I Wake up Screaming* (1941) and *Laura* (1944). Columbia, however, did not gamble on a recognizably *noir*-type movie until late in 1945 with *My Name Is Julia Ross*, and even then, true to studio policies, Joseph H. Lewis directed the film on a shoestring. Yet once the genre's popularity and profitability were demonstrated, Columbia became one of the most prolific and consistent producers of *film noir*, averaging nearly three such films a year during *noir*'s heyday (1946-1957), when only RKO and United Artists exceeded that output.[3]

One reason for Columbia's commitment to the genre is that *noir* fitted in with the studio's budgetary policies. Because a typical *noir* took place in a modern-day city, no special period sets or costuming were needed, and nearby locales could be employed. Since the action often occurred at night and was shot in low-key light, whatever sets were necessary, interior or exterior, could be minimal. Thanks to their contemporary subjects, *noir* plots could easily be taken from newspaper and magazine articles (*The Undercover Man* [1949], *The Killer That Stalked New York* [1951], *The Garment Jungle* [1957]). And with their emphasis on the small, human story, usually that of a desire repressed and then unleashed (see Fritz Lang's *Human Desire* [1954]), casts could be pared down. In short, a typical *noir* could usually be done relatively cheaply, quickly, and with a minimal commitment of the studio's resources—quite in line with the tested Columbia formula for success.

Because the studio tended to hire people on short-term contracts and to use actors and directors whose contracts with other studios had run out, Columbia *noir* displays a wide variety of talent. Among male leads, Glenn Ford is a notable exception; he starred in six *noirs* at Columbia. While Rita Hayworth was the studio's biggest female star in this era, she appeared in only two *noirs*. Still, only Gloria Grahame and Dorothy Malone played in more, each appearing in three. Since Columbia often served as a proving ground for young directors and a brief refuge for experienced but out-of-favor older ones like Orson Welles and Fritz Lang, it is no surprise that such a variety of directors contributed to this body of films. Joseph H. Lewis, often described as the quintessential B director, contributed three films, while Lang, Nicholas Ray, and several others produced two *noirs* apiece.

Still, in terms of style and iconography, Columbia produced some of the most typical and even archetypal *noirs*. In fact, when J.A. Place and L.S. Peterson set out to describe a consistent, identifying "visual style" for the form, they turned to two Columbia releases, *In a Lonely Place* (1950) and *The Big Heat* (1953), for many of their illustrations, and especially to suggest *noir*'s abiding fascination with low-key lighting, the use of framing devices, and a tendency for unbalanced composition.[4] Part of the reason for this classical *noir* look is that, on the technical side, at least, the studio maintained a level of consistency. Cinematographer Burnett Guffey, for example, lent his talent and stabilizing hand to sixteen of these films, while Robert Peterson worked as art designer on eight of them.

Iconographically, the Columbia *noirs* are no less distinctive. Glenn Ford proved an especially appropriate *noir* protagonist, with his consistent image of the tough but vulnerable male who would prove easy prey for the black widows of the genre. Nearly archetypal is a film like *Framed* (1947), with its scheming waitress who lures Ford into an embezzlement scheme and almost leads him to destruction.[5] Humphrey Bogart, working as a Warners loan-out and later as head of his own production company doing projects for Columbia, made several *noirs* for the studio (including *Dead Reckoning* [1947], *Knock on Any Door* [1949], *In a Lonely Place* [1950]), bringing with him his nearly mythic image of the alienated yet unfailingly moral loner. Rita Hayworth's image proved no less paradigmatic or powerful. As Janey Place notes, *film noir* created a most atypical image for the American cinema, that of an "erotic, strong, unrepressed (if destructive) woman" marked by an unusual "access to her own sexuality (and thus to men's) and the power that this access unlocked."[6] In *Gilda* (1946), Hayworth, the American serviceman's favorite pin-up during the war, embodied this strong sexual presence, especially with her famous "Put the Blame on Mame" striptease, wherein, as Richard Dyer puts it, she managed to project an "eroticism for herself as well as for the spectator."[7] And as Elsa Bannister in *The Lady from Shanghai* (1948), she demonstrated the destructive power latent in that unrepressed sexuality as she used her allure to manipulate and eventually destroy the various men in her life, thus becoming the paradigm of the *noir* femme fatale.

In narrative form as well, Columbia *film noir* seems to echo the trends established by the mainstream of the genre. The voice-over/flashback narrative, which critics often describe as a *noir* hallmark, shows up in many of Columbia's films and takes various forms. Both *Gilda* and *Dead Reckoning*, for example, employ an embedded or partial voice-over to set part of their stories at a temporal remove, after the fashion *Double Indemnity* had made popular. *The Lady from Shanghai* uses an all-embracing voice-over—one that begins with the film's opening image and continues to its close—to set its narrative entirely in the form of a flashback.

Of course, voice-over implies a subjective dimension to the story, and that tendency helped spur another sort of narrative development in the postwar era. Thus films like MGM's *Lady in the Lake* (1946) and Warners' *Dark Passage* and *Possessed* (1947) employed subjective camera for all or major portions of their narratives. Following this lead, Columbia produced its own subjective narrative with *The Dark Past* (1949), while it also tried to depict the workings of the psyche in more conventionally shot films like *In a Lonely Place* (1950) and *M* (1951).

Another popular *noir* form was the semidocumentary, which relied on location shooting, newsreel footage, true-life stories, and a voice-of-god narrator. Largely innovated by producer Louis de Rochemont at Twentieth Century-Fox, this approach proved quite popular for a time, resulting in films like Fox's *Boomerang* (1947) and *Call Northside 777* (1948), Universal-International's *The Naked City* (1948) and *City across the River* (1949), Paramount's *Union Station* (1950), and MGM's *The Asphalt Jungle* (1950), among many others. Columbia too tried this naturalistic approach with Joseph H. Lewis's *The Undercover Man* (1949). Suggesting far less of a social consciousness than the films of Fox or Universal-International, though, *The Undercover Man* simply retold what was by this time a familiar story: the successful effort to put gangster Al Capone—here referred to as "the Big Man"—in prison. While location footage would figure more and more in Columbia's *noirs*, the studio developed few films in this particular realist trend and concentrated instead on the kind of brooding, interior narrative that RKO specialized in.

While in their general style and form Columbia's *noirs* largely "follow the pack," developing patterns similar to, and following the same styles as, the major studios' efforts in this vein, they also at times did far more. Columbia's *noirs* helped stretch the form in the ways they pushed—wittingly or unwittingly—at its boundaries and even at those of conventional American cinematic practice. Partly because Columbia was emulating the products of the major studios, its films often seem to pull together the traits of many other *noirs*, combining them in a mix that, while effective, so exaggerates the form's elements as to reveal an instability typical of the darkest *noir* narratives. That instability is rooted in the form's reliance on a sort of melodramatic romanticism, a pattern that results in stories that capitalize on the darker, disturbing upwellings in our culture but end up reconciling many of those problems or exiling the most transgressive characters beyond the social pale. In their later form, several Columbia *noirs* would shake loose those unstable elements to produce challenging visions of the American scene. And it may well be in this somewhat unexpected way that Columbia's contributions to *film noir* will prove most notable.

Consider Humphrey Bogart's first *film noir* for the studio, *Dead Reckoning*. Writing about *Casablanca* (1942), Umberto Eco argues that its enduring popularity is largely the result of its being a sort of accidental "collage." It successfully throws together a familiar variety of stock characters, mannered attitudes of the period, and predictable events; as a result, "it is not *one* movie. It is 'the movies.'"[8]

In a similar way, *Dead Reckoning* is "the movies," or at least "the *films noirs*," although this result hardly seems accidental. Rather, in keeping with the studio's penchant for mining where others had already struck gold, the film seems designed to evoke much of what has gone before it.

In fact, *Dead Reckoning* is often cited as prototypical for the way it treats the *noir* female—here, the beautiful yet dangerous Coral Chandler (Lizabeth Scott), who has killed several men and is finally destroyed by returning war hero Rip Murdock (Bogart) after she lures his best friend to his death. What makes Coral's character so resonant is not just the pattern she enacts—that of the now familiar duplicitous and deadly female—but the extremes to which the character is stretched. Coral is not only the murderous black widow, all the more dangerous because of her beauty and deceptive nature, but also the wronged innocent, needing to be rescued from corruption and misunderstanding. Coral is literally a widow and someone around whom death seems a common occurrence; she is also constantly dressed in white, accepted by other sympathetic characters and bullied by the conventionally evil gangsters in a way that warrants our sympathy. If at times she recalls Brigid O'Shaughnessy of *The Maltese Falcon* (1941) and Vivian Sternwood of *The Big Sleep* (1946), it is hardly accidental. In fact, posturings, speeches, and plot events loudly (and brazenly) echo these earlier—and successful—Bogart/Warners vehicles.

The plots of both *Dead Reckoning* and *The Big Sleep* turn on a missing friend and blackmail. In the former, Rip's war buddy, Johnny Drake, disappears en route to receive the Congressional Medal of Honor, and Rip trails him to a small Florida town, where he meets Johnny's girl, Coral, whom casino owner Martinelli (Morris Carnovsky) is blackmailing. In *The Big Sleep*, detective Philip Marlowe, in trying to keep blackmailers away from the Sternwood sisters, finds himself drawn into searching for an old friend, Sean Regan. Here, too, Vivian Sternwood is being blackmailed by a casino owner, Eddie Mars. Underscoring these broad parallels is a series of scenes that seem more than accidentally similar. Vivian Sternwood and Coral Chandler both sing at the casinos; both engage in a bit of reckless roulette playing, and in each instance the Bogart character helps the woman walk away a winner; in both films the girl takes the place of the male "buddy" in helping Bogart defeat the casino owner and his sadistic henchman. Consequently *Dead Reckoning* seems to encourage us to "read" Coral Chandler in terms of Vivian Sternwood, as the strong woman in trouble, needing help and, in return, promising to be a most satisfyingly sexual replacement for the absent male buddy.

Even in its resonances to *The Maltese Falcon* and other films, *Dead Reckoning* is disturbing. For Coral Chandler, like Brigid O'Shaughnessy before her, is finally shown to be the most deceptive character in this world. In both films, Bogart's character tests the girl, even asks others he trusts what they think of her, and they corroborate his initially positive assessment. Yet Brigid and Coral prove to be murderers—the former of Spade's partner, Miles Archer, the latter of her husband. The discovery of that guilt then puts both Spade and Rip in a quandary, as each must weigh his love for the "black widow" against moral right. Just as Spade gets the details "straight" for the police and then tells Brigid, "You killed Miles and you're going over for it," so does Rip affirm that "We've got to be all square with John Law," and tells Coral, "You're going to fry." Their reasoning too is the same, as Spade explains that "when a man's partner is killed, he's supposed to do something about it," and Rip echoes him with "when a guy's pal is killed, he oughta do something about it." While Brigid challenges Spade, charging, "You don't love me," and Coral asks Rip, "Don't you love me?" the male characters can only try to explain just how difficult that moral choice is. Spade's rejoinder is, "I'll have some rotten nights after I've sent you over, but that'll pass," while Rip replies, "That's the tough part of it, but it'll pass." Both films leave us with this sense of personal loss, even as they affirm the need for that greater moral code in spite of what the individual may feel.

What *Dead Reckoning* suggests, then, is a kind of schizophrenic tale, as it veers from one *noir* narrative pattern to another. While it may prompt us to read its semiotic within one group of generic conventions, it also sets about, as Marc Vernet puts it, "hollowing out the fiction and shooting it full of holes."[9] This result might well be expected from a studio's tendency to mine as many profitable veins as possible, but we should hardly dismiss the end simply because of the means. The creation of a character like Coral Chandler is in itself notable. Certainly it well suits the darker and more complex situation of postwar America, especially as it brings into focus the American male's ambiguous attitude toward the female, as he returned from the war to find his job occupied by a woman and the traditional family roles suddenly challenged. At the same time, *Dead Reckoning* points to the more complex narrative situation facing the moviegoers of that era—an emerging period when the conventional formulas would no longer hold, when our expectations would frequently be dashed, and when no character would prove a safe or comfortable repository for our empathy or identification.

In a similar vein, we might consider an even more challenging narrative, *The Dark Past*, which also harks back to other ground-breaking efforts by the major studios and manages to pull them together effectively. As previously noted, *The Dark Past* reflects earlier attempts to use subjective camera. Robert Montgomery had already directed and starred in MGM's *Lady in the Lake*, which employed subjective camera for nearly its entirety to approximate the sort of interior narrative in the Raymond Chandler novel on which it was based. As a result, we inhabit the protagonist's perspective—our point of view is his—for almost the entire film. And while *Lady in the Lake* met with only limited success, it anticipated a brief trend among *noirs*, with the Bogart vehicle *Dark Passage* probably the best example.

A remake of an earlier Columbia movie, *Blind Alley*, *The Dark Past* seems to have learned from such previous attempts at subjectivity as *Murder, My Sweet* and *Spellbound* (1945), each of which uses distorted images to *imply* the protagonist's perspective. The former represents detective Philip Marlowe's drugged stupor with a smoked glass, and his lapsing into unconsciousness with an animated "black pool" that blots out the image; the latter depicts the events of a haunting dream with a surreal landscape designed by Salvador Dalí. Later efforts, *Lady in the Lake* and *Dark Passage*, rely mainly on establishing the camera as the protagonist and placing the viewer within the world depicted. While the former approach sought to convey a state of mind, the latter focused on how the characters occupied a real physical world. Yet each technique leaves something to be desired. The former's artificiality, its nearly theatrical intrusion into cinematic reality, called attention to its basically *metaphoric* status. And the latter's insistence on our identification with the protagonist ran counter to what we experience in such films—which is, ultimately, our sense of *difference* from the character whose point of view we share.

The Dark Past meets these problems almost head-on. In fact, it combines both techniques with a far more conventional manner of suggesting subjectivity—voice-over—while remaining mindful of the sense of distance that invariably accompanies these cinematic effects. Its focus is pointedly double, as it tells the story of a police psychiatrist, Dr. Andrew Collins (Lee J. Cobb), and an escaped psychopathic killer, Al Walker (William Holden). The introductory subjective scenes are motivated by the psychiatrist; they represent his perspective as he goes to work at the police station. The later are Walker's, as he recounts a dream that has haunted him and that, we are led to believe, holds the key to his antisocial behavior. Linking both is a voice-over/flashback narrative as Collins describes the case to a police detective. That auditor is important, for he becomes our stand-in, a model of our placement in the narrative, suggesting an alternative to the sort of forced identification at which other subjective efforts labored—in this instance, an alternative to identifying with either the psychiatrist or, more disturbingly, the killer.

The film begins with Dr. Collins's morning bus trip to work. It is shot subjectively, but that characteristic is never announced, not marked by the multiple looks of outward regard that usually signal a subjective point of view. In fact, the voice-over provided by Collins almost seems to deny the singularity of our perspective. It describes the general anonymity of a large town and notes how people seem to have "no names, no faces. I'm one of the people too." The narrative thus quickly motivates that voice's lack of identity, its absence of "face," even as it begins to suggest a deeper sense of difference here, as the voice-over qualifies its initial observation with, "Yet for all the similarity of our routine, we're none of us the same. We're as different as the print of our thumbs." That note, in turn, introduces a slow tracking shot through the bus, as if someone were moving from front to rear, seeking a seat, as the narrator speculates on the occupations and concerns of the passengers. Only with the bus's arrival outside Central Police Station are we conventionally cued into the nature of this point of view. Here policemen look into the camera, salute, and otherwise address this mobile perspective, while the narrator in response interrupts his monologue on "difference" to return the greetings. The narrative then puts a name on this vague personification, as the camera enters an office and a hand reaches down to pick up a paper beside a name plate reading, "Dr. Andrew Collins."

What the film has done is anticipate the difficulty involved in such subjective sequences and turn it into capital. The basic problem is one of placement, or identification, as that technique forces the viewer into a position within the narrative that is his own yet not his own. In effect, it fashions a kind of mystery of identification that the viewer is forced to play, and one that can easily sidetrack the narrative itself. But *The Dark Past* incorporates that mysterious sense of placement. Just as the nameless, faceless narrator plays what he terms a "guessing game" on the way to work, so do we begin guessing at the identity of the one through whose eyes we are seeing. Moreover, the narrator encourages that response, offhandedly noting, "No, I'm not a policeman, not a detective either," as we track past several offices in the police station. More important, it engages that same attitude in its subsequent exploration of the mysteries of human identity, that is, in its efforts to demonstrate just how much about the self always remains hidden—"off-screen."

As a detective succinctly puts it, "I know, doc. You think everything is in the mind."

That skeptical detective then becomes our new, more stable placement in the narrative, as Collins sets out to explain the mysteries of identity with his flashback account of the case of Al Walker. While his voice-over attests to the subjective nature of all that we see, it is also clearly an account *to* someone: to an identified character and to us. When we finally return to a fully subjective camera sequence with Walker's dream, it is from a different angle than when the film began. It comes to us stabilized through a series of filters (a flashback within a flashback), as Walker relates his puzzling dream to Collins, who is in turn analyzing it and recounting it to the detective—and to us. As a result, we get our subjective experience and our conventional vantage as well. We get to share a killer's perspective, yet we avoid the difficulties of identification or guilt.

Al Walker's dream recalls, by turns, the metaphoric, Dalí-designed dream sequence of *Spellbound* and the more straightforward subjective camera technique seen in the film's opening. While we get no surrealist imagery here, the sequence does use a wide-angle lens, flat lighting scheme, and forced perspective to distort the images and craft a pointedly abnormal world. Yet the hesitantly moving, low-angle point of view precisely suggests how Al Walker the boy would have seen things. This combination well suits what is going on here, for while Walker's dream is indeed metaphoric, it is in the process of being interpreted, its unreality being rendered real. As Collins tells him, "Everything in your nightmare is a substitute for something else," so "if we could only find out what those symbols stand for, we'd know what your dream means." We watch, therefore, as the real begins to emerge from a symbolic field. In turn, a fluidly tracking, subjective camera complements this emergence by engaging what I have termed the subjective's mystery of identification. But it is a mystery in the process of being solved, for Collins labels the dream, and thus the subjective sequence as well, a drama of identity. Its images reveal a boy, Walker, who has helped the police gun down an older man, his father, who has come between the boy and his mother; and the psychiatrist easily reads their Oedipal pattern: "That's what you wanted—to take your father's place."

By incorporating its subjective elements into its own tale of identity, *The Dark Past* accomplishes what few of its subjective camera predecessors did: it effectively integrates those techniques with its narrative thrust. A metaphoric representation of subjectivity—Walker's dream—becomes part of the pattern of blockage and repression with which the psychiatrist and his subject are struggling. At the same time, the mystery of identification to which subjective camera often gives rise is here used to suggest a larger pattern of identification woes that seem to abound in the modern world and to underlie many psychic ills and much aberrant behavior. While the film ends with a plea for understanding, even of a killer like Al Walker, it is a plea well supported by the problem of identity its subjective techniques have effectively dramatized.

Those techniques push at the very boundaries of the cinematic. They point to the off-screen space we occupy, our own artificial placement in every film narrative, and thus trouble the reality illusion that classical film narratives have traditionally tried so hard to fashion. Yet that difficulty seems to have generated less resistance at Columbia than at many of the larger studios, if we are to judge by the reflexive or self-referential elements that would begin surfacing in a number of its *noirs*. While Paramount produced the definitive *noir* examination of the film industry in Billy Wilder's *Sunset Boulevard* (1950), Columbia released two of the most self-conscious and ultimately subversive works in the *noir* canon: Orson Welles's *The Lady from Shanghai* and Nicholas Ray's *In a Lonely Place*.

While Welles's film does not focus on the film industry, its resonsances to his career, to that of his wife, Rita Hayworth, and to the movie business are unmistakable. As James Naremore has noted, Welles's reworking of his wife's image for *The Lady from Shanghai*, cutting her hair short and dying it blond, dressing and posing her "in near parodies of calendar-girl fashion," seems to comment generally on "Hollywood's synthetic sexuality"[10] and more particularly on Hayworth's real-life image as pin-up girl and movie siren. At the same time, the film's protagonist, who is seduced by that glamorous figure and eventually finds himself plunged into a hall of mirrors, surrounded by multiple images, offers parallels to both Welles's life and the plight of the typical filmgoer. It is a peculiarly Wellesian trope for the lure of cinematic art, for the seductive way in which it can work its will on both film artist and audience, and for the dangers implicit in that lure.

While Nicholas Ray's movie takes a far less subtle approach to the film industry, the very straightforwardness of its treatment is itself noteworthy. *In a Lonely Place* derives from a 1947 Dorothy B. Hughes novel which, although set in Hollywood, little concerns itself with the film industry. That setting simply provides a context for the action by establishing a kind of modern American obsessiveness—with success and image—that points toward the darker and more dangerous obsessions of the novel's protagonist. The film, in contrast, takes the movies and their practices as its chief focus. The protagonist, Dix Steele (Humphrey Bogart), is an accused murderer who has frequently been arrested for beating up his girlfriends and acquaintances. More than just the novel's pathological character, though, he is a screenwriter who has been driven to his current isolated and violent state, the film implies, by his work in the movie industry, an industry that compels him to write what he does not want to write; that turns all his efforts into formulaic projects requiring no thought on his part, that has transformed him, as he puts it, into little more than "a popcorn salesman," and that has even made him something of an expert on murder ("I've had a great deal of experience with this sort of thing. I've killed dozens of people—in pictures"). What the film suggests is a level on which the film industry itself becomes a kind of pathological force, operating, unchecked and dangerously, on the popular psyche.

This image of Hollywood is obviously unflattering and seems an unlikely product of a system that has traditionally tried to deflect attention from both the film apparatus and the film business. The industry has simply considered it good business to disguise the fact that it is manufacturing and selling us our dreams. Yet this sort of portrait shows up increasingly in the output of Columbia and, along with a film like *Sunset Boulevard*, helped open the way for a growing number of works that examine the film industry in particular and popular modes of communication in general. Following this lead were *The Glass Web* (1953), *The Big Knife* (1955), and *The Sweet Smell of Success* (1957), as well as works in other veins that examine the very media by which we communicate our cultural "truths" and produce the popular images that dominate our lives.

In many ways, Columbia might be seen as simply following the pack with its *films noirs*, as taking a trail already blazed by the major studios it had always aspired to join. Yet even in the act of following, it seems to have managed, in the best corporate tradition, to distinguish its own product. Fritz Lang's work for the studio, for example, certainly pushed the level of acceptable violence (*The Big Heat*) and the depiction of human emotions (*Human Desire*) beyond normal Hollywood practice. And films like *Dead Reckoning*, *The Dark Past*, *The Lady from Shanghai*, and *In a Lonely Place* stretched the boundaries of both the *noir* form in particular and classical film practice in general. Of course, *film noir*, which many saw as a kind of deviant form, thanks to its often stylized focus on crime and corruption, probably lent itself to such stretching. But it is to Columbia's credit that it developed the sort of film that clearly played at the margins of conventional cinematic practices. The result is, on the one hand, a noteworthy addition to the *noir* canon; on the other, evidence that Columbia in the late 1940s and early 1950s helped reshape Hollywood's story patterns and techniques.[11]

NOTES

1. *Film noir's* status as a genre is frequently debated, generally because it seems to depend so heavily on the conventions of recognized genres like the

crime film, and because, unlike many other genres, it seems a largely time-bound phenomenon, limited to the 1940s and 1950s. While the focus of this chapter keeps me from pursuing that debate, current scholarship and the appearance of numerous *films noirs* in recent years suggest that the form might profitably be thought of as a distinct genre.

2. Douglas Gomery, *The Hollywood Studio System* (New York: St. Martin's, 1986), 165-66.

3. For much of the information on titles and release dates, I have relied on Alain Silver and Elizabeth Ward, *Film Noir: An Encyclopedic Reference to the American Style* (Woodstock: Overlook Press, 1979), and Robert Ottoson, *A Reference Guide to the American Film Noir* (Metuchen, N.J.: Scarecrow, 1981).

4. J.A. Place and L.S. Peterson, "Some Visual Motifs of Film Noir," *Film Comment* 10, no. 1 (1974): 30-35.

5. Ford had a curiously ambiguous posture. At times, when filmed with the typical *noir* low-key lighting, dressed in rumpled or working-class outfits, and with his close-cropped hair, he took on the image of the rugged individual, while at other times he could be nearly feminized, as in a film like *Gilda*. If both potentials were implicit in Ford's character, Columbia seems to have recognized and capitalized on them, for his later roles especially ally a more traditionally masculine character with what might be described as a feminine vulnerability.

6. Janey Place, "Women in Film Noir," in *Women in Film Noir*, ed. E. Ann Kaplan (London: BFI, 1980), 36.

7. Richard Dyer, "Resistance through Charisma: Rita Hayworth and *Gilda*," in *Women in Film Noir*, 97.

8. Umberto Eco, "*Casablanca*: Cult Movies and Intertextual Collage," *SubStance* 14, no. 2 (1985): 10.

9. Marc Vernet, "The Filmic Transaction: On the Openings of Film Noirs," trans. David Rodowick, *Velvet Light Trap* 20 (1983): 6.

10. James Naremore, *The Magic World of Orson Welles* (New York: Oxford Univ. Press, 1978), 160.

11. The following Columbia movies are typically classified as *films noirs*: *Between Midnight and Dawn* (Joseph H. Lewis, 1950), *The Big Heat* (Fritz Lang, 1953), *The Brothers Rico* (Phil Karlson, 1957), *The Burglar* (Paul Wendkos, 1957), *Convicted* (Henry Levin, 1950), *The Crimson Kimono* (Sam Fuller, 1959), *The Dark Past* (Rudolph Maté, 1949), *Dead Reckoning* (John Cromwell, 1947), *Drive a Crooked Road* (Richard Quine, 1953), *Framed* (Richard Wallace, 1947), *The Garment Jungle* (Vincent Sherman, 1957), *Gilda* (Charles Vidor, 1946), *The Harder They Fall* (Mark Robson, 1956), *Human Desire* (Fritz Lang, 1954), *In a Lonely Place* (Nicholas Ray, 1950), *Johnny O'Clock* (Robert Rossen, 1947), *The Killer That Stalked New York* (Earl McEvoy, 1951), *Knock on Any Door* (Nicholas Ray, 1949), *The Lady from Shanghai* (Orson Welles, 1948), *The Lineup* (Don Siegel, 1958), *M* (Joseph Losey, 1951), *The Mob* (Robert Parrish, 1951), *My Name Is Julia Ross* (Joseph H. Lewis, 1945), *Night Editor* (Henry Levin, 1946), *The Night Holds Terror* (Andrew Stone, 1955), *Nightfall* (Jacques Tourneur, 1957), *Pushover* (Richard Quine, 1954), *The Reckless Moment* (Max Ophuls, 1949), *Scandal Sheet* (Phil Karlson, 1952), *711 Ocean Drive* (Joseph M. Newman, 1950), *The Sniper* (Edward Dmytryk, 1952), *So Dark the Night* (Joseph H. Lewis, 1946), *The Undercover Man* (Joseph H. Lewis, 1949), and *Underworld U.S.A.* (Sam Fuller, 1961).

4

RITA HAYWORTH AT COLUMBIA, 1941-1945

The Fabrication of a Star

WILLIAM VINCENT

To say that Rita Hayworth came along at the right time in Columbia's history is to mythologize the event. Actually, she was a manufactured product—trained, honed, hyped, and market-tested before Harry Cohn decided to put her in her first leading role, Sheila Winthrop in *You'll Never Get Rich* (1941). From the beginning Hayworth was the perfect example of the fabricated Hollywood star. There was nothing new in this; as Carl Laemmle said, "The fabrication of stars is the fundamental thing in the film industry."[1] What are interesting in Hayworth's case are the process of fabrication, the image that emerged from it, the way Columbia presented that image during the war years, and the extent to which the image reflected Hayworth's personal life.

Hayworth has been the subject of two biographies which, if they do not entirely rise above the level of gossip, incorporate a good deal of revealing material from those who knew and worked with her.[2] One thing they make clear is that, with Hayworth, the fabrication process began when she was twelve. On moving to California with his wife and children in 1931, her father, Eduardo Cansino, a well-known Spanish dancer, decided to make his daughter, Margarita, his partner in the "Dancing Cansinos." Cansino "groomed her to be sexually provocative onstage, while offstage she remained the same shy, withdrawn child she had always been."[3]

Thus the disjunction between her public image and her private self was formed early. Hayworth's shyness was undoubtedly exacerbated by the fact that her father made her not only his dancing partner but perhaps his partner in incest, too.[4] Certainly the repetitive patterns of her life can be seen to have originated in the problematic relationship with her father: her dependence on older men and her anxiety to please them by letting them take control.

The Dancing Cansinos entertained American tourists in Tijuana and Agua Caliente, and after the performance Eduardo would present his daughter to some of the wealthier and more influential patrons, particularly those from Hollywood. Eventually his efforts paid off, and Margarita was spotted by an executive from Fox. A screen test resulted, followed by a six-month contract and her screen debut in *Dante's Inferno* (1935). After a succession of small roles failed to advance her career, and her benefactor at Fox was ousted, her contract was not renewed.

At this point Eddie Judson entered her life. Old enough to be her father and with no visible means of support, Judson took over the fabrication of Hayworth's image. He got her a contract at Columbia and then married her. Hayworth "readily allowed Eddie to take over every aspect of her life, to dictate her smallest and most personal decisions."[5] Deciding to redo her look, he had her hairline raised and her hair color changed to its characteristic red.[6] Her name, which had already been shortened from Margarita to Rita Cansino, was further altered to free her from being typed as a Latin. She was now Rita Hayworth. Meanwhile, she was appearing in B movies—twelve between 1937 and 1938. She took diction and voice lessons, acting lessons, tennis lessons, riding lessons. At night she and Judson would go to the best night spots so she could be seen by the "right" people. Judson hired one of the best press agents; consequently, "the photographers invariably began to take her picture because . . . she was usually the smartest young woman in the room. By 1940 there had been more than 3,800 stories filed on her and her photograph had been reproduced over 12,000 times."[7] Hayworth may even have gotten her first big break—a part in Howard Hawks's *Only Angels Have Wings* (1939)—by parading herself in a provocative dress at the Trocadero on a night Hawks and Harry Cohn were having dinner there.[8]

Her success as a *femme fatale* in *Only Angels Have Wings* made Cohn take notice, and he and Columbia took over from Judson the job of grooming and promotion. As Cohn's biographer has noted, "The ascending stardom of Rita Hayworth provided a new and stimulating experience for Harry Cohn. Never before had he been able to discover and develop—and often to profit from—a star of the top rank."[9] His interest in Hayworth was both proprietary and fatherly; there were suspicions that he harbored a sexual interest as well. Since Judson had, perhaps in continuation of her father's practice, arranged for her to sleep with men who could be useful to her career, it would not be surprising if Cohn had similar expectations, but nothing came of them except for an almost pathological jealousy on his part.[10]

Once Cohn decided to make Hayworth a star, she was brought along slowly, with good parts in a succession of B movies and some loan-outs. The latter—to Warners for *The Strawberry Blonde* (1941) and *Affectionately Yours* (1941), and to Fox for *Blood and Sand* (1941), *My Gal Sal* (1942), and *Tales of Manhattan* (1942)—were particularly welcome to

Cohn, who not only made money on Hayworth but also profited from her growing fame. *Blood and Sand* was especially successful, and as Doña Sol, Hayworth stole the film from Tyrone Power and Linda Darnell. Once again, as in *Only Angels Have Wings*, she played the *femme fatale*, a type that would be suspended for the duration. Concurrently, her image as a sex object was consolidated by her picture in *Life* (11 August 1941), where she appears in a black lace negligee, soft pillows behind her, looking inscrutably over her shoulder at the camera, and with one finger hooked provocatively into her décolletage. This picture would become one of the most popular pin-ups of the war.

There was, however, another Hayworth, the one who dominated her 1941-1945 Columbia musicals: *You'll Never Get Rich* (1941), *You Were Never Lovelier* (1942), *Cover Girl* (1944), and *Tonight and Every Night* (1945).[11] In these, Hayworth is a forthright modern woman, spunky and sarcastic but also a bit sentimental and vulnerable. Her sex appeal is unself-conscious—totally contrary to the Doña Sol and postwar Gilda/Elsa Bannister/Carmen image—but nonetheless powerful for it. To imagine a *femme fatale* as the main character in a full-fledged 1940s musical is to imagine a variation on the genre not possible until the 1970s and 1980s. In part, then, Hayworth's second persona was determined by genre, in part also by wartime sensibilities that dictated what was acceptable in terms of character types the stars could play. A million men may have had Rita Hayworth in a negligee pinned to their footlockers, but that Hayworth was not an image their wives back home were prepared to accept on the silver screen.

The 1941-1945 musicals are variations on the basic plot of the classic Hollywood musical in which a couple overcome obstacles to their union.[12] In *You'll Never Get Rich*, Hayworth is Sheila Winthrop, appearing in the chorus of a revue that Robert Curtis (Fred Astaire) is choreographing for Martin Cortland. The philandering Cortland buys Sheila a diamond bracelet, which she refuses. When Cortland's wife discovers the bracelet, he is forced to lie, claiming that Curtis bought it for Sheila. After Cortland persuades Curtis to back him up, deception and misunderstanding multiply until everything is resolved by the on-stage wedding of Sheila and Curtis that happens to be performed by a real justice of the peace. The tired plot incorporates elements typical of the classic 1930s musical: deception, misunderstanding, overreaction, manipulation, and coincidence (which is usually interpreted as fate). The dramatic trajectory resembles nothing so much as a dance of alternating advance and withdrawal on the part of the two main characters until they come together once and for all at the end.

The film's production values do not make up for the script's deficiencies. Since Cohn was paying a lot for Astaire's services, he decided to hold costs down elsewhere: black-and-white photography, no designer dresses for Hayworth, no white sets. The direction was entrusted to Sidney Lanfield, a journeyman director who delivered a straightforward narrative and little more. What saves *You'll Never Get Rich* are the performances, Cole Porter's score, and the dancing. The musical numbers were intended primarily to showcase Astaire's talent: three duets with Hayworth, two solos with ensemble, and one typical Astaire sequence. Two of the duets with Hayworth—an exuberant rehearsal for "The Boogie Barcarolle" and the sensual "So Near and Yet So Far"—make one understand why *You'll Never Get Rich* led many to believe Astaire had at last found a suitable replacement for Ginger Rogers.

These two duets exemplify what Babington and Evans call "the laws of condensation that operate in the dreamlike world of numbers" in which "the most intense meanings are registered."[13] In the first duet, the stirring of romantic interest is expressed by pure *joie de danser;* in the second, both the lyrics and the dance become metaphors for the rapture and pain of romantic love. On the whole, though, if Babington and Evans are right that in most great musicals the numbers both condense and intensify plot, theme, and character, then the fact that few of the numbers in *You'll Never Get Rich* have anything to do with plot, theme, or character accounts, in part, for the film's weakness.

Although made in 1941, *You'll Never Get Rich* is still very much a peacetime picture. No mention is made of the war, nor is Curtis apprehensive about being drafted. In fact, he goes off to boot camp singing "I'm Shooting the Works for Uncle Sam," and nothing in the army camp suggests a potential wartime footing.

There is also no wartime atmosphere in *You Were Never Lovelier* (1942), in which the plot is again set in motion by the meddling of an older man. Eduardo Acuña, a Buenos Aires hotel owner whose daughter Maria (Hayworth) "has an ice cube for a heart," decides to warm it by sending his daughter flowers from an unknown admirer. When Robert Davis (Fred Astaire), an out-of-work dancer, delivers the flowers, Maria believes he is the admirer—the Lochinvar of her adolescent fantasies. Again there is the basic plot of attraction and withdrawal, and the elements of deception, misunderstanding, overreaction, manipulation, and coincidence. The most interesting plot variation is also the most distasteful—the father's somewhat incestuous meddling in his daughter's love life. Not surprisingly, the whole family is given to meddling, from the mother, who tries to visit her eldest daughter on her honeymoon, to Maria's sisters, who are anxious to get her married off so they can marry in turn (the father's rule being that his daughters must marry in order of birth). Apart from this aspect, the plot is very much a 1930s product.

Like *You'll Never Get Rich, You Were Never Lovelier* is primarily

Astaire's film; his Robert Davis is no different from his Robert Curtis. Similarly, Hayworth's Maria is not unlike her Sheila. Despite references to Maria's being old-fashioned ("Maria's as old-fashioned as a hoop skirt"), it is clearly a modern woman we see when Hayworth and Astaire go into an up-tempo, slightly jitterbuggy rendition of "The Shorty George," which was Columbia's attempt to resurrect the old Astaire trademark of introducing a new dance in every film.

Although *You Were Never Lovelier* was shot in black and white and the direction entrusted to another journeyman director, William Seiter, the production values were stronger. The most obvious improvement was in the sets and costumes, particularly the gowns Irene created for Hayworth. Especially beautiful is Hayworth's costume for the "I'm Old Fashioned" sequence; the gown shows off Hayworth's shoulders and back and thrusts her breasts forward in a manner that is anything but old-fashioned.

Jerome Kern's score is more sentimental than Porter's was in *You'll Never Get Rich*, but that suits the theme of old fashionedness. While there are still songs that add nothing in the way of intensification and condensation, there is a greater integration of the music with the plot than there was in *You'll Never Get Rich*. "Dearly Beloved," sung first by Davis and reprised by Maria, establishes a common theme in the musical: lovers brought together by fate ("Dearly beloved / How clearly I see / Somewhere in heaven / You were fashioned for me"). When first heard, the song presages the as-yet-unborn mutual attraction of the couple; when heard the second time, it expresses Maria's awakening to love as she dances dreamily around her bedroom and sinks languorously on the bed. "I'm Old Fashioned" develops the idea implicit in the lyrics ("I'm old fashioned / I love the moonlight") and gives rise to the couple's first rapturous dance together. And if the words to "The Shorty George" are silly and, from a contemporary perspective, racially offensive, the number expresses that *joie de danser* that brought out the best in both Astaire and Hayworth. The title song ("You were never lovelier / Dreams were never lovelier") marks the full realization on Robert's part of his love for Maria, reinforcing the idea of the dreamlike nature of the loved one and love itself.

You Were Never Lovelier shows even less awareness of World War II than *You'll Never Get Rich*. One suspects the reason Buenos Aires was chosen as the setting, aside from the film's being based on an Argentine source, is that it allows the romance to unfold without a single reference to the war. Certainly no explanation is offered as to why Robert is following the horses in the Argentine rather than serving his country.

Cover Girl (1944) does acknowledge that a war is on, but not immediately; its primary concern is whether Rusty Parker (Hayworth) should choose Broadway over Brooklyn and theatre impresario Noel Wheaton (Lee Bowman) over nightclub owner Danny McGuire (Gene Kelly). When Rusty's picture appears on the cover of *Vanity*, she becomes an instant celebrity, although she had previously been a singer at Danny McGuire's Brooklyn club. John Coudair, *Vanity's* publisher, decides to save Rusty from obscurity at Danny's by wooing her, not as he had wooed her grandmother Mirabelle (also played by Hayworth) but by means of a surrogate, Noel Wheaton. Once again there is a plot that depends on the familiar elements of deception, misunderstanding, overreaction, manipulation, and coincidence. The situation in *Cover Girl* differs from that of the previous two films because Danny and Rusty are in love from the beginning. As in *You Were Never Lovelier*, there is a curious twist in the manipulation used, but again it boils down to an older man's attempt to dictate a young woman's romantic life for his own selfish or voyeuristic pleasure. The most glaring coincidence—that Rusty should be Mirabelle's granddaughter and her spitting image (inevitable with Hayworth playing both parts)—is one audiences of the period had seen so many times in one form or another that they may have come to believe it.

Hayworth looks lush in Technicolor. She is beautifully costumed, and because of the flashbacks where she appears as Mirabelle, she is seen in both contemporary and period clothes and hairstyle. The script does not demand much of her by way of acting, and she is up to most of it except for a feeble drunk scene. She lip-synchs her songs well (Hayworth's singing was always dubbed by, among others, Nan Wynn, Martha Mears, and Anita Ellis.) As a dancer, she is at her best with Kelly in "Put Me to the Test" and the dreamlike "Long Ago and Far Away," and with Kelly and Phil Silvers in "Make Way for Tomorrow," which shows off her superb athleticism. Her solos are less successful, not because of lack of ability on her part but because of uninspired choreography that is forgivable in the two turn-of-the-century numbers, which are self-consciously old-fashioned, but not in the title number. The "Cover Girl" sequence begins well enough with a succession of "cover girls" in close-up and medium shot who then freeze into one magazine cover after another. The colors are intense and supersaturated; the poses are witty and elegant. But then Rusty appears rushing down a zigzag ramp, holding her diaphanous dress so that it streams out behind her. After some maneuvering with a corps of male dancers, she runs back up the ramp, with the dancers following her and throwing their hands up in rhythmic unison. For a film that was meant to showcase Hayworth's talent and beauty, the effort is all rather pointless.

The score, as in *You Were Never Lovelier*, was composed by Jerome Kern, with lyrics by Ira Gershwin. It is not a great score, but it has its moments. "Make Way for Tomorrow" expresses the optimism and self-confidence of the three main characters as they dance down a soundstage Brooklyn street. Danny's "Alter-Ego Dance" does not capture the character's internal debate with his conscience so much as his (and Gene Kelly's) narcissism. "Long Ago and Far Away" is a paean to the mystic power of love ("Long ago and far away / I dreamed a dream one day, / And now that dream is here beside me"). Again we hear the affirmation of the myth that forms the basis of the classical musical: love is eternal, preordained, and the only means of satisfying human longing.

The title song embodies a second theme of the film, a theme that, on the level of plot, it seems to deplore, but that on the level of spectacle it embraces wholeheartedly: feminine beauty is more important than feminine talent ("Life's incomplete / Until I meet / That girl on the cover"). What could be more appropriate to the Pin-Up Girl age? Never mind that the song—like most songs in the pre-*Oklahoma!* (1943) stage of the musical—brings the narrative to a halt. Yet in this sequence, one can see the great advantage the musical has over other genres in presenting the woman as spectacle. In classic cinema, the woman's "visual presence tends to work against the development of the storyline, to freeze the flow of action in moments of erotic contemplation."[14] Since musical plots are so simple and predictable, interruptions for erotic contemplation are easily accommodated.

The "Cover Girl" song is also perfect for a Hayworth film. One wonders how Margarita Cansino would have replied had someone said to her, as Danny says to Rusty, "You're going to be a star, but you have to make it on your feet, not your face." For all Hayworth's dancing talent, it was her (remade) face that first attracted attention and sustained her success long after her dancing had faded. So much of her success depended on her appearing on the covers of *Look*, *Time*, and *Life* as well as the fan magazines, and on that famous pin-up that so enraptured Orson Welles when he saw it in South America that he said, "When I come back *that's* what I'm going to do!"[15] How revealing is Welles's use of "that." It brings to mind Coudair's words in *Cover Girl*: "Beauty like hers demands . . . money to put *it* [italics mine] in the proper setting." Could there be two clearer demonstrations than the reduction of the Hayworth persona to a "that" and an "it" of Laura Mulvey's thesis that woman-as-spectacle is simply a fetish object to the male?

Hayworth is less obviously a spectacle in *Tonight and Every Night* (1945), although she is again a showgirl. The idea for the film came from London's Windmill Theatre, which remained in operation throughout the Blitz. The theater in *Tonight and Every Night* puts on variety shows starring the American Rosalind Bruce (Hayworth) and the British performers Judy Kane (Janet Blair) and Tommy Lawson (Marc Platt). Tommy has a secret yen for Rosalind, while Judy has the same for him. Into their lives comes Paul Lundy (Lee Bowman), an RAF squadron commander, who naturally becomes attracted to Rosalind, especially after she sings "You Excite Me." When Paul must go on a secret mission, his father, a minister, gives Rosalind Paul's bible in which they find Rosalind's picture in the middle of First Corinthians, across from "It is better to marry . . ." (the complete sentence does not appear on the screen). Both Reverend Lundy and Rosalind interpret this as a marriage proposal. When Paul returns, Rosalind is ready to leave with him for Canada until Judy and Tommy are killed in a raid. Rather than have the evening's performance cancelled, Rosalind steps into Judy's part in the finale, and she and the company sing "Tonight and Every Night" as the film ends.

Although *Tonight and Every Night* received respectful reviews because of British director Victor Saville's smooth style, as a film it is more interesting than good. It deliberately violates several canons of the genre, particularly in ending with the deaths of Judy and Tommy. It also makes the least use of the standard elements of the classic musical (deception, misunderstanding, manipulation, etc.). Attraction-withdrawal, which generally provides the plot tension, is so insignificant here that it is unnoticeable. As a result, *Tonight and Every Night* is more believable than the other Hayworth films, but less dramatic—and certainly less mythic.

In the absence of tension, the film must rely more heavily on performance. The acting is generally solid, except for some atrocious English accents by the mostly American cast. But aside from Hayworth, none of the principals—Blair, Platt, or Bowman—has much personality; since Bowman neither sings nor dances, the love between Rosalind and Paul cannot be expressed in song and dance. Moreover, Hayworth is not at her best, perhaps because she was several months pregnant, perhaps because she was having difficulty in her marriage with Orson Welles, or perhaps because she was simply tired. Her dancing is heavy-footed; certainly Jack Cole's choreography makes few demands of her. Cole himself has pointed out that, at this stage in her career, she was no longer practicing every day, a factor that might explain the routines he created for her.[16] Hayworth also has no one of the magnitude of Astaire or Kelly to bring out her best. Marc Platt was being groomed for stardom and had a considerable talent, but his main number is a solo danced to the radio. Hayworth does one number with Cole ("What Does an English Girl Think of a Yank"), but he overshadows her, and there is no rapport between them.

Although Jule Styne and Sammy Cahn wrote the songs, they are mostly without distinction. The one that captured Hayworth's eroticism was the samba, "You Excite Me," in which she does not so much have to dance as rotate her pelvis and look sexy in Jean Louis's two-piece, sequin-covered outfit. The sequence gives Paul Lundy the "wrong" idea about Rosalind; it was intended to give the audience the same idea.

"The Boy I Left Behind" typifies the film's reversal of the genre's conventions. Judy and Rosalind appear as two army recruits, reminiscing about their boyfriends on the home front. The number is meant as a reminder of one of the film's central themes: the war effort involves women as well as men. As Reverend Lundy tells Rosalind, "It's nice to know my daughter's a soldier as well as my son."

The title song condenses and intensifies this theme. Sung by Judy, it begins with a newsreel depicting typical Britons, some of whom are invited to step out and join in the number, moving from screen to stage. People from all walks of life sing out in affirmation of the wartime spirit exemplified by the theater itself: "We'll go on and on and on and on, tonight and every night." Unlike Hayworth's previous three musicals, *Tonight and Every Night* makes the war its focus. Every aspect of the film—romance, entertainment, and spectacle—is justified in the name of the war effort and the troops' morale. Thus the film opens with servicemen from all the allied forces waiting in line to see the show. From the opening image it is clear that what is being celebrated is not just British but international; and when Rosalind takes over Judy's part in the finale, it is clear that love, the prime mover in the musical, must relinquish its primacy for the duration. Thus *Tonight and Every Night* is in keeping with Hollywood's World War II philosophy: a movie spectacle of any sort is a necessary and valuable part of the war effort.

Tonight and Every Night was Hayworth's last film of the war years. She was about to move into a new phase of her career—out of the musical and into "straight" roles.

Her four wartime films for Columbia (*You'll Never Get Rich, You Were Never Lovelier, Cover Girl, Tonight and Every Night*) present a Hayworth who, for the most part, is forthright, moral, modern—but not really independent. She does not signify, as Bette Davis and Katharine Hepburn do, a challenge to the patriarchy. Nor does "Hayworth" signify the suffering heroine of the woman's film; in fact, Hayworth never made a woman's film, despite its popularity in the 1940s. In three of her four wartime films, Hayworth plays a show girl, a type in which "the gaze of the spectator and that of the male characters in the film are neatly combined."[17] Even Rosalind Bruce, the most liberated of the four characters, is defined in terms of her performance for the appreciative gaze of the male audience. Furthermore, a male is the narrative center in three of the four movies; the issue is always whether Robert Curtis (*You'll Never Get Rich*), Robert Davis (*You Were Never Lovelier*), or

Danny McGuire (*Cover Girl*) will solve the "problem" the Hayworth character presents. These films also corroborate the thesis that, in the classic Hollywood film, the male gaze is the privileged one and the male's role is "the active one of advancing the story." [18] The exception is *Tonight and Every Night*, where there is no central male character; but there is no main female character, either. Both are subordinate to something higher—the war. [19]

It was partially because of the war that the characters Hayworth played were carefully kept under control; like other films of the era, they can be seen as incorporating the male's uneasiness about his absence from home and the female's newfound personal and economic freedom. In that light, one can read the switch to the new Hayworth image, *femmes fatales*, as a postwar unleashing of both the "true" Hayworth persona and the "true" feelings of American men toward these women the war had created.

In three of the four films she made between 1946 and 1948, she appears as a *femme fatale* married to an older man. In *The Lady from Shanghai*, Elsa (Hayworth) is married to Arthur Bannister (Everett Sloane), who represents "the crippled father, the Law, weakened by insufficient manliness." [20] This description is equally applicable to Ballin Mundson (*Gilda*) and either the Colonel or Garcia (*The Loves of Carmen*), or to Cortland (*You'll Never Get Rich*), Acuña (*You Were Never Lovelier*), Coudair (*Cover Girl*), and Reverend Lundy (*Tonight and Every Night*) in a different but relevant way. It is the task of the Hero to rescue the Maiden from the Father.

Thus, one way to read these films is as metaphors for the struggle of father and son for the female; another is to see them as the passing of the female from father (or surrogate father) to son (or surrogate son) to neutralize her threat. Although *Cover Girl* insists that Rusty should make up her own mind, the film never allows her to do so. Sheila (*You'll Never Get Rich*) is repeatedly subjected to deception; even her marriage is arranged without her knowledge. Maria (*You Were Never Lovelier*) is deceived by both her father and Robert. Rusty (*Cover Girl*) is subjected to manipulation by almost everyone, even the watchman at Danny's club; when she goes back and finds it closed, the watchman implies it is her fault. Rosalind (*Tonight and Every Night*) is subject to the constraints of war.

The Hayworth woman is always under the control of men. She is controlled by their language: men call her "chicken," "kid," "beautiful" (as a noun), "child," "lover." She is also controlled by the male narrative. In the wartime as well as the postwar films, the narrative always focuses on the male—on the working out of *his* problem, the resolution of *his* quest for wholeness, *his* remasculinization—whether it is Robert Curtis (*You'll Never Get Rich*), who learns to look at a woman other than the way a butcher looks at a lamb chop, or Don José (*The Loves of Carmen*), who confronts Carmen with a knife, only to be taunted with "You're not man enough!"

Even in her only non–*femme fatale* movie of the 1946-48 period, *Down to Earth* (1947), a musical reworking of Columbia's earlier success *Here Comes Mr. Jordan* (1941), the Hayworth woman is subject to the male. The silver-haired Mr. Jordan, a stand-in for the Deity and as patriarchal a figure as one can find, allows Terpsichore (Hayworth) to descend to earth to show a Broadway producer (Larry Parks) what a musical about the Muses should really be like. Initially the producer yields to her suggestions, which result in a highbrow financial flop, but it is *she* who finally comes around to *his* way of thinking and agrees to sacrifice art for commercialism. Terpsichore's action saves not only the show but the producer's life, which had been threatened by gangsters. For her sacrifice, Mr. Jordan tells her that when the producer dies, they will be reunited in the clouds.

In *Cover Girl*, after Rusty's picture appears on the cover of *Vanity*, "Genius" (Phil Silvers) remarks, "Can you imagine a star being born to a couple of parents like me and Danny?" The line is an attempt at humor, but looked at objectively it expresses what Hayworth's career was all about. If ever a star was born of men—Eduardo Cansino, Eddie Judson, Harry Cohn, Orson Welles, and the patriarchal studio system—it was Rita Hayworth. She was the fabrication of men to serve men's needs. "She reflected what the men wanted. . . . Unfortunately, that's the way she thought it should be."[21] Perhaps that's why she was recognized as the Love Goddess: she was everything a *man* could desire.

NOTES

1. Edgar Morin, *The Stars*, trans. Richard Howard (New York: Grove Press, 1960), 134.

2. John Kobal, *Rita Hayworth: The Time, the Place and the Woman* (New York: Norton, 1977); Barbara Leaming, *If This Was Happiness* (New York: Viking, 1989). Kobal includes extensive interviews with many of Hayworth's co-workers, particularly those behind the camera, and had the added advantage of interview material from Hayworth herself. Leaming's is particularly useful in that it includes information from Hayworth's second husband, Orson Welles. A third biography, James Hill, *Rita Hayworth* (London: Robson Books, 1983), deals almost exclusively with Hill's own relationship with the star, which culminated in his becoming her fifth husband.

3. Leaming, *If This Was Happiness*, 18.

4. Ibid., 17; the information came from Welles.

5. Ibid., 34.

6. Kobal, *Rita Hayworth*, 76-77.

7. Ibid., 81.
8. Ibid., 95.
9. Bob Thomas, *King Cohn: The Life and Times of Harry Cohn* (New York: Putnam, 1967), 217.
10. Leaming, *If This Was Happiness*, 59-60; see also 51 for Orson Welles's remark, "Her first husband was a pimp. Literally a pimp."
11. *You'll Never Get Rich*: director, Sidney Lanfield; producer, Samuel Bischoff; cinematography, Philip Tannura; screenplay by Michael Farmer and Ernest Pagano; songs by Cole Porter; dances by Robert Alton. Cast: Fred Astaire (Robert Curtis), Rita Hayworth (Sheila Winthrop), Robert Benchley (Martin Cortland), Frieda Inescort (Julia Cortland), John Hubbard (Tom Barton), Osa Massen (Louise).

You Were Never Lovelier: director, William Seiter; producer, Louis Edelman; cinematography by Ted Tetzlaff; screenplay by Michael Farmer, Ernest Pagano, and Delmer Daves; songs by Jerome Kern and Johnny Mercer; dances by Val Raset. Cast: Fred Astaire (Robert Davis), Rita Hayworth (Maria Acuña), Adolphe Menjou (Eduardo Acuña), Barbara Brown (Delfina Acuña), Leslie Brooks (Cecy Acuña), Adele Mara (Lita Acuña), Xavier Cugat (as himself).

Cover Girl: director, Charles Vidor; producer, Arthur Schwartz; cinematography by Rudolph Maté; screenplay by Virginia Van Upp; songs by Jerome Kern and Ira Gershwin; choreography by Val Raset and Seymour Felix. Cast: Rita Hayworth (Rusty Parker/Mirabelle), Gene Kelly (Danny McGuire), Phil Silvers ("Genius"), Otto Kruger (John Coudair), Eve Arden ("Stonewall" Jackson), Lee Bowman (Noel Wheaton), Leslie Brooks (Maureen Martin), Jess Barker (John Coudair as a young man).

Tonight and Every Night: producer and director, Victor Saville; cinematography by Rudolph Maté; screenplay by Lesser Samuels and Abem Finkel; songs by Jule Styne and Sammy Cahn; choreography by Jack Cole and Val Raset. Cast: Rita Hayworth (Rosalind Bruce), Lee Bowman (Paul Lundy), Janet Blair (Judy Kane), Marc Platt (Tommy), Florence Bates (May Tolliver), Leslie Brooks (Angela), Professor Lamberti (The Great Waldo).
12. Bruce Babington and Peter William Evans, *Blue Skies and Silver Linings: Aspects of the Hollywood Musical* (Manchester: Manchester Univ. Press, 1985), 16-17.
13. Ibid., 24, 15.
14. Laura Mulvey, *Visual and Other Pleasures* (Bloomington: Indiana Univ. Press, 1989), 19.
15. Leaming, *If This Was Happiness*, 79.
16. Kobal, *Rita Hayworth*, 181.
17. Mulvey, *Visual and Other Pleasures*, 19.
18. Ibid., 20.
19. How far the war itself is a product and projection of the patriarchy is very much to the point here.
20. E. Ann Kaplan, *Women in Film: Both Sides of the Camera* (New York: Methuen, 1983), 70. One curious aspect of this study is that the author refers throughout to "Hayworth" when describing the character Hayworth is playing. When Kaplan refers to males, she invariably uses the characters' names rather than the names of the actors. This suggests that either consciously or unconsciously Kaplan is acknowledging that it is Hayworth's mystique that gives the role resonance. And it is a new "Hayworth" at that in *The Lady from Shanghai*, with Welles having publicly and willfully altered her image by cutting her hair and dyeing it blonde. If rumors about his intention to use *The Lady from Shanghai* to get even with Hayworth for their marital experiences are true, then

this act can be seen as the reverse of the Samson and Delilah story—in other words, as an attempt to control the dread of woman's destructiveness by the deliberate manipulation of her image.

21. Make-up artist Bob Schiffler, as quoted in Leaming, *If This Was Happiness*, 39.

5

JUDY HOLLIDAY
The Star and the Studio
RUTH PRIGOZY

The brief career of Judy Holliday is one of the anomalies of film history: she played dumb blondes, but her IQ was in the near-genius range; she won an Academy Award, but her subsequent film career never even approached her early success; she played roles that emphasized her sexual appeal, yet she was big-boned, small-bosomed, and tended to be overweight. She was hailed for her brilliant portrayal of a dumb blonde, yet spent the rest of her life alternately rejecting that image and retreating behind the safety a familiar role provides. As early as 1951, shortly after she was nominated for an Oscar, she confessed that her aim was "never to play a dumb blonde again."[1] Her lifelong ambition was to part company from Billie Dawn, the role in *Born Yesterday* that had brought her fame both on Broadway and in Hollywood. "She's a darned good dame, honest and brave and nobody's fool and I'm duly grateful to her, but this thing could go on forever. . . . I started off as a moron in 'Kiss Them for Me,' worked up to an imbecile in 'Adam's Rib,' and have carved my current niche as a noble nitwit. Now I want a part where I can use my own hair, my own voice, and maybe even be literate."[2]

A perfectionist and consummate professional, insecure and filled with self-doubt about her film-acting ability, she flowered briefly under the compassionate tutelage of George Cukor and the uncharacteristic sympathy of Harry Cohn. Indeed, Judy Holliday, a major Columbia star of the 1950s, embodies the conflicts and contradictions of an era that saw the end of the studio system and the introduction of technology that would alter film production and distribution in America and throughout the world. Since Columbia could not compete with studios like Fox and Paramount as they embraced new processes to bring audiences back to the theaters, Cohn had Holliday's films shot in black-and-white and in standard screen ratio; naturally they were not big-budget.

Cohn relied on his actors' star quality, which eventually he saw in Holliday; thus it is to his credit that after his initial refusal to consider her for the movie version of the play in which she had scored such a personal triumph, he tried to select properties suited to her talent, provided legal assistance when she was summoned to appear before the House Committee on Un-American Activities (HUAC),[3] and finally became her friend and confidant. July Holliday's career—brief, brilliant, and tragic (she died in 1965 after making only eight films)— demonstrates the tensions existing within American attitudes toward sex, marriage, success, and democratic ideals. Her career faltered not because she failed to break out of a familiar mold but because 1950s America could not accommodate a woman who fit no previous conception of cinematic womanhood. Between Marilyn Monroe and Kim Novak at one extreme, and Grace Kelly and Audrey Hepburn at the other, Holliday posed a challenge that probably no American studio could meet at the time. It would be more than another decade before actresses like Diane Keaton and Goldie Hawn would achieve success in the new, post-studio Hollywood. Thus Holliday's career—her achievements as well as her failures—is emblematic of the struggles of independent women to transcend narrow cultural definitions.

Although Holliday's film career began at Fox with bits in *Winged Victory* (1944), directed by George Cukor, *Greenwich Village* (1944), and *Something for the Boys* (1944), it was at MGM that she made her first important movie and her very last one: *Adam's Rib* (1949) and *Bells Are Ringing* (1960), respectively. In between, she did six films for Columbia and made several appearances on the stage, notably in *Born Yesterday* and *Bells Are Ringing*. Her stage work was crucial to her development as a screen actress; indeed, were it not for *Born Yesterday*, Garson Kanin's 1946 hit Broadway comedy, her career might have taken a different direction.[4]

Harry Cohn's reluctance to cast Judy Holliday in the film has been well chronicled.[5] He searched for two years for an actress to play Billie Dawn, settling at last on Rita Hayworth, who disappointed him by marrying Ali Khan before filming began. Because of the special efforts of Garson Kanin, Katharine Hepburn, and George Cukor, who provided Holliday with a small but meaty role in *Adam's Rib* (1949), Cohn agreed to cast her in the film, a decision that would affect the mutual destinies of star and studio.

In reassessing her career at Columbia, we find that one of its oddest aspects was her relationship with Harry Cohn, which got off to a decidedly inauspicious start when, at the first meeting, he commented, "Well, I've worked with fat asses before." That she was able, despite her acute sensitivity to her appearance, to return to the studio testifies to her determination to succeed in the role she had made her own. (A recent stage revival with Madeline Kahn seemed an *hommage* to Judy Holliday rather than a fresh interpretation.) Her Columbia contract, for which she bargained astutely, called for one film a year for the standard seven years, but after the completion of each film she would be permitted to work in any other medium of her choice except film. She was also given some power of selection over her assignments, with Cohn retaining veto power. Thus the films she made at Columbia reflect her own perception of her talent, her desire to vary her roles, her acceptance of the limitations that Columbia imposed on her, and, finally, Harry Cohn's awareness of both the problems and the potential she offered the studio.

Two additional factors were significant in her career at Columbia: winning the Academy Award for *Born Yesterday* in 1950 and her appearance before the House Committee on Un-American Activities in 1952. And in addition to Harry Cohn and Garson Kanin, her film career owed its success to her artistic collaboration with George Cukor, who directed five of her films.

Judy Holliday's films at Columbia fall into two distinct groups: those in which she played Billie Dawn and her "dumb blonde" heirs (*Born Yesterday*, *It Should Happen to You* [1954], and *The Solid Gold Cadillac* [1956]); and a group of films one might call "The Marriage Cycle" (*The Marrying Kind* [1952], *Phffft!* [1954], and *Full of Life* [1957]), where she attempted roles that required her to discard mannerisms associated with the comic persona she had perfected and assume a maturity embodying, however obliquely, ideals of domesticity prevalent in the 1950s. Her final film, *Bells Are Ringing*, owes much to the film personas developed in both groups. It is not Vincente Minnelli, the script by Comden and Green, or the Jule Styne score that viewers remember; *Bells Are Ringing* is, simply and elegantly, Judy Holliday carrying the production on her shoulders and creating in Ella Peterson, a character who matches Billie Dawn in intelligence, dynamism, and audacity. Indeed, Billie Dawn and Ella Peterson are Holliday's personal bookends: each role encapsulates her art at a particular moment in a brief career that began, auspiciously, with the small but unforgettable role of Doris Attinger in George Cukor's *Adam's Rib* (1949).

In her first major comedy, she established the outlines of the persona she would develop and refine in later films. Doris Attinger not only offered her the opportunity to display the comic gifts she had mined nightly for three years on the stage in *Born Yesterday*, but also gave her the confidence to explore other, deeper nuances of performance that would become explicit in her domestic comedy-dramas. Cukor worked closely and compassionately with her, assuring her when her confidence seemed to falter, of his unquestioned faith in her talent. Her rapport with the film's stars, Spencer Tracy and Katharine

Hepburn, and her abiding friendship with writer Garson Kanin led to a performance that even today critics recall as having stolen the movie from the principals. (She did not, in fact, steal it. Hepburn generously stepped back to allow Holliday the freedom that her comic genius needed. It was, of course, all part of the plan to convince Harry Cohn that he had to cast her as Billie Dawn.)

As Doris, Holliday first appears at the beginning of *Adam's Rib*, standing amid the rush-hour crowd in a flowered hat, carrying a large floppy pocketbook and eating a hamburger. After following and finding her husband, Doris stops outside the door of his mistress's apartment, holds a gun at arm's length, and reads the instructions before beginning to shoot wildly. Apart from Doris's screams during the shooting, the sequence is played in pantomime; in Holliday's best films, her gift for mime alternates with the verbal delivery for which she is perhaps best known.

Holliday has two big scenes in *Adam's Rib*: the jail interview with Amanda (Katharine Hepburn), which is actually a four-and-a-half-minute take, and the courtroom sequence, where she is questioned first by Amanda and then by Adam (Spencer Tracy). In both, we can identify characteristics associated with the Holliday persona as dumb blonde and average housewife: the display of uncertainty beneath bravura, as the voice rises, turning statements into questions; the casually dropped, irrelevant remarks; and above all, her timing— shifting at precisely the right moment from lower middle-class housewife to hurt, angry, and genuinely pathetic woman whose maternal tenderness, jealousy, and disbelief have driven her to violence. Holliday's ability to convey a depth of feeling lacking in most comedians separates her from every other actress with whom she has been compared.

Although *Born Yesterday*'s Billie Dawn is Holliday's most celebrated role, it also proved a burden, for she was never completely able to escape the stereotype. Yet here the problem is less intrusive than it is in her subsequent films. All of them, however, reveal an unresolved tension between her persona and the overt as well as implicit messages in the films' texts. Her obvious intelligence (usually recognized by the end of each film) and her extraordinary screen presence are in marked contrast to the destinies her scriptwriters envisioned for her. At the end of *Born Yesterday* she becomes a dutiful wife to a bland William Holden (in an impossible role); in *It Should Happen to You* she discards her foolishness and, we suspect, her distinctiveness as well, when she becomes Jack Lemmon's wife. In film after film, she is forced to conform to the image of 1950s woman. Clearly not a sex symbol (even in her black negligee in *Born Yesterday* she exudes a healthy prettiness), she was consistently forced, by the film's end, to discard, disguise, or harness the traits that made her a screen icon.

Born Yesterday is appealing today only for her performance. Produced during the McCarthy era, it tried to reassert the New Deal populism associated with Frank Capra's 1930s films. The warning against American fascism is so encumbered by traditional liberal rhetoric that it seems too innocent for the shrewd Billie Dawn to embrace without some skepticism. Indeed, the real problems of the fifties—racism, the subordination of women, fear of atomic fall-out—are not even hinted at. Broderick Crawford's Harry Brock is without nuance; as Paul, Holden, as he often did in an undemanding role, depended on his looks and charm. Because Holliday's performance is such a revelation, however, viewers can overlook what is awkward and dated in the script and revel in her achievement.

Until her first line, "Whaah?" in a voice that "miraculously fused the innocence of extreme girlishness with the sound of an out-of-tune kazoo,"[6] she creates through the famous hip-swaying walk, with back perfectly straight, head held high, nose in the air, and dark eyes staring blankly, an indelible portrait of an expensive floozy. The fur coats she wordlessly tosses, as well as the cigarette holder she ostentatiously fingers, illustrate how astutely she knew how to use props. Despite her battles with weight, she was remarkably light-footed. In the little dance during the visit of the senator and his wife, and with variations in virtually all of her films, she made an art of body movement. In *Born Yesterday*, and later in *It Should Happen to You* and *Bells Are Ringing*, her walk frequently changes; with her head down and slightly forward, frowning, she shows her determination by charging ahead like a machine with a newly fired engine.

The gin game, which broke up the house on Broadway, loses none of its brilliance on the screen. Billie's single-minded concentration, her mockery of Harry's rage, her humming and singing, which infuriate and distract him, and her determination to collect her winnings convey at once her character, the nature of their relationship, and the ultimate outcome of the plot.

Perhaps the most important aspect of the Judy Holliday persona, both in variations of Billie Dawn and in her roles as housewife, is her vulnerability. That quality was apparent in *Adam's Rib*, but in *Born Yesterday* it adds a dimension to the film that the script does not suggest. We first notice her pain when Harry reviles her in front of Paul in the first sequence. She is wounded but conceals it with bravado: the slow, hip-swaying walk now suggests her courage, her refusal to sink to his level. Later, after Harry hits her, her eyes express how deeply she has been hurt. Her ability to shift her mood quickly from comic to serious is one of her greatest technical gifts. Here, her pain and disgust are apparent as she runs out of the room, but she has the last word, and it is a famous rejoinder—"Would you do me a favor, Harry? Drop dead"—that again shifts the mood, now tenuously melodramatic, back to comedy.

Although Judy Holliday did not play ethnic parts (and in the 1950s ethnic diversity found expression primarily in stereotypes), her own Jewish background enhanced her comic roles. When she raises her voice questioningly at the end of declarative sentences, she is echoing Yiddish cadences. In *Born Yesterday* the pattern was established, but in other films, it detracted from her efforts to create new characters. Audiences waited for the familiar speech patterns, and scriptwriters and directors tended to rely on a comic delivery that had already been tested. Harry Cohn's plans for Judy Holliday did not include ethnic roles. When she failed to conform to his idea of glamour, he made her into the average American girl, an image that was only partially successful. Judy Holliday had an appealing directness and honesty that made audiences love her—she was the idealization of the ordinary—but she could never contain her energy and intelligence in roles that demanded she be "average." Nevertheless, Billie Dawn's revelations to Paul about her father's simple life and moral standards, as well as her admonition to Paul to discard inflated language and say what he means, are a vindication of American values.

Another version of Billie Dawn, this time in the guise of a small-town girl who wants to achieve fame in the big city, is the role of Gladys Glover in *It Should Happen to You* (1954), again written by Garson Kanin and Ruth Gordon and directed by George Cukor. Judy Holliday needed a hit, for her career had been badly damaged by the HUAC inquiry in 1952 and by the commercial failure of her previous film, *The Marrying Kind* (1952). Like Billie Dawn, Gladys is lovable, shrewd, pragmatic, and short-sighted until a young man educates her in the appropriate human values. Unlike Billie, she does not have a coarse veneer, and neither the writers nor the director suggest that her sexual experience has been anything but innocuous, as befits a 1950s heroine. However, the repetition of her Billie Dawn mannerisms led some reviewers (who liked the film) to comment on her reliance on them.[7]

It Should Happen to You capitalizes on the viewer's familiarity with Billie Dawn and subtly redefines her persona. Gladys Glover is the classic naif, adrift in the big city, victimized by mercenary forces she doesn't understand. Ultimately, however, through her essential decency, she triumphs over the sophisticates who exploit her understandable if foolish desire to achieve worldly recognition and thereby acquire an identity.

The film is notable on several counts: George Cukor's direction, which, from the first sequence when both the camera and Jack Lemmon observe Judy Holliday, captures her visual appeal; Lemmon's performance, a rare instance of a leading man playing perfectly to her strengths yet retaining his own distinctive charm; Holliday's effectiveness as a romantic heroine, despite the daffiness of the character's self-promoting schemes; and the revelation that her underlying vulnerability marks her as totally unlike the Lucille Ball/Lucy Ricardo persona with which hers has been compared. In the one sequence involving physical comedy (where she is made up to be the "before" in a "before/after" weight-loss advertisement), she is not funny. Indeed, her vulnerability makes the viewer cringe at the cruelty inherent in the kind of masquerade that was pivotal in Lucille Ball's depiction of a lovable clown. Harry Cohn's vision of his star as the average American girl found its best expression in this film, but Judy Holliday's slavic cheekbones, her distinctive walk, her brief but pithy remarks, which always deflate the rhetoric of sophisticates, mark her as anything but average.

It Should Happen to You is successful on two levels: romantic and comic. The rapport between Judy Holliday and Jack Lemmon is captured indelibly in a sequence that seems to be unrehearsed in its spontaneity. (Cukor actually shot several takes.) Pete (Lemmon) is improvising on a piano at a bar as Gladys hums along with him, leaning her head on his shoulder. They join in a duet, "Let's Fall in Love," reprised at the end of the film, which their effortless grace transfigures into a moving love scene. Ironically, her romantic encounters with Peter Lawford (with whom she was involved off-screen) are tepid and unconvincing, not only because of his stuffy role but also because of Lawford's inability to compete with her vital screen presence.

The television scenes are witty parodies of 1950s staples: the Walter Winchell–type gossip show, *This Is Your Life*, and the celebrity panel discussion. Judy Holliday's literal teleprompter reading is a hilarious take-off of television's attempts to sensationalize an average American's overnight fame. And her no-nonsense answers to questions about love and marriage on a panel show featuring Ilka Chase and Constance Bennett is a delightful satire of television wisdom. Yet for all of its sly ridicule of celebrity worship and show-business commercialism, *It Should Happen to You* plays it safe. Questions involving sexuality, identity, success, and family are all resolved within the strictures of 1950s morality. Again, for the actress, the message conflicted with the persona: there was a revolutionary spark in Judy Holliday that few of her scripts permitted to flourish. Although the film was successful as a comeback vehicle, neither Judy Holliday nor Columbia was willing to depart measurably from a proven formula for success. Despite her public statements to the contrary, she was reluctant to risk abandoning completely the comic image associated with her in films, as she later did, disastrously, on stage in *Laurette*.[8] And despite Harry Cohn's sincere efforts to find new scripts that might suit her talents, Columbia's quest for roles worthy of her ultimately proved fruitless.

The Solid Gold Cadillac (1956) was her last attempt to resurrect a version of Billie Dawn. Adapted from the play by George S. Kaufman and Howard Teichmann, the film featured Judy Holliday as Laura Partridge, the role created on Broadway by the sixty-nine-year-old Josephine Hull. Several studios bid for the rights, envisioning the property as a starring vehicle for Shirley Booth at Paramount, Marilyn Monroe at Fox, or Judy Holliday at Columbia. Harry Cohn won, and his star greeted the acquisition of the property with enthusiasm. The film was reviewed favorably by most critics, but it is Holliday's least effective performance in the Billie Dawn style. She is less physically attractive than in any other film and relies on old mannerisms to such a degree that Pauline Kael's remarks seem accurate even to Holliday's most loyal admirers: "Judy Holliday brings the role her familiar cartoon mixture of wide-eyed primordial simplicity and complacent urban abrasiveness. She's a funny woman, yet lacking in variety; her truculent voice and glassy eyes and shrewd innocence are wonderful in a sketch but a little monotonous in a starring role like this one. However, the fault here isn't primarily hers: it's in the formula Broadway comedy, with its predictable situations and sledgehammer laugh lines."[9] Richard Quine's direction is uninspired, and Holliday's distaste for Paul Douglas, which dated back to their Broadway appearance in *Born Yesterday*, created additional tension on the set. Despite its popularity in England, box-office success in the United States, and generally good reviews, *The Solid Gold Cadillac* makes it evident that Holliday's identification with Billie Dawn had trapped her, and the vehicles which she, Kanin, and Cukor selected, as well as those sought by Columbia, could not provide the breakthrough she needed.

The fault lay not merely in her reluctance to give up Billie Dawn but also in the paucity of scripts for independent or even slightly off-beat actresses. Judy Holliday neither looked nor acted like 1950s women; she was hindered by the conformity of a decade whose most interesting films were late *film noir* explorations of a society whose conventionality and faith in technocracy were thin veneers covering social dissolution: Robert Aldrich's *Kiss Me Deadly* (1955), Orson Welles's *Touch of Evil* (1958), Joseph H. Lewis's *The Big Combo* (1955), or a fearless farce like Billy Wilder's *Some Like It Hot* (1959), which dared to examine sexual roles and morality from a comic perspective atypical of the era. The few films in which she relinquished the Billie Dawn pose offer evidence that she was a versatile actress who, had she lived, might have developed her comic genius and dramatic skills along the lines of her idol, Laurette Taylor.

The Marrying Kind (1952) was a departure for Holliday; the role of Florence Keefer allowed her to create a character who bore no relation to Billie Dawn. With director George Cukor constantly bolstering her confidence, she began to think of herself as an actress, not simply a comedienne. Garson Kanin and Ruth Gordon created the role for her, and it demanded that she show Florence's development from a young, happily married working-class girl to a despairing wife and mother, whose early dreams were dashed by the tragedy of her son's drowning and the inability of her marriage to absorb the loss. The Kanins' script and Cukor's direction are imaginative, blending comedy, pathos, and fantasy in an unusual narrative structure. As Florence and Chet Keefer (Aldo Ray) tell the divorce-court judge the story of their marriage in flashback, their voice-over narration is often in contrast to the visualization.

Surprisingly, the comic moments are the weakest: the "meet-cute," Florence's luncheon for her sister and sister-in-law, and the call from the quiz show host when Florence struggles to find the right answer. Here Holliday drew on her Billie Dawn mannerisms. The plot, however, required her to play a lower- to middle-class (at least in aspirations) wife who was warm, intelligent, courageous, and independent—which she did by relegating Billie to the background and becoming Florence. She was so convincing, in fact, that the *Village Voice* (26 October 1982) singled out her performance as a model for feminists in an unlikely era.

The Marrying Kind deals tentatively with the mechanization of contemporary life. Machinery—symbolized by the conveyor belt Chet rides in the post office and the ball bearings that represent success (Chet's idea is to make roller skates using ball bearings) and failure (someone else develops the idea)—is in conflict with human needs and values. Although Chet's brother-in-law lectures Chet about the importance of home and marriage as opposed to making money, the advice comes from a man who is ungainly, crude, and unappealing. Florence's sister and brother-in-law are equally unattractive, but they can afford a home that is spacious and elegant—quite the opposite of the Keefers' cramped flat. Florence blames Chet's ambition and neglect of her for the failure of their marriage, yet she is a willing partner to his ball bearings scheme, never questioning the success myth behind the dream of the good life.

The proper role of women, particularly wives and mothers, comes under similar scrutiny but with an inconclusive resolution; in fact, the film's message is confusing, not only about the meaning of success but also in its view of marriage, class attitudes, and values. Chet is adamant that his wife not work lest his manhood be threatened by her employment. Later, when he is ill and she is forced to work, she says, sincerely, that if she should be forced to choose between home and job, home is where she belongs. *The Marrying Kind* seems to be preaching a 1950s sitcom philosophy: Be happy with your lot even if you are poor; value your mate; regard marriage as a stable and life-affirming institution; remember that women belong at home and that men must respect and nurture women's maternal and wifely virtues. This philosophy, however, is completely at odds with Holliday's characterization. When Florence slams the door after a fight with Chet, leaving him with their child, she behaves like a modern Nora. It is difficult to imagine her returning to the life we have witnessed. But the ending shows the couple, now reunited, leaving the judge's chambers together. Despite Aldo Ray's immensely likable performance, Chet is clearly not the type to make Florence happy. The complexity of Holliday's performance works against the film's resolution, which is strangely unsatisfying.

Nevertheless, there is a sequence in *The Marrying Kind* that is among the best in any of her films. Florence, at peace with herself, strums a ukelele and sings "Dolores" at the family picnic, minutes before learning that her son has drowned. The scene then dissolves to the judge's chamber, where Florence lays her head down on the table and sobs uncontrollably. It is a moment of genuine pathos, played with restraint by both actors, and sensitively directed by Cukor. The sequence suggests that with the right script and director, the vulnerability beneath Holliday's comic facade might have led her to serious drama.

We will probably never know the thinking behind Columbia's naming a film *Phffft!* (1954), but the title was only one of its problems. The studio tried to rekindle the successful teaming of Judy Holliday and Jack Lemmon, but when the producers added to the cast their new sex symbol, Kim Novak, they lost the gentle chemistry that Holliday and Lemmon might have brought to the screen once again. Neither of them found much room to develop beyond the constricted roles in George Axelrod's screenplay.

Phffft! is a comedy of remarriage, but it bears no resemblance to such sparkling examples of the genre as *The Awful Truth* (1937) or *The Lady Eve* (1941). The divorce of Nina and Robert Tracy is merely the catalyst for the principals' sex romps, as approved by the smarmy virtue of 1950s censors. Jack Carson, repeating the role of the leering "friend" of the family he played so well in *Mildred Pierce* (1945), is merely vulgar as sexual advisor to newly divorced Robert Tracy. Kim Novak, pretty and sexy, reveals how much she needed a good director to elicit a creditable performance (like Hitchcock in *Vertigo* [1958] or

Wilder in *Kiss Me, Stupid* [1964]). Yet she is undeniably the center of the film, and Holliday has little opportunity to develop her role beyond its narrow limits. Lemmon has the thankless role of a would-be playboy (modeled after the "swingers" celebrated in Hugh Hefner's *Playboy*), clumsily and reluctantly attempting the seductions that Frank Sinatra accomplished so smoothly in *The Tender Trap* (1955).

Nevertheless, Holliday has moments in the film that are suggestive of new directions she might have taken had the studio been able to find appropriate vehicles for her. In *Phffft!* she plays a successful TV soaps writer who marries a rising young lawyer. The couple is upper class, with a chic apartment and obligatory summer home in Connecticut (where the closing scenes take place), and for the first time Holliday plays an educated woman. But the script offers her few opportunities to do more than posture and repeat old routines. She still drops her punchlines with impeccable timing ("I'm gonna be passion's play-thing"), but she is not required to do anything more than look attractive which she does, without the familiar bouffant dresses and slightly frowsy hairdo) and extract whatever sympathy Mark Robson's direc-tion and George Axelrod's hackneyed script permit. She does have one memorable comic moment, however, at the TV studio, when she lip-synchs the words of her script. It is a fine example of her gift for pantomime, wasted in this strained effort.

The failure of *Phffft!* is traceable not only to lackluster direction, a dull script, and one-dimensional characters but also to the values of the 1950s, particularly as they relate to sex and marriage. The message here is clear: no extramarital sex (although the film is loaded with verbal and visual innuendo—the major prop is a murphy bed); marriage is a valuable institution; a woman may have a successful career, but she is unfulfilled unless she marries. All of these ideas are familiar legacies of countless Rosalind Russell and Irene Dunne movies of the 1930s and 1940s, but in postwar America the issues are too close to the surface to be brushed off with antique farce.

Full of Life (1957) was Holliday's least successful film and the one she personally found the most objectionable. Although she altered the role of Emily from the original screenplay, her alterations were, as one biographer notes, "essentially cosmetic additions to a plot run through with cheap sentimentality and a frightening helping of ethnic schmaltz." [10] Ideologically the film is ultraconservative even for the conformist 1950s. It is anti-intellectual, patriarchal, antifeminist, and, most difficult for the actress to accept, a glorification of conventional religion—in this case Catholicism. Images of growth, fecundity, and solidity (orchards, hearths) are associated with Emily and her Italian father-in-law, played by basso Salvatore Baccaloni as if he were on stage at the Metropolitan Opera. The son, Emily's husband (Richard Conte), a writer who has lost touch with his ethnic and religious roots, is associated with the sterility and mechanization of suburban life. Emily is pregnant, and her anxieties are resolved when she accepts the values of her Italian father-in-law, even the childbirth superstitions imported from the old country. Despite the sentimentality, the bland direction by Richard Quine, and the irritating mugging by Baccaloni, Holliday nevertheless succeeds in adding to her developing mature persona. She is so thoroughly likable, unpretentious, and intelligent, that without resorting to any of her comic mannerisms, she quietly dominates the film. In *Full of Life*, we get a glimpse of the actress as an articulate, sensitive woman in control of herself and her relationships with others. Unfortunately, as in the other films in which she plays domestic roles, the script does not provide her with the opportunity her new persona requires. The limitations are not only in the script, which relegates her to domesticity, but also in the cinematography and direction. Quine rarely shoots a close-up of his star but rather limits her screen presence to medium and long shots that mute her distinctiveness.

Full of Life was the last film for Columbia, which realized, as did she, that they had come to the parting of the ways. Although Holliday owed Columbia another movie, the studio did not prevent her from making *Bells Are Ringing* at MGM three years later. After the failure of *Full of Life*, she was eager to return to New York; she felt uncertain about her future in the new Hollywood, where even her own studio had entered the wide-screen competition with *Picnic* (1955). Her relationship with Harry Cohn did not end, however; he visited her often in New York, and their friendship continued until his death.

After a 924-performance run on Broadway, *Bells Are Ringing*, which opened in New York in November 1956, was acquired by MGM, to be produced and directed by the familiar team of Arthur Freed and Vincente Minnelli. The weakness in the script was apparent to all the principals; just as she had done on the stage, Holliday made up for its deficiencies by sheer force of personality and comic genius. *Bells Are Ringing*, not a great musical by any standard, is nevertheless a triumph for Holliday, who displays the versatility that won her accolades a decade earlier as Billie Dawn, deepened by the emotional maturity she acquired from her marriage-cycle roles at Columbia. As Ella Peterson, she is again the naif, but the character's insecurity about her own identity, which prompts her to play a variety of roles as a telephone operator for an answering service, meshes perfectly with the actress's own self-doubts. Ella Peterson is a version of Judy Holliday as she experiments with multiple personalities that connect her to the world outside the Manhattan basement apartment where she works. Despite the wide-screen, full-color treatment, the film, as Stephen Harvey notes, is "the least pompous of movie musicals in that age of 'Glorious

Technicolor, Breathtaking CinemaScope and Stereophonic Sound' tweaked by Cole Porter's lyric." [11]

Minnelli's direction allowed Holliday to display the physical grace that appeared only intermittently in her other films. In the "Just in Time" duet with Dean Martin, she shifts from comedy to pathos imperceptibly, her face registering the wide-eyed expression of Billie Dawn in one moment and the romanticism of Florence Keefer in the next. In her rendition of the climactic "I'm Goin' Back," she does a true vaudeville turn complete with imitations of Jimmy Durante and Al Jolson. Although *Bells Are Ringing* was well received when it opened at the Music Hall, it did poorly abroad and became Minnelli's least profitable picture since *The Pirate* (1948).[12] But for Holliday it was significant as a showcase for her multiple talents, celebrating her skill as a musical comedy performer and actress and revealing her vulnerability and intelligence. The two Judy Hollidays were now one, and she was ready for the more challenging roles she had earned. The years at Columbia had not been wasted, for in her last film she recreated herself once again out of the triumphs and disappointments of her six movies as a contract player.

A year later she was diagnosed as having cancer, which she battled until her death in 1965 at forty-two. Her last performances were abortive stage ventures, although she never stopped looking for suitable screen properties.

The Judy Holliday years at Columbia provide a fascinating insight into the effects of economics and ideology on a star and her studio. Both were locked into patterns neither had envisioned, and their fates were ultimately interconnected. Columbia has continued, if in name only; Judy Holliday's film career was tragically brief.

NOTES

1. Helen Markel Herrmann, "Hey-Hey-Day of a 'Dumb' Blonde," *New York Times Magazine*, 4 March 1951, 16.

2. Ibid.

3. Larry Ceplair and Steven Englund, *The Inquisition in Hollywood: Politics in the Film Community, 1930-1960* (Garden City: Anchor Press/Doubleday, 1980), 396.

4. Her theatrical career began auspiciously in 1945 when she won the Clarence Derwent Award for her comic role in *Kiss Them for Me*.

5. See Gene D. Phillips, *George Cukor* (Boston: Twayne, 1982), 108-9, and Gary Carey, *Judy Holliday: An Intimate Life Story* (New York: Seaview Books, 1982), 94-101.

6. *Newsweek*, 16 June 1965, 87.

7. *Films in Review*, 5 (March 1954): 144: "George Cukor well directs the one talent of Judy Holliday in this kidding by Garson Kanin about an ingenious

blonde from Binghamton who has been led to believe that having her name on every tongue is an end in itself."

8. *Laurette*, based on the life of Laurette Taylor (whose ability to blend bravado and pathos made her an inspiration to Holliday, who could do the same), never reached New York, although it was written by Stanley Young and directed by José Quintero. It opened in New Haven on 26 September 1960 and closed 1 October.

9. *New Yorker*, 29 Jan. 1990, 23.

10. Will Holtzman, *Judy Holliday* (New York: Putnam's, 1982), 179.

11. Stephen Harvey, *Vincente Minnelli* (New York: Museum of Modern Art and Harper & Row, 1989), 152.

12. Ibid., 151.

6

AN INTERVIEW WITH DANIEL TARADASH

From Harvard to Hollywood

BERNARD F. DICK

Today, law degrees are common in Hollywood, but not so in the 1930s. In 1938 it was unusual for someone with a Harvard law degree to show up at Columbia, of all studios, to work on the screen version of Clifford Odets's *Golden Boy*. But Daniel Taradash was neither a typical lawyer nor a typical screenwriter.[1] Despite his prestigious degree, he never practiced law; and while other East Coast writers went west for the money, Taradash went because he had won a playwriting contest. The theatre was his first love, and when he had finished *Golden Boy*, he planned to return to New York and write plays. Eventually one of his plays reached Broadway, but that was not until 1960, after he had become an Oscar-winning screenwriter. The play, *There Was a Little Girl*, a shocker about a rape and its aftermath, was a failure, although it won some good notices for the star, Jane Fonda.

Not surprisingly, Taradash's scripts have been mainly adaptations of novels (among them *From Here to Eternity* [1953], *Desirée* [1954], *Hawaii* [1966]) and plays (*Golden Boy* [1939], *Picnic* [1955], *Bell, Book and Candle* [1958]). *Storm Center*, one of his rare ventures into the original screenplay, was the most outspoken attack on McCarthyism to appear on the screen in the 1950s; written in 1951, filmed in 1955, and released the following year, *Storm Center* would have been truly incendiary if it had come out at the beginning of the decade instead of two years after McCarthy's censure; on the other hand, no studio would have made *Storm Center* in 1951. Still, the burning of the library sequence, in which the world's great books go up in flames because a boy believes his favorite librarian is a Communist sympathizer, remains a horrifying example of retaliation based on ignorance, anger, and a false sense of betrayal.

Taradash's finest script won him an Oscar: *From Here to Eternity*, a touchstone among adaptations. By eliminating some characters from James Jones's novel, conflating others, and limiting the narrative focus to five (Warden, Karen, Alma, Prewitt, and Maggio), Taradash retained the novel's essence while exercising an adaptor's rights with the accidents. For example, despite Fatso's brutal treatment of Maggio in the stockade, Maggio does not die in the novel, as he does in the film; in the novel, it is Blues Berry who dies at Fatso's hands. To build Maggio into a tragic as well as an empathetic figure, Taradash has Maggio die Berry's death in a scene that Frank Sinatra played so movingly that he won an Oscar for best supporting actor.

In the novel, Karen is not childless, as she is in the film. To make Karen's life even emptier than it was in the novel, Taradash makes her unable to have any children. Jones's Karen could not have any *more* children because of a hysterectomy necessitated by venereal disease transmitted by her philandering husband.

Of the many stories intertwined in the novel, Taradash concentrated on two: the ill-starred romances of Karen, the commanding officer's wife, and Sergeant Warden; and Prewitt and the prostitute Lorene, whose real name is Alma. By alternating between the two love stories, Taradash established the film's rhythm, which director Fred Zinnemann preserved. Taradash did not so much write as compose the script, so that one story balances the other; thus a scene with Karen and Warden will often be followed by one with Alma and Prewitt, as if their affairs were occurring simultaneously and each couple knew the other. Only the former is true. While Warden obviously knew Prewitt, Karen knows him only by name and has never met Alma.

At the end of the film, after the climactic attack on Pearl Harbor, Karen and Alma find themselves on the promenade deck of a ship heading for the United States. Prewitt has been killed, and Warden has returned to his true love, the U.S. Army. The irony does not end here. Not knowing to whom she is speaking, Alma describes Prewitt's "heroic" death, although he was shot while trying to return to his outfit. When Karen and Alma cast their leis into the water and watch them drift away, it is evident they will never return to Hawaii. But the receding leis suggest something more: they represent all that remains of relationships in which two couples were reduced to two singles, never knowing their lives were interconnected.

The following interview took place in Daniel Taradash's Beverly Hills home on 7 June 1989.

DICK: I gather it was Rouben Mamoulian who was responsible for your coming to Columbia in 1938.[2]

TARADASH: Yes. Others have claimed credit, but without Mamoulian I doubt I would have—or at least not so early.

DICK: Was it because Columbia was wooing promising writers? I ask because I know you had won a playwriting contest.

TARADASH: The contest was sponsored by an organization called the Bureau of New Plays, which was financed by a number of studios. The Bureau also sponsored a playwriting contest in which the finalists were invited to participate in a playwriting course. The course itself was rather informal, but a number of important people, including Theresa Helburn of the Theatre Guild, Lee Strasberg, John Gassner, John Mason Brown, and Robert E. Sherwood, would come in and lecture. While it may have seemed altruistic of the studios to put up the money for such a program, the aim was really to get young writers to Hollywood. Lewis Meltzer and I came out of that course. Meltzer had a play open and close in Boston with Ina Claire, so he was invited to be in the course without participating in the contest. Mamoulian, who, as you know, was both a stage and film director, heard about the contest, in which I was one of the winners. He was about to direct *Golden Boy* at Columbia and came to New York to get Clifford Odets to do the script, but Odets was madly in love with Luise Rainer at the time, and doing the script of his own play held no interest for him. Eve Ettinger, Columbia's New York story editor, told Mamoulian about the course and suggested he look at some of the students' work. Mamoulian liked what Lew Meltzer and I had written and told us he wanted to hire us for about a week. Each of us had to write a few scenes for a *Golden Boy* screenplay. When Mamoulian read our efforts, he said he could not choose between us, so he hired us both. And that's how Lew Meltzer and I got on the Columbia payroll at $200 a week—an excellent salary for beginners; it's also how we both got screen credits for *Golden Boy*.

DICK: The play ends tragically, yet you and Meltzer gave the film a happy ending. Whose idea was this?

TARADASH: Mamoulian had a definite idea as to how he wanted the picture done. For example, he wanted the scene at the end with the family of the black fighter who died in the ring. Mamoulian was really in charge; Harry Cohn had some involvement, but not much. It was really Mamoulian's picture. He obviously knew movie audiences did not want Lorna and Joe to die at the end, as they did in the play.

DICK: You've been quoted as saying that, contrary to popular opinion, Harry Cohn liked writers.

TARADASH: I'm sure of it. Remember, he's famous for saying, "I kiss the feet of talent." I can tell you from experience that at a story conference with a producer, a director, and a writer, he would almost always talk to the writer—rarely to the producer. He also chose writers as executive producers—Sidney Buchman, Virginia Van Upp.

DICK: Was there a writers' building at Columbia as there was at Paramount?

TARADASH: Not a writers' building as such, just a building where the writers were. It was a frame building with a little patio.

DICK: After *Golden Boy* you don't have another Columbia credit until *Knock on Any Door* (1949).

TARADASH: After *Golden Boy* I wanted to go back to New York and complete a play I had started in the course. Columbia wanted Meltzer and me to stay; he did, but I was allowed to return to New York before finishing out the last three months of my contract. When I came back, I was punished by being put into Sam Katzman's unit to work on a film called "The Sing Sing Story," which was never made. Columbia didn't pick up my option, so I did not return until 1949. Again, it was Eve Ettinger. I was in New York, and Eve called me and said she had a script called *Knock on Any Door* that Bob Lord was producing for Santana Productions for a Columbia release.[3] No one was happy with the original script, so she asked if I would come out and work on it. Since it was a Santana production, Cohn had nothing to do with it, and I rarely saw him.

DICK: It's not commonly known that you wrote *Storm Center* before *From Here to Eternity*.

TARADASH: I even wrote it before *Picnic*, even though it came out after *Picnic*. To be brief, I met a writer by the name of Elick Moll when I was at Fox writing the Marilyn Monroe movie *Don't Bother to Knock* in 1951. Elick and I were interested in doing an original script. He had written a story called "Two Dozen Roses," which we thought would make a good movie; it was about a man who mistakenly sent two dozen roses to his mistress instead of his wife. I showed it to my wife, who thought it was garbage. Well, so much for "Two Dozen Roses." Then I happened to be reading *Saturday Review* and came upon a letter about an Oklahoma librarian who had been fired for refusing to remove a controversial book from her library. I told Elick the story would make a great movie. Certainly no one in Hollywood would be writing that kind of script; this was 1951. Elick wondered if we could sell it. I thought of Stanley Kramer, who was a known liberal and was about to strike an independent production deal with Columbia. And if not Kramer, then Julian Blaustein, whom I knew from Harvard. Eventually it was Blaustein who produced the film—in 1956. Then, as often happens, another project intervened, *Rancho Notorious*. When I received the offer to work for Fritz Lang, I was making $1,000 a week. I decided that if I liked the story and could get $1,500, I'd do it, but then I would come back and finish "The Library," as *Storm Center* was then called. As soon as I finished *Rancho Notorious* for Lang, I went back to "The Library." By that time Kramer was at Columbia, and the film was slated for his company. Irving Reis was scheduled to direct, but he died in 1952. I thought it would be a brilliant public relations coup if Mary Pickford, "America's Sweetheart," played the liberal librarian. I went to Pickfair and read the entire script to her. She was transfixed and immediately agreed to do it. The wardrobe had been ordered and construction had started on the sets. Pickford came to one rehearsal and never returned. In the meantime, Hedda Hopper, who may have been just a gossip columnist to some but nonetheless had enormous power, persuaded her to disassociate herself from a movie made by Stanley Kramer, "The Red." Unfortunately, Kramer's company only gave Columbia one hit, *The Caine Mutiny,* so he left with a settlement but with "The Library" as one of his unfilmed projects. That was about 1955. In the meantime I had won an Oscar for *From Here to Eternity* and had finished *Picnic,* so I was certainly *persona grata* at Columbia. I was supposed to direct *Picnic,* but I told Blaustein that I'd give up *Picnic* if I could do *Storm Center* first. As you know, Joshua Logan directed *Picnic.* Still, there was Harry Cohn. If Kramer had still been at Columbia, there would not have been a problem since he could have done what he wanted as long as he came in on budget. But Cohn neither liked the script nor the subject matter. Finally, Julian and I were in Cohn's office, along with Ben Kahane, the vice president. We told Cohn we had Bette Davis for the lead and for less than her usual salary. We also told him the movie would be controversial. Finally Cohn said, "Take $900,000 and go make your goddamn picture." Kahane was furious. "Harry, you can't do this," he said. "You have an obligation to Columbia; this picture is a certain flop." Cohn replied, "Columbia has had flops before, but never one with such enthusiasm." *Storm Center* may have been a flop, but [cinematographer] Nestor Almendros told me he went into the business because of it.

DICK: *Eternity* was controversial also. How did you solve the problems the novel presented?

TARADASH: It was controversial in a different way. Apart from a few plot details and the language, the problems were not insurmountable. Eve Ettinger was still story editor, and I told her I could do it; I also talked with producer Buddy Adler. Finally, we all met in Cohn's bedroom, which was not unusual since Cohn often held meetings there. I told him I would change some of the incidents in the novel to make a more dramatic movie. I told him I would have Maggio die and Prewitt play taps as a kind of requiem. That really excited Adler and Cohn because they could see that my changes had great dramatic potential.

I had actually solved most of the problems before the script reached the Hays—or then I guess it would have been called the Johnston—office. You must remember this was a novel that ran 859 pages, 150 of which took place in a stockade where American soldiers exemplified man's inhumanity with brutal sadism rarely, if ever, described with such rage. Then there was the job of combining and eliminating characters, of selecting the high points and spotting them where they would be most effective in the screen story, and at the same time trying to be true to the author's vision. I knew that no matter what changes I made, I had to remain true to Jones's philosophy, as expressed by Prewitt, that "if a man don't go his own way, he's nothin'." It's the old idea that character is destiny.

As we say in Hollywood, I "licked" the book, which means I somehow found a way to defy gravity. Censorship was skirted because the Production Code officials liked the screenplay immensely and, out of character, tried to help rather than hinder us. The army, also impressed by the script and mollified by a change I had made in advance in a one-page scene, loaned us soldiers and equipment and the use of Schofield Barracks in Hawaii. Interestingly, the army showed *Eternity* everywhere, but the navy banned it as "derogatory to a sister service."

One reason we had so few censorship problems with the script was that Geoffrey Shurlock, who used to be Joe Breen's assistant, respected good scripts and loved *Eternity*. Still, I thought there might be a problem with some of the dialogue. For example, I had a scene when Prewitt comes to Alma's house and says, "This is just like bein' married"; and she says, "It's better." The next time you see the movie, watch for it; it's there.

DICK: Did Cohn read the script?

TARADASH: *Read* it? We had so many story conferences with Cohn that I nearly lost my mind. He would go over and over the dialogue. Often he would come up with a helluva idea, or something that would at least make you think. Sometimes his ideas were bad. For example, I had a scene in which Alma tells Prewitt she has to marry a proper man and live in a proper house because if you're proper, you're safe. "Proper" was in the novel. Cohn objected to "proper." "Use 'respectable,'" he insisted. We argued about it. I gave in even though I thought "respectable" was a meaningless word as well as a cliché.

Yet Cohn could come up with a good idea. I decided that Prewitt should play taps, but Cohn felt he had to play it before Maggio's death so that the audience would know he could play the trumpet. Of course, Prewitt couldn't play Taps twice, so I worked out a scene in which he plays some riffs during the "Re-enlistment Blues" number in the barracks.

DICK: Did the film's length bother Cohn?

TARADASH: As I recall, the final screenplay timed out at two hours and four minutes. And Harry Cohn's edict was that we must cut four or five pages. To our screams of resistance, Cohn shouted, "No Columbia picture ever ran over two hours." This, of course, was not entirely true, since *Lost Horizon* in its original version and *Mr. Smith Goes to Washington* did. Still, Cohn was adamant: "I don't give a goddamn how good this one is! I don't care if it makes a fortune! It's not going to run more than two hours!" *From Here to Eternity* runs exactly one hour and 58 minutes.

NOTES

1. On Taradash's career, see Jay Boyer, "Daniel Taradash," *DLB*, 1986, 44:370-77.
2. For Mamoulian as stage and screen director, see Tom Milne, *Mamoulian* (Bloomington: Indiana Univ. Press, 1969).
3. Santana was Humphrey Bogart's production company, later bought by Columbia.

7

ON THE WATERFRONT
"Like It Ain't Part of America"
ADAM J. SORKIN

It is no longer a question as to whether *On the Waterfront* is about informing. The film presents as its central character a man who becomes an informer, depicts him in such a way as to win the audience's sympathy, and imagines his difficult decision to testify in open hearings as growth toward self-knowledge and maturity. Terry Malloy (Marlon Brando) begins as a loner, a chip-on-the-shoulder tough, uneducated as well as unreflecting. He is first shown as a loyal and unambitious stooge for waterfront union boss Johnny Friendly (Lee J. Cobb). Soon, however, influenced by the local parish priest and the sister of the longshoreman whose murder he had unknowingly set up, Terry finds himself unable to resist becoming engaged in a painful inward struggle. His innate sense of fairness combined with a rebellious honesty impels him not only to acknowledge to himself his complicity in the murder but also to confess it to the priest, Father Barry (Karl Malden), and the victim's sister, Edie Doyle (Eva Marie Saint), whom he comes to love. Finally, after the killing of his older brother, Charley (Rod Steiger), Terry decides to testify before the Crime Commission by which he has been subpoenaed, despite the waterfront's moral absolute, "D 'n D . . . Deaf 'n dumb." [1] Terry's informing is the crucial step in his own, and the story's, development.

There is no doubt that the film's historical context lends a special gravity to the act of giving information and naming names. In *On the Waterfront*, informing is repeatedly scorned as being a pigeon or a stoolpigeon, as stooling, squealing, spilling one's guts, singing like a canary, ratting, cheese-eating (extended visually to birdseed-eating, with birdseed a euphemism for the then unrepeatable "shit-eating"). On the positive side, it is termed "testifyin' for what you know is right," "fight[ing] . . . with the truth," "gettin' the facts to the public," "tell[ing] . . . the . . . story the way the people have a right to hear it." Early 1950s America had an obsession with exposing what many during this age of Cold War paranoia saw as the imminent threat of domestic Communist subversion, and the period was beset by a corresponding media-inflamed addiction to identifying purported Un-Americans. This inquisition was exposed to many Americans in its unsavoriness during the Army-McCarthy hearings, which took place in the months just before the movie premiered (22 April-17 June 1954); coincidentally, a Senate motion to censure Senator Joe McCarthy was introduced two days after *On the Waterfront* opened in New York.[2] But national anti-Communism remained at a high pitch. The comparison made by a dock worker to Father Barry—"The waterfront's tougher, Father. Like it ain't part of America"—is the movie's most explicit reminder of its immediate political connection. That the waterfront is Un-American implies that the union mobsters' conspiratorial secrecy and their strong-arm tactics are analogous to the international Communist conspiracy's much feared covert agendas and the party's reputed iron-willed discipline of members. Furthermore, such investigative proceedings as Senator Estes Kefauver's nationally televised 1950-1951 hearings into organized crime and the sensational New York Anti-Crime Commission findings about waterfront racketeering during the same period were the headline-garnering counterparts of the anti-Red crusading of the House Committee on Un-American Activities (particularly known for its incursions into the entertainment industry), Pat McCarran's Senate Internal Security Subcommittee, and McCarthy's Senate Permanent Subcommittee on Investigations.[3]

That the movie's concern with informing is imbued with a private, biographical urgency on the part of its creators is also no longer a question. Both the screenwriter of *On the Waterfront*, Budd Schulberg, and the director, Elia Kazan, who collaborated closely on the screenplay, had appeared before HUAC as friendly witnesses. (So, for that matter, had cast member Lee J. Cobb.) Schulberg's and Kazan's cooperation with HUAC has colored recent interpretations of the film. Victor Navasky considers *On the Waterfront* "the definitive case for the HUAC informer," while Peter Biskind sees it as espousing a centrist position, implicitly mythicizing social control and serving as a "weapon of the witch-hunt, a blow struck in the ideological and artistic battle between those who talked and those who didn't."[4] These positions are reductive but enlightening, particularly about the more or less unified movie that reaches its denouement when Terry fingers Johnny Friendly to the Crime Commission. But the eighteen or so minutes remaining seem anticlimactic. To Nora Sayre, they are "a festival of bathos" that "reverberates with a deceptive optimism"; worse is Lindsay Anderson's charge that the closing sequence is "implicitly (if not unconsciously) Fascist" and "demagogic dishonesty."[5]

There is some validity to the criticism that the conclusion is overwrought, especially in contrast to the relatively brief courtroom scene preceding it. Kazan himself feels he shot the conclusion "too insistently."[6] *On the Waterfront* is more than a parable about informing, however; aesthetically, it is neither political commentary nor self-justification. Nor, for that matter, is it a proletarian coming-of-age story or an exemplary fairy tale. Although Penelope Houston once suggested that *On the Waterfront* is "a significant, almost a definitive, example of a type of film which traditionally finds Hollywood at its most expert: the melodrama with a stiffening of serious issues," it is more properly heroic romance, the kind of quest story that Northrop Frye finds closest to "wish-fulfillment dream."[7] The black-and-white moralism of the romance fits well with the American film's penchant for moral clarity, and the romance's well-defined patterns of action and simplistic characterization (an exception is Terry) dovetail with the personal-political allegory. From this perspective, the final sequence— Terry's vengeful return to the shape-up, his fight with Johnny Friendly, his savage beating by the union thugs, and his walk to lead the rank and file to work—is formally definitive. Moreover, it is appropriate that Terry lead the camera back to the waterfront, the locus of the opening scene and the terrain of the movie's title—*On the Waterfront*, not *In the Hearing Room*. The final sequence concludes with an economy deriving from heroic necessity, though perhaps a little too neatly for authenticity of atmosphere. Still, the ending effectively subsumes the issue of informing, transforming it into a crucial stage in the development of Terry Malloy, not just as fictive person but also as hero.

Victor Navasky's *Naming Names* is a central document for understanding informing in mid-century America.[8] As Navasky points out, in contrast to the despised Judas figure in Christianity, the even worse unclean eater of human flesh in Jewish traditions, and the traitor of popular culture (as in John Ford's *The Informer* [1935] and various prison movies), the 1950s saw a rehabilitation of the image of the giver of testimony about friends and comrades. Through the media, the informer was vindicated as a patriot and held up as a role model for society; similarly, the naming of names became a test of credibility and character. Confession also became a sign of onerous personal necessity, a kind of hellish duty on the way to maturity—a view that the most influential of the period's informers, Whittaker Chambers, expounded in religious terms.[9] In short, during the McCarthy era the informer became a savior of secular society.

The moral presumption against informing was, of course, never absolute. Navasky remarks that it was always complicated by social obligations to report crimes, legal obligations to testify in court, and the Christian mandate to bear truthful witness to the state according to conscience—all counterarguments mustered in *On the Waterfront* to load the scales on Terry's behalf. What the movie does not suggest is that the kind of testimony it is implicitly justifying was clouded by very pertinent questions about the legitimacy and intentions of the Red-hunting committees and loyalty-security boards as part of what was more frequently a rite of condemnation than a forum for investigation.[10] Such doubts should have remained strong, however much the individuals who attacked their former beliefs, associations, and colleagues might believe in the need to counter a perceived Communist threat. This is a point Arthur Miller in part implies in *The Crucible* (1953), written immediately after Kazan testified, supposedly in answer to the director's actions and values, and to which *On the Waterfront* itself can be seen as Kazan's responding shot in "an artistic duel."[11]

The fact that neither Schulberg nor Kazan opted to testify before being named by others suggests that they were themselves not completely willing witnesses in their HUAC appearances, but it does not necessarily imply insincerity when they eventually spoke out. Their unwillingness, whether conscious or unconscious, is transferred to Terry Malloy, but the situation for Terry is clarified as to the rightness of his testifying. Many commentators have noticed that the film presents informing as Terry's sole course of honorable action.[12] Not only do Father Barry and Edie encourage him to speak out, citing reasons of legality, just revenge, conscience, and solidarity with his fellow workers, but the situation is set up so that when he does testify, he is more than just speaking out against former comrades and disavowing former allegiances: he is accusing a criminal whose clandestine actions he was privy to and abetted. Beyond this, he is identifying a tyrant who himself ordered Terry to spy on the workers' meeting in the church basement, who used him in rubbing out Edie's brother, and who executed Terry's own brother for trying to protect an increasingly skeptical Terry. In fact, those in the film who advise Terry not to give evidence are, first, the union racketeers and thugs, including his brother, whom the plot conveniently disposes of so as not to force Terry to confront being traitor to his own flesh and blood; and second, the boys in the gang Terry started, the Golden Warriors. The admonition not to snitch is represented as childish convention and mob discipline, always backed by the threat of violent enforcement.

In their testimony to HUAC, both Schulberg and Kazan admitted Communist party membership in the 1930s, gave evidence about the party, denounced Communism, voiced opposition to totalitarianism and secrecy as antidemocratic, and identified fellow members as part of the ritual ceremony of public degradation and expiation which Navasky notes served the double purpose of purging guilt and reinforcing consensus while stigmatizing outsiders, particularly political outsiders, as deviants.[13] Schulberg testified voluntarily, having sent a telegram to HUAC two days after he was himself named by a witness. He spent much of his May 1951 session recounting the Communist party's attempts to make writers toe the ideological line, especially as exemplified by pressures on him to make his novel *What Makes Sammy Run?* (1941) acceptable to the theoreticians and strategists, and on a reviewer for party papers who first praised the novel and then promptly recanted and condemned it. For this, Schulberg was thanked by Francis Walter for "one of the most constructive statements that I have heard since I have been a member of this Committee."[14]

Kazan, accorded celebrity treatment, appeared twice: by subpoena in January 1952 in executive session, when he wouldn't implicate others; and, when he changed his mind, in an April executive hearing released to the press the next day. At this second session he went much further, appending a minutely detailed *apologia* to explain, production by production, that his entire career supported American democracy against Communism. He also published a statement as a paid *New York Times* advertisement the day after the text of his second session was released. Immediately after his HUAC appearances, Kazan, with his prominence and his self-sought publicity, was seen by many as "the ultimate betrayer," was dubbed "Looselips" by Zero Mostel (Terry is correspondingly called a "rubber-lipped ex-tanker" by his brother), and was accused of selling out for a fat contract.[15] For his cooperation, Kazan was also commended by Representative Walter: "It is only through the assistance of people such as you that we have been able to make the progress . . ." etc.[16] This praise of both Kazan and Schulberg is echoed in *On the Waterfront* by the committee counsel thanking the protagonist: "You've done more than break the Joey Doyle case. You have begun to make it possible for honest men to work the docks with . . . peace of mind."

The project that led to *On the Waterfront* was one that gripped Kazan and "answered a need. . . . It was my reply to the beating I'd taken." Thus Kazan was motivated by what he admits was "a desire for revenge."[17] It was not until after both he and Schulberg had testified and both had separately worked on crime-on-the waterfront scripts that they began to collaborate.

Kazan had first begun working on a waterfront movie in 1949-50 with Arthur Miller, with whom he had a complex friendship and close professional relationship that did not survive their different attitudes toward testifying and informing. The story has been told most recently in the memoirs of the two participants, *Elia Kazan: A Life* and Miller's *Time Bends*, which differ slightly in emphasis and details.[18] Miller's completed script, *The Hook*, based on his knowledge of the Red Hook waterfront in Brooklyn, was rejected by Harry Cohn in 1951, ostensibly because Miller refused to make the union officials of the screenplay Communists instead of gangsters. In truth, Miller and Kazan both point out that Cohn, in effect, gave Roy Brewer of the International Alliance of Theatrical and Stage Employees political veto power, and, as Miller stresses, Brewer would not stand for the script's implicit attack on the International Longshoremen's Association of Joseph P. Ryan, Brewer's close friend (who would later go to Sing Sing for his crookedness as ILA head).[19] Brewer's use of anti-Communism as a weapon to accomplish other agendas is characteristic of the period's Red-baiters. In any case, according to Miller, his pulling out of the project was principled. According to Kazan, Miller simply abandoned it after a minor difficulty because the playwright had been "panicked" by fear of some personal or political exposure.[20] Miller's work eventually provided the material for his 1955 play *A View from the Bridge*, which is unambiguous in its condemnation of informing.[21]

Meanwhile, Schulberg became involved in his own script with Harry Cohn's nephew Jack Curtis, based on reporter Malcolm Johnson's 1949 Pulitzer Prize–winning *New York Sun* exposés of waterfront racketeering, and he too had come to a dead end when Cohn would not approve their proposed *The Bottom of the River*.[22] In 1952 Schulberg and Kazan met and, discovering their shared background in a waterfront crime film as well as common attitudes toward Communism and informing, agreed to team up. Schulberg soon began earnest on-the-scenes investigations in Hoboken, where the movie eventually was shot. In spring 1953, however, the ensuing script, *The Golden Warriors*, got turned down by every major studio, twice by Columbia. Then one night Kazan and Schulberg, disconsolate over the rejection of a script they believed in, crossed paths in the Beverly Hills Hotel with producer Sam Spiegel. Lucky for them, Spiegel was in need of a project, if only to keep earning his producer's salary. After Schulberg narrated the plot to him as he lay in bed barely awake, Spiegel resuscitated the proposal, planned as a low-budget United Artists film with a former Hoboken kid, Frank Sinatra, in the lead. Spiegel later conned Marlon Brando into starring, welching on Sinatra but, with a bigger name under contract, getting Columbia to back the project.[23] Spiegel was a major factor in the film's success: it won eight Oscars, including Best Screenplay, Best Director, Best Actor, and Best Supporting Actress.[24]

Kazan has spoken a number of times about his decision to testify and name names to HUAC, most importantly in his 1988 autobiography and his 1971–1972 conversations with French critic Michel Ciment. In both he identified himself with Terry Malloy and Terry's story, but his attitude has not always been the same. He is at his most confident in his autobiography, where he discusses the parallel between Anthony "Tony Mike" de Vincenzo, Terry's real-life model, who had testified under subpoena to the New York Waterfront Crime Commission, and himself: "I did see Tony Mike's story as my own, and that connection did lend a tone of irrefutable anger to the scenes I photographed and to my work with actors. When Brando . . . yells . . . "I'm glad what I done—you hear me?—glad what I done!" that was me saying, with identical heat, that I was glad I'd testified as I had." [25]

On the Waterfront was, to Kazan, "a film about myself" [26] in other ways, too, as his earlier comments to Ciment indicate. In these interviews, Kazan recognizes the same relationship to the main character but is less positive in describing Terry's reactions: "He felt ashamed and proud of himself at the same time. . . . He also felt it was a necessary act. He felt like a fool, but proud of himself because he found out that he was better than the other people around him. That kind of ambivalence." [27] Earlier, Kazan offers an even more negative self-assessment of his decision to inform: "Well, I don't think there is anything in my life toward which I have more ambivalence, because, obviously, there is something disgusting about giving other people's names." [28]

Ambivalence, which Kenneth Hey considers the thematic center of the entire production, [29] is not so much a description of the film's implicit meaning as a key to the shaping of the story and the portrayal of Terry Malloy until he appears before the Crime Commission. Kazan found a similar ambivalence in Brando, with his "deep hostilities, longings, feeling of distrust" kept in check behind an "outer front." Kazan understood such ambivalence: "That's my own taste." [30] Invariably, he understood Brando. This underlying rage and energy as they show in performance, as a behavioral tension, define Brando's genius.

For Schulberg, likewise, although he has never spoken about the issue with Kazan's emotion or acted with Kazan's self-proclamation (Kazan himself appreciates Schulberg's "greater objectivity" [31]), Terry can be seen as representing his own experience. Discussing with Navasky his testifying and naming of others, both of which he vehemently defended, Schulberg told of coming to grips with leaving the Communist party, which he describes in terms of the three stages in Arthur Koestler's *The God That Failed*. "First, you argue inside yourself. . . . Second, you go out of the Party, but you feel that to make it public would play into the hands of reaction. . . . Third . . . you realize you have not been true to yourself." [32] It is not stretching analysis to note that these stages correspond exactly to the experience of Terry Malloy. Terry is tormented first with guilt after setting up the death of Joey Doyle; then with doubt after meeting Edie and Father Barry. Second, in a process somewhat overlapping with the first stage, Terry distances himself from the mob psychologically; he is not quite conscious of what he has done, although his lack of commitment is all too apparent to both the viewer and the mob. This is the motivation for the famous taxi ride scene in which his older brother, Charley the Gent, tries to convince Terry "to dummy up." Terry refuses and for the first time must ask if it was Charley who ruined his boxing career and sold away his future. Although "pushin' thirty," Terry is still the "kid" who had to throw his big chance in the ring for the sake of the mob's bets. It is obvious that in his heart, albeit not in his head, he has decided to break with the criminal union. Third, when Terry accuses Johnny Friendly of three killings—Joey Doyle's, Dugan's, and Charley's—he experiences self-realization: "I was rattin' on myself all them years. I didn't even know it. . . . I'm glad what I done to you!"

It is clear that Schulberg identified with Terry Malloy's struggle and its outcome more unequivocally than did Kazan. The film has the director's stamp on it, however, and Kazan's conflicting emotions are particularly evident after the hearing. For the Terry Malloy the audience sees in the final sequence is no longer the vital, mumbling, sideways-glancing figure that energized the screen previously. At the hearing, Brando, in coat and tie, is all slicked up—or rather slicked down—and his Terry is uncharacteristically quiescent as he sits in the much constricted space. (Even the frame he occupies is sometimes masked and narrowed by foreground objects.) Afterward, Terry becomes subdued on the surface, less the mobile essence of hostility held tensely and expressively in check. The Brando of "the tough-guy front and the extreme elegance and gentle cast of . . . behavior"—the phrases are Kazan's, who knew well "the extraordinary element" he was blessed with as director[33]—has partially gone out the window.

In the closing sequence, Terry, not surprisingly, seems deprived of his credibility, and Brando, of the dynamic essence of his screen achievement. Ambivalence is the fulcrum on which the film's center of gravity shifts, and in a sense it is transferred to a deeper tension between the Brando characterization in a slice-of-life drama and a new plot imperative to make Terry a hero.

The imposed cathartic violence of the closing sequence is necessary for Terry to reclaim his filmic space as well as his role as protagonist. At the same time, the movie itself, along with Terry, is made to conclude morally and emotionally on the right side—the approved outcome in terms of the black-and-white dichotomy between, on the one hand, the state, the church, love, conscience, and the investigative and judicial processes, and, on the other, the thugs and thieves. What Brando did earlier with subtlety and intimacy is now accomplished with broader physical action in collusion with plot and camera manipulation that can be compelling but, unlike the best screen acting, are less, not "more real than life."[34] After he informs, Terry is diminished in his human complexity; the purposeful Terry seems a different kind of character, one too explicitly designed to fit the director's conception of "a man who has sinned and is redeemed."[35] But with the loss of the edginess that was his nature, it is not so much sins that are redeemed as the screen.

This lost Terry is the tormented existential outsider who has formed his identity on powerlessness and lack of ambition and sees all life as a racket. This Terry is Terry the Other, whose depiction presents a paradigm of what Pauline Kael calls "The Glamour of Delinquency"— his mumbling working-class charisma adumbrating the Dionysian hipster that a few years later Norman Mailer would call "the white negro" and "philosophical psychopath."[36] This lost Terry remains the inarticulate adolescent—Terry the ever-shifting physical presence, aptly an ex-prizefighter always moving and feinting with body or eyes. Before the hearing he appears in utter stillness only in his place of refuge, the rooftop, and when concentrating on Edie with what the audience reads from his physical language, from his pleading and tone of voice, as both awe and a kind of instinctive courtliness all the more charming for their oblique expression.

Juvenile delinquency, cultural historians have pointed out, "loomed disproportionately large" in the 1950s, a decade that might be accused of having had a "fixation on delinquents."[37] During the two years after *On the Waterfront* was released, another Kefauver committee held hearings on the corruption of youth by comic books, TV, movies, and literature.[38] Navasky has noted the significance of the discovery of deviance in this period's sociology;[39] social deviants—not in the form of the blacklisted, but delinquents and urban toughs, from working class kids to middle class drop-outs—became money-making cultural icons for Hollywood in this age of surface conformism. Before the Beats and the hip, before the hegemony of rock music and its youth sub-cultures, Brando and James Dean, along with lesser imitative screen celebrities, were popularized into what Sayre calls "Hollywood's sub-stitute for a counterculture."[40] Terry's disaffection formed a cynosure of interest for the film's original audience in just these terms, a fact upon which Kael zeroed in.[41]

One of the most interesting questions about the film is why Edie finds Terry appealing. Edie herself begins as a storybook common-place: a wholesome young female on the brink of womanhood, girl-ishly innocent but with more than a little fire beneath the exterior. Educated by the Sisters of St. Anne in Tarrytown, cloistered, as it were, in the country, where the crickets would make the city-bred Terry nervous, Edie has already internalized patterns of self-restraint and socially approved channels of self-release, as well as modes of behavior that seem to elude Terry except maybe in his self-denying passivity before the mob. Her collars may link her with the emissary of organized religion, Father Barry, but in contrast an outspoken directness bubbles up in her from the start, and her role as catalyst is an asset to the plot. It is her stinging challenge to the priest's formulaic condolences that makes him turn his Christianity outward into an active social gospel, and it is her plunging into the melee for a work tab for her father that leads to her first meeting with Terry as they wrestle for it. This independent streak of self-possession also allows her to go out with Terry to a saloon, her initiation into drink, and to talk with him alone on the rooftop, where, in the open and more or less private spaces she discovers the more vulnerable side of Terry. She also shows a sensual depth when she and Terry engage in their only passionate kissing after Terry arrives from his taxi ride with Charley and all-too-symbolically breaks her apartment door down, cornering her. But Edie, to use Terry's phrase, is still a "nice thing," and, as Eva Marie Saint plays her, appears remarkably prim in her white slip even while admitting to Terry that she loves him.

But the question remains, why does Edie do these things in the first place? Surely not just because no woman can resist a Marlon Brando, or because story conventions demand a love plot, as if the character knows she is destined to be Terry's eventual reward! Is it the future teacher in Edie? The idealist who would have treated Terry "with a little more patience and kindness" in school, not punishment? The animal-lover who dotes on six-toed kittens? Spelled out in the script, it is all these, as well as her search for her brother's killer. Visually, however, the basis of Terry's appeal to Edie must be his fundamental difference that forms the vital center of Brando's impersonation. After all, Edie is attracted before she has any notion that Terry is in any way linked to her brother's death, and she admits remembering him fondly as the schoolboy troublemaker he was. Just as she plays a choral role appraising action and ideas as morally right or wrong, so too is Edie an internal audience responding to Terry's anti-heroic, delinquent glamour, the toughness softened by the tender inflection given by the "look in his eye." Moreover, not unexpectedly, his delinquent glamour has a frankly sexual appeal—an allure that, for pure 1950s heroines, usually had to be interdicted, just as, in the phrase of Michael Rogin, the Cold War evoked a "demonology" of difference in condemning the subversive, which the era did with the help of testimony such as Kazan's and Schulberg's.[42] Immediately after talking to her father about Terry's look, Edie turns to a mirror and impulsively lets down her hair while telling Pop that Terry wants to see her again. The effectiveness of Terry's (and Brando's) magnetism, which also spoke to the mass audiences of On the Waterfront, derives, therefore, from the film's complex acceptance of Brando's ambivalence as a mode of seductive if demonized otherness, an ambivalence that disappears, as if exorcised by the ritual of informing, when the plot turns Terry from an apparent rebel without a cause into an unlikely instrument of politically meaningful action in the last sequence. Rogin argues that America's mid-century demonology opposed the subversive to woman-as-mother-figure "empowered morally," a double-edged role, but otherwise subordinated.[43] So it is telling that, after the hearing, Edie's relationship to Terry changes as she acts in a more proprietary and protective—negatively, a more maternal—way. By then, however, she has been transformed into a minor and ineffectual blocking agent whom later scenes only include symbolically.

Brando's acting style is highly naturalistic in the sense, so congenial to the cinematic medium, of providing visible and audible correlatives of found inner feeling, exhumed passions, or "emotional recall" in Group Theatre or later Actors Studio thinking.[44] This style, which is that of most of the main players of *On the Waterfront*, fits Terry's hand in Edie's glove with the movie's minute attention to the prosaic details of working-class life, behavior, and attitudes and its almost journalistic exposé of working conditions, hiring practices, union exploitation, and mob operations. For the purpose of establishing the look of documentary authenticity, Kazan and his crew worked on location on the Hoboken waterfront, using actual longshoremen for extras and a cadre of ex-boxers for Johnny Friendly's associates. Likewise, the effect of Boris Kaufman's smoky black and white cinematography is the creation of an artificial verité style that supports the film's claim to mimetic realism and a cool rhetoric.[45] The intent of Schulberg's preparatory on-site research for anecdotes, character types, mannerisms, and waterfront dialect, a process he describes in his afterword to the published final shooting script, was similar, as was his basing of events and situations on Malcolm Johnson's prize-winning newspaper articles. In particular, Schulberg points out, the film's Father Barry was modeled on a real-life Reverend John Corridan; the impassioned sermon about "Christ . . . in the shape-up" was, Schulberg assures the viewer, "taken almost verbatim from Corridan's daring Sermon on the Docks."[46] That Father Barry seems to have stepped out of the familiar "Irish priest" mold into a movie deriving, at least in part, from the 1930s gangster film is a measure of the ease with which research can be transformed into cinematic local color.

Such undercutting of the representational style is characteristic of romance, which as a story-telling mode permits many an "artful" and fanciful "conjuring trick" (to borrow phrases from Lindsay Anderson's condemnation of the last sequence[47]). Romance subverts the transparent mimeticism that is apprehended as photographic verisimilitude.

Frye remarks, in passing, that the politics of this imaginative schema tends to be the projected ideals of the dominant social and intellectual classes.[48] Anderson's criticism of the film's "fundamental falsity of conception" misses the target; it is not a subtext of right-wing political conservatism, nor ambivalence about informing, but romance's very nature and its penchant for fabulousness and, to the world of the here and now, "spurious" heroics that undermine the character of the story as artifice.[49]

The tension that most affects the viewer's response to On the Waterfront is between two kinds of stories and story-telling. One, which dominates most of the picture, is realistic narrative—an individual's development from personal failure to informer to union renegade and on (improbably, according to this tale's internal logic) to what Kazan calls "self-redemption."[50] The second is the paradigm of the heroic romance that underlies Schulberg's and Kazan's crafting of their main character's choices and actions to result in desired triumph.

As a romance, On the Waterfront evidences many of the genre's elements; the protagonist's guilt, his dilemma about testifying, his resistance to his brother's wrong advice, his decision not to confront his nemesis Johnny Friendly with a gun, and even his appearance in the courtroom take place on his "perilous journey" or agon, what Frye describes as the first stage of the romance in its complete form. Terry's single combat against impossible (though not quite superhuman) odds with an antagonist backed by loyal, hulking creatures can be viewed as the hero's pathos or "death-struggle," the next stage. His seeming loss is "a point of ritual death" containing a third aspect, the mythic rending into pieces, or sparagmos. Finally, Terry's transformation into leader of the longshoremen is a kind of miraculous rebirth that is the anagnorisis or "recognition of the hero."[51] Thus Terry frees himself from ordinariness because of qualities the viewer can identify with the rebellious self. His antisocial glamour now becomes the ennobling factor in his exaltation as well as his elevation in stature. And having endured trials and gone on to triumph, he also wins the maiden.

Not only does the plot take shape as heroic romance but many of the genre's trappings function in the movie, although they are muted because of their inclusion as part of a contemporary setting. There are signifying animals—here the pigeons, communicating eloquently to Edie at least, though not magically talking. There are loyal helpers, particularly Father Barry. There are talismans of preternatural power, such as Joey's jacket, which must be passed on to Terry before he can triumph. There is the implicit attribution of divinity to the hero, now Other in superior nature, as in the often intrusive Christian iconography.[52] If there is no danger-fraught passage through a shadowy forest, there is instead survival on the edge of the continent—the lawless and dark waterfront, a kind of underworld repeatedly said to be "down" in terms of the movie's symbolic topography and hence a subterranean realm to which the protagonist descends and from which he reappears before the climax. Finally, Terry's world has trinities enough to invoke a mystic's blessing: the omen-bearing Crime Commission agent appears out of nowhere three times before Terry testifies; three men become martyred before Terry acts; three men wear Joey's charmed windbreaker, Terry being the last; Terry is the third opponent to speak out against Johnny Friendly; and thrice Terry rescues Edie from danger.

On the level at which made-up characters get individualized by names, backgrounds, actions, feelings, and values and placed in a represented world, Terry's story is best described as a moral and psychological pilgrimage not so much to informing as to what is suggested by its root: forming. Terry begins as an *un*formed human being, not just confused but misguided. He is paralyzed by his disowned individuality and *de*formed in his narrow sense of human connection and social utility, which is true to the crime world's creed of negation—"I don't know nothin', I ain't see nothin', and I'm not sayin' nothin'." His initial characterization as a social deviant and deficient human being means he must be *re*formed.

For this to happen, Terry must be converted in more than allegiances. His decision to own up to the Crime Commission is synonymous with maturation, and to *in*form comes to mean its etymological parts: "to form within." His testimony is merely the outward sign of salvation within. His newly enlightened conscience has led him to *con*form to higher values that, to his creators and their mouthpieces, give meaning to the heroic outcome of the plot. For instance, Terry learns from Edie that no one is isolated, and from Father Barry that his soul is more important than his physical existence and that all men are brothers. By the time he honors his subpoena and betrays Johnny, Terry has accepted new definitions; at the end, when Johnny accuses him of ratting, Terry shouts: "From where you stand, maybe. But I'm standing over here now."

Up to this point in his life, Terry has done only what others wanted of him. He became a stooge for the mob as his brother set him up to be after he was through taking dives in the ring. Now he becomes a stoolie for justice, as Father Barry, Edie, and the Crime Commission investigators urge him. Though saved, Terry is still a nobody; in fact, he is a pariah to his fellow workers. It is from this low point that the cult of heroism beckons to and transforms him. Before he goes "to shape" for the last time, he says, "I ain't a bum, Edie. . . . I'm just goin' to go down there and get my rights."

Terry's growth goes much further than Father Barry and Edie

anticipated. To them, Terry's story is his private, then public, confession; hence, Edie tries to reassure him after the session in court, "It's all over." But the viewer knows that a different confrontation is Terry's destiny. For a long time Terry has fought inward change; now he repudiates the centrist limitations Father Barry and Edie have educated him to accept. Thus he *performs*, not as scorned outcast or the victim of bland values who might have fled west with Edie, but as a "somebody," empowered and granted the guts—(in)formed!—by the different set of narrative conventions that disempower her. The outcome, of course, is as fixed as Terry's big fight. In the theatrical sense of the term, Terry convincingly plays the role Kazan and Schulberg have designed for him: hero.

In the final sequence, Terry acts on his own. Assisted by Father Barry as a novice convert to the heroic order, Terry manages to "stand up . . . all the way." It is a compelling moment captured in such seductive, subjective camera work that all Terry has to do is walk. His staggering walk climaxes the film in terms of an action that, from the beginning, when he entered in line with four mobsters and then continued walking his own way, has been the visual mode of a man in personal transition.

The viewer is clearly supposed to regard Terry's triumph as not merely personal. In contrast to Johnny Friendly, who will not fight Terry man-to-man but summons his "cowboys" to back him up, the new Terry has the downtrodden behind him, of their own will, though they are too intimidated to fight. At the end, the audience sees the longshoremen, too, disobey the union leadership. Kazan is not misinterpreting when he says that the ending shows "a new potential leader."[53] But the center of the movie's emotional power is elsewhere than in celebrating a new reform boss of an erstwhile "trigger local." The necessity of Terry's heroic stature, propelled by the ritual pattern of the story, does not become necessity within the dock workers' world, in which the corrupt are eloquent and persuasive: "I'll be back," Johnny bellows. What completes the film is the heroic-melodramatic romance in which informing comes to mean more than the waterfront environment can sustain.

On the Waterfront finally redeems informing by reconceptualizing it as the path to heroic achievement. Thus it is deeply ironic that the final image has such powerfully dispiriting negative implications. With the very last shot of the heavy iron door closing inexorably upon the workers of the realistic narrative and the hero of the romance, the film descends from the extraordinary to the ordinary—to the unidealized world of hard work, ignorance, poverty, threats, kick-backs, knock-offs, and victims. But it just ain't part of Kazan's America for the film to make much of this last return of ambivalence upon its creators.

NOTES

On the Waterfront (1954). Screenplay, Budd Schulberg, based on articles by Malcolm Johnson; producer, Sam Spiegel; director, Elia Kazan; photography, Boris Kaufman; score, Leonard Bernstein. Cast: Marlon Brando (Terry Malloy), Eva Marie Saint (Edie Doyle), Karl Malden (Father Barry), Lee J. Cobb (Johnny Friendly), Rod Steiger (Charley Malloy), Pat Henning ("Kayo" Doyle), John Hamilton ("Pop" Doyle), Martin Balsam (Gillette).

1. All quotations are from the movie. The dialogue as acted and recorded differs in many small ways from the final shooting script, the specifics of which Kazan can be said nonetheless to have respected in his direction. The script was published as Budd Schulberg, *On the Waterfront: A Screenplay* (Carbondale: Southern Illinois Univ. Press, 1980).

2. For a full treatment of these hearings and the Ralph Flanders motion, see David Oshinsky, *A Conspiracy So Immense: The World of Joe McCarthy* (New York: Free Press, 1983), 416-94. Kazan incorrectly indicates in *Elia Kazan: A Life* (New York: Doubleday, 1988), 528-29, that *On the Waterfront* opened in April; but the *New York Times* reviewed it 29 July 1954, 18, as having been unveiled at the Astor Theatre the day before.

3. The Kefauver hearings are summarized in Joseph Bruce Gorman, *Kefauver: A Political Biography* (New York: Oxford Univ. Press, 1971), 74-102. The New York waterfront hearings are noted in Daniel Bell, *The End of Ideology: On the Exhaustion of Political Ideas in the Fifties* (Glencoe, Il.: Free Press, 1960); see especially 183-85. David Caute, *The Great Fear: The Anti-Communist Purge under Truman and Eisenhower* (New York: Simon and Schuster, 1978) remains the best overview of this period's sordid history; see 88-103 for an overview of HUAC, 104-8 for McCarran's SISS and the McCarthy Committee, 485-538 for the efforts against show business. Standard about the film industry is Larry Ceplair and Steven Englund, *The Inquisition in Hollywood: Politics in the American Film Community, 1930-1960* (Berkeley: Univ. of California Press, 1983).

4. Victor S. Navasky, *Naming Names* (New York: Viking, 1980), 209; Peter Biskind, *Seeing Is Believing: How Hollywood Taught Us to Stop Worrying and Love the Fifties* (New York: Pantheon, 1983), 163, 170.

5. Nora Sayre, *Running Time: Films of the Cold War* (New York: Dial, 1982), 160-61; Lindsay Anderson, "The Last Sequence of *On the Waterfront*," *Sight and Sound* 24 (Jan.-March 1955): 128, 130.

6. Michel Ciment, *Kazan on Kazan* (New York: Viking, 1974), 108.

7. Penelope Houston, review of *On the Waterfront*, *Sight and Sound* 24 (Oct.-Dec. 1954): 85; Northrop Frye, *Anatomy of Criticism* (Princeton: Princeton Univ. Press, 1957; repr., New York: Atheneum, 1967), 186.

8. Navasky, *Naming Names*, x-xxiii.

9. Whittaker Chambers, *Witness* (New York: Random House, 1952). See especially "Forward in the Form of a Letter to My Children," 3-22.

10. Caute's comprehensive study, *The Great Fear*, makes the often neglected point that beneath the well-known congressional committees, a wide-ranging apparatus of federal, state, local, industry, and community boards effected purges from the civil service, the military, and the state department, from state, city, and town governments, and from the unions, schools, school boards, colleges, newsrooms, and civic groups as well as from stage, screen, and the broadcast media.

11. Kenneth Hey, "Ambivalence as a Theme in *On the Waterfront* (1954): An Interdisciplinary Approach to Film Study," *American Quarterly* 31 (Winter 1979): 463.

12. See, for instance, Navasky, *Naming Names,* 210; Sayre, *Running Time,* 159; Biskind, *Seeing Is Believing,* 170.

13. Navasky, *Naming Names,* in particular Chapter 10, "Degradation Ceremonies," 314-29.

14. Eric Bentley, ed., *Thirty Years of Treason: Excerpts from Hearings before the House Committee on Un-American Activities* (New York: Viking, 1971), 457.

15. Navasky, *Naming Names,* 206-7; part of the bitterness, Navasky observes, was the accurate sense that, though the very successful Kazan could probably not have broken the blacklist in 1952, "no person was in a better strategic position to try . . . to mount a symbolic campaign against it" (200). And probably most strongly opposing this was the Turkish-born Anatolian Greek's self-image as an outsider and his deep-seated yearning, "passionately, to be an American" (Kazan, *A Life,* 28).

16. Bentley, *Thirty Years,* 495.

17. Kazan, *A Life,* 487.

18. Arthur Miller, *Time Bends: A Life* (New York: Grove, 1987; repr., New York: Harper Perennial, 1988), 143-56, 299-310; Kazan, *A Life,* 409-15.

19. See Bell, *End of Ideology,* Chapter 9, "The Racket-Ridden Longshoremen: The Web of Economics and Politics," 159-90, for a history and analysis of the New York waterfront, labor corruption, the ILA, and Ryan (whose takings are detailed, 383, note 47).

20. Kazan, *A Life,* 415.

21. Miller, *Time Bends,* 149.

22. Johnson's articles became a book, *Crime on the Labor Front* (New York: McGraw-Hill, 1950). Johnson's material was in fact optioned to Curtis, for whom Schulberg worked up his first script. The best synopsis of the three versions and the differences between the Miller and Schulberg and Schulberg-Kazan treatments can be found in Thomas H. Pauly, *An American Odyssey: Elia Kazan and American Culture* (Philadelphia: Temple Univ. Press, 1983), 182-92.

23. Kazan relates this anecdote in his *A Life,* 508-12, with less complicity in Spiegel's deceiving Sinatra (513-17) than when Schulberg tells it (*Screenplay,* Afterword, 149-51).

24. For a full list of awards, see Hey, 692. Schulberg also won Screen Writers Guild honors.

25. Kazan, *A Life,* 500.

26. Ibid.

27. Ciment, *Kazan on Kazan,* 110.

28. Ibid., 83.

29. Hey, "Ambivalence," 668.

30. Stuart Byron and Martin L. Rubin, "Elia Kazan Interview," *Movie* 19 (Winter 1971-72): 7.

31. Kazan, *A Life,* 500.

32. Navasky, *Naming Names,* 245.

33. Kazan, *A Life,* 525.

34. Ibid., 146.

35. Ibid., 528.

36. Pauline Kael, "The Glamour of Delinquency," *I Lost It at the Movies* (Boston: Little Brown, 1965; repr., New York: Bantam, 1966); Norman Mailer, "The White Negro," *Advertisements for Myself* (New York: Putnam, 1959; repr., New York: Putnam-Berkley Medallion, 1966), 311-31, quotation 316.

37. Douglas T. Miller and Marion Nowak, *The Fifties: The Way We Really Were* (Garden City: Doubleday, 1977), 280; Sayre, *Running Time,* 112-14.

38. Gorman, *Kefauver,* 197-98. Kefauver, though a prominent member, did

not become committee chair until 1955, when the Democrats gained control of Congress.

39. Navasky, *Naming Names*, 320.

40. Sayre, *Running Time*, 114.

41. Kael, "Glamour of Delinquency," 45-46. Kazan also observed that this same popularity among "tough-guys" was noticeable even before the movie's opening, when "somebody quipped that if the three hundred people in line that first morning had been booked and taken to police headquarters, the crime rate would have plummeted" (*A Life*, 528).

42. Michael Rogin, "Kiss Me Deadly: Communism, Motherhood, and Cold War Movies," *Representations* 6 (Spring 1984): 2.

43. Ibid., 6.

44. Kazan, *A Life*, 144.

45. The creation of the seemingly unartificial style is discussed by Kaufman in Edouard L. de Laurot and Jonas Mekas, "An Interview with Boris Kaufman," *Film Culture* 1 (Summer 1955): 4-5.

46. Schulberg, *Screenplay*, Afterword, 143-44, 152.

47. Anderson, "Last Sequence," 129.

48. Frye, *Anatomy of Criticism*, 186.

49. Anderson, "Last Sequence," 129-30.

50. Kazan, *A Life*, 528, stipulates that informing itself was "Terry's act of self-redemption"; Byron and Rubin, "Elia Kazan Interview," 7.

51. Frye, *Anatomy of Criticism*, 187, 192.

52. The Christian symbols are much pointed to throughout criticism and include the vague crosses in ships' masts in the establishing shot and in the background shadows at other times, the analogue of the stoning of the saints during Father Barry's shipboard oration about Christian duty and the murders being a crucifixion, the passing on of Joey's relic, the stigmata of Terry's bloody hand and later his bloodied head, the removal as from the cross of his murdered brother from the stevedore's hook, and not least of all Terry's baptism and his lurching *via dolorosa*. In the same spirit, for that matter, it was in "the Garden" that Terry took a fall in the match what would have given him a shot at the title. The symbols, Kael caustically notes, together provide "the *look* of meaning," p. 44.

53. Ciment, *Kazan on Kazan*, 105.

8

ANATOMY OF A MURDER
Life and Art in the Courtroom
JEANINE BASINGER

Many of history's most celebrated movie directors have been unable to resist the cinematic challenge of the courtroom drama. Where lesser talents might shrink from the restrictions imposed by contained space, controlled dialogue, monitored behavior, and limited decor, successful directors seem to be morbidly fascinated by them. Is it some secret impulse to self-destruct on screen, or perhaps the urge to solve a series of filmmaking obstacles? Whatever it is, film abounds in excellent courtroom dramas, many directed by the best in the industry: Alfred Hitchcock (*The Paradine Case* [1948]); Billy Wilder (*Witness for the Prosecution* [1957]); and John Ford (*Sergeant Rutledge* [1960]), whose *Dr. Bull* (1933), *Young Mr. Lincoln* (1939), and *The Sun Shines Bright* (1953) have lengthy trial sequences. George Stevens made the murder trial the dramatic centerpiece of *A Place in the Sun* (1951); Frank Capra treated an insanity hearing in *Mr. Deeds Goes to Town* (1936) and a Senate debate in *Mr. Smith Goes to Washington* (1939) as if they were formal trials; Mervyn LeRoy recreated the Leo Frank case in *They Won't Forget* (1937). There are heavenly courts (*Stairway to Heaven* [1945]), Ku Klux Klan-like courts (*Black Legion* [1936]), and courts in which criminals try one of their own (*M* [1930]). There are Oscar-winning attorneys (Gregory Peck in *To Kill a Mockingbird* [1962]) and Oscar winning criminals (Susan Hayward in *I Want to Live!* [1958]). There are scene stealers in courtrooms (John Barrymore slyly intoning "She'll fry" in *True Confession* [1937]) and on juries (Henry Fonda in *Twelve Angry Men* [1957]). If *Jagged Edge* (1985), *The Verdict* (1987), and *Presumed Innocent* (1990) are any indication, the genre is in no danger of extinction.

Of all the courtroom movies, none may be greater than *Anatomy of a Murder*. Certainly it is fair to say that no film shows greater respect for the accuracy of trial behavior or for the letter of the law than *Anatomy*, whose producer-director, Otto Preminger, was the son of an Austrian attorney.[1] As a child, Preminger was taken to trials, and allowed to watch the proceedings. All his life Preminger was drawn to stories about investigations or situations in which people had to make decisions based on evidence presented from opposing viewpoints. Issues of fact, deliberation, and justice recur in his films. *Laura* (1944), *Fallen Angel* (1945), and *Where the Sidewalk Ends* (1950) concern attempts to solve murders by people who are emotionally involved in the case. *Exodus* (1960), *Rosebud* (1975), and *The Human Factor* (1979) portray international political situations in which no one can win but in which sides still have to be taken. Furthermore, Preminger's films themselves are trial-like in the sense that the audience is asked to become a jury. A balance of information is presented; the viewer is then invited to consider the plot as evidence and to accept the premise that no one image contains an explanation. The response Preminger wants is not "Are these people good or bad?" but rather "How did they get this way?" and, finally, "With whom did I most sympathize?" and "Who do I think is right?" Viewers are treated like adults who can and will make up their minds, and often Preminger audiences end up with widely divergent views about the character most or least deserving of sympathy. His films, Preminger once said, are about people who are "infinite shades of gray."

Not all films lend themselves to this type of presentation. Thus Preminger was always looking for properties that would afford him the chance to make the kind of balanced and mature film he preferred. In August 1957 he read the galleys of a book that was to be called *Anatomy of a Murder.* He knew it was his kind of story and immediately negotiated for the rights, so that when the book came out and was an instant bestseller, Preminger was in on the ground floor. In July 1958 he finally had the screen rights; by then, *Anatomy* had been a bestseller for sixty-five weeks and a Book-of-the Month Club selection. Its author, "Robert Traver," was actually John Voelker, a Michigan State Supreme Court justice who knew the places and people about whom he wrote. Readers felt the sting of truth in his words while at the same time enjoying his storytelling.

As one of Hollywood's new breed of independent producer-directors, Preminger was in a strong position in the late 1950s. A shrewd businessman as well as an artist, he formed his own production company as the studio system began to crumble. Preminger took advantage of the fact that the "new" Hollywood was a town where strong individuals like himself could make independent releasing deals with the studios, as Preminger then did with Columbia. At the time he was preparing for *Anatomy*, he had already made *Bonjour Tristesse* (1958) for Columbia and would go on to make four more films for the studio: *Porgy and Bess* (1959), *Advise and Consent* (1962), *The Cardinal* (1963), and *Bunny Lake is Missing* (1965).

After securing the film rights to *Anatomy*, Preminger selected Wendell Mayes to adapt it. Mayes's previous credits included working with Billy Wilder on *The Spirit of St. Louis* (1957) and with Audie Murphy on *To Hell and Back* (1955). Preminger and Mayes had never worked together before, and Preminger had his own way of collaborating with writers: "My attitude toward writers is unlike that of other directors. I never ask for screen credit, in spite of the fact that I participate very actively on the writing of the screenplay. It is the director's job, and my job as a director, to direct everything—even the writer, just as I direct actors, and this means working with writers for hours at a time and re-writing scenes. The script has to be completely filtered through my brain and through my emotions if I want to direct it."[2]

Preminger and Mayes adapted *Anatomy* in this way, working closely on a daily basis while Preminger was involved in preproduction on *Porgy and Bess*. After principal photography began on *Porgy*, the two men worked together on *Anatomy* only in the evenings, and this mutually beneficial method continued when they collaborated later on *Advise and Consent* and *In Harm's Way* (1964).

Anatomy told a long, complicated story. Adapting it was a challenge, but Preminger knew it was a natural for the movies. It had an engrossing plot about a rape and a murder, and colorful, believable characters whose lives were interrelated but in unpredictable ways. More important, the novel showed a deep respect for, and a detailed knowledge of, the law, and it was set in a little known area of America, the Upper Peninsula of Michigan. Preminger felt he could exploit these two features to the fullest and make a film that was not just another courtroom melodrama.

With a finished script in hand, Preminger went into preproduction. First he visited Upper Michigan to see what it looked like and to scout possible exteriors. Just as the novel had been written under a pseudonym, it was also set in the fictitious town of Iron City, Michigan. The novel described the area as "wild, harsh and broken land . . . with a forlorn look in the late winter." As soon as Preminger saw the bleak landscape with its grim skies and weathered buildings, he decided the only place to film the exteriors would be in their original setting. When his art director, Boris Leven, accompanied him on a second trip, Leven became equally excited. Then Preminger made the bold decision to shoot the entire film, exteriors and interiors, on location. "It's not only the look of the place that I wanted to get on the screen," Preminger insisted. "I want the actors to feel it, to absorb a sense of what it's like to live here . . . to smell it. *Anatomy* is a story that requires reality."[3] "Reality" became Preminger's guide during filming, not only in terms of locations but also in casting, costuming, lighting, and sound recording.

After a thorough location search, Preminger and Leven decided on two Michigan towns, Ishpeming and Marquette, to represent Iron City. In Ispheming they selected the library and railroad station; in Marquette, the hospital, the jail, and the courtroom. For the leading character's home and law office, they had no trouble finding what they wanted: Justice Voelker's own law office, which was also the home where he had been born, was the perfect choice.

By deciding to film in Upper Michigan, hardly a common site at the time, Preminger guaranteed the visual honesty and realism he wanted. The decision also meant that viewers could look at the settings and form their own opinions about them. The spaces on the screen would not be sets, designed to define the characters living in them and pointing toward a single visual interpretation. A movie set represents the thinking of the mind or minds that create it; the *Anatomy* "sets" were a nonspecific jumble of places brought about by many minds over the years—minds that had no intention of using them to make a meaningful statement.

Having convinced Columbia of the need for total location shooting, Preminger then turned to casting. Allowing the audience to question who is really guilty was one of Preminger's primary goals; thus he needed supporting actors who not only excelled at their craft but were also not associated with previous roles that might prejudice viewers. When actors have established screen personas, it is difficult for them to play against type or appear in roles other than their customary ones. John Wayne's presence in a movie, for instance, immediately triggers an association with Hero/Good Guy. Preminger, by extending the realism of location shooting into casting, found actors who, at the time, were not well known to moviegoers—George C. Scott as Dancer, the slick out-of-town attorney; Orson Bean for the small but crucial role of Dr. Smith, the psychiatric witness. Whenever possible, he cast someone who corresponded to the public's idea of the character.

He chose Kathryn Grant to play Mary Pilant, for example, because she looked as if she came from a small town. Grant's inexperience made her performance look so uncomplicated that it was impossible for an audience to determine whether she was a "bad girl" who looked innocent or a "good girl" the locals perceived as wicked. After carefully selecting the unknowns, Preminger rounded out the cast with established players whose personas *could* be put to use: Eve Arden as the wise-cracking secretary and Arthur O'Connell as the drunken older lawyer.

The three pivotal roles were the most difficult to cast: Lt. Manion, the accused; his wife, Laura; and the defense attorney, Paul Biegler. In the book, Laura Manion was forty-one. Preminger's initial choice was Lana Turner, then about thirty-nine. Because she was the right age and still had star power, Turner seemed ideal. But trouble developed almost immediately between the strong-willed Preminger and his leading lady, who was used to, and had earned, star treatment. Turner felt she should have some input into the way she would look on the screen; in particular, she wanted a say about her wardrobe, believing it was necessary for her to wear the kind of glamorous clothes with which she had long been associated. Preminger, on the other hand, felt it would compromise the character (an army officer's wife) as well as the film's realism: "We had a conflict because I selected a pair of slacks, and she didn't want to wear them. . . . She wanted to have her costumes done by Jean Louis. I felt that the wife of a second lieutenant couldn't afford Jean Louis."[4] Turner bowed out of the film, making headlines and having no regrets. Recalling their clash years later, Turner remarked, "God forbid that I should ever be so hungry that I would ever think of working for Mr. Preminger."[5]

After Turner's departure, Preminger decided against casting a name, preferring someone who could blend sexuality and innocence. He settled on Lee Remick, whose ability to look both trashy and wholesome, to seem both dangerous and vulnerable, gave the character of Laura everything Preminger could have hoped for.

To play the leading role of Biegler, however, Preminger wanted a star. In James Stewart he found the right combination of a box-office draw and one of the most talented and versatile actors in the business. Yet anyone who read the novel would probably agree that Stewart's name is not necessarily the one that comes to mind for Paul Biegler. Preminger's casting of Stewart in an offbeat role was part of a tradition the director had established early in his career of making unusual choices, sticking by them, and finally proving he was right. For example, Twentieth Century-Fox had opposed his casting Clifton Webb as Waldo Lydecker in *Laura*, yet that performance is not only the one for which Webb is remembered but also the one that helped elevate *Laura* to its present classic status.[6]

Many associated with *Anatomy* found Stewart a strange choice, but Preminger thought otherwise. What seemed right to him was Stewart's ability to handle emotional outbursts as well as down-to-earth naturalism. Although Stewart is often thought of as an "all-American guy," there is a passion, a dangerous (even violent) quality lurking beneath some of his most famous characterizations. Capra capitalized on that quality in *Mr. Smith Goes to Washington* and *It's a Wonderful Life* (1946); Hitchcock, in *Rope* (1948) and *Vertigo* (1958); and particularly Anthony Mann in a series of westerns depicting Stewart as an angry, vengeful hero.[7] Preminger was interested in depicting both sides of the Stewart persona—the side that would be believable as a small-town Michigan lawyer and the side that suggested the character might be no better than he should be—canny, shrewd, and not to be reckoned with lightly.

For the third main character, Lt. Frederick Manion, Preminger cast the New York actor Ben Gazzara, whose only previous screen credit was Columbia's *The Strange One* (1957), in which he played a young, sadistic military school student. Although most moviegoers were not familiar with Gazzara's work, his screen presence was dynamic; moreover, his acting had a menacing quality that kept the audience in doubt. With Gazzara in place, Preminger had his cast, each of whom was precisely right for his or her part. Yet there was one bit of casting that turned out to be a coup: the casting of a real judge as Judge Weaver, who in the film tries the case. It was the final touch of realism, and a newsmaking event in itself.

During 1954 the American public had been mesmerized by the Army-McCarthy hearings, one of the first televised events of national importance. The presiding judge had been Justice Joseph N. Welch, a dapper man with an incisive wit and elegant articulation. His no-nonsense, straight-talking approach had captured the public's respect, especially when he lashed out at McCarthy, saying, "Have you no sense of decency, sir, at long last? Have you no sense of decency?"

In a stroke of casting genius, Preminger persuaded Welch (persuasion being largely financial) to play the trial judge in the film. Preminger could not have made a better decision; the result was some well-earned pre-release publicity. Moreover, Welch turned out to be a good enough actor to do what was required for the role but not such a good actor as to lose his identity. Welch was never false, never actorish. He was never inside the fiction. He simply sat at the center of the trial, on the bench where he belonged in life as well as in the plot, totally believable because he *was* a justice who knew how to listen, how to act in the literal sense, how to proceed. Everything he did was ironically reinforced by the fact that many who saw him in *Anatomy* had seen him in an earlier, similar "role," albeit in a different medium, as a real-life justice.

With cast, script, and locations ready, Preminger began filming. He always felt the core of the story, as well as the key to its meaning, lay in the long and complex trial sequence: in the way it addressed rape, the American legal process, courtroom theatrics, and jury objectivity. Can a jury, chosen at random, weigh evidence fairly? Is it possible to find out truth at a trial? *Anatomy* transcends the level of courtroom melodrama because everyone associated with it understood that, in addition to the engrossing plot, there were other levels of meaning. Preminger, therefore, decided to film the trial first, and in sequence, and to use locals for jury and spectators, thus preserving the integrity of action, dialogue, and space.

Preminger's decision broke with standard practice; it required great effort from his crew and cast, and perhaps more from the non-professionals who were playing the jurors and spectators. Everyone rallied; by photographing the action in sequence, Preminger allowed both cast and crew to become familiar with one another, the setting, and courtroom etiquette. A strong sense of realism began to prevail; it was as if a trial were really in progress.

The trial illustrated Preminger's directorial philosophy: "Don't forget that the essential factor is not technique, but *what* we want to tell and *what* we want to do, and *how* we want to present it in order to involve audiences in matters of consequence, in patterns of human behavior."[8] Preminger sought objectivity, not as it is commonly perceived, not in terms of what the viewer sees on the screen, but in terms of decisions the viewer makes about what is on the screen. This sense of objectivity combined with Preminger's desire to involve the audience in decisions about the characters and their motives led Preminger to a technique that became his trademark: the long take. Perhaps it was inevitable that Preminger, himself an actor as well as a stage director, would choose a mode of cinematic expression that favors actors.[9] The long take allows an actor to build a characterization, to become comfortable in the space explored by the camera, to find natural moments to pause, move, and control pace. There is a coherence to a scene shot in long take akin to what actors experience when they create roles on the stage; it is also a method to which most actors respond well.

The long take favors both performance and viewers. Just as an actor has a better opportunity to find coherence in a scene as well as a chance to exercise his or her intellect, so does an audience. Viewers allowed to relate to filmed space as a whole judge it for themselves. If a scene is broken up by montage, the process creates a specific meaning for the viewer. A long take allows a viewer to make choices, to see parts of the scene—a rose on the table, the nervous tic of an actor—as discoveries made individually in time. Since it was Preminger's intention to allow viewers to experience the lengthy trial in *Anatomy*, with its many suspects and contradictory testimonies, as a single event, he chose the long take as the main way of photographing the sequence. The result is singular; not only is the trial perhaps the most brilliant on film, it is also unlike any other movie trial.

The three most common questions filmmakers ask themselves when they set out to shoot a trial sequence are: How can I generate excitement? How can I offset the problem of lengthy testimonies? How can I find variety within the courtroom itself? There are standard ways of answering these questions. As to the first, the desire to generate excitement can lead to clichés—someone bursting into the courtroom crying, "Stop!"; a sudden breakdown by the guilty party as the camera tracks in on the character, who then begins to confess. The desire to offset long speeches on the witness stand may be satisfied by that trusty cinematic device, the flashback. In *Witness for the Prosecution*, Billy Wilder uses the flashback to take the viewer out of the courtroom, as does John Ford in *Sergeant Rutledge*. While ostensibly remaining in the courtroom for valuable testimony, a film can still take the viewer as far away as postwar Germany (*Witness*) or a cavalry attack (*Sergeant Rutledge*). The method is one of visualizing what the witness is saying instead of asking the audience to listen to the testimony. Finally, variety within the courtroom may be achieved by having members of the jury or spectators become reactive characters.

The reactive character is standard in classic Hollywood cinema: a character in a scene reacts in a way that cues the audience as to how to think and feel about the action. Reactive characters are especially useful in trial movies. By cutting to specific jurors or colorful courtroom visitors, filmmakers can achieve variety, tempo, humor, and relief from tedium; they can also indicate the way the trial is progressing. If the audience does not fully understand the proceedings, the reactors in the movie do! These characters, who often have no real function in terms of the plot and who appear only at the trial, can reflect opinion, trigger response, and, most important, reflect change of attitude. In the hilarious trial scene in *The Lady from Shanghai* (1948), the courtroom visitors include several Asians, gossips of both sexes, a leering man whose interests are clearly prurient, the "lady" herself (a blonde Rita Hayworth), and a woman in a veiled hat whose sanity is clearly questionable. This weird collection continues the bizarre tone that was set at the beginning; the spectators at the trial also furnish a subtext: there's no justice here. In fact, the man on trial has himself been framed!

Preminger more or less avoids these clichés. Although he builds suspense by having McArthy, who has not driven in years, brave the highways to bring in valuable evidence, he treats the unexpected entrance of Mary Pilant into the courtroom with great simplicity. There *are* surprises and revelations, but they come largely from the testimony itself and not from histrionics. As for flashbacks, there is not a single one. Obviously, if Preminger's goal was to maintain balance, objectivity, and realism, flashbacks would be inappropriate. If the viewer were allowed to see the crime Laura Manion describes in her testimony, he or she would have no questions about what actually happened. The viewer's entire relationship to the trial would change. Not having seen the event through flashback, the viewer has no choice but to listen carefully to Laura's description of it and try to determine if she is telling the truth. The viewer must listen to *all* the testimony to form a judgment; in other words, Preminger forces the audience to become a jury. In so doing, it begins to pay closer attention to details: Lt. Manion's effete cigarette holder, Laura Manion's lovely hair when it is revealed, the fishing fly that Biegler fashions as he listens.

As far as reactive characters are concerned, there are none; there is not one close-up of a juror or a spectator. There are no knitting mothers or gum-chewing reporters; there is no one to influence opinion, no one to explain who won a legal point or even what it was. There is, however, sound from the people in the courtroom: tittering about Laura's panties that are brought in as evidence, expressions of surprise when certain information is revealed. There are also two medium close-ups of Mary after she decides to visit the trial late in the film; Mary, however, is one of the key players in the courtroom drama, not a reactive character. The close-ups reveal nothing of her inner feelings, nor do they shed light on the alleged rape; in fact, they do little more than establish Mary's presence and her obvious concern.

Richard McGuinness has pointed out that one way Preminger achieves objectivity in movies without trial scenes is to use a proxy audience as a way of keeping the viewer from resorting to traditional responses.[10] McGuinness speculates that if Preminger were doing a trial scene, he would probably use the jury itself as a proxy audience. This is not the case in *Anatomy*, where the jury is an almost distanced group; it is true, however, of an earlier Preminger film, *Angel Face* (1952), which has a short but vital trial scene in which Preminger uses the jury to tell the viewer how *not* to react; he does so by using the wrong reaction. As we see the jury weighing evidence incorrectly, substituting sentiment for sense, we do the reverse. If there is a proxy audience in *Anatomy*, it is probably the justice himself, who illustrates how we all should listen, weighing everything carefully and not prejudging. And even then, we would probably not know the whole story.

After *Anatomy* had been filmed, Preminger added two elements to it in postproduction that enhanced its appeal: imaginative credits by the great Saul Bass and an outstanding original jazz score by the legendary Duke Ellington, who also plays a small role in the movie. Both the credits and the score reflect the open-ended narrative. Bass created a simple set of line drawings, black and white, of a body cut into six parts (trunk, head, two arms, two legs) that must be connected for the sake of completeness. Visually, they recall the chalk drawings investigators use to mark the spot where a murder victim has been found; they also suggest a murder, a puzzle, and the need for an explanation.

The jazz score was appropriate for several reasons. Attorney Biegler is not only a jazz fan but also an amateur jazz musician who pounds away at the piano while waiting for the verdict. Jazz, therefore, was already in the narrative line. Jazz is also not a "content" kind of music; it does not instruct audiences as to how they should feel; thus it has the objectivity for which Preminger was striving. Jazz's improvisitory quality and intricacy seem right for a film in which the law is open to individual interpretation—or jamming—by the two opposing lawyers. The fragmentation, suggested by the titles and the score, thus provides an analogy for the situation Biegler faces: pieces that must be gathered and assembled by one who must make his own story (or melody) out of them.

Preminger felt that the fact that *Anatomy* was Ellington's first film score was an asset. Ellington moved out to Michigan to confer with Preminger and his staff. His presence there resulted in his playing the small role of Pie-Eye, the local jazz musician. Ellington's name proved to be a box-office draw; in fact, the film itself opened to excellent reviews. Thus no one was surprised when the 1959 Oscar nominations were announced and *Anatomy* was nominated in seven categories: Best Picture, Best Actor, Best Supporting Actor (two in that category— George C. Scott and Arthur O'Connell), Best Screenplay Based on Another Medium, Best Cinematography, and Best Editing. Ironically, the man who bought the book, assembled the cast and crew, and put them all together to make a movie that would acknowledge the respect for the law he had learned from his father—Otto Preminger—was not nominated. It was not the first time, of course, nor would it be the last (cf. *Driving Miss Daisy* in 1990) in which a movie is nominated for Best Picture but its director receives no nomination at all.

In the end, *Anatomy* won no Oscars: *Ben Hur* swept all the major categories except Best Screenplay (*Room at the Top*) and Best Cinematography (*The Diary of Anne Frank*). The National Board of Review named *Anatomy* to its Ten Best List, and the New York Film Critics chose Stewart as Best Actor and honored Wendell Mayes for Best Screenplay. The 450 movie critics of America voted it one of the year's ten best, and it was also one of the top grossers of 1959.

Today, *Anatomy* is still popular; it is a perennial on television and college campuses. It has proved so popular on television that Preminger, a pioneer in demanding that TV respect his work, brought a lawsuit against a station that cut *Anatomy*: "If the owner of a TV station shows ANATOMY OF A MURDER," Preminger said, "it should be the ANATOMY OF A MURDER that I made, and the way I showed it in theatres should be the way it is shown everywhere."[11] Preminger believed the right of final cut had to be extended to include television showings. He specifically singled out two common abuses: cutting a movie's running time and excising scenes deemed censorable. While he was never against showing movies made for the big screen on the small screen, he was against cutting them indiscriminately for any reason. One can only imagine how Preminger, who died in 1986, would have felt about colorization and panning/scanning, two alteration methods common today.

Anatomy's popularity has not been diminished by television restrictions or the passing of time. The movie does not date; as the years go by, its brand of intelligent filmmaking, in which audiences are treated as an adult group of thinking people, seems more and more uncommon. Its complexity continues to challenge; its balance and clarity seem ahead of its time, as one observes the unprejudicial way women particularly are revealed as both strong and weak, manipulative and innocent, victimized and victimizing. Viewers realize they are watching more than a murder mystery; they are watching how the American legal system, a man-made set of laws, really works. It is strange how often Anatomy has been called a mystery. There is no mystery as to who committed the only murder in the film: Lt. Manion, who shot the man he believes raped his wife. The question is not "Did he do it?" but "Was the act of murder justified or not?" If there is "reasonable cause," the law states, then Manion can be judged "not guilty." Thus, the search conducted in Anatomy is not for a killer but for the truth. What really happened, and who is to blame?

Ultimately, Anatomy becomes a battle of wits between a slick city attorney (Dancer) and a country lawyer (Biegler). As the story unfolds, the men exchange legal blows. They are worthy adversaries; both win battles, although neither wins the war. Under the shrewd and watchful eye of Judge Weaver, they step around the limited courtroom space, neatly tricking each other while remaining within the law and accepted legal practice. The audience watches transfixed, coming to understand, perhaps for the first time, that it is not the "story" that each lawyer is after but the part of the "story" that will enhance his case.

Biegler moves carefully, seeking to open up information. He ferrets out the bare facts: a man has shot someone who gave his wife a ride home from a bar. When he interviews the accused, Biegler cautiously outlines the ways he could defend his client: If it was not murder (if it was a suicide or an accident); if the accused did not do it; if the accused was legally justified (that is, if he was protecting his home or acting in self-defense); if the killing was excusable.

These are the only legal bases for defense. Skillfully, cunningly, but without transcending legal and moral boundaries, Biegler points out to Manion that the first two possibilities simply are not true. The third is out because Manion waited too long after he learned about the ride home and possible rape before he shot the victim; moreover, he did not catch the dead man raping his wife. Biegler quietly waits until Manion figures it out for himself: only the fourth is possible. Manion, then, must find a justifiable legal reason for the murder and present it to

Biegler. If he can do that, Biegler, who has planted the idea in his mind, can morally defend him.

Once he is hired, Biegler soon becomes aware of the pitfalls. Laura Manion was apparently raped, but did she invite it with her flirting and tight clothes? Had she used other men to make her husband jealous? Had a similar situation occurred before? Laura has a black eye, and her clothes were torn. But was it her husband who beat her? Lt. Manion has a history of violence. Was the dead man a popular figure in the town or are the rumors true that he kept a young mistress and was also violence-prone? Does Laura love her husband or is she afraid of him? Is theirs a love story or a sordid relationship?

While Biegler tries to bring out facts that will help Manion, Dancer seeks to reveal those that will not. Dancer seeks professional testimony that will blacken Manion's character and make the jury question both his honesty and his love for his wife. After the facts are established, Biegler uses them to reveal the witnesses' emotions—but only those emotions that will win his case. Preminger directs the proceedings with limited histrionics but not with limited drama. Underneath one set of facts lies another, and the viewers as well as the lawyers are digging for it. Unexpected information turns up that neither lawyer can suppress: the victim had an illegitimate daughter; Manion had been in trouble with the military police; Manion had beaten up his wife before. Conflicting and enticing facts tumble out.

Biegler finally wins partly because, unlike Dancer, he lives in the town where the trial is taking place and knows the kind of people who are on the jury. He knows how to woo the judge by making him a special fishing lure and presenting it to him as if it were a spur-of-the-moment idea. Perhaps he wins because he is what Preminger wishes his audience to be: flexible and open, or, as Biegler says, "As a lawyer, I've had to learn that people aren't just good or bad, but people are many things."

As his drunken old lawyer pal, Parnell McArthy, observes, "Criminal trials are from their very nature intensely partisan affairs—primitive, knockdown, every-man-for-himself combats; the very opposite of detached, scientific determination." Yet that detachment is what the law counts on to work. As he, Biegler, and Maida (Eve Arden) wait for the verdict, McArthy philosophizes about juries in the best speech in the film: "Twelve people go off into a room. Twelve different minds, twelve different hearts, twelve different walks of life. Twelve sets of eyes, ears, shapes and sizes. These twelve people are asked to judge another human being as different from them as they are from each other. And in their judgment, they must become as one mind: unanimous. It's one of the miracles of man's disorganized soul that they can do it. And in most instances do it right well. God bless juries."

God bless juries who, like film audiences, do the best they can with what they are given. In *Anatomy* the audience is given the chance to *be* a jury. Yet after feeling secure in the knowledge that justice was done, they face the same irony Biegler does. When he and McArthy drive to the Manions' trailer, they find it gone. The Manions have skipped town without paying the fee, leaving behind a broken high-heeled shoe and unanswered questions. What was the true story and who was to blame? *Anatomy* is a perfect lesson in the law and a piece of first-class movie entertainment.

NOTES

Anatomy of a Murder (1959). Director, Otto Preminger; screenplay, Wendell Mayes, based on the novel by Robert Traver (pseud.); photography: Sam Leavitt; music: Duke Ellington; titles: Saul Bass. Cast: James Stewart (Paul Biegler), Lee Remick (Laura Manion), Ben Gazzara (Lt. Frederick Manion), Joseph N. Welch (Judge Weaver), Kathryn Grant (Mary Pilant), Arthur O'Connell (Parnell McArthy), Eve Arden (Maida Rutledge), George C. Scott, (Claude Dancer), Orson Bean (Dr. Smith), Duke Ellington (Pie-Eye).

1. Preminger's father held a position in Austria equivalent to that of Attorney General in the U.S.

2. Gerald Pratley, *The Cinema of Otto Preminger* (New York: A.S. Barnes, 1971), 69.

3. Richard Griffith, *Anatomy of a Motion Picture* (New York: St. Martin's, 1959), 25.

4. Pratley, *Cinema of Otto Preminger*, 128.

5. Lou Valentino, *The Films of Lana Turner* (New York: Citadel Press, 1976), 265.

6. Preminger was also responsible for replacing Peggy Cummins with Linda Darnell in *Forever Amber* (1947) even though Cummins had been brought from England specifically for the role. By casting an Iowa farm girl, Jean Seberg, in *St. Joan* (1957), a decision he alone defended, he gave her international celebrity.

7. On the Mann-Stewart collaborations, see Jeanine Basinger, *Anthony Mann* (Boston: Twayne, 1979), 97-128.

8. Pratley, *Cinema of Otto Preminger*, 186.

9. On the screen Preminger appeared in *The Pied Piper* (1942), *They Got Me Covered* (1942), *Margin for Error* (1943), and *Stalag 17* (1953). He was also famous for playing "Mr. Freeze" on the Batman TV show. His best known stage productions were *The Moon Is Blue* (1951) and *Critics Choice* (1960).

10. Richard McGuinness, "Otto Preminger," *On Film* 1 (1970): 36.

11. Pratley, *Cinema of Otto Preminger*, 186.

9

COLUMBIA AND THE COUNTERCULTURE
Trilogy of Defeat
SYBIL DELGAUDIO

For those who rely only on memory, the counterculture of the 1960s was energetic, idealistic, radical, and optimistic; for those who rely only on movies, it was wrongheaded, laughable, hopeless, and dead. The New Hollywood, which appeared to challenge the traditions of classic Hollywood (and seemed to spring, at least in part, from the cultural defiance of the period), was identified in the early and mid-1970s by such scholars as Peter Lloyd and Thomas Elsaessar, who suggested that linear narrative, generic conventions, and motivated heroes were being replaced by looser structures, less predictable characters, ambiguity, and other identifiable borrowings from the international art cinema.[1] Encouraged by the success of the French New Wave, studios began distributing foreign films whose refreshing iconoclasm and commercial success encouraged American moviemakers to be less faithful to the Hollywood formula. This alleged liberalization was accompanied by a corresponding relaxation of the Production Code (entirely replaced in 1968 by the voluntary MPAA rating system); both appealed to a new audience of younger, more affluent, and better educated filmgoers.

More recent historians, however, have argued that while the New Hollywood certainly borrowed from the European art cinema of the 1960s and 1970s by experimenting with disjointed narrative and minimal motivation, the Hollywood model remained intact: "Classical premises of time and space remain[ed] in force, with only minor instrumental changes [and] classical film style and codified genres swallow[ed] up art-film borrowings."[2]

Using *The Conversation* (1974) as a model, David Bordwell, Kristin Thompson, and Janet Staiger showed how the New Hollywood controlled narrative potential and character ambiguity by keeping innovation within "classical boundaries" and "a coherent genre framework."[3] Whatever Hollywood took from the art cinema, it merged with the standard conventions of narrative, style, and genre to absorb what was borrowed and to subdue the "disruptiveness of the art cinema."[4]

Also contributing to the defeat of difference was the underlying support for the dominant ideology of the period. Thus some American films of the 1960s and 1970s were decidedly two-faced; on the one hand they dramatized countercultural values for an apparently sympathetic audience; on the other, they undermined those values, however subliminally, by presenting them within the parameters of Hollywood moviemaking (that is, by maintaining stylistic conventions), depicting their ultimate failure, or subjecting them to ridicule and satire.

Three Columbia films illustrate how difficult if not impossible it is for an industry like the movies, which promotes the interests of the dominant class, to endorse the counterculture. *Easy Rider* (1969), *Bob & Carol & Ted & Alice* (1969), and later *The Big Chill* (1983) form an interesting trilogy in their depiction of the counterculture and their denial of its viability.

When *Easy Rider* premiered it received almost universal acclaim from critics, who hailed its stars, Peter Fonda and Dennis Hopper (also its director), as voices of a new generation. Honored at Cannes and Edinburgh and singled out by the National Society of Film Critics, *Easy Rider*, made for a mere $375,000, became Columbia's fourth highest grossing movie of the 1960s, and by 1991 had earned over $19 million. Since the film was independently made, Columbia agreed to distribute and market it with some say about the final cut—the original being twice its ninety-four-minute release length.[5] Reviewers dubbed *Easy Rider* "New Hollywood," and the industry scrambled to capitalize on its success by the usual method of cloning: the result was a spate of low-budget, youth-oriented movies aimed at a market sympathetic to European aesthetics and a general but apparent opposition to the mainstream.[6] On the surface, at least, *Easy Rider* signalled an American "New Wave," a movement in film aesthetics and production that appeared to affirm the 1960s counterculture.

In retrospect, *Easy Rider*'s apparent sympathy for the counterculture is, as David E. James has suggested, "finally reducible to and incorporable into the dominant ideological field."[7] To James, the film celebrates drugs, free love, and the excitement of the open road only insofar as those activities are seen as "infractions" subject to retribution. While the film's style may suggest alternative cinema, it is essentially conventional, and its values are eventually discredited. As James puts it, "The counterculture hippies reject the city for a technologically primitive, communal agrarianism to which the technological dependence of the film medium is fundamentally alien. . . . A real endorsement of the commune would have brought the film to a halt there. It

184 COLUMBIA AND THE COUNTERCULTURE

would have meant abandoning the film's real destination, arresting both the death trip of Captain America and the success of *Easy Rider* in the commercial cinema."[8]

Finally, James interprets "We blew it!" as "an allegory of the failure . . . to make a film adequate to the ideals of the counterculture."[9] While *Easy Rider* was originally an independent production, its distribution by Columbia made use of industry apparatus, thus neutralizing the possibility of alternatives in terms of practice, style, or content.[10]

Chris Hugo has suggested that *Easy Rider*, for all its trend-setting, was by no means progressive: its narrative structure was conventional as was its theme, the picaresque journey; its morals were puritanical (retribution for drug dealers); the male bonding recalls Howard Hawks's buddy movies and Jack Kerouac's road novels. *Easy Rider*, then, is merely a "re-working of old Hollywood traditions to suit contemporary notions of what was fashionable," and ends by "break[ing] no new ground, [either] formally or thematically."[11]

Generically, *Easy Rider* is classifiable and familiar. Reminiscent of the road movie, it also evokes the popular male buddy movies of the period, such as *Butch Cassidy and the Sundance Kid* (1969) and *Midnight Cowboy* (1969). Even more directly, the film recalls the western with its use of such names as Wyatt (Earp) and Billy (the Kid) and the parallel suggested in an early scene between a rancher shoeing his horse and his contemporary counterparts changing a tire on their bike.[12] Most genre movies, with their familiar iconography, conventions, archetypal characters, and formulaic plots, are monolithic in their view of tradition; the western, one of the most recognizable of film genres, is also one of the most traditional. By implying that *Easy Rider* is a quasi western, the filmmakers have ensured its structural conservatism, shrouding its so-called iconoclasm in tradition and thereby containing its surface mission.

Easy Rider, a 1960s cultural artifact, becomes, in retrospect, a self-parody partly because of its faddishness. The clothes are particularly representative of the 1960s, when attire became an antiestablishment reaction to the mainstream. In fashion history, there is probably no better example of the incorporation of sociopolitical values into clothing than the 1960s look. Miniskirts, tie-dyed fabrics and denim, long hair, love beads, low-waists, and bell-bottoms all made their way into the mainstream of American fashion. Since 1960s fashion had gone to such an extreme, it was inevitable that it would be replaced by a more sober look that called attention to the mutability of fashion signs and the impermanence of fads.

Further, the film's morality—in the sense of the main characters' gaining their "freedom" to embark on their journey by dealing drugs—has also been reevaluated; drugs no longer represent the freedom they did in the 1960s, nor can dealers any longer escape the judgment of society. Even the arty camera work and loose structure, reminiscent of the French New Wave, have been validated by such mainstream successes as *The Graduate* (1967) and *Bonnie and Clyde* (1967).

Finally, *Easy Rider* is self-defeating because it is self-conscious; by communicating extremes in terms of both message and style, the film denies the possibility of real alternatives, burying its values in the datedness of cultural faddism.

Bob & Carol & Ted & Alice uses broad satire to mock countercultural values by focusing on the lives of two California couples trying vainly to become more "modern." While most critics reacted favorably to the film, some found it "sniggering" and attacked the New York Film Festival for opening with it.[13] Hollis Alpert suggested that the conflicting responses were the result of differences in the viewing experience; seeing *Bob & Carol* with an audience instead of at a critics' screening, where reviewers are too busy taking notes to laugh when they should, clarifies the film's point of view.[14] John Simon argued that the film could be taken "as a daring comedy essentially affirming the sexual revolution, or as a daring comedy essentially satirizing [it]."[15]

It was Arthur Schlesinger who made the most provocative assessment of the movie: "The film is not Now at all" but, in fact, "an old-fashioned romantic comedy disguised as a blue picture."[16] To Schlesinger it was a conservative film whose bourgeois values were decked in contemporary trappings.

The sexy updating of the old "change partners" plot appealed to Mike Frankovich, who produced the film. Frankovich, who headed production at Columbia from 1964 to 1968 and then became an independent producer releasing through Columbia, disliked cerebral pictures and was certain he knew what the public wanted. Using his ability to identify with characters as a measure of a film's potential success ("They have to be people like me or like people I know"[17]), Frankovich managed to turn out films that reflected the social concerns of the period (*To Sir, with Love* [1967], *Guess Who's Coming to Dinner* [1968]) and proved to be box office hits. But Frankovich's own generational conservatism (he was fifty-eight when he produced *Bob & Carol*), coupled with his exceptional business acumen, explains his attraction to the script and his willingness to make a movie that explored trendy countercultural values while at the same time subverting them.

Like *Easy Rider*, *Bob & Carol* presents the counterculture as a fad by satirizing the way the middle class attempts to deal with liberation. By poking fun at such 1960s ideas as emotional self-awareness, sexual freedom, and partytime drug use, the film then subjects them to ridicule and ends by affirming their impermanence. The satire revolves around the notion of incongruity, first expressed in the film's title with its ambiguous reference to both the individual and the group. Since so much of the countercultural search for self was based on both the individual (finding oneself, individual therapy) and the group (encounter sessions, group awareness, communal living), the equal emphasis given to both in the title implies the impossibility of reconciliation. At the end, when Alice (Dyan Cannon) proposes an orgy to Bob (Robert Culp), Carol (Natalie Wood), and Ted (Elliott Gould), it is the individuals who cannot function in a group situation, and the "orgy" is waived in favor of a less threatening and more retrograde Tony Bennett concert.

The film's first images—high-angle shots of Bob and Carol traveling in their sports car to an Esalen-like institute—are juxtaposed with the music of Handel's Hallelujah Chorus to make a visual-aural statement about misplaced faith. The encounter session itself is filled with platitudes about "feelings"; a man in his sixties wants to "continue to grow," while a woman expresses her wish for a "better orgasm." While the couple overcome their initial discomfort and skepticism about the session (Bob is there only to make a documentary; Carol is there because Bob is there), their radical change seems as incredible and ridiculous to their friends as it does to the viewer. Ted and Alice are persuaded to express their true feelings about the length of Bob's hair or the appropriateness of Carol's outfit as the film mocks the absurdity of applying encounter techniques to everyday life. Alice's reaction to Bob's extramarital affair (she is outraged by both his infidelity and Carol's apparent acceptance of it) underscores the incongruity of retaining one's composure after an admission of adultery.

These middle-class California trendies are merely trying out the counterculture as they would the latest fashions; like the clothes of *Easy Rider*, those of *Bob & Carol* are emblematic of the ephemeral 1960s. Moreover, the characters' attempts at progressivism are often overreactions to their own discomfort. When Bob returns from a business trip to discover that Carol has been unfaithful to him, his immediate reaction is visceral: he wants to kill the guy. It is only when he begins to reevaluate his feelings in light of what he has learned in encounter sessions that he accepts Carol's lover, even offering him a conciliatory drink in their bedroom. Again, the inappropriateness of Bob's "enlightened" reaction, in contrast to his more "human" one, accentuates the incongruity of his response; his demeanor is once again a comment on the failure of the counterculture to meet the needs of individuals who have lived most of their lives in the mainstream.

The film concludes with the strains of "What the World Needs Now Is Love, Sweet Love," while the four main characters lead a Felliniesque processional into a mingling crowd. Bob and Carol and Ted and Alice have, at least for the present, relinquished their alternative lifestyle for something more traditional. The final scene reflects their inability to regard transient notions as anything other than fads.

The Big Chill is the most direct of these three films about the failure of the counterculture. Set in the present, it is an evaluation of the counterculture as seen through the collective and individual eyes of a group of pre-Yuppie friends gathered for the funeral of one of their own. Less nostalgic than defensive, the film conveys an almost unrelieved sense of disillusionment and lost possibilities. Even Columbia's marketing of *The Big Chill* reduced the 1960s to trivial pursuits: "How much love, sex, fun and friendship can a person take? They're eight old friends who haven't seen each other since the 'sixties. Searching for something they've lost. And finding all they need is each other. . . . In a cold world, you need your friends to keep you warm." [18]

Generally well received, *The Big Chill* still prompted Pauline Kael to say that it would be hated by "anyone who believes himself to have been a revolutionary or a deeply committed radical during his student demonstration days." [19] But it does not take a radical to realize that commitment can be reduced to fad by reevaluating and reordering priorities, and can be justified by rationalization—an activity that occupies most of the characters in the film.

Beginning with an image of death, *The Big Chill* intercuts shots of the friends reacting to the news of Alex's suicide with shots of the body being prepared for burial by a mortician. This is the first of several references to sexual liberation as a countercultural value. Here, sex is linked with death in a series of ambiguous close-ups that resemble, for a while, the aftermath of a sexual encounter, as a woman (the mortician) appears to dress a man (Alex's corpse). Since Alex seems to have been a member of a group whose values remained relatively intact, his death becomes a metaphor for the death of the counterculture; his friends puzzle over his suicide just as they do over the loss of their old beliefs. Here, more than in the other two films, hindsight contributes to the reclassification of 1960s values as fad, just as rationalization and selective memory lessen the degree of remorse for their demise.

In one scene, Meg (Mary Kay Place), an unmarried attorney whose disillusionment stems from her discovery that her clients are more guilty than she thought, rationalizes her reordering of priorities: what is most important to her now is having a baby. Searching for an appropriate partner, she expresses her feelings about the 1960s, thereby articulating the film's thesis: "Sometimes I think I put that time down . . . pretend it wasn't real . . . so I can live with how I am now."

The other characters exercise varying degrees of denial about the way they have changed, but almost all have sold out in one form or another: Harold (Kevin Kline) is a successful shoe store owner; Sarah (Glenn Close), his wife, is a physician who questions the significance of their past; Sam (Tom Berenger) is a television actor in a *Magnum P.I.-*like series; Michael (Jeff Goldblum) was a promising journalist who now writes for *People*; Karen (JoBeth Williams) is a housewife and mother who seems not to have been reconciled with her choices (which included giving up writing); and Nick (William Hurt) is a cokehead, impotent from an injury in Vietnam and still in search of answers. The press highlighted the film's sense of disillusionment, thus justifying its theme of the rationalization of compromise. Some critics tried to associate the actors' personal experiences with their characters; for example, JoBeth Williams was portrayed as a once-committed Brown University graduate who gave up her dream to work in community theater for the "practicality" of Hollywood: "I remember saying, 'I will only do Art, but I will never do entertainment' . . . but there are all sorts of considerations out here—like you need the exposure, you need the money—that never occurred to you in college."[20]

Others in the cast (Tom Berenger, Kevin Kline, Glenn Close, William Hurt) discussed their identification with the characters, all agreeing that *The Big Chill* had forced them to examine their own choices. Director Lawrence Kasdan reduced commitment to peer pressure and mob psychology: "I think the atmosphere was so heavily politicized you could not avoid being involved . . . and having an army of cops bearing down on you with tear gas—it made it easy to believe you were doing something important. And sometimes we were—I'm not cynical about that, but I don't think it necessarily sprang from any deep-rooted convictions."[21]

Kasdan's assessment of the counterculture is as superficial as his direction, which shifts from one pair of characters to another in a series of audiovisual bytes that trivialize consideration and preclude evaluation: according to one critic, "the result is a film about reflection that nowhere contains the space for reflection—that actively tries to snuff reflection out."[22]

Finally, *The Big Chill*, whose title ostensibly crystallizes the collective cooling of once hot idealism, avoids complete rejection of the counterculture (a gesture required to avert guilt) by maintaining that Nick, its reluctant remnant, is in a farmhouse nearby. But the gesture is perfunctory and futile, since it is unlikely that Nick, impotent and defeated, can succeed in reviving a dream that has been relegated to the periphery by those who consider it more dead than deferred.[23]

As illustrated by these three Columbia releases, the counterculture existed in Hollywood films only to be defeated, and the defeat was usually self-induced by characters who had a sense of their own disillusionment. "We blew it," says Wyatt in *Easy Rider*. So did the counterculture, according to Hollywood.

NOTES

Easy Rider (1969). Screenplay, Peter Fonda, Dennis Hopper, and Terry Southern; photography, Laszlo Kovacs; director, Dennis Hopper. Cast: Peter Fonda (Wyatt), Dennis Hopper (Billy), Jack Nicholson (George Hanson), Luana Anders (Lisa), Karen Black (Karen).

Bob & Carol & Ted & Alice (1969). Screenplay, Paul Mazursky and Larry Tucker; photography, Charles Lang; music, Quincy Jones; director, Paul Mazursky. Cast: Natalie Wood (Carol), Robert Culp (Bob), Elliott Gould (Ted), Dyan Cannon (Alice).

The Big Chill (1983). Screenplay, Lawrence Kasdan and Barbara Benedek; photography, John Bailey; music, Meg Kasdan; director, Lawrence Kasdan. Cast: William Hurt (Nick), Meg Tilly (Chloe), Tom Berenger (Sam), JoBeth Williams (Karen), Mary Kay Place (Meg), Jeff Goldblum (Michael), Kevin Kline (Harold), Glenn Close (Sarah), Don Galloway (Richard).

1. Cf. David Bordwell, Janet Staiger, and Kristin Thompson, *The Classical Hollywood Cinema: Film Style and Mode of Production to 1960* (New York: Columbia Univ. Press, 1985), 373.

2. Ibid., 375.

3. Ibid., 377.

4. Ibid., 375.

5. Introduction to *Easy Rider*, ed. Nancy Hardin and Marilyn Schlossberg (New York: New American Library, 1969), 15. In the fall of 1990 the film's producers, Burton J. Schneider and Bob Rafelson, sued Columbia for refusing to return negatives, prints, and outtakes (*Variety*, 12 Nov. 1990, 4). If there is ever a restored *Easy Rider*, it may then be possible to see how "new" the New Hollywood really was.

6. Chris Hugo, "*Easy Rider* and Hollywood in the '70's," *Movie* 31/32 (Winter 1986): 67.

7. David E. James, *Allegories of Cinema: American Film in the Sixties* (Princeton: Princeton Univ. Press, 1989), 15.

8. Ibid., 17-18.

9. Ibid., 17.

10. Ibid.

11. Hugo, "*Easy Rider* and Hollywood," 71.

12. Anthony Macklin, "*Easy Rider*: The Initiation of Dennis Hopper," *Film Heritage* 5 (Fall 1969): 7.

13. Cf. Pauline Kael, review of *Bob & Carol & Ted & Alice* in *Film 69/70*, ed. Joe Morgenstern and Stefan Kanfer (New York: Simon and Schuster, 1970), 50.

14. Hollis Alpert, "A Critical Situation," review of *Bob & Carol & Ted & Alice* in Morgenstern and Kanfer, *Film 69/70*, 47.

15. John Simon, "What the World Doesn't Need Now," review of *Bob & Carol & Ted & Alice*, in Morgenstern and Kanfer, *Film 69/70*, 59.

16. Arthur Schlesinger, Jr., "Innocence Updated," review of *Bob & Carol & Ted & Alice* in Morgenstern and Kanfer, *Film 69/70*, 57. Schlesinger notes that the film could have been made twenty years earlier with Jack Carson and Ronald Reagan; in 1969 "fornication replaces kissing, bare bosoms replace cleavage, pot replaces liquor . . . but the essential innocence remains."

17. Chris Welles, "Behind the Silence at Columbia Pictures—No Moguls, No Minions, Just Profits," *New York*, 7 Sept. 1970, 44.

18. Newspaper ad for *The Big Chill*, *New York Times*, 10 Oct. 1983, C 14.

19. Pauline Kael as quoted in Brian Cronenworth, "He Knew What He Wanted," *American Film*, Jan./Feb. 1989, 50.

20. JoBeth Williams as quoted in Michiko Kakutani, "Lawrence Kasdan's *Big Chill* Will Begin the N.Y. Film Festival on Friday," *New York Times*, 19 Sept. 1983, sec. 2: 6.

21. Ibid.

22. Dave Kehr, "Saluting the Sixties," review of *The Big Chill*, *Chicago*, Oct. 1983, 140.

23. One might compare *The Big Chill* with two independently made films, *Return of the Secaucus 7* (1980), which deals with a reunion of 1960s radicals, and *Between the Lines* (1977), which portrays a group of 1960s activists working at a counterculture newspaper threatened by a takeover. Both are more loosely structured, more open-ended than *The Big Chill* and less willing to relegate countercultural beliefs to fad. As independent productions, neither follows the typical Hollywood formula, and their attempt to speak to the ideological convictions of their more limited audience allows them to take a more radical stance.

10
TAXI DRIVER
Bringing Home the War
LES KEYSER

In 1987, United Artists released *You Talkin' to Me?*, a political fable about an ethnic New York actor who idolizes Robert DeNiro in *Taxi Driver* yet is lured by greed, ambition, and lust into being the spokesperson for a Christian family broadcasting empire and preaching racism to laid-back surfers on the West Coast. This low-budget, law-and-order melodrama, whose villain, Peter Archer, could easily be a Jimmy Bakker clone, was produced by the aptly named "Second Generation Film Productions" and acknowledged its enduring debt to *Taxi Driver*'s director, Martin Scorsese, star Robert DeNiro, writer Paul Schrader, and producers and artistic consultants Michael Phillips, Julia Phillips, and Julie Cameron. In its numerous subplots, *You Talkin' to Me?*—whose title comes from DeNiro's famous monologue in *Taxi Driver*—not only criticizes the social and economic scene in 1980s America but also provides a sharp commentary on the difference between the independent film and the Hollywood product.

Coming a decade after *Taxi Driver, You Talkin' to Me?* reveals three aspects of *Taxi Driver* that critics originally overlooked or under-emphasized: *Taxi Driver* is social criticism of the highest order, excoriating America's needless involvement in Vietnam and boldly testifying to the havoc President Lyndon Johnson's "guns and butter" politics wrought, especially in urban centers. *Taxi Driver* also confronts the issues of class and gender in America, pinpointing the chasm between the haves and the have-nots, between white establishment yuppies and homeless drifters and outsiders. Finally, *Taxi Driver* exemplifies the polarization of American popular art between mindless entertainment and thoughtful cinema.

The central dilemma in *You Talkin' to Me?* is the perennial one of artistic integrity: Should Bronson Green (Jim Young) stick to his ideals, keep his dark hair and swarthy Robert DeNiro complexion, and struggle for recognition in New York, or should he sell out to Tinseltown, give agents the blonde look guaranteed to pack theaters, and content himself with the pleasures of wealth?

In the early 1970s Martin Scorsese was mulling the same choices. His earlier films, *Who's That Knocking at My Door?* (1968) and *Mean Streets* (1973), revealed his artistic integrity and spiritual angst. It was well known that Little Italy, Catholicism, and loneliness haunted this frail, asthmatic New York University *Wunderkind*. Yet Scorsese had capitulated to the industry by directing *Boxcar Bertha* (1972), a bloody *Bonnie and Clyde* spinoff, for exploitation king Roger Corman, and by fashioning a star vehicle for Ellen Burstyn with *Alice Doesn't Live Here Anymore* (1975). The followup film to *Boxcar Bertha* and *Alice* shaped his career irrevocably.

Scorsese frequently lamented the choice confronting him: "The question of commercialism is a source of worry. Must one make a choice? Must it be a matter of either setting your sights on winning an Academy Award and becoming a millionaire or making only the movies you want to make and starving to death?"[1] In the 1970s, the answer was all too obvious. George Lucas made over $300 million in domestic rentals for *Star Wars* (1977) and *The Empire Strikes Back* (1980); Steven Spielberg, over $200 million for *Jaws* (1975) and *Close Encounters of the Third Kind* (1977); and Francis Ford Coppola, over $100 million with *The Godfather* (1972) and *The Godfather, Part II* (1974). Science fiction and the gangster film were in; philosophy, sociology, and theology were out. Hollywood's famous dictum was still in force: for messages, try Western Union.

Against this backdrop of escalating budgets, Columbia's commitment to *Taxi Driver*, a low-budget production with seemingly little appeal to mainstream America, is amazing. In 1972, Paul Schrader, an academic critic turned screenwriter, drafted the first script of *Taxi Driver* in ten days because, as he told interviewers, the material leaped from his head like an animal. Schrader, who was raised in a strict Calvinist household and had never seen a film until he was eighteen, had just experienced a series of major crises: his wife was divorcing him, his mistress was deserting him, and his ulcerative condition worsened as a result of a six-month binge during which he wandered the streets and slept in porno theaters, nursing his loneliness, self-loathing, and despair. Around the time of his emergency hospitalization, Schrader, who had been reading the French existentialists, also came upon the story of Arthur Bremmer, the misfit who shot George Wallace after failing to assassinate several other political figures. Schrader had also listened carefully to Harry Chapin's song "Taxi," about a cabbie's lost youth, failed romance, and shattered dreams. Sartre, Bremmer, and Chapin coalesced in a scenario of existentialism, violence, class consciousness, despair, longing, and thwarted love—in short, *Taxi Driver*.

Michael and Julia Phillips, whose Malibu beachfront house provided a salon for young aspiring talents like Schrader, Peter Boyle, Steven Spielberg, Scorsese, Brian DePalma, Al Pacino, John Milius, and Robert DeNiro, were impressed by *Taxi Driver* and immediately optioned it. But the Phillipses, too, were torn between their desire to make a political statement as they had in *Steelyard Blues* (1972) and their love of commercial success, so obvious in their second project, the Oscar-winning *The Sting* (1973).

It was the Phillipses' influence that had led Schrader to develop the initial outline for *Close Encounters*. Yet *Taxi Driver* sat on the shelf; it was a great script but seemingly unproducible. For awhile there was the possibility of a *Taxi Driver* with Jeff Bridges, directed by Robert Mulligan. But once the Malibu set saw *Mean Streets*, it became evident that *Taxi Driver* belonged in the hands of DeNiro and Scorsese. DeNiro, in fact, had been working for years on his own screenplay about a would-be political assassin wandering the streets of New York. And Scorsese, who loved *film noir* and had been impressed by Paul Schrader's 1972 essay in *Film Comment*, "Notes on Film Noir," remarked that Schrader's script was one of the finest he had ever encountered. Everyone was on board for the project and so committed to it that they willingly took large pay cuts. Scorsese's longtime advisor and agent, Harry Ufland, urged him to continue working on *New York, New York* (1977), which was then in preproduction, instead of pursuing the adventures of an urban misfit. DeNiro also came under intense pressure; his Oscar for *The Godfather, Part II* had greatly improved his salary prospects. He was getting offers that paid ten times as much as *Taxi Driver* and that demanded much less preparation and labor. Paul Schrader was being courted on every side, and the Phillipses seemed to be involved in every major deal in Hollywood.

All this notoriety for the four principals finally propelled *Taxi Driver* into production. The proposed budget of $1.3 million, which eventually swelled to $1.9 million, made this a package Columbia could not turn down. David Begelman knew a bargain when he saw one. Thus in July 1975 *Taxi Driver* went into production on the streets of New York during one of the hottest summers on record and at a time when it appeared that financial crises, racial strife, and political incompetence were about to sink New York once and for all. The city was on the ropes, and within the year the *Daily News* would print one of the twentieth century's best remembered headlines: "Ford to New York: 'Drop Dead.'"

The actual shooting of *Taxi Driver* proved physically difficult and emotionally draining. Even a native New Yorker like Scorsese felt tension and despair crowding every street corner. Normally an apologist for the Big Apple, Scorsese admitted that the summer of 1975 was "a down point for New York, and it shows in that film, in the mood of it. It was so hot you could see the violence shimmering in the air, taste it in your mouth, and there we were in the middle of it. . . . You can't always paint New York as a summer festival. It's a rough city, though probably no rougher than any other big city where there are a lot of people and some of them are angry."[2] Complicating things further was the low budget. Studio representatives lurked around the set, always suggesting further economizing.

Things came to a boil during the second week of filming when rainstorms made location shooting all but impossible. As various Columbia personnel suggested bringing key scenes indoors and ignoring the urban backdrop, Scorsese exploded and shut the production down at lunch. That night he threatened to walk off the project, but Columbia relented. So long as he kept to budget, he could do as he wished; the studio's risk was minimal, so the director's freedom remained intact. Only in the editing stage did studio pressure mount again. Scorsese had promised a specific date for completion; to make the deadline, the editing had to be speeded up. The last two weeks, Scorsese has remarked, were like working for Roger Corman again. Everything was rushed to open the film on schedule.

Except for the hectic pace of postproduction, Scorsese enjoyed a freedom few other young directors would ever achieve in 1970s Hollywood. A New Yorker who lauded his heritage in the acclaimed short *Italian-American* (1974), Scorsese hammered home his personal statement as he brought to the screen a script he loved so much he could have written it himself. Thus many saw as Scorsese's alter ego his *compare*, Robert DeNiro, another exile from Little Italy struggling to express himself in Hollywood. Because he was willing to work on an extremely tight budget, Scorsese could turn *Taxi Driver* into his most powerful commentary yet on the madness of Vietnam and its effect on the American psyche.

Scorsese had long been an outspoken critic of the war. He had dazzled European intellectuals with his gory and macabre 16 mm fable *The Big Shave* (1967), made in graduate school. A blistering allegory of America's involvement in imperialistic wars, *The Big Shave* showed a young man methodically shaving his own face away in a bloody machismo ritual of self-destruction. America, the film implied, was slitting its own throat in Vietnam by allowing the military to pursue a suicidal course of expansionism, "destroying" villages to "save" them. For those too blind to understand, the symbolic bloodbath in an empty bathroom concluded with a sink full of human blood and the title "Viet 67."

Shortly thereafter, as an instructor in New York University's film school, Scorsese allowed his apartment to become the center for radical filmmakers organizing against the war. One of their projects, *Street Scenes 1970*, credited to the New York Cinetracts Collective, had the youthful Scorsese as production supervisor and postproduction director. The film was so accomplished that it was screened at that year's New York Film Festival.

The studios were still hesitant about tackling Vietnam. Except for Warners' *The Green Berets* (1989), in which John Wayne gleefully scorched hordes of "gooks," the studios found it easier to make their war epics about World War II and Korea—*Tora! Tora! Tora!*, *Patton*, and *M*A*S*H*. Even when *Taxi Driver* was released, Hollywood was still studiously avoiding criticism of American incursions in Southeast Asia. Julian Smith's book *Looking Away: Hollywood and Vietnam* (1975) had as its basic concern "how Hollywood has averted its eyes from the war" and argued that in the few American fiction films dealing with Vietnam, every one "supported our involvement."[3] Scorsese was clearly swimming against the tide with a movie about an urban terrorist who admits he is a Vietnam veteran and who frequently dons his combat jacket with its fading black stencilled identification, "Travis Bickle," and its prominent battle patch celebrating the infamous King Kong Brigade. This combat patch later finds ironic counterpoint in the pin Travis purloins from the Palantine campaign, "We are the people."

Interestingly, most commentators and critics ignored Scorsese's rather obvious political criticism. Normally astute analysts like Robert Kolker assert that *Taxi Driver* "withholds any political, social, or even psychological analysis of Travis Bickle."[4] And this, despite the fact that Scorsese hired a former Special Forces officer with a background in psychology as a consultant to assist him in demonstrating how Vietnam would have shaped Travis's everyday habits, the way he moved, the way he talked, the way he avoided eye contact and other human communication. Scorsese wanted audiences to see that Travis had brought this dirty little war home with him and that Americans were all now "waist deep in the big muddy."

Scorsese is most explicit about Vietnam's importance to *Taxi Driver* and to Travis Bickle: "It was crucial to Travis Bickle's character that he had experienced life and death around him every second he was in south-east Asia. That way it becomes more heightened when he comes back; the image of the street at night reflected in the dirty gutter becomes more threatening. I think that's something a guy going through a war, any war, would experience when he comes back to what is supposedly 'civilization.'"[5] Focusing even more sharply on the war's effect, Scorsese argues that "Bickle was affected by Vietnam: it's held in him and then it explodes. And although at the end of the film he seems to be in control again, he gives the impression that any second the time bomb might go off again" (62).

Both Schrader and Scorsese labor assiduously in *Taxi Driver* to link the ticking clock of Travis's explosive personality to the minefields and rice paddies of Vietnam. For example, the large scar on Travis's back featured so prominently in the film provides a physical emblem of his deeper, more extensive mental wounds. Travis complains of insomnia and worries about the cancer devouring his stomach; veterans' hospitals are overcrowded with restless men tortured by their fears of carcinoma; battle fatigue often expresses itself in sleeplessness, chronic self-absorption, and psychosomatic illnesses. In Schrader's original script, Travis confesses to Andy, the gun salesman, that he was "all around" in Vietnam, "one hospital and then the next." Also, in Schrader's script, the descriptive material, intended to be read by director and performer, suggests how appropriate Scorsese's metaphor of a time bomb was for *Taxi Driver*. In his notes, Schrader compares Travis to an overwound spring: "The clock spring cannot be wound continually tighter. As the earth moves toward the sun, Travis Bickle moves toward violence."[6] Clues to the progression can be found in the porno houses Travis frequents, in his constant threats to Sport, the pimp, and his henchman, and in his combative posture with other cabbies. Among the subtle clues of his Vietnam hangovers are his unfiltered Camel cigarettes (these assertively masculine cigarettes could easily be field stripped in combat zones with no telltale filter residue), his penchant for purifying shoe polish in the flames (an old army spit-and-polish ploy for perfect shoeshines), and the K-bar knife he straps to his leg (only the Special Forces used this particular weapon in Vietnam). When Travis reaches out to others, he quickly hides behind his military experience. At breakfast with Iris, the young prostitute (Jodie Foster), for example, he brags that his real mission in life is "top secret" because he's "doing something for the Army" and just driving a cab part time. And in his pathetic anniversary card to his parents he again lies that he cannot send his address because his work for the army "demands utmost secrecy." Unfortunately, the army has crippled Travis, and he doesn't realize it; that is his utmost secret.

In a 1976 interview Scorsese confessed to journalist Gregg Kilday his own impatience with viewers who ignored all these details and complained there was no explanation for Travis's murderous explosion: "We knew all the background—the scars on his back, the way he lights the shoe polish to get rid of impurities—Special Forces in Vietnam. It's all there. Some people can't get it completely, some people do. You can't make a movie for everybody. And spell it out for everybody. . . . This picture just takes the idea of macho and takes it to its logical conclusion, graphically, pornographically, insane."[7] The Code and Rating Administration (CARA) decided that the concluding sequence of *Taxi Driver* was too graphic and insisted that Scorsese soften the color of the bloodbath before it would issue the film an "R" rating. America obviously could take only so much catharsis; too much of the war was not welcome on American shores.

The most disturbing moments in *Taxi Driver* actually come after the shooting stops. Travis, wounded in the neck like so many of Scorsese's demented saints, recovers from his injuries and, like Alex in *A Clockwork Orange* (1971), another famous "cure," finds himself a celebrity, hailed for his bold attack on pimps and drug dealers. Newspapers all join in adulation for the courageous cabbie, and even Betsy (Cybill Shepherd), the sophisticated career woman who rejected his earlier advances, is anxious to ride in his cab again. Instead of being labeled insane or ostracized, Travis is lionized by a populace eager for an apocalyptic savior. The central irony of *Taxi Driver* is, as Pauline Kael has observed, "that the city is crazier than he is."[8]

In this dramatic turnabout, Scorsese reveals his deeper themes in *Taxi Driver*. Like British psychiatrist R.D. Laing, Scorsese posits Travis's insanity as a logical response to a world spinning out of control. As presidential aspirant Charles Palantine (Leonard Harris) reminds Travis and all the "little people" he wants to vote him into office, "We the people suffered in Vietnam; we still suffer from unemployment, crime, and corruption." Like Kurtz in Conrad's *Heart of Darkness*, who goes to the jungle to spread light only to become convinced that the solution is to "exterminate the brutes," Travis Bickle has always been faithful to his own vision, exterminating in Vietnam and then stamping out the criminals at home. He seems fixated on his dream of a rain that will wash all the filth from the world and end his suffering. He is intent on eliminating all the suffering in Vietnam and on the Lower East Side; he will exterminate if that is what it takes to save.

Scorsese's focus on the insanity of the war abroad and the war at home provides an unsparing condemnation of hustlers like Palantine and the upwardly mobile professionals who manage his campaign. One true sign of Travis's irrationality is his idealization of Betsy, whom he sees as an "angel" rising out of the "open sewer" of New York; a radiant presence so alone and aloof that "they cannot touch her." Like many of Scorsese's protagonists, Travis has been duped by a Madonna-whore complex. The blonde Betsy is every bit the opportunist that the child prostitute Iris is; Betsy just has a lot more intelligence and a few more dollars. Schrader's script is especially pointed in its description of Betsy: "Beneath that cover girl facial there is a keen, though highly specialized, sensibility: her eyes scan every man who passes her desk as her mind computes his desirability: political, intellectual, sexual, emotional, material. Simple poise and status do not impress her; she seeks out the extraordinary qualities in men. She is, in other words, a star-fucker of the highest order." Scorsese makes the identification between Betsy and New York City hookers in a subtle scene after Travis takes her to his idea of a movie for couples, a porno feature entitled *Swedish Marriage Manual,* which explains the reproductive system with graphic examples. Betsy rushes from the theater, then grapples momentarily with a bewildered Travis. In the next few seconds, Betsy finds herself alone, standing next to a blonde prostitute with a remarkable physical resemblance to herself. Betsy, momentarily transfixed by this *doppelganger,* then rushes into a cab. Wordlessly, Scorsese has spoken volumes about sexual oppression, class consciousness, and a polarized society. New York City, Scorsese intimates, has become like a third-world country, like Vietnam; its denizens are overly rich or overly poor, free or enslaved, black or white, educated or ignorant. The middle class and the middle ground have been eliminated; it is a Marxist apocalypse, with haves confronting have-nots for possession of the streets.

Critic Colin Westerbeck describes how this dichotomy manifests itself in Travis's two romantic interests, Iris and Betsy: "Betsy is a goddess from the haut monde"; Iris, "a lost soul from the demi-monde . . . is a demonic reincarnation of the untouchable Betsy, even looking vaguely like her." To Westerbeck, Travis's switch from Betsy to Iris parallels his movement from the pleasure principle of sexuality to the death urge of violence. Travis confuses sexual energy with violent hatred, the destruction of life with its creation, as he dreams of salvation through sacrifice and expiation through retribution.[9] While Westerbeck's interpretation is valid, *Taxi Driver* fans had blood lust, not Freudianism, on their minds. Scorsese, who friends say chuckles through screenings of *Taxi Driver,* was so shocked by the way some audiences reacted to it that he found it uncomfortable to watch the movie in a theater. In *You Talkin' to Me?* the protagonist Bronson Green is physically ejected from a screening of *Taxi Driver,* and the ushers who throw him out observe that *"Taxi Driver* fans are all freaks."

There does seem to be some evidence that *Taxi Driver* may have powers not yet fully understood, somewhat like Mick Jagger's rendition of "Sympathy for the Devil," a piece of music that seems uniquely cursed since Altamont. Consider, for example, Frank Rich's confession in his review of *Taxi Driver*: "My reaction to the movie has scared me as much as the movie itself, and I was afraid that if I tried to talk out my feelings, I'd reveal obscene, intimate details about my psyche that, before that night, I couldn't remember having thought before. . . . Snatches of the film—visual, musical, and verbal—play over and over again in my mind, and some nights *Taxi Driver* slips into my dreams and blasts open hidden, normally repressed crannies of my consciousness."[10] Rich, who was eventually to become the principal drama critic for the *New York Times,* wrote few such notices before his ascendancy; rarely does any movie critic accuse a film of blasting open repressed crannies of consciousness. But *Taxi Driver* had such an effect on many viewers—so many, in fact, that when the defense offered its final summary in the trial of John Hinckley, who shot President Reagan in 1981 because of his obsession with *Taxi Driver* and his unrequited love for Jodie Foster, it showed the jury *Taxi Driver*. Hinckley was found not guilty on grounds of insanity. Little did Martin Scorsese or Columbia Pictures know what they had wrought when they teamed up on *Taxi Driver*; they had indeed brought the war back home.

NOTES

Taxi Driver (1976). Screenplay, Paul Schrader; music, Bernard Herrmann; photography, Michael Chapman; director, Martin Scorsese. Cast: Robert De-Niro (Travis Bickle), Cybill Shepherd (Betsy), Jody Foster (Iris), Peter Boyle ("Wizard"), Albert Brooks (Tom), Leonard Harris (Charles Palantine), Harvey Keitel ("Sport").

1. As quoted in Guy Flatley, "Martin Scorsese's Gamble," *New York Times*, 8 Feb. 1976, 34.

2. Martin Scorsese, "Tapping the Intensity of the City: Creativity as a Natural Resource," *New York Times Magazine*, 9 Nov. 1986, 85.

3. Julian Smith, *Looking Away: Hollywood and Vietnam* (New York: Scribner's, 1975), 20.

4. Robert Phillip Kolker, *A Cinema of Loneliness* (New York: Oxford Univ. Press, 1988), 194.

5. David Thompson, ed., *Scorsese on Scorsese* (London: Faber and Faber, 1989), 62; hereafter cited in text.

6. Draft script, 29 April 1975, n.p.

7. Gregg Kilday, "Martin Scorsese: Virtuoso of Urban Angst," *Los Angeles Times*, 14 March 1976, calendar: 32.

8. Pauline Kael, *When the Lights Go Down* (New York: Holt, 1979), 135.

9. Colin Westerbeck, "Beauties and the Beast: *Seven Beauties* and *Taxi Driver*," *Sight and Sound*, Summer 1976, 137-38.

10. Frank Rich, "*Taxi Driver*," *New York Post*, 14 Feb. 1976, 16, 58.

11
LAWRENCE OF ARABIA, 1962, 1989
"It Looks *Damn* Good"
GENE D. PHILLIPS

David Lean's *Lawrence of Arabia* (1962), which chronicles the life of Thomas Edward Lawrence, the British officer who became a legendary leader of the Arab people during World War I, has won wide and continued public acceptance since its original release, when it garnered seven Academy Awards, including Best Picture and Best Director.

At the time of its premiere, in December 1962, *Lawrence of Arabia* ran 222 minutes. When the film went into nationwide release in 1963, producer Sam Spiegel had excised 20 minutes from it to allow for an additional showing each day. Further trims were also made when it was reissued in 1971. A quarter of a century after its initial release, film archivist Robert Harris got permission from Columbia to restore *Lawrence of Arabia* to its original length. He eventually recovered the missing footage from the studio vaults, and a restored version was released theatrically in 1989 to renewed critical and popular acclaim.

Lean decided to film the life of T.E. Lawrence when the screen rights to *The Seven Pillars of Wisdom* (1935), Lawrence's autobiographical account of his Middle East exploits during World War I, became available in the late 1950s. The rights were originally owned by Sir Alexander Korda, who died in 1956. When Lean acquired them, he assigned blacklisted screenwriter Michael Wilson, who had worked on Lean's previous film, *The Bridge on the River Kwai* (1957), to do a preliminary draft of *Lawrence of Arabia*, based on *The Seven Pillars of Wisdom*. Wilson worked on the project for more than a year before he was replaced by playwright Robert Bolt, who specialized in dramas (*A Man for All Seasons* [1960], *Vivat, Vivat Regina!* [1970]) focusing on a personal narrative played out against the background of epic historical events—just the sort of material at which Lean excelled, as *Kwai* had proved. Bolt retained the overall structure of Wilson's original draft as well as some of Wilson's scenes. Since the blacklist had prevented Wilson (and Carl Foreman) from receiving screenplay credit for *Kwai* as well as from receiving Oscars when their film won in the category of "screenplay based on material from another medium," Wilson would naturally be uncredited for his work on *Lawrence of Arabia*. But at least his contribution is now known.

Bolt hoped to clarify the Lawrence enigma by extensive background reading. "I found the authorities contradicted one another," he recalled; and so he returned to *The Seven Pillars of Wisdom* as his principal source, "even though it contains long passages of dubious veracity" in which Lawrence tends to romanticize his adventures in Arabia.[1]

The finished film begins with a prologue set in 1935 portraying Lawrence's death in a motorcycle crash on an English country road. This is followed by a scene of the impressive memorial service held shortly afterward in Lawrence's honor. With that, the film goes back to World War I, when Lawrence (Peter O'Toole) was a British intelligence officer stationed in Cairo, and then proceeds to dramatize Lawrence's life from that point on.

Lawrence manages to convince his superiors to let him seek out the Bedouin chief Prince Feisal (Alec Guinness) in the desert and help him unite the Arab tribes against their common enemy, the Turks, with whom the British are also at war. Lawrence becomes the charismatic leader of the Arabs, spurring them on to victory against the Turks; then he champions Arab nationalism in order to gain their political independence from the British after he discovers that his own countrymen are using the Arabs as pawns in their political maneuvers in the Middle East.

But Lawrence unfortunately turns out to be a man defeated by his own capacity for greatness. As the Arabs begin to treat him like a god, he becomes vain, egocentric, and erratic. The most brilliant scene in the film shows us how Lawrence has become mesmerized by the adulation of his Arab warriors. After he and his men have destroyed a Turkish train, Lawrence jumps atop one of the cars to accept the cheers of his men. As he stands there wearing the dazzling white robes of a Bedouin chief, he is suddenly stunned by a bullet that just misses wounding him critically. He looks down to see that a dying Turk is firing at him from the ground. An expression of amazement crosses Lawrence's face; he has been jolted into realizing that he is, after all, still a mortal and not the god his warriors believe him to be.

Lawrence comes to an even deeper realization of his limitations when he is captured by the Turkish bey (José Ferrer), a local official in Derea, a town occupied by the Turks. He is taken into custody while wandering incognito through the town on a scouting expedition. When Lawrence repels the bey's advances, the bey has him tortured. The experience is profoundly disillusioning for Lawrence, for it forces him to recognize not only the fundamental frailty of human flesh but also that he, like other men, has a breaking point. Indeed, he admits to an Arab friend afterward that, under torture, he would have told the enemy whatever it wanted to know. As Michael Anderegg writes, "Lawrence finally comes face to face with his simple mortality" and with what Lawrence himself terms his "ration of common humanity." [2]

Filled with self-doubt, Lawrence asks his superior, General Allenby (Jack Hawkins), to allow him to return to regular military service. But Allenby tells Lawrence his mission is too vital to the war effort, and sends him back to lead his Arabs once more.

Lawrence's subsequent attacks on the Turks become increasingly savage as he "resorts to barbaric violence after he loses faith in himself." [3] He participates in the senseless slaughter of a whole caravan of Turkish soldiers at Tafas, an attack that he launches with the cry of "No prisoners." Admittedly, these same Turks have themselves just destroyed a nearby Arab village; yet Lawrence realizes after the massacre of the soldiers that he is becoming as sadistic as the enemy.

Lawrence of Arabia is a masterpiece of understatement. Often feelings are only hinted at and words are left unarticulated in order to let the viewer gradually discover the full implications of the story as it unfolds. Characteristically, Lean has succeeded in compressing much of the meaning of a given scene into cinematic imagery, as he does in the scene just mentioned, in which Lawrence faces up to his own streak of sadism after the massacre at Tafas. As the scene develops, Lawrence stares fixedly at the knife which he has just used in the course of the slaughter. This image of Lawrence staring at his own reflection in the blade of his knife is meant to recall an earlier scene in which he did the same thing but under different circumstances. On that occasion Lawrence had just donned for the first time his chieftain's robes. Dressed in white, the traditional sign of purity and innocence, he admired his handsome reflection in his shiny new knife. Later, after the massacre, his once-spotless robes are caked with blood and dirt, an emblem of the way he has soiled his character by vile, savage deeds. Moreover, the visage he now stares at in his blood-smeared knife blade is no longer that of the heroic figure he had gazed upon before but that of the chieftain of a marauding band of desert thugs.

Besides coming to the realization of how ruthless he has become, Lawrence also sees that his attempts to form a Pan-Arabia are doomed to frustration by the factiousness of the Arab tribes and the continued meddling of the British in Arab affairs. He therefore decides once and for all to return to the ranks of the British army and go back to England, to live out the balance of his military life in obscurity. As he is driven to the airport, a truckload of British soldiers pass him on the road; none of them recognizes him, implying that Lawrence is already becoming a forgotten man. Lean underscores this point by cutting to a shot of Lawrence's face as seen through the dusty windshield of the car. His tarnished image has already begun to fade, for his moment of glory has passed.

Lawrence's tragedy lies in his being robbed of the dignity that might have accompanied an honorable defeat by the fatal flaws in his character that have been exposed by the crises he has faced. Lawrence, the would-be hero, is stubbornly determined to surmount staggering odds; but he is revealed in the process to be a self-deluded man who is as dedicated to his own self-esteem as to the principles he is championing.

Lean has never ceased to be concerned with the individual and his ability—or lack of it—to measure up to life's demands; Lawrence is a case in point. Yet Lean presents him throughout as a character who deserves our compassion, even though he is eccentric to the point of neurosis.

To make *Lawrence of Arabia,* Lean went on location to Jordan and Morocco, where he photographed the desert in striking images that vividly communicate to the viewer the experience of living in relentless heat. Lean's ability to immerse his audience in the environment of the story he is telling is epitomized in the breathtaking shot of the blazing sun slowly rising on the horizon over the rim of the desert, which stretches into the measureless reaches of space, dwarfing man and his petty pretensions by comparison.

Such awesome images need to be seen on the wide screen of a movie theater to be fully appreciated. More than one film critic mentioned this fact when reviewing the restored version of *Lawrence,* which was released in its original 70 mm format in 1989. The restoration of *Lawrence* to its original length was no easy task for Robert Harris, who supervised the undertaking, aided by Lean and by editor Anne V. Coates, who also won an Oscar for the film. Harris had to sift through more than two tons of film cans to piece together the missing footage from various prints, some of them imported from Europe.

"Most of the additions are transitional passages or establishing shots, rather than new scenes," notes Janet Maslin, "more like clauses in a sentence than whole sentences." [4] For example, some transitional footage has been restored at the end of the motorcycle sequence and at the beginning of the following scene, the memorial service for Lawrence, and this material provides an excellent example of Lean's acute visual sense. The fateful death scene concludes with a restored close-up of the goggles Lawrence was wearing when he crashed; they are seen dangling from the branch of a tree. This shot is succeeded by a restored close-up of Lawrence's bust in the crypt of St.

Paul's Cathedral in London. Then the camera pulls back to show two of the mourners attending the ceremonies as they discuss whether or not Lawrence really deserves all of the pomp and circumstance that have surrounded his passing. By juxtaposing Lawrence's death with the memorial that followed it, Lean ironically contrasts the inglorious demise of a forgotten war veteran on a back country lane with the "instant immortality" conferred upon him by the elaborate service, along with the heroic bust so prominently on display.

Admittedly, none of the segments Harris has reinstated are particularly significant in themselves; but each contributes additional details that help fill out Lawrence's portrait. For example, in its depiction of the aftermath of the massacre of an Arab village by Turkish soldiers, already mentioned, the film now lingers at greater length on shots of the victims, with Arab women and children clearly visible among the dead. Lawrence is appalled at the sight of these innocent victims, left behind to rot by the Turkish soldiers who can still be seen marching away into the distance; this restored footage helps explain, if not excuse, Lawrence's slaughter of that same Turkish regiment.

By the same token, Janet Maslin adds that "the torture scene, though essentially the same, now includes outdoor reaction shots of Lawrence's friend Ali (Omar Sharif) that indicate that the episode lasted from morning until night."[5] The indication of the prolonged duration of Lawrence's torture by the Turkish bey's men further explains why the experience had such a lasting effect on Lawrence, psychologically as well as physically.

Despite the additional nuances and clarifications that surface in the restored version, the fact remains that it was never the intention of Lean and his collaborators to explain away all of the ambiguities surrounding the enigmatic T.E. Lawrence. Various commentators on Lawrence's life, for example, have suggested that he was a repressed homosexual, but the film does not attempt to settle this debate. For one thing, censorship restrictions in the 1960s were tougher than later on and would not have permitted a director to be very frank in dealing with homosexuality. Lean does show Lawrence taking under his wing two desert urchins who become his constant companions, but the director does not exploit the homosexual implications of this situation. In fact, as Roger Ebert observes, apropos of Lawrence's relationship with the two youngsters, "none of the other characters in the movie seem to notice."[6]

Lean's fellow English director Carol Reed once told me that he likewise soft-pedaled the notion that Michelangelo may have been homosexual in his film about the artist, *The Agony and the Ecstasy* (1965), because there was nothing conclusive about this in any of the sources. "I didn't think that it was right to write into the screenplay something that historians themselves weren't sure about," he explained. Lean may well have felt the same way about his film on Lawrence. As a matter of fact, both Lawrence's autobiography and the volume of his collected letters are inconclusive on this point; so there seems to be no reason why the movie should have sought to resolve this controversy.

Furthermore, Michael Wilson stated in an early synopsis of the screenplay that the possibility that Lawrence was homosexual should not be "placed at the center of the riddle" of Lawrence's personality. Accordingly, with reference to the torture sequence, he said that there was "little to be gained from dramatizing the notion that Lawrence finally succumbs to the bey's advances," as some commentators on Lawrence's life have contended. "This does not mean," Wilson concluded, "that we should omit any suggestion of the bey's homosexuality."[7] Wilson's approach to the torture scene was followed in the final shooting script, as is apparent from the above discussion.

Another disputed point Lean's film does not seek to settle is whether or not Lawrence's death was a suicide, born of the discouragement and depression that marked his later years. Certainly Lean's depiction of Lawrence's death at the beginning of the film suggests that perhaps it was not entirely accidental. There is a curious smile on Lawrence's face as he recklessly careens along a country road, gathering speed all the while. When he swerves to avoid hitting someone coming down the road in the opposite direction, he inevitably loses control of the cycle and crashes into a ditch. As Anderegg notes, Lawrence comes across in this scene as "brave but foolhardy; a thrill-seeker who seems to invite disaster," someone possessed of self-sacrificial bravado.[8] In short, Lawrence, to some degree at least, may have been unconsciously courting death at the time it overtook him. And so, in death as in life, the man and his motives remain ambiguous. But that is as it should be; for in the last analysis, *Lawrence of Arabia* endures as a thought-provoking motion picture precisely because the central figure continues to be something of a mystery to the end.

When Lean took a look at the restored print of his film, he decided to snip out a few frames here and there that he thought slowed down the pace; by doing so he brought the running time to 217 minutes, slightly under the original 222 minutes. Lean explained that, since he was an editor before he became a director, he has always been ruthless in spying out superfluous footage in his films. In fact, when he trimmed one particular shot from *Lawrence*, Harris begged him to leave it in. "David," he pleaded, "that's such a gorgeous shot; how can you cut it?" Lean responded, "This movie is *full* of gorgeous shots. One less won't ruin it." After finally viewing the finished print of the restored *Lawrence*, Lean remarked in his laconic fashion, "I must say, it looks *damn* good!"

When one considers the positive public response to many of Lean's movies, underscored by the successful theatrical rerelease of *Lawrence* some twenty-five years after its premiere, it is evident that few directors have commanded such a large portion of the mass audience. Indeed, Lean seems to have possessed a sixth sense that over the years enabled him to guess what the public would like. In the case of *Lawrence* he had the foresight to gamble $15 million on a project that at the outset seemed at best unpromising. "It was a very expensive film," Omar Sharif observed recently, "with no love story, no action really, if you come to think of it—no great battles—just a lot of Arabs going around the desert on camels." Moreover, the actor playing the title role was not yet an established star, "and the leading character was an anti-hero"; hence, Sharif concludes, he would never have guessed, while making the film, that it would be such an enduring success.[9]

Referring to the popularity of his films, Lean has said that if movies like *Lawrence* have pleased a lot of people, presumably it means that he is something of a common denominator. Like the average filmgoer, Lean explained, "I like a good strong story. I like a beginning, a middle, and an end." He went on to say, "I like to be excited when I go to the movies. I like to be touched. And I like a good yarn, I suppose." Commenting on Lean's words, William Bayer, in his essay on *Lawrence*, notes, "No amount of critical analysis will sum up the aesthetic of David Lean better than that quotation. Lean does not merely pay lip service to well-constructed, exciting stories. He makes them." His greatest achievement, in a career that has included *Great Expectations* (1946) and *The Bridge on the River Kwai*, says Bayer, is unquestionably *Lawrence of Arabia*, "one of the most exciting adventure stories ever to fill a screen."[10]

Elsewhere Lean has said of himself, "I'm a picture chap. I like pictures, and when I go to the movies I go to see pictures. I think dialogue is nearly always secondary in a movie. It's awfully hard, when you look back over the really great movies that you see in your life, to remember a line of dialogue. You will not forget the pictures." One movie for which Lean's statement certainly holds true is *Lawrence of Arabia*.

Peter O'Toole recalls in Stephen Silverman's book on Lean that, on the first day of shooting, Lean turned to him and said, "Pete, this could be the start of a great adventure." Reminded of this remark in 1989, Lean commented, "And it was."[11]

NOTES

Lawrence of Arabia (1962). Producer, Sam Spiegel; director, David Lean; screenplay by Robert Bolt; cinematography by E.A. Young; music by Maurice

Jarre. Cast: Peter O'Toole (Lawrence), Alec Guinness (Prince Feisal), Anthony Quinn (Auda Abu Tayi), Jack Hawkins (General Allenby), José Ferrer (Turkish Bey), Anthony Quayle (Colonel Brighton), Claude Rains (Mr. Dryden), Arthur Kennedy (Jackson Bentley), Donald Wolfit (General Murray), Omar Sharif (Sherif Áli Ibn el Kharish).

1. Ivan Butler, *The Making of Feature Films: A Guide* (Baltimore: Penguin, 1971), 40-41.

2. Michael Anderegg, *David Lean* (Boston: Twayne, 1984), 112.

3. Michael Sragow, "David Lean's Right of 'Passage,'" *Film Comment* 21 (Jan.-Feb. 1985): 25.

4. Janet Maslin, "*Lawrence* Seen Whole," *New York Times*, 29 Jan. 1989, sec. 2: 13. See also Roy Frumkes, "The Restoration of *Lawrence of Arabia*," *Films in Review* 40 (April 1989): 204-10, and 40 (May 1989): 285-91.

5. Maslin, "*Lawrence* Seen Whole," 13.

6. Roger Ebert, "*Lawrence* Remains a Visionary Epic," *Chicago Sun-Times*, 17 March 1989, sec. 2: 37.

7. Wilson's remarks are given in Vito Russo, *The Celluloid Closet: Homosexuality in the Movies*, rev. ed. (New York: Harper, Row, 1987), 133-34.

8. Anderegg, *David Lean*, 117.

9. Allen Barra, "At Long Last, the Real Lawrence," *American Film* 14 (March 1989): 44; Frumkes, "Restoration," 287.

10. Gerald Pratley, "Interview with David Lean," in Andrew Sarris, ed., *Interviews with Film Directors* (New York: Avon, 1969), 321; William Bayer, "*Lawrence of Arabia*," in *The Great Movies* (New York: Grosset and Dunlap, 1973), 137.

11. Harlan Kennedy, " 'I'm a Picture Chap,'" *Film Comment* 21 (Jan.-Feb. 1985): 28; Stephen M. Silverman, *David Lean* (New York: Abrams, 1989), 138.

12

A SOLDIER'S STORY
A Paradigm for Justice
JIM WELSH

A Soldier's Story (1984) must be considered a breakthrough film for Columbia and Hollywood in general. It told a story about black soldiers and utilized a predominantly black cast at a time when no such pictures were being made. It preceded *The Color Purple* (1985) and the later films of Spike Lee. At the end of the decade it was followed by *Glory* (1989). Not only was *A Soldier's Story* "the first serious drama about American blacks released by Hollywood in close to a decade"; it also helped establish "media visibility" for blacks in the 1980s in both film and television.[1] Although nominated for Best Picture, *A Soldier's Story* lost to *Amadeus* (1984). Still it is noteworthy that the film earned the Academy nomination and that one of director Norman Jewison's earlier movies, *In the Heat of the Night* (1967), was the "only problem film about racial discrimination against blacks to have won Best Picture" to that time.[2] If any director could make *A Soldier's Story* successfully, it was Norman Jewison. It was also appropriate that the black playwright Charles Fuller was chosen to adapt his 1981 Pulitzer Prize–winning drama *A Soldier's Play* for the screen.

The setting of both play and movie is a Louisiana army base in 1944. A black soldier, Master Sergeant Vernon C. Waters (Adolph Caesar), has been murdered. The general assumption is that his death was racially motivated—probably a Klan execution. Because of the tension between the base and the civilian community, Colonel Nivens (Trey Wilson) has not ordered a full investigation. When Captain Richard Davenport (Howard E. Rollins, Jr.) is sent to conduct one, Nivens cannot believe he will be impartial. For one thing, Davenport is black, and Nivens is convinced the killers are white.

As it happens, Davenport is both impartial and thorough: he discovers that the men feared and despised Waters, who had driven one of them, C.J. Memphis (Larry Riley), to suicide after having him imprisoned on a trumped-up charge. It gradually dawns on Davenport that Waters may have been murdered by his own men. But Davenport knows that justice, not race, is the issue and is determined to solve the crime. The solution gives the impression that justice has been done, even though Fuller makes clear in a flashforward at the end of *A Soldier's Play* that the entire all-black 221st Smoke Generating Unit's "C" Company is doomed. As Davenport explains in the play's final monologue, "The entire outfit—officers and enlisted men—was wiped out in the Ruhr Valley during a German advance."[3] At the end of *A Soldier's Play* the mystery has been solved, justice done, and the black company sent abroad to die—an ironic triumph for race relations. *A Soldier's Story*, as we shall see, concludes differently.

A Soldier's Story was the first project Jewison completed in what was to have been a seven-picture contract with Columbia. In the 1960s he had planned to film William Styron's *The Confessions of Nat Turner* (1966) but "was discouraged by blacks who found fault with the white novelist's approach."[4] Understandably, Jewison would be attracted to Fuller's play which, like Styron's novel, was a Pulitzer Prize winner dealing with black themes. Jewison worked with Fuller in bringing *A Soldier's Play* to the screen, retaining and refining the flashback structure and opening up the work to achieve a richer evocation of time and place. Fuller originally wanted "to put blacks and whites on stage as people" and not "do just the usual black and white confrontation piece."[5] He achieved his aim in the screenplay as well. Similarly, the justice theme was transferred to the film version, which depicted for a mass audience the role of black soldiers and officers in the armed forces—hardly a familiar subject in the movies.

During the Civil War black soldiers served in the liberating Union army as it invaded the South, particularly after the Emancipation Proclamation of 1 January 1863. On 26 January, Secretary of War Stanton granted permission to Governor John Andrew of Massachusetts to establish a black volunteer regiment with white commissioned officers, the 54th Massachusetts Infantry under the command of Colonel Robert Gould Shaw, a Boston abolitionist, who, with recruiting assistance from Frederick Douglass, had trained 1,000 combat-ready soldiers by 28 May 1863.[6] Additional black regiments were later raised by other northern states, and by 22 May a Bureau of Colored Troops had been established within the War Department for the further recruitment of black regiments.

Meanwhile, the 54th Massachusetts Regiment fought the Confederate army with valor and distinction at Fort Wagner on Morris Island, near Charleston, South Carolina, on 18 July 1863. Colonel Shaw led the attack and was one of the 247 killed.[7]

Such examples of bravery and sacrifice under fire during the Civil War, though recognized by Union leaders, could not counteract a tradition of racism, prejudice, and discrimination as the battle for civil rights was waged into the next century. At the time World War I was being fought, Secretary of War Baker gave assurances that the army "would be free of racial discrimination and that black soldiers would be justly treated," but in actuality "blacks confronted gross prejudice and discrimination at every stage."[8] One such example is remembered by Vernon Waters in Fuller's play.

The situation did not begin to improve until World War II; by January 1940 "there were only five Negro officers in the Regular Army."[9] During World War II there were documented incidents of black soldiers' being victimized by racism in the South. For example, Ned Turman, a black soldier, was shot and killed by a military policeman at Fort Bragg, North Carolina, and was eulogized in a ballad published in the Pittsburgh *Courier*, 31 January 1942: "They say this is a war / For Freedom Over There. / Say, Mr. F.D.R. / How 'bout some Freedom Here? / 'Twas a Fort Bragg M.P. shot him down / One evening when he was leaving town."[10] And there is the reverse racist side of the situation dramatized by Fuller; Waters, repelled by blacks who behave like ethnic stereotypes, thinks like a white racist and is murdered by his own people. It was not at all uncommon for black soldiers on leave to be shot and killed by white police, military or civilian, in the South. The War Department had a policy of white supremacy and racial separatism while waging war against "an enemy dedicated to conquering the world in the name of racist ideology," an absurdity that did not go unnoticed in the black community.[11] One of the blues songs C.J. Memphis sings in *A Soldier's Story* makes a parallel point: "Well, it's a low down dirty shame. / They say we fightin' Hitler, / But they won't let us in the game. / Lord, left home to join this army; / Won't somebody tell me who's to blame?" Such treatment caused a morale problem for black soldiers, a fact that is entirely glossed over by the final sequences of *A Soldier's Story* as the exuberant black troops go happily marching off to war. The play's conclusion is not nearly so upbeat as the film's, but otherwise *A Soldier's Play* has been carefully adapted to the screen.

The design of the play is abstract and theatrical; the film opens up the play and carefully modulates time between present (Davenport's investigation) and past (as witnesses reconstruct the events leading to the murder). The overture-like credits sequence takes the viewer to locales that could not have been represented on stage. The film opens, for example, in a black nightclub, Big Mary's, with Patti LaBelle singing a jazz-blues number while the opening credits roll, establishing time and place and signaling to the audience that the film will be mainly about black Americans in the deep South; it also establishes the character of Waters, who was drinking heavily the night he was killed.

Although the viewer first sees Waters as a pathetic drunk, the witnesses Davenport interrogates do not. To Wilkie (Art Evans), for example, Waters was "all spit and polish." But the Waters who stumbles out of the bar in the credits sequence has lost all sense of dignity and self-respect, blaming himself—and rightly—for C.J.'s death. As the credits sequence concludes, we hear the line that opens the play ("They still hate you!") and witness the murder—but not the murderer. The visual style is mainly realistic except for the killing: a montage shows the weapon in close-up and Waters falling backward in slow motion, as the sound of the shot is extended and distorted. Jewison then cuts to the barracks to introduce the other soldiers and the white officer, Captain Taylor (Dennis Lipscomb).

In contrast to the barracks world stands the redneck microcosm that greets Davenport on his arrival. Sleeping in the back of a segregated bus, Davenport is awakened by a white driver who addresses him as "boy"—hardly appropriate for one of Davenport's education and rank. When Davenport gets off the bus, the rednecks crane and gawk, obviously unaccustomed to black officers. As the bus pulls away, the frame is dominated by a blue bench bearing a "For Whites Only" inscription in white letters.

Initially race even affects the relationship between Davenport and Taylor, his white counterpart, who fears the investigation will lead to racial unrest. "People around here have never seen a black officer. Come to think of it, I never saw a black until I was twelve or thirteen years old," Taylor muses. Later, Taylor's decency is revealed as he and Davenport gradually gain respect for each other as coequals in an integrated army. At least that is the illusion the film creates. In fact, however, more than a decade would pass before the goal of black integration would be achieved. By October 1953, 95 percent of the black troops were integrated,[12] and by the end of 1954 "segregation had been officially eliminated from the internal structure of the active military forces."[13] Hence integration was not to be accomplished until the end of the Korean War. In the play, Peterson tells C.J., "White folks'll neva' integrate no army." The more optimistic C.J. believes integration will come about, and he is right.

Thereafter, the film generally follows the play, dramatizing past action by the use of conventional flashbacks as the soldiers give their accounts. Hence the play's major themes—racism, identity, and justice—are scrupulously maintained: justice as it relates to the investigation, and racial justice as it applies to the black troops, who, as co-equals, must bear the consequences of their conduct.

The play's thesis is more implied than stated, though C.J. Memphis, the strapping ballplayer and guitar-picker (combining two of the stereotypes for blacks as athletes and musicians), defends Waters to

Peterson, the man who eventually murders him: "Callin' names ain't nothing, I know what I is. Sarge ain't so bad—been good to me . . . plus I feel kinda sorry for him myself. Any man ain't sure where he belongs must be in a whole lotta pain." [14]

C.J. is perceptive, despite his country-boy handkerchief-head persona. Waters has misread black history and chooses to imitate the white man, turning his back on his own culture and heritage. C.J. is a potent reminder of what he has rejected. It appears that Waters had Wilkie frame C.J. so Waters could throw him in the brig to teach him a lesson. What Waters does not realize is that, although C.J. is physically strong, he is psychologically weak. After C.J.'s suicide, Waters feels responsible, and his guilt drives him to drink; hence his drunken state during the credits sequence. C.J. has caused Waters to lose his self-respect (artificially created because of his racial confusion) and his dignity.

Adolph Caesar, who played Waters on stage and in the film, explains his character as follows: "Part of the problem that we faced as black people is that historically we believed that we could not move forward unless we became like white people. What I wanted to convey in *A Soldier's Story* was that it doesn't have to be so. We will move forward if we have something to contribute. *A Soldier's Story* is as much about black people's misunderstanding of history as it is about racism in the '40's." [15]

So is *A Soldier's Play*, which works an effective contrast between Waters, who has rejected his identity, and Davenport, an emblem of black pride who goes about his unrelenting quest for truth and justice. Davenport has "something to contribute."

The Davenport/Waters contrast, then, establishes two responses to the dilemma of being black in America. The Davenport/Taylor contrast shows how white America can both accept and respect black Americans for what they can contribute. The Waters/Peterson contrast sets up still another duality that is explained far better in the film than in the play. Peterson hates and resents Waters, but Waters respects Peterson for his spunk and spirit after they fight and Waters demolishes him. Although Peterson does not know it, Waters plans to recommend him for promotion. What Fuller suggests is that the two men have a great deal in common. This commonality is emphasized by the expanded action of the screenplay in a way not evident in the original.

Fuller's play is structured around a series of interviews that tell the story and define Waters's character in flashback. The play is not a conventional murder mystery, since in this instance it is more important to learn about the victim than to discover the murderer's identity. Nonetheless the mystery is solved by Davenport's interrogation of Private Smalls, followed by a monologue in which Davenport explains that Peterson was captured "a week later in Alabama." The staging makes it impossible for both Smalls and Peterson to be present on stage in the same time-frame. The stage is divided into three playing areas, one representing the barracks, another an office and the interrogation room; Fuller describes the third as "limbo," a place where past action can be conveniently dramatized. Aside from opening up the action, the film follows the play faithfully until the climax, which is redesigned to good effect.

In the play, while Davenport extracts the confession from Smalls in the office, Peterson reenacts the murder of Waters in the "limbo" area. Since film can easily handle parallel action, both Smalls and Peterson can be brought into the present time-frame; first Smalls, the weaker of the two, then Peterson after Smalls has confessed. The film dramatizes Smalls's attempt to escape on a freight train, which he barely misses in the rain. Then the film speeds up the capture of Peterson to effect a final confrontation between Davenport and Peterson immediately after Smalls has been apprehended and questioned. In the film Peterson confesses by saying, "I didn't kill much." This confrontation not only enhances the drama but allows Davenport to clarify the message for the mass audience. Belligerent to the end, Peterson defends himself by saying he killed Waters "for justice, for C.J., for everybody." Enraged by such arrogance, Davenport responds: "Who gave you the right to judge, to decide who is fit to be a Negro and who is not?"

What the film makes clear is that this was also Waters's mistake, his fatal flaw. Waters had passed the same kind of judgment on C.J., causing his suicide. Thus the film leaves no doubt that Waters and Peterson have a great deal in common. Waters paid for his mistake. In a just world, Peterson also will pay.

The film effectively dramatizes and explains Waters's frame of reference through a conversation with Wilkie at Big Mary's bar while C.J. is playing the guitar and singing in the background. Waters explains that he is offended by what he thinks C.J. represents, an ignorant country black who subordinates himself entirely to white authority. Waters is embarrassed by C.J., as he makes clear to Wilkie by telling him about an incident in France during World War I:

> Do you know the damage one ignorant Negro can do? We were in France during the First War, Wilkie. We had won decorations, but the white boys had told all the French gals we had tails. And they found this ignorant colored soldier. Paid him to tie a tail to his ass and parade around naked making monkey sounds. They sat him on a big round table in the Café Napoleon, put a reed in his hand, a crown on his head, a blanket on his shoulders, and made him eat bananas in front of them Frenchies . . . called him Moon-

shine, King of the Monkeys. And when we slit his throat, you know that fool asked us what he had done wrong?[16]

As Waters delivers this key speech from the play, the camera moves in to capture his face in close-up, then pulls out to a two-shot revealing Wilkie's horrified response reflected in the mirror behind the bar. Given this confession, there is justice in Waters's execution, since he himself was implicated in this murder; but Peterson has no information about the confession, nor does he have the right to take the law into his own hands and act as executioner. Peterson murders Waters out of spite, malice, and revenge.

Waters believes in the goal of racial equality and hopes to attain in the Second World War what he was unable to attain in the First: "The First War didn't change nothin' for the Negro, but this one is going to change everything," Waters tells C.J. after C.J. has been framed by Wilkie and imprisoned. Waters cynically considers C.J. "one less fool for the race to be ashamed of." But what Peterson does to Waters is no different from what Waters had done to Moonshine. Although Waters feels no regret about Moonshine's murder, C.J.'s suicide troubles his conscience, which gives Waters a tragic potential Peterson lacks.

The action of A Soldier's Story operates in two spheres, past and present. The present is a mystery in the contemporary sense in that dramatic interest is sustained by the process of investigation and detection. The past, on the other hand, represents a fully developed subplot employing most of the characters of the framing present; the present represents a play-within-a-play, the nature of which is tragic. Waters is the tragic protagonist who, acting on principle and (he thinks) for the best, makes an error in judgment (motivated by racial pride) in his treatment of C.J., whom he presumes to reform and improve by punishment.

Waters miscalculates, however. C.J. is not so strong as he seems and cracks under confinement, failing to understand Waters's motives. The punishment drives him to suicide which, in turn, works destructively on Waters's conscience, transforming a once proud leader into a drunken derelict. Waters reaches a point of recognition and discovery at exactly the time he is murdered. He seems to understand the fallacy of his success formula, grasping what should have been obvious all along—that it is difficult, if not impossible, for a black man to play by the rules of the white power structure and still achieve his goals. This discovery forms the context of his dying words, "They still hate you!"

Waters, then, makes an error in judgment that brings about another's death. Because he is potentially a man of conscience, he suffers for his mistake. His values are shaken and destroyed; his final punishment is death. There is a brute sense of justice that is satisfied by

Waters's death, but his murderer has made the same presumptuous mistake by taking the law into his hands. The present also has tragic potential since Waters and Peterson are parallel figures sharing the same flaw. The film's restructuring of the events completes the tragic cycle by making the present action more clearly Peterson's tragedy. Davenport, the agent of justice, is devastated after having done his duty. He is left in a reflective pose beside a rain-streaked window after Smalls and Peterson have been taken away. The rain coursing down the window is reflected on his face; then, almost imperceptibly, a tear runs down his cheek. Davenport weeps for Peterson. Thus the film not only captures but also enhances the play's tragic potential.

The play is deceptive. Although it seems to be a murder mystery, it is a tragedy in disguise. By the end the solving of the mystery seems secondary. The issue of black identity is central; understanding it requires the spectator to examine the victim's identity as well as the murderer's. And in the course of investigating the case, Davenport is forced to come to grips with his own identity and then assert it in the service of justice.

Davenport, however, knows who he is. Convinced of his ability and worth, he is able to stand up to the white supremacist Nivens, who dismisses Waters's death as "just another black mess of cuttin', slashin' and shootin.'" Davenport manages, as well, to win the respect of Taylor, who also reveals racist tendencies ("being in charge just doesn't look right on Negroes"). Taylor is at least openminded and, ultimately, fair.

Peterson, the murderer, hates Waters for his honky pretensions, even though he is no better than Waters in his presumption. Peterson has the courage to challenge Waters by asking, "What kinda colored man are you?" Waters humiliates Peterson by beating him man to man, but he secretly admires Peterson's "spunk." Waters rightly senses a kinship with Peterson but fails to understand the depth of his hatred. Peterson, on the other hand, cannot get beyond his own hatred of Waters and what Waters represents—a selling out to the dominant race by attempting to take on its values.

While *A Soldier's Story* is, for the most part, faithful to the original, it betrays the play's tone by omitting Davenport's concluding speech and ending on a note of optimism as the black troops are sent to the European theatre. The ending of *A Soldier's Play* offers a different message about racial justice. Waters is mistakenly regarded as a war hero when his remains are sent home, and none of the others survive combat. C.J.'s significance is reduced and trivialized as his name is attached to "a style of guitar pickin' and a dance called the C.J." The play's conclusion is bitterly ironic, suggesting a world in which justice is haphazard and certainly not total. The film, by contrast, offers images that suggest unity and equality. The justice Davenport achieves becomes emblematic for the race.

The film's conclusion might be faulted as a triumph of wish-fulfillment, but the goal of an integrated army was surely to come; moreover, it is difficult to fault the way the film restructures the play and clarifies its discourse. The major themes of the play are impressively orchestrated. Even Herbie Hancock's musical score suggests the theme of integration. The opening music is thoroughly black—the jazz-blues at Big Mary's. Midway through the film C.J. plays country blues on his guitar. The final music is white parade music that gives way to a big band rendering of "St. Louis Blues," played with a marching beat that suggests the sound of the Glenn Miller Orchestra—black music integrated into a style in keeping with the period and the military setting, black music transformed into mainstream American music in which the black influence is still dominant.

A Soldier's Story opened to generally favorable reviews, despite the opinion of one journalist that it "doesn't have any particular application to racism,"[17] a charge refutable by internal evidence. Nivens clearly represents the white supremacist conditioning of the Deep South, as does Lieutenant Byrd, who brutalizes the drunken and defenseless Waters. Byrd is also offended and hostile when he is later ordered to cooperate with Davenport's investigation. Moreover, both Waters and Peterson are obviously spokesmen for interracial prejudice and inverted racism. Though ultimately the theme of racism may be secondary to that of justice, it is still important.

Budgeted at a mere $5 million (half the average in 1984) and finally costing around $6 million, *A Soldier's Story* earned $30 million for Columbia, becoming the studio's third highest moneymaker that year.[18] The film, which was carefully marketed to liberal audiences in urban areas, went on to capture three Oscar nominations: Best Adapted Screenplay, Best Supporting Actor (Adolph Caesar), and Best Picture. It was a true crossover success, appealing to both white and black audiences because, as Columbia's marketing head, Ashley Boone, noted, it was "a good movie and good movies make money."[19] More important, *A Soldier's Story* marked the beginning of a renascence of black films in the 1980s; it is also an outstanding example of film adaptation.

NOTES

A Soldier's Story. Director, Norman Jewison; screenplay by Charles Fuller, based on his play *A Soldier's Play;* cinematography, Russell Boyd; music, Herbie Hancock. Cast: Howard E. Rollins, Jr. (Captain Davenport), Adolph Caesar

(Sergeant Waters), Art Evans (Private Wilkie), David Alan Grier (Corporal Cobb), David Harris (Private Smalls), Dennis Lipscomb (Captain Taylor), Larry Riley (C.J. Memphis), Robert Townsend (Corporal Ellis), Denzel Washington (Private First Class Peterson), Patti LaBelle (Big Mary), Wings Hauser (Lieutenant Byrd), Scott Paulin (Captain Wilcox), John Hancock (Sergeant Washington), Trey Wilson (Colonel Nivens).

1. Carol Cooper, " 'Soldier's Story' Salute," *Film Comment* 20 (Nov.-Dec. 1984): 17.

2. Emanuel Levy, *And the Winner Is . . . The History and Politics of the Oscar Awards* (New York: Ungar, 1987), 131.

3. Charles Fuller, *A Soldier's Play*, in *The Bedford Introduction to Literature*, ed. Michael Meyer (New York: St. Martin's, 1987), 1622. All further citations are from this edition.

4. Cooper, " 'Soldier's Story' Salute," 17.

5. *Contemporary Authors*, 108: 168.

6. Jack D. Foner, *Blacks and the Military in American History: A New Perspective* (New York: Praeger, 1974), 37.

7. The story of this black regiment was told in Tri-Star's *Glory* (1989).

8. Foner, *Blacks and the Military*, 111.

9. Richard M. Dalfiume, *Desegregation of the U.S. Armed Forces* (Columbia: Univ. of Missouri Press, 1969), 64.

10. Quoted in ibid., 73-74.

11. Ibid., 74-75.

12. Ibid., 218-19.

13. Foner, *Blacks and the Military*, 194.

14. Fuller, *A Soldier's Play*, 1600.

15. Quoted from the Columbia Pictures press kit.

16. Fuller, *A Soldier's Play*, 1618.

17. Francis Wheen, "Done to Death," *New Statesman*, 15 March 1985, 35.

18. Brent Staples, " 'Soldier's' Success," *New York Times*, 8 Jan. 1989, Sec. 2: 13.

19. As quoted by David Ansen and David Friendly, "A Revival of Black Movies?" *Newsweek*, 7 Jan. 1985, 50.

13

THE LAST EMPEROR
A Subject-in-the-Making
JANICE MOUTON

Pu Yi, the emperor who was not an emperor, the Chinese ruler who was not Chinese, the subject as yet unconstituted as a subject—this Pu Yi now appears in Bernardo Bertolucci's *The Last Emperor*, searching for the past, searching for the Self.

What kind of undertaking is this? Does a search for a past and a Self imply that such things are there to be found? Isn't history just "in our minds" or "what we think happened?"[1] As for the Self, does it even belong to the order of being? Isn't it, rather, something about which we say, "that's not it" and "that's still not it"?[2] Perhaps we should say instead that the issue here is the process of creating a past, of creating a Self (history-in-the-making, subject-in-the-making). Or can this intense and unsettling process be an end in itself? "Know thyself" gives way to the responsibility to engage in an unending "Search for thyself." Bertolucci has never been daunted by the demands of such a search. Taking risks and following his own obsessed vision have marked his work from the beginning, and *The Last Emperor* is no exception.

In this film, however, the subject of the search is no longer Italian; the context is no longer European. In assuming the position of the Westerner gazing Eastward, of the European viewing the Other, we (director and spectator) join a long and troubled "Orientalist" tradition: "You know it, don't you, who have directly or indirectly written accounts of *The Nature of the Non-Western World*, *How Natives Think*, and *The 'Soul' of the Primitive*. Of *The Savage Mind* and *The Sexual Life of Savages*. Of *Primitive Mentality* and *The Making of Religion*. Then, of 'Asian Westernism' and 'African Philosophies.' Striving for the Other's mind and redefining the intangible is 'human.' You can no doubt capture, tame, and appropriate it to yourself, for language as a form of knowing will always provide you with Your other."[3]

Side by side with Western anthropologists, sociologists, and historians stand Western artists—busily creating an Orient as "a place of romance, exotic beings, haunting memories and landscapes, remarkable experiences."[4] That these representations rely very little on an Orient of empirical reality becomes obvious upon a moment's reflection. (Consider Puccini's *Madama Butterfly* and Delibes's *Lakmé*; remember Cary Grant in *Gunga Din* [1939] and Yul Brynner in *The King and I*; [1956] and, lest one assume that "things are getting better," think of Steven Spielberg's *Empire of the Sun* [1987]). Quite simply the Orient has served the West as a deep and recurring image of the Other. As "contrasting image, idea, personality, and experience,"[5] this Orient, although fashioned by our own imaginative creation, has helped us define ourselves. It emerged according to a "logic" governed by "a battery of desires, repressions, investments, and projections."[6]

How might this be otherwise? Must the fact that we are exterior to the Oriental world prevent us from ever looking in that direction or doom us to perpetual silence on that subject? Is there no means by which we can question our representations of the Other? No way to deconstruct the voyeur/object relationship? Is it not possible to affirm difference without reenacting the old patterns of dominance and submission? This is a challenge that cannot be ignored; these are questions that demand positive answers. In *The Last Emperor* we have an example of a filmmaker who meets the challenge, carrying out his work on the project in conjunction with the equally important task of exploring the processes of personal and socio/historical subject formation.[7]

Bertolucci has said, "Every new film I make is affected by a sort of decree ordering me to change, by a fear of repetition that forces itself on me."[8] And while we are far from the Italian landscape and the specter of Italian fascism as we saw it in *The Spider's Stratagem* (1970), *The Conformist* (1971), and *1900* (1977), far from Italian opera as we heard it in *Before the Revolution* (1964) and *Luna* (1979), we do nonetheless recognize familiar markers of the filmmaker's work: again he explores the absent father/surrogate father construct; again he works on the project of rethinking historical meanings and reexamining historical consciousness; again he engages in the loss-of-Self/realization-of-Self dynamic in connection with identification with and separation from the Mother. And yet again he uses the flashback structure to give form to his work—a structure which, together with the musical patternings, functions to create an overall film rhythm, complemented by the color modulations, the interplay of visual and sonic motifs, and the back-and-forth of the narrating voices.

Already a master of the flashback, in *The Last Emperor* Bertolucci reinvents the structure in such a way as to create a new kind of film story: a multi-vocal story, the life story of Pu Yi as seen, spoken, written, and filmed by many different storytellers. He himself refuses to speak *for* or *about* his subjects: rather he gives them the voice. At the same time, however, conscious of the inevitable superimposition of the filmmaker-self on the filmed other, Bertolucci acknowledges his own presence, particularly through the intricate, self-conscious flashback structuring, but also through the use of film-within-the-film, titles, the presence of filmmakers/picturetakers, and the inclusion of quotes from earlier films.[10]

Although most of Pu Yi's years are represented in the film, what the spectator is faced with here is everything other than a straight chronological rendering of time as so often is the case in films dealing with historical topics. Bertolucci opens with a shot that immediately focalizes the subject: Pu Yi (John Lone) regards his likeness in a mirror and sees the other-self as non-self. As he slashes his wrists in the next shot he attempts to obliterate his actual, physical self, to join that mirror image in the realm of the non-living. This attempt is thwarted by the intervention of the prison governor, Jin Yuan (Ying Ruocheng), as he calls out the first of a refrain-like series of "Open the door[s]." He brings Pu Yi back from being nothing to *being*, one of many steps on a very long path whose final realization of being is "model citizen."[11] It is Jin Yuan's responsibility to guide one accused of being a "counter-revolutionary, a collaborator, and a traitor" through a reeducation program reflecting both Enlightenment and Marxist philosophies. At an introductory session in the Fushun prison the governor spells this out to his inmates: "We believe that men are born good. We believe that the only way to change is to discover the truth and look at it in the face. That is why you are here. You will begin by writing the story of your life; confess your crimes; your salvation lies entirely in the attitude you take. I advise you to be frank and sincere."

Thus by confessing—by writing and by speaking—Pu Yi is placed in the position of "subject-in-the-making." His search for himself as a subject threatened with obliteration by the flowing away of his life's blood, a subject threatened with oblivion by the fading away of his life's memories—this subject now seeks the Self and continues to do so for the duration of the film. The filmmaker also embarks on this search, as do we, the viewers, along with the film's prison governor and inter-rogators. And as Pu Yi's written and spoken words contribute to the reconstitution of the subject, so too do those of a great number of other characters who peopled his life from his birth in 1905 to his release from prison in 1959.

These stories are structured into thirteen flashbacks, of three dif-ferent sorts in terms of focalization and purpose. The first two are externally focalized (that is, not from the point of view of one—or even several—characters) and serve a referential purpose: here we are treated to the magnificence of the imperial court and initiated into some of its "exotic and mysterious" practices. Beginning with the low-angle shot of the grotesquely made-up Dowager Empress on her throne (one of Bertolucci's veiled tributes to Nicholas Ray[12]) and including the spectacle of thousands of kow-towing eunuchs in brilliantly colored garb; from an extreme long shot of the Forbidden City, with its stunning architecture and vast expanse to detailed sequences focused on the care and feeding of the new child Emperor, the three-year-old "Lord of Ten Thousand Years"—this wealth of visual display comprises the first two flashbacks. Here, too, we see representations of the loss of the Mother which Pu Yi was forced to endure early in life: repeated positionings of the mother behind veils, screens, and closed doors (though we hear the continuing refrain "Open the door," the doors do not open for Pu Yi), as well as the literal separation first from his biological mother, then from his wet-nurse mother. He is also called upon to replace the Father, succeeding to his uncle's throne at three when his father goes into a kind of retirement. Throughout these first two flashbacks identity is ambiguous and constantly questioned: Pu Yi is certain neither of who he is nor of who he is to become. Nor can he count on those around him—people appearing and disappearing, playing and changing roles, giving and reversing opinions.

The next two flashbacks (numbers 3 and 4) are primarily focalizations by Reginald Fleming Johnston (Peter O'Toole), who served as Pu Yi's English tutor between 1919 and 1924 and whose book *Twilight in the Forbidden City* provided important information not only to Bertolucci in making the film but also to the Fushun prison officials in carrying out Pu Yi's interrogation and reeducation. Flashback 3 cuts from a close-up of Fleming's book in the hands of one of the prison's investigating officers to a high-angle shot of the Peking streets, with the continuous voice-over of Johnston reading: "After a few years the Chinese Republic had become as corrupt as the old Empire. It fell quickly into the hands of ambitious generals and corrupt bureaucrats. By May 1919 when I received my appointment, China was in turmoil. The era of the Warlords had begun."

Again we see flashback material fulfilling a referential purpose: the audience is told of the May 1919 student demonstrations against the government and made aware of the degree to which Pu Yi is isolated from the world outside the Forbidden City, since he too finds out about these events only from Johnston. True, he can hear shouts, gunshots, and horses' hooves, but all he can see is the interior surface of the Forbidden City walls topped by their sheltering tile roofs. When Pu Yi expresses to Johnston his wish to go beyond the walls, to "see the 'city of sound,'" a eunuch guard intervenes.[13] These flashbacks also privilege Johnston's voice as one of the components of the historical record and at the same time place it within a context. Johnston is a member of a class, a member of a race, and a citizen of an interested nation; a tall, blue-eyed, top-hatted English gentleman whose dubious mission it was to make the Chinese Emperor into a copy of an "English gentleman." In a sense we can see the Johnston figure as displacing Bertolucci and ourselves from the position of Western imperialist. We are spared from occupying that site since the position is "already filled." It remains to us to view that traditional dominant/submissive relationship critically, from outside the structure itself.[14]

Beginning with flashback 5 and continuing to the end of the film we see Pu Yi's own focalizations. Here Pu Yi is on trial for his life—a product of history producing a new understanding of that history.

Structured as they are into the prison interrogation format, these flashbacks join a long tradition of "trial testimony" flashbacks.[15] In *Flashbacks in Film*, Maureen Turim discusses early examples of this type, describing how they "create an atmosphere where guilt, innocence, condemnation, or clemency are the constant undercurrents of each scene related. The film's spectators become the trial's jury, witnessing both the courtroom drama and an imaginary recreation of the circumstances involved in the crime."[16] Early movies such as Mauritz Stiller's *The Woman on Trial* (1927) and Alexander Korda's *The Night Watch* (1928) present imagery in the flashbacks without making a distinction between narrated testimony and objective account. Nor, as Turim points out, are they interested in questioning subjectivity or faulty memories, or in problematizing overlapping and contradictory versions.[17] Undoubtedly the best known film of this sort is Akira Kurosawa's *Rashomon* (1950), whose flashback portrayal of four different versions of an attack by a robber on a samurai and his wife provides—according to how one wishes to view it—"a philosophical statement on relative truth values and subjectivity . . . a discourse on lying . . . [or] a deconstructive play with the mechanisms of fiction."[18]

Bertolucci's is no less an undertaking as he uses flashbacks to represent the many voices that participate in telling a life story, and as he calls into question the effects of ideologies—whether traditional Chinese Imperial, nineteenth-century Western colonial, Japanese militarist and expansionist, or modern-day Maoist—on subject-formation and historical understanding. But he rigorously avoids taking the traditional "stance of the White Man" vis-à-vis the Other. Instead, he involves himself with his characters and his audience in the search for knowledge—not "power-knowledge" but rather "knowledge-for-use," the kind one needs to become a useful citizen. This is not knowledge that is accumulated and stored; it is knowledge that unsettles and changes. In seeking, Bertolucci listens to many voices, reads many writings, and includes them all in the film, exemplifying Trinh T. Minh-ha's observation that "the more ears I am able to hear with, the farther I see the plurality of meaning and the less I lend myself to the illusion of a single message." [19]

The interrogation structure with its minimalist prison setting as the narrative present clearly throws the balance of interest in the direction of the flashback material, although it is the interaction of this material with the character's current mental state that constitutes the film's structure. We are not so much rereading the present in terms of what we find out about the past as we are reforming/reconstituting the subject—forming a new subject—in the light of rethinking the past. This is an altogether different technique from the kind one finds in films where flashbacks serve to reveal the role of the past in character formation, often from a deterministic point of view. Bertolucci's approach is the opposite. His subject is a subject-in-the-making; his investigation centers on how we recreate, by rethinking the past from a new perspective, the subject of that past story, at the same time that we alter our understanding of the story itself. This way of looking at history was already evident in Bertolucci's earlier film 1900, which "comprehends the historical past as a particular set of possibilities that can be fulfilled in the future." [20]

The fifth flashback begins with another call to "open the door." That Pu Yi actually does push open the interrogation room door leads us to expect other "openings" as well, openings that Bertolucci will represent through writing. The scene itself begins with writing, as Pu Yi writes the Chinese characters of his name, "Aisin-Gioro Pu Yi," in white chalk on the floor. Next the interrogator reads the black-ink Chinese characters Pu Yi has written on the pages of his confession book, and finally as Pu Yi speaks the court scribe also writes with black ink on a white page. To write is to become; to write is to express; to write is to allow a new reality to emerge.

When we hear Pu Yi claim that while he was still within the Forbidden City he wanted reform, the film flashes back to a sequence exemplifying the reforms Pu Yi claims to have wanted. At the same time, since the Party, as we have just learned from the interrogator, "already knows everything about [him]," what we see cannot be taken as a representation of his subjective memory alone. It is, rather, a presentation of a dialectical process wherein his past activities are reexamined for their "reformist" vs. their "counter-revolutionary" motivation. In a rare instance of voice-over narration, Pu Yi says, "The Forbidden City had become a theater without an audience. So why did the actors remain on stage? It was only so they could steal the scenery piece by piece." This, in fact, reflects an opinion of Johnston's that Pu Yi adopted and acted on. His attempt to reform the Imperial Household Department, however, so threatened those concerned that they simply resorted to arson rather than face a reckoning.

The ambiguity of Pu Yi's position is graphically portrayed in these sequences. True, he "wanted reform," and we see him enacting it when he expels the palace eunuchs after the fire. But as we see him from low angle standing on high, garbed in the imperial yellow and gazing down as his command is being carried out, we perceive the "counter-revolutionary," the deposed emperor who indeed wishes to rule again. In this back and forth between look and voice, action and motivation, Bertolucci again represents the past as a "set of possibilities," historical subjects as "in-the-making."

From this shot Bertolucci cuts back to the narrating present. As we pick up the interrogation process again, Pu Yi is just admitting apologetically, "I forgot what I was saying." Although the interrogator declares that he is "wasting [their] time" and immediately launches into questions about Pu Yi's connections with the Japanese, this simple "I forgot what I was saying" arouses the spectator's interest. What is there he does not wish to remember? Why does Pu Yi forget at this point? Totally cut off from the world as he had been until then, whatever he thought or said would have been based on the slightest of information and would scarcely have mattered. Johnston describes and criticizes "the evil results of the revolutionary compromise . . . whereby the Emperor was deprived of political power but left with his empty title and the enormously expensive and barren privilege of maintaining an unnecessary and otiose court."[21]

The next flashback, which presents material that Pu Yi indicates he would prefer to forget, brings us to 1924. We now begin to see Pu Yi play some role in world events, and it is for this reason that the period is of greater interest in terms of the rethinking, reconstruction process of the film.

On 5 November 1924, Pu Yi was expelled from the Forbidden City by order of Feng Yuxiang, a northern warlord who was occupying Peking at the time. The film makes a great deal of the question of Pu Yi's "going over" to the Japanese. We see the interrogators accusing him of covering up the truth. Pu Yi himself in the course of the interrogation accuses Johnston of lying, since in his book he claims, "The endeavor to make out that the Emperor had been kidnapped by the Japanese is wholly untrue. He left Tientsin and went to Manchuria of his own free will." There is a flashback where the empress, Wan Jung (Joan Chen), pleads with him not to collaborate with the Japanese ("Do you not see? The Japanese are using you!") There is incriminating evidence from Pu Yi's valet, also a prisoner in the process of reeducation, who withdraws his story out of deference to his former employer only to have the interrogator throw their confession books at them, screaming "You're both lying."

On the one hand, these contradictory accounts emphasize that there is no self-contained historical world "out there" to be discovered; they also serve to focus on the reconstruction of the past as a process that is itself an object for critical inquiry.[22] In fact, there appear to be fewer contradictions in the story than its filmic telling suggests. Over a ten-year period, Pu Yi actually made four separate "moves," each occurring in a different context. Since the film elides the time periods between the so-called "moves," it can build up what comes to seem like a single, decisive "move." After he was ousted from the Forbidden City, Pu Yi spent some time under guard at his father's palace. Since this was not a secure arrangement, negotiations began with various ministers and other members of the diplomatic corps so that he might be accommodated by one of the foreign legations. Despite a number of complications, he did, in fact, go to the Japanese Legation in Peking where, again, he remained for a short time. At the end of February 1925 he moved to the Japanese Concession in Tientsin. Although the film does take an anti-Japanese position in interpreting this series of events, at the time it may well have seemed as if there was little to choose between the English and the Japanese, since dating from the Opium War (1839-1842) the British presence in China had been at least as damaging to Chinese interests as had the Japanese.

As political chaos continued in Peking, and as Tientsin took on the image of a cosmopolitan social center, the real political fate of the country was being decided in the power struggle between the Kuomintang, headed by Chiang Kai-shek (after the death of Sun Yat-sen in 1925), and the Communists under the leadership of Chen Duxiu, Zhou Enlai, Mao Zedong, and others. Throughout the decade 1925-1935, when the Kuomintang and the CCP were debating and acting on such issues as land distribution, union organization, foreign interests on Chinese soil, and policy toward the northern warlords, Pu Yi played no role whatsoever.[23] The movie accounts for his never establishing any ties with Chiang Kai-shek and the KMT on the grounds of his refusal to forget the grave-desecration incident.[24] This deed, committed by some of Chiang's soldiers, loomed large in Pu Yi's mind as a heinous crime—the Dowager Empress's body hacked to pieces, her jewels stolen—and fed his sense of his own difference from the Chinese, strengthening his will to look on himself as the defender of his ancestral line, of the Manchurian people, and finally of Manchuria as the political entity "Manchukuo."

In September 1931 the Japanese, having perpetrated the "Mukden Incident" in order to facilitate their takeover of Manchuria, approached Pu Yi, requesting that he collaborate with them in setting up the new state. At first their overtures were rejected, but gradually, through the efforts of his personal advisors and continued pressure from the Japanese, Pu Yi became convinced it would be advisable to go to Manchuria. Thus on 10 November 1931 he left his Tientsin residence (in the trunk of a car, to avoid being seen) and traveled by boat to Manchuria. Upon his arrival he assumed the anomalous title "Chief Executive" and was forced to wait until 1934 to be crowned Emperor of Manchukuo. In this capacity he became the first of four puppet rulers set up by the Japanese on Chinese soil for the primary purpose of serving Japan's economic interests.

Through a combination of flashbacks and ellipses, not only is the curiosity/suspense level elevated but also a case is being made—history is being read—to show the seductive power of the Japanese who, by playing on Pu Yi's vanity and ambition, got him to work against the interests of his own people.

In the prison sequence between flashbacks 11 and 12 there is an extraordinary example of Pu Yi's resistance of memory: as he sits at a table in his cell writing his confession, he dips his pen into the ink bottle, and, as he withdraws the pen, suddenly the bottle tips over and a wash of black ink floods the screen. It is at this moment, while blotting the ink, that Pu Yi tells his cellmates in a weary and bitter voice, "You're all pretending. You're just pretending that you have changed. You worked in Amakasu's private office. You're still the same people. People do not change." The Cell Leader silences him initially with the claim that "The Party teaches us to be new men. We're working for a new China," after which he calls for the guard. This interim scene ends in the narrative present with the Cell Leader beating on the door and crying, "Guard, Guard," while Pu Yi sits despondently, saying, "I let it happen. I let it happen."

In spite of this extremely personal bridge to flashback 12, it begins with a scene that Pu Yi did not witness: the birth and death of his wife's child, followed by a subjective memory sequence of his own, where for the third time massive red doors close on him. This time his "Open the door" is uttered so faintly that it is as if he is merely a shadow-Self issuing a shadow command. On the other side of the closed and guarded doors the hospital van carries the Empress Wan Jung to an unknown destination where she can "recuperate"—another loss of the Mother, another blurring and diminishing of the Self.

The horror of the content at the personal level represented in this flashback is paralleled by that of the public and political horror from the same period, and is presented as a documentary film, screened in the prison as a part of the inmates' reeducation process. Here we see Bertolucci employing yet another mode of telling, adding yet another kind of voice to his multivocal story. We view this film as the inmates view it, as members of the audience just as Pu Yi is a member of the audience: horrified yet somehow distanced from the information presented about Nanking, about Pearl Harbor, about germ warfare. When

Pu Yi the inmate in the audience recognizes Pu Yi the Emperor of Manchukuo on the screen, the overpowering force of representation literally draws him out of his seat. No longer is he being asked to assimilate "information"; now he encounters himself as Subject—as Subject-in-the-making. The intensity of this confrontation equals that of the ink spilling over the confession book which begins the sequence, and prepares the viewer for the next scene: a discussion between Jin Yuan, the governor of the prison, and Pu Yi concerning nothing less than the nature of personal responsibility and the possibility of personal change.

Unlike those accused of war crimes in Europe whose refrainlike denials, "Ich bin nicht schuld" ("not guilty"), have marked our aural memories, Pu Yi now, because of his reeducation, claims full responsibility on all counts. The prison governor comes to him as he works in the garden, confronting him with his having confessed to everything, even to what he did not do. "Perhaps," says Jin Yuan, "you think we're here to teach men to lie in a new way. Why did you sign every accusation against you?" To this Pu Yi answers, "I was responsible for everything." Whereupon the governor responds, "You are responsible for what you do." Pu Yi then begs to be left alone, accusing the governor of having saved him "to be a puppet in your play; you saved me to be useful to you." The exchange closes with Jin Yuan having been given the last word: "Is that so terrible? To be useful?" This eloquent closing question, is, of course, another invitation to Pu Yi and to the audience to continue the inquiry as to what constitutes the Self in relation to society, and to ponder the meaning of subject formation through time.

That the film does not conclude at this point, however, underscores Bertolucci's conviction that the past extends into the present and the future. In fact, time moves out of its linear pattern altogether into circularity and timelessness. When we see another student demonstration in the streets—reminiscent of the demonstrations of 1905, 1912, and 1919 (and from the perspective of 1990, tragically, also that of 1989)—we are reminded of the way in which history repeats itself and of the fact that history is still in the making, that as "useful citizens" we still have political work to be done. Beyond this we move back into the Forbidden City, into the realm of an altogether mysterious and marvelous cricket whose presence reminds us of the path we have traveled—through lived time and reexamined time—and whose continuing presence suggests the path ahead; before Pu Yi magically disappears, he gives this cricket to a small Chinese boy wearing the familiar red neck-scarf. This is the kind of moment about which Bertolucci has said, "The proposal made in that episode steps out of any real historic context and that moment represents, for me, the real thrust of the film, where it goes beyond the narrative level, beyond the moment. Utopia becomes reality for a flash. . . . I believe that making the emotion of a Utopian situation come alive is one way of doing politics.[25]

Another way of doing politics is represented in the final scene. As a group of uncomprehending Western tourists listens to a tour guide's patter about Pu Yi and his life in the Forbidden City, the viewer realizes that Pu Yi's search for the past, his search for the Self, cannot be reduced to a simplistic recitation of facts. Rethinking the past, reconstituting the Self is an ongoing process, an exploration that continues to shape the present and the future.

NOTES

The chapter title uses Julia Kristeva's term from "Oscillation between Power and Desire," *New French Feminisms,* ed. Elaine Marks and Isabelle de Courtivron (Amherst: Univ. of Massachusetts Press, 1980), 167.

The Last Emperor (1987). Screenplay, Mark Peploe with Bernardo Bertolucci, photography, Vittorio Storaro; music, Ryuichi Sakamoto, David Byrne, Cong Su; director, Bernardo Bertolucci. Cast: John Lone (Pu Yi), Joan Chen (Wan Jung), Peter O'Toole (Reginald Johnson), Ying Ruocheng (the Governor), Ryuichi Sakamato (Amaksu), Victor Wong (Chen Pao Shen), Dennis Dun (Big Li), Maggie Han (Eastern Jewel), Jade Go (Ar Mo), Richard Vuu (Pu Yi, age three), Tijger Tsou (Pu Yi, age nine), Wu Tao (Pu Yi, age fifteen).

1. John King Fairbank, *The Great Chinese Revolution: 1800-1985* (New York: Harper & Row, 1986), 38; or, as stated by Mike Merrill in an interesting discussion with Herbert Gutman in which they oppose the idea of history as foreordained, as inevitable, *Visions of History*, ed. Henry Abelove et al. (New York: Pantheon Books, 1976), 199, "We can change the way we think about our history, and if we do, we can change that history itself."

2. Julia Kristeva uses these phrases in regard to "woman" in "Women Can Never Be Defined," *New French Feminisms,* 187.

3. Trinh T. Minh-ha, *Woman, Native, Other* (Bloomington: Indiana Univ. Press, 1989), 53.

4. Edward W. Said, *Orientalism* (New York: Vintage Books, 1979), 1.

5. Ibid.

6. Ibid., 8.

7. Three other works, a drama and two films, deserve mention as interesting attempts in very different ways at changing the old structures that have been fabricated by generations of white European males: Jean Genet's *Screens* (1966), Michelangelo Antonioni's *Chung Kuo, China* (1972), and Joris Ivens's *The Story of the Wind* (1989). The latter, shot on location in China when the director was in his eighties (just prior to his death) is an especially brave attempt "to do the impossible—to film the invisible wind," as the pre-credits title has it.

8. Bertolucci quoted in Robert Phillip Kolker, *Bernardo Bertolucci* (London: British Film Institute, 1985), 68.

9. For a brilliant discussion of *The Spider's Stratagem* see David Bordwell, *Narration in the Fiction Film* (Madison: Univ. of Wisconsin Press, 1985), 88-98. Another useful study on flashbacks is Brian Henderson's "Tense, Mood, and Voice in Film (Notes after Genette)," *Film Quarterly* 36, no. 4 (Summer 1983): 4-17.

10. One of the commonplaces of writing on Bertolucci is, of course, the repeated claim that "he is his own main character," "he is the real star of the movies he makes," "his films are primarily about himself," or "his presence is 'always there.'" See, for example, David Lapin, "After the Revolution? Conversation with Bernardo Bertolucci," *Literature/Film Quarterly* 12, no. 1 (1984): 22-25; Joan Mellen, "Bernardo Bertolucci: 'I am not a moralist,'" *The Cineaste Interviews: On the Art and Politics of the Cinema*, ed. Dan Georgakas and Lenny Rubenstein (Chicago: Lake View Press, 1983), 33-40.

11. This story is told by Pu Yi himself in *From Emperor to Citizen: The Autobiography of Aisin-Gioro Pu Yi*, 2 vols. (Peking: Foreign Language Press), 1964-1965.

12. Bertolucci has always been a great admirer of Ray and on more than one occasion (see, for example, the movie discussion sequence in *Before the Revolution*) he includes direct references to Ray or quotes directly from his films. When Ray died in 1979, Bertolucci delivered the eulogy at the memorial service, using Proust's words for its title: "The boundless frivolity of people about to die." Text in Wim Wenders, *Nick's Movie* (Frankfurt: Zweitausendeins, 1981).

13. In a brief but perceptive note on *The Last Emperor* in the *Chicago Reader* (Fall 1987, multiple issues), Jonathan Rosenbaum observes that Bertolucci uses Pu Yi's "remoteness from China as an objective correlative of our own cultural distance as Westerners."

14. In this and many other instances throughout the film I believe that Bertolucci is deconstructing and critiquing colonialist attitudes and the tradition of Orientalism. Thus I find an accusation such as the following by Fatimah Tobing Rony facile and wholly unfair. "*The Last Emperor's* opium-dream-like oneiricism, although self conscious, descends into old stereotypes about China and Orientalism: that is Oriental cruelty, sensuality, and lack of rationality." See his review of *The Last Emperor* in *Film Quarterly* 42 (Winter 1988-1989): 51.

15. In addition to participating in the trial-testimony tradition of flashbacks, *The Last Emperor's* interrogation flashbacks can also claim certain commonalities with films whose flashbacks are structured into the psychoanalytic session, where with the aid of the analyst/interrogator the patient/prisoner's repressed or forgotten memory material is called forth and interpreted, resulting in the one case in a "cure" and in the other in "reeducation." In both cases the spectator has available to him/her the positions of the analyst/interrogator and the patient/prisoner.

16. Maureen Turim, *Flashbacks in Film: Memory and History* (New York: Routledge, 1989), 53.

17. Ibid., 54.

18. Ibid., 201.

19. Trinh, *Woman, Native, Other*, 30.

20. Robert Burgoyne, "Temporality as Historical Argument in Bertolucci's *1900*," *Cinema Journal* 28, no. 3 (Spring 1989): 57.

21. Reginald Fleming Johnston, *Twilight in the Forbidden City* (London: Victor Gollancz, 1934), 209.

22. See Anton Kaes, "In Search of Germany," *From Hitler to Heimat* (Cambridge: Harvard Univ. Press, 1989), 105-35, for an interesting discussion of Alexander Kluge's *The Patriot*, a film which "deals with history from the perspective of the present, shedding new light not only on the past (as a prelude to the present) but also on the present itself in its historical dimension" (108).

23. For further reading on these developments, see Fairbank's *The Great Chinese Revolution*, and Jonathan D. Spence, *The Search for Modern China* (New York: Norton, 1990).

24. Pu Yi himself says the report of this grave-robbery "gave me a shock worse than the one I had received when I was expelled from the palace" (*From Emperor to Citizen*, 195).

25. Bernardo Bertolucci, "The Poetry of Class Struggle," (interview with Fabio di Vico and Roberto Degni) in *Cineaste Interviews*, 146. Bertolucci's comment was made originally in reference to the final 25 April 1945 scene in *1900*.

FILMOGRAPHY
The Columbia Features, 1920-1991
Compiled by BERNARD F. DICK

Columbia's first incarnation (August 1920-January 1924) was as the CBC Film Sales Company. While it is customary to designate 10 January 1924 as the official birthdate of Columbia Pictures, one should remember, first, that "Columbia" was the name of a special type of CBC film (other types included "Perfection" and "Waldorf") that started to appear in 1923; and second, that early in 1924 Columbia also became part of the name of CBC's first film exchange, Columbia Pictures Corporation, which shortly replaced CBC as the name of the company.

The following list includes only features, not shorts, a great many of which are enumerated in Ted Okuda, with Edward Watz, *The Columbia Shorts: Two-Reel Hollywood Film Comedies, 1933-1958* (Jefferson, N.C.: McFarland, 1986). For the Columbia serials, see Roy Kinnard, *Fifty Years of Serial Thrills* (Metuchen, N.J.: Scarecrow Press, 1983); 101-27. Directors are listed below for all films.

For 1921-1926, these symbols are used:
* = Distributed by CBC
** = First CBC production
*** = A film in the Columbia series

1921

The Heart of the North (Quality Film Productions), Harry Revier
Life's Greatest Question (Quality Film Productions), Harry Revier
The Victim (Goebel Productions, reissue)

1922

**More to Be Pitied Than Scorned*, Edward Le Saint
Only a Shop Girl, Edward Le Saint

1923

The Barefoot Boy, David Kirkland
***Forgive and Forget*, Howard M. Mitchell

Her Accidental Husband, Dallas M. Fitzgerald
****Innocence*, Edward Le Saint
****The Marriage Market*, Edward Le Saint
****Mary of the Movies*, John McDermott
Temptation, Edward Le Saint
****Yesterday's Wife*, Edward Le Saint

1924

The Battling Fool, W.S. Van Dyke
The Beautiful Sinner, W.S. Van Dyke
****Discontented Husbands*, Edward Le Saint
The Fatal Mistake, Scott Dunlap
A Fight for Honor, Henry MacRae
****The Foolish Virgin*, George W. Hill
****The Midnight Express*, George W. Hill
****One Glorious Night*, Scott Dunlap
****Pal O'Mine*, Edward Le Saint
The Price She Paid, Henry MacRae
****Racing for Life*, Henry MacRae
Tainted Money, Henry MacRae
****Traffic in Hearts*, Scott Dunlap
Women First, Reeves Eason

1925

After Business Hours, Mal St. Clair
****The Danger Signal*, Erle C. Kenton
An Enemy of Men, Frank Strayer
The Fate of a Flirt, Frank Strayer
The Fearless Lover, Henry MacRae
Fighting the Flames, Reeves Eason
Fighting Youth, Reeves Eason
A Fight to the Finish, Reeves Eason
A Fool and His Money, Erle C. Kenton
The Great Sensation, Jay Marchant
The Handsome Brute, Robert Eddy
Justice of the Far North, Norman Dawn
****The Lure of the Wild*, Frank Strayer
The New Champion, Reeves Eason
The Price of Success, Tony Gaudio
Sealed Lips, Tony Gaudio
****S.O.S. Perils of the Sea*, James P. Hogan
Speed Mad, Jay Marchant
****Steppin' Out*, Frank Strayer
****The Unwritten Law*, Edward Le Saint
When Husbands Flirt, William Wellman
Who Cares, David Kirkland

1926

The Belle of Broadway, Harry O. Hoyt
The Better Way, Ralph Ince
The False Alarm, Frank O'Connor
****Ladies of Leisure*, Thomas Buckingham
The Lone Wolf Returns, Ralph Ince
Obey the Law, Alfred Raboch
Remember, David Selman
Sweet Rosie O'Grady, Frank Strayer
The Thrill Hunter, Eugene De Rue
The Truthful Sex, Richard Thomas
When the Wife's Away, Frank Strayer

1927

Alias the Lone Wolf, Edward H. Griffith
The Bachelor's Baby, Frank Strayer
Birds of Prey, William J. Craft
The Blood Ship, George B. Seitz
By Whose Hand?, Walter Lang
The Clown, William J. Craft
The College Hero, Walter Lang
Fashion Madness, Louis Gasnier
For Ladies Only, Henry Lehrman
Isle of Forgotten Women, George B. Seitz
The Kid Sister, Ralph Graves
The Opening Night, Edward H. Griffith
Paying the Price, David Selman
Pleasure before Business, Frank Strayer
Poor Girls, William J. Craft
The Price of Honor, Edward H. Griffith
Rich Men's Sons, Ralph Graves
The Romantic Age, Robert Florey
Sally in Our Alley, Walter Lang
The Siren, Byron Haskin
Stage Kisses, Albert Kelly
Stolen Pleasures, Phil Rosen
The Swell-Head, Ralph Graves
The Tigress, George B. Seitz
Wandering Girls, Ralph Ince
The Warning, George B. Seitz
The Wreck, William J. Craft

1928

After the Storm, George B. Seitz
The Apache, Phil Rosen
Beware of Blondes, George B. Seitz
Broadway Daddies, Fred Windemere

Court-Martial, George B. Seitz
The Desert Bride, Walter Lang
Driftwood, Christy Cabanne
Golf Widows, Erle C. Kenton
Lady Raffles, Roy William Neill
The Matinee Idol, Frank Capra
Modern Mothers, Phil Rosen
Name the Woman, Erle C. Kenton
Nothing to Wear, Erle C. Kenton
Object—Alimony, Scott Dunlap
The Power of the Press, Frank Capra
Ransom, George B. Seitz
Restless Youth, Christy Cabanne
Runaway Girls, Mark Sandrich
Say It with Sables, Frank Capra
The Scarlet Lady, Alan Crosland
The Sideshow, Erle C. Kenton
Sinner's Parade, John G. Adolfi
So This Is Love, Frank Capra
The Sporting Age, Erle C. Kenton
Stool Pigeon, Renaud Hoffman
The Street of Illusion, Erle C. Kenton
Submarine, Frank Capra
That Certain Thing, Frank Capra
Virgin Lips, Elmer Clifton
The Way of the Strong, Frank Capra
The Wife's Relations, Maurice Marshall
A Woman's Way, Edmund Mortimer

1929

Acquitted, Frank Strayer
The Bachelor Girl, Richard Thorpe
Behind Closed Doors, Roy William Neill
The Broadway Hoofer, George Archainbaud
Broadway Scandals, George Archainbaud
The College Coquette, George Archainbaud
The Donovan Affair, Frank Capra
The Eternal Woman, John P. McCarthy
The Faker, Phil Rosen
The Fall of Eve, Frank Strayer
Flight, Frank Capra
The Flying Marine, Albert S. Rogell
Hurricane, Ralph Ince
Light Fingers, Joseph Henaberry
The Lone Wolf's Daughter, Albert S. Rogell
Mexicali Rose, Erle C. Kenton
The Quitter, Joseph Henaberry
The Song of Love, Erle C. Kenton
Trial Marriage, Erle C. Kenton

Wall Street, Roy William Neill
The Younger Generation, Frank Capra

1930

Africa Speaks, Walter Futter
Around the Corner, Bert Glennon and Patterson McNutt
Brothers, Walter Lang
Call of the West, Albert Ray
Charley's Aunt, Al Christie
The Dawn Trail, Christy Cabanne
For the Love o' Lil, James Tinling
Guilty?, George B. Seitz
Hell's Island, Edward Sloman
Ladies Must Play, Raymond Cannon
Ladies of Leisure, Frank Capra
The Last of the Lone Wolf, Richard Boleslawski
The Lone Rider, Louis King
Madonna of the Streets, John S. Robertson
The Melody Man, Roy William Neill
Men without Law, Louis King
Murder on the Roof, George B. Seitz
Personality, Victor Heerman
Prince of Diamonds, Karl Brown and A.H. Van Buren
Rain or Shine, Frank Capra
A Royal Romance, Erle C. Kenton
Shadow Ranch, Louis King
Sisters, James Flood
Soldiers and Women, Edward Sloman
The Squealer, Harry Joe Brown
Sweethearts on Parade, Marshall Neilan
Temptation, E. Mason Hopper
Tol'able David, John Blystone
Vengeance, Archie Mayo

1931

Arizona, George B. Seitz
The Avenger, Roy William Neill
Border Law, Louis King
Branded, Louis King
The Criminal Code, Howard Hawks
A Dangerous Affair, Edward Sedgwick
The Deadline, Lambert Hillyer
The Deceiver, Louis King
Desert Vengeance, Louis King
Dirigible, Frank Capra
Fifty Fathoms Deep, Roy William Neill
The Fighting Fool, Lambert Hillyer
The Fighting Marshall, D. Ross Lederman

The Fighting Sheriff, Louis King
The Flood, James Tinling
The Good Bad Girl, Roy William Neill
The Guilty Generation, Rowland V. Lee
The Last Parade, Erle C. Kenton
The Lightning Flyer, William Nigh
The Lion and the Lamb, George B. Seitz
Lover Come Back, Erle C. Kenton
Meet the Wife, A. Leslie Pearce
Men in Her Life, William Beaudine
The Miracle Woman, Frank Capra
The One Way Trail, Ray Taylor
Pagan Lady, John Dillon
Platinum Blonde, Frank Capra
The Range Feud, D. Ross Lederman
Shanghaied Love, George B. Seitz
The Sky Raiders, Christy Cabanne
Subway Express, Fred Newmeyer
Ten Cents a Dance, Lionel Barrymore
The Texas Cyclone, D. Ross Lederman
The Texas Ranger, D. Ross Lederman
The Secret Witness, Thornton Freeland

1932

American Madness, Frank Capra
As the Devil Commands, Roy William Neill
Attorney for the Defense, Irving Cummings
The Big Timer, Edward Buzzell
By Whose Hand?, Ben Stoloff
Cornered, Reeves Eason
Daring Danger, D. Ross Lederman
Deception, Lewis Seiler
End of the Trail, D. Ross Lederman
Fighting for Justice, Otto Brower
Final Edition, Howard Higgin
Forbidden, Frank Capra
Forbidden Trail, Lambert Hillyer
Hello Trouble, Lambert Hillyer
Hollywood Speaks, Edward Buzzell
The Last Man, Howard Higgin
Love Affair, Thornton Freeland
McKenna of the Mounted, D. Ross Lederman
Man against Woman, Irving Cummings
The Menace, Roy William Neill
The Night Club Lady, Irving Cummings
Night Mayor, Ben Stoloff
No Greater Love, Lewis Seiler
No More Orchids, Walter Lang
Ridin' for Justice, D. Ross Lederman

The Riding Tornado, D. Ross Lederman
Shopworn, Nick Grinde
South of the Rio Grande, Lambert Hillyer
Speed Demon, D. Ross Lederman
Sundown Rider, Lambert Hillyer
The Texas Cyclone, D. Ross Lederman
Three Wise Girls, William Beaudine
This Sporting Age, Andrew W. Bennison and A.F. Erickson
Two Fisted Law, D. Ross Lederman
Vanity Street, Nick Grinde
Virtue, Edward Buzzell
War Correspondent, Paul Sloane
The Western Code, J.P. McCarthy
White Eagle, Lambert Hillyer
Washington Merry Go Round, James Cruze

1933

Air Hostess, Albert S. Rogell
Ann Carver's Profession, Edward Buzzell
Before Midnight, Lambert Hillyer
Below the Sea, Albert S. Rogell
The Bitter Tea of General Yen, Frank Capra
Brief Moment, David Burton
Child of Manhattan, Edward Buzzell
The Circus Queen Murder, Roy William Neill
Cocktail Hour, Victor Schertzinger
Dangerous Crossroads, Lambert Hillyer
East of Fifth Avenue, Albert S. Rogell
The Fighting Code, Lambert Hillyer
Fog, Albert S. Rogell
Hold the Press, Phil Rosen
King of the Wild Horses, Earl Haley
Lady for a Day, Frank Capra
Let's Fall in Love, David Burton
Man of Action, George Melford
Man's Castle, Frank Borzage
Master of Men, Lambert Hillyer
My Woman, Victor Schertzinger
Night of Terror, Ben Stoloff
Obey the Law, Ben Stoloff
Police Car 17, Lambert Hillyer
Rusty Rides Alone, D. Ross Lederman
Silent Men, D. Ross Lederman
Soldiers of the Storm, D. Ross Lederman
So This Is Africa, Eddie Cline
State Trooper, D. Ross Lederman
Straightaway, Otto Brower
The Thrill Hunter, Lambert Hillyer
What Price Innocence?, Willard Mack

When Strangers Marry, Clarence Badger
The Whirlwind, D. Ross Lederman
The Woman I Stole, Irving Cummings
The Wrecker, Albert S. Rogell

1934

Above the Clouds, Roy William Neill
Against the Law, Lambert Hillyer
Among the Missing, Albert S. Rogell
Behind the Evidence, Lambert Hillyer
Beyond the Law, D. Ross Lederman
Black Moon, Roy William Neill
Blind Date, Roy William Neill
Broadway Bill, Frank Capra
The Captain Hates the Sea, Lewis Milestone
The Crime of Helen Stanley, D. Ross Lederman
The Defense Rests, Lambert Hillyer
The Fighting Ranger, George B. Seitz
Fugitive Lady, Albert S. Rogell
Fury of the Jungle, Roy William Neill
Girl in Danger, D. Ross Lederman
Hell Bent for Love, D. Ross Lederman
The Hell Cat, Albert S. Rogell
I'll Fix It, Roy William Neill
It Happened One Night, Frank Capra
Jealousy, Roy William Neill
Lady by Choice, David Burton
The Lady Is Willing, Gilbert Miller
The Line-Up, Howard Higgin
A Man's Game, D. Ross Lederman
The Man Trailer, Lambert Hillyer
Men of the Night, Lambert Hillyer
Mills of the Gods, Roy William Neill
The Most Precious Thing in Life, Lambert Hillyer
Name the Woman, Albert S. Rogell
The Ninth Guest, Roy William Neill
No Greater Glory, Frank Borzage
Once to Every Woman, Lambert Hillyer
One Is Guilty, Lambert Hillyer
One Night of Love, Victor Schertzinger
The Party's Over, Walter Lang
The Prescott Kid, David Selman
Shadows of Sing Sing, Phil Rosen
Sisters under the Skin, David Burton
Social Register, Marshall Neilan
Speed Wings, Otto Brower
That's Gratitude, Frank Craven
Twentieth Century, Howard Hawks
Voice in the Night, C.C. Coleman, Jr.

The Westerner, David Selman
Whirlpool, Roy William Neill
White Lies, Leo Bulgakov
Whom the Gods Destroy, Walter Lang

1935

After the Dance, Leo Bulgakov
Air Hawks, Albert S. Rogell
Atlantic Adventure, Albert S. Rogell
The Awakening of Jim Burke, Lambert Hillyer
The Black Room, Roy William Neill
The Best Man Wins, Erle C. Kenton
The Calling of Dan Matthews, Phil Rosen
Carnival, Walter Lang
The Case of the Missing Man, D. Ross Lederman
The Cattle Thief, Spencer Bennet
Champagne for Breakfast, Mel Brown
Crime and Punishment, Josef von Sternberg
Death Flies East, Phil Rosen
Eight Bells, Roy William Neill
Escape from Devil's Island, Albert S. Rogell
A Feather in Her Hat, Alfred Stantell
Fighting Shadows, David Selman
The Gallant Defender, David Selman
The Girl Friend, Edward Buzzell
Grand Exit, Erle C. Kenton
Guard That Girl, Lambert Hillyer
Heir to Trouble, Spencer Bennet
If You Could Only Cook, William Seiter
I'll Love You Always, Leo Bulgakov
In Spite of Danger, Lambert Hillyer
Justice of the Range, David Selman
Lawless Riders, Spencer Bennet
Let's Live Tonight, Victor Schertzinger
The Lone Wolf Returns, Roy William Neill
Love Me Forever, Victor Schertzinger
Men of the Hour, Lambert Hillyer
One Way Ticket, Herbert Biberman
Party Wire, Erle C. Kenton
The Revenge Rider, David Selman
Riding Wild, David Selman
She Couldn't Take It, Tay Garnett
She Married Her Boss, Gregory LaCava
Square Shooter, David Selman
Superspeed, Lambert Hillyer
Swellhead, Ben Stoloff
Together We Live, Willard Mack
Too Tough to Kill, D. Ross Lederman
Unknown Woman, Albert S. Rogell

Unwelcome Stranger, Phil Rosen
Western Courage, Spencer Bennet
Western Frontier, Albert Herman
The Whole Town's Talking, John Ford

1936

Adventure in Manhattan, Edward Ludwig
Alibi for Murder, D. Ross Lederman
And So They Were Married, Elliott Nugent
Avenging Waters, Spencer Bennet
Blackmailer, Gordon Wiles
The Cattle Thief, Spencer Bennet
Code of the Range, C.C. Coleman, Jr.
Come Closer, Folks, D. Ross Lederman
Counterfeit, Erle C. Kenton
Counterfeit Lady, D. Ross Lederman
The Cowboy Star, David Selman
Craig's Wife, Dorothy Arzner
Dangerous Intrigue, David Selman
Devil's Squadron, Erle C. Kenton
Don't Gamble with Love, Dudley Murphy
End of the Trail, Erle C. Kenton
Final Hour, D. Ross Lederman
Hell-Ship Morgan, D. Ross Lederman
Heroes of the Range, Spencer Bennet
Killer at Large, David Selman
The King Steps Out, Josef von Sternberg
Lady from Nowhere, Gordon Wiles
Lady of Secrets, Marion Gering
Legion of Terror, C.C. Coleman, Jr.
The Man Who Lived Twice, Harry Lachman
Meet Nero Wolfe, Herbert Biberman
Mine with the Iron Door, David Howard
The Music Goes 'Round, Victor Schertzinger
More Than a Secretary, Alfred E. Green
Mr. Deeds Goes to Town, Frank Capra
The Mysterious Avenger, David Selman
Panic on the Air, D. Ross Lederman
Pennies from Heaven, Norman Z. McLeod
Pride of the Marines, D. Ross Lederman
Roaming Lady, Albert S. Rogell
Secret Patrol, David Selman
Shakedown, David Selman
Stampede, Ford Beebe
Theodora Goes Wild, Richard Boleslawski
They Met in a Taxi, Alfred E. Green
Trapped by Television, Del Lord
Tugboat Princess, David Selman

Two Fisted Gentleman, Gordon Wiles
You May be Next, Albert S. Rogell

OUTSIDE PRODUCTIONS

[Originally, outside productions were films made for the studio by producers who were often given studio space for their production units; later Columbia began to use the term to include films it was only distributing.]

Central Films
Vengeance, Del Lord

Larry Darmour
North of Nome, William Nigh
Ranger Courage, Spencer Bennet
Rio Grande Ranger, Spencer Bennet
The Unknown Ranger, Spencer Bennet

1937

All American Sweetheart, Lambert Hillyer
The Awful Truth, Leo McCarey
Counsel for Crime, John Brahm
Criminals of the Air, C.C. Coleman, Jr.
A Dangerous Adventure, D. Ross Lederman
The Devil Is Driving, Harry Lachman
Devil's Playground, Erle C. Kenton
Dodge City Trail, C.C. Coleman, Jr.
A Fight to the Finish, C.C. Coleman, Jr.
Find the Witness, David Selman
The Frameup, D. Ross Lederman
The Game That Kills, D. Ross Lederman
Girls Can Pay, Lambert Hillyer
I'll Take Romance, Edward H. Griffith
I Promise to Play, D. Ross Lederman
It Can't Last Forever, Hamilton McFadden
It Happened in Hollywood, Harry Lachman
It's All Yours, Elliott Nugent
League of Frightened Men, Alfred E. Green
Let's Get Married, Alfred E. Green
Life Begins with Love, Ray McCarey
Lost Horizon, Frank Capra
Motor Madness, D. Ross Lederman
Murder in Greenwich Village, Albert S. Rogell
The Old Wyoming Trail, Folmer Blangsted
One Man Justice, Leon Barsha
Outlaws of the Prairie, Sam Nelson
Paid to Dance, C.C. Coleman, Jr.
Parole Racket, C.C. Coleman, Jr.
Racketeers in Exile, Erle C. Kenton
The Shadow, C.C. Coleman, Jr.

She Married an Artist, Marion Gering
Speed to Spare, Lambert Hillyer
Thunder in the City, Marion Gering
Trapped, Leon Barsha
Two Fisted Sheriff, Leon Barsha
Venus Makes Trouble, Gordon Wiles
Westbound Mail, Folmer Blangsted
When You're in Love, Robert Riskin
Woman in Distress, Lynn Shores
Women of Glamour, Gordon Wiles

OUTSIDE PRODUCTIONS

Central Films

Across the Border, Leon Barsha
Death Goes North, Frank McDonald
Convicted, Leon Barsha
Manhattan Shakedown, Leon Barsha
Murder Is News, Leon Barsha
Woman against the World, David Selman

Larry Darmour

Law of the Ranger, Spencer Bennet
Outlaws of the Orient, Ernest B. Schoedsack
The Rangers Step In, Spencer Bennet
Reckless Ranger, Spencer Bennet
Roaring Timber, Phil Rosen
Trapped by G-Men, Lewis D. Collins
Trouble in Morocco, Ernest B. Schoedsack
Under Suspicion, Lewis D. Collins

Coronet Pictures

Headin' East, Ewing Scott
Hollywood Round-Up, Ewing Scott

1938

Adventure in Sahara, D. Ross Lederman
Blondie, Frank Strayer
Call of the Rockies, Alan James
Cattle Raiders, Sam Nelson
City Streets, Albert S. Rogell
Colorado Trail, Sam Nelson
Extortion, Lambert Hillyer
Flight to Fame, C.C. Coleman, Jr.
Highway Patrol, C.C. Coleman, Jr.
Holiday, George Cukor
I Am The Law, Alexander Hall
Juvenile Court, D. Ross Lederman
The Lady Objects, Erle C. Kenton
Law of the Plains, Sam Nelson

The Little Adventuress, D. Ross Lederman
Little Miss Roughneck, Albert Scotto
The Lone Wolf in Paris, Albert S. Rogell
The Main Event, Danny Dare
No Time to Marry, Harry Lachman
Penitentiary, John Brahm
Rio Grande, Sam Nelson
Smashing the Spy Ring, Christy Cabanne
South of Arizona, Sam Nelson
Squadron of Honor, C.C. Coleman, Jr.
Start Cheering, Albert S. Rogell
There's Always a Woman, Alexander Hall
There's That Woman Again, Alexander Hall
West of Cheyenne, Sam Nelson
West of the Sante Fe, Sam Nelson
When G-Men Step In, C.C. Coleman, Jr.
Who Killed Gail Preston?, Leon Barsha
Women in Prison, Lambert Hillyer
You Can't Take It with You, Frank Capra

OUTSIDE PRODUCTIONS

Sunset Productions
Heroes of the Alamo, Harry Fraser

Larry Darmour
Crime Takes a Holiday, Lewis D. Collins
Flight into Nowhere, Lewis D. Collins
In Early Arizona, Joseph Levering
Making the Headlines, Lewis D. Collins
Phantom Gold, Joseph Levering
Pioneer Trail, Joseph Levering
Reformatory, Lewis D. Collins
Rolling Caravans, Joseph Levering
Stagecoach Days, Joseph Levering
The Strange Case of Dr. Meade, Lewis D. Collins

Coronet Pictures
California Frontier, Elmer Clifton
Law of the Texan, Elmer Clifton
The Overland Express, Drew Eberson
The Stranger from Arizona, Elmer Clifton

David L. Loew
The Gladiator, Edward Sedgwick
Wide Open Spaces, Kurt Neumann

Sol Lesser
Terror of Tiny Town, Sam Newfield

1939

The Amazing Mr. Williams, Alexander Hall
Behind Prison Gates, Charles Barton
Beware, Spooks!, Edward Sedgwick
Blind Alley, Charles Vidor
Blondie Brings Up Baby, Frank Strayer
Blondie Meets the Boss, Frank Strayer
Blondie Takes a Vacation, Frank Strayer
Cafe Hostess, Sidney Salkow
Coast Guard, Edward Ludwig
First Offenders, Frank McDonald
Five Little Peppers, Charles Barton
Golden Boy, Rouben Mamoulian
Good Girls Go to Paris, Alexander Hall
Homicide Bureau, C.C. Coleman, Jr.
Konga, the Wild Stallion, Sam Nelson
The Lady and the Mob, Ben Stoloff
Let Us Live, John Brahm
The Lone Wolf Spy Hunt, Peter Godfrey
The Man They Could Not Hang, Nick Grinde
The Man from Sundown, Sam Nelson
Missing Daughters, C.C. Coleman, Jr.
Mr. Smith Goes to Washington, Frank Capra
My Son Is a Criminal, C.C. Coleman, Jr.
My Son Is Guilty, Charles Barton
North of Shanghai, D. Ross Lederman
North of the Yukon, Sam Nelson
Only Angels Have Wings, Howard Hawks
Outpost of the Mounties, C.C. Coleman, Jr.
Outside These Walls, Ray McCarey
Parents on Trial, Sam Nelson
Riders of Black River, Norman Deming
Romance of the Redwoods, Charles Vidor
*Scandal Sheet,*Nick Grinde
Spoilers of the Range, C.C. Coleman, Jr.
The Stranger from Texas, Sam Nelson
Taming of the West, Norman Deming
Texas Stampede, Sam Nelson
Those High Grey Walls, Charles Vidor
The Thundering West, Sam Nelson
Western Caravans, Sam Nelson
A Woman Is the Judge, Nick Grinde

OUTSIDE PRODUCTIONS

Larry Darmour

Frontiers of '49, Joseph Levering
The Law Comes to Texas, Joseph Levering
Lone Star Pioneers, Joseph Levering

Trapped in the Sky, Lewis D. Collins
Whispering Enemies, Lewis D. Collins

Harefield Productions
Clouds over Europe, Tim Whelan

1940

Angels over Broadway, Ben Hecht
Arizona, Wesley Ruggles
Babies for Sale, Charles Barton
Before I Hang, Nick Grinde
Beyond the Sacramento, Lambert Hillyer
Blazing Six Shooters, Joseph H. Lewis
Blondie Has Servant Trouble, Frank Strayer
Blondie on a Budget, Frank Strayer
Blondie Plays Cupid, Frank Strayer
Bullets for Rustlers, Sam Nelson
Convicted Woman, Nick Grinde
The Doctor Takes a Wife, Alexander Hall
The Durango Kid, Lambert Hillyer
Escape to Glory, John Brahm
Five Little Peppers at Home, Charles Barton
Five Little Peppers in Trouble, Charles Barton
Girls of the Road, Nick Grinde
Girls under 21, Max Nosseck
Glamour for Sale, D. Ross Lederman
He Stayed for Breakfast, Alexander Hall
His Girl Friday, Howard Hawks
I Married Adventure, Osa Johnson
Island of Doomed Men, Charles Barton
The Lady in Question, Charles Vidor
The Lone Wolf Meets a Lady, Sidney Salkow
The Lone Wolf Keeps a Date, Sidney Salkow
The Lone Wolf Strikes, Sidney Salkow
The Man from Tumbleweeds, Joseph H. Lewis
The Man with Nine Lives, Nick Grinde
Men without Souls, Nick Grinde
Military Academy, D. Ross Lederman
Music in My Heart, Joseph Santley
Nobody's Children, Charles Barton
Out West with the Peppers, Charles Barton
The Phantom Submarine, Charles Barton
Pioneers of the Frontier, Sam Nelson
Prairie Schooners, Sam Nelson
The Return of Wild Bill, Joseph H. Lewis
The Secret Seven, James Moore
So You Won't Talk?, Edward Sedgwick
Texas Stagecoach, Joseph H. Lewis
Thundering Frontier, D. Ross Lederman

Tillie the Toiler, Sidney Salkow
Too Many Husbands, Wesley Ruggles
Two-Fisted Rangers, Joseph H. Lewis
West of Abilene, Ralph Ceder
The Wild Cat of Tucson, Lambert Hillyer

OUTSIDE PRODUCTIONS

Frank Lloyd Pictures, Inc.

The Howards of Virginia, Frank Lloyd

Larry Darmour

Ellery Queen, Master Detective, Kurt Neumann
Fugitive from a Prison Camp, Lewis D. Collins
The Great Plane Robbery, Lewis D. Collins

1941

Across the Sierras, D. Ross Lederman
Bedtime Story, Alexander Hall
The Big Boss, Charles Barton
The Blonde from Singapore, Edward Dmytryk
Blondie Goes Latin, Frank Strayer
Blondie in Society, Frank Strayer
Confessions of Boston Blackie, Edward Dmytryk
The Devil Commands, Edward Dmytryk
The Face behind the Mask, Robert Florey
Go West, Young Lady, Frank Strayer
Hands across the Rockies, Lambert Hillyer
Harmon of Michigan, Charles Barton
Harvard Here I Come, Lew Landers
Here Comes Mr. Jordan, Alexander Hall
Her First Beau, Theodore Reed
Honolulu Lu, Charles Barton
I Was a Prisoner on Devil's Island, Lew Landers
King of Dodge City, Lambert Hillyer
The Lone Wolf Takes a Chance, Sidney Salkow
Meet Boston Blackie, Robert Florey
The Medico of Painted Springs, Lambert Hillyer
Mystery Ship, Lew Landers
Naval Academy, Erle C. Kenton
North from the Lone Star, Lambert Hillyer
The Officer and the Lady, Sam White
Our Wife, John Stahl
Outlaws of the Panhandle, Sam Nelson
Penny Serenade, George Stevens
The Pinto Kid, Lambert Hillyer
Prairie Stranger, Lambert Hillyer
The Return of Daniel Boone, Lambert Hillyer
The Richest Man in Town, Charles Barton

Riders of the Badlands, Howard Bretherton
Roaring Frontiers, Lambert Hillyer
The Royal Mounted Patrol, Lambert Hillyer
Secrets of the Lone Wolf, Edward Dmytryk
Sing for Your Supper, Charles Barton
The Son of Davy Crockett, Lambert Hillyer
Sweetheart of the Campus, Edward Dmytryk
The Stork Pays Off, Lew Landers
Texas, George Marshall
They Dare Not Love, James Whale
This Thing Called Love, Alexander Hall
Thunder over the Prairie, Lambert Hillyer
Three Girls about Town, Leigh Jason
Time Out for Rhythm, Sidney Salkow
Two in a Taxi, Robert Florey
Two Latins from Manhattan, Charles Barton
Under Age, Edward Dmytryk
You Belong to Me, Wesley Ruggles
You'll Never Get Rich, Sidney Lanfield

OUTSIDE PRODUCTIONS

Larry Darmour
Ellery Queen and the Murder Ring, James Hogan
Ellery Queen and the Perfect Crime, James Hogan
Ellery Queen's Penthouse Mystery, James Hogan
The Great Swindle, Lewis D. Collins

Irving Asher Productions, Ltd.
Missing Ten Days, Tim Whelan

Robert Sherwood
Adam Had Four Sons, Gregory Ratoff

Charles Rogers
Adventure in Washington, Alfred E. Green
She Knew All the Answers, Richard Wallace

Gregory Ratoff
The Men in Her Life, Gregory Ratoff

Lester Cowan
Ladies in Retirement, Charles Vidor

1942

Alias Boston Blackie, Lew Landers
Atlantic Convoy, Lew Landers
Bad Men of the Hills, William Berke
Blondie for Victory, Frank Strayer
Blondie Goes to College, Frank Strayer

Blondie's Blessed Event, Frank Strayer
The Boogie Man Will Get You, Lew Landers
Boston Blackie Goes Hollywood, Michael Gordon
Bullets for Bandits, Wallace W. Fox
Cadets on Parade, Lew Landers
Canal Zone, Lew Landers
Counter-Espionage, Edward Dmytryk
The Daring Young Man, Frank Strayer
The Devil's Trail, Lambert Hillyer
Down Rio Grande Way, William Berke
Flight Lieutenant, Sidney Salkow
Junior Academy, Lew Landers
Hello Annapolis, Charles Barton
The Lady Is Willing, Mitchell Leisen
Laugh Your Blues Away, Charles Barton
Lawless Plainsmen, William Berke
The Lone Prairie, William Berke
The Lone Star Vigilantes, Wallace W. Fox
Lucky Legs, Charles Barton
A Man's World, Charles Barton
The Man Who Returned to Life, Lew Landers
Meet the Stewarts, Alfred E. Green
My Sister Eileen, Alexander Hall
A Night to Remember, Richard Wallace
North of the Rockies, Lambert Hillyer
Not a Ladies Man, Lew Landers
Overland to Deadwood, William Berke
Parachute Nurse, Charles Barton
Pardon My Gun, William Berke
Prairie Gunsmoke, Lambert Hillyer
Riders of the Northland, William Berke
Riding through Nevada, William Berke
Sabotage Squad, Lew Landers
Shut My Big Mouth, Charles Barton
Smith of Minnesota, Lew Landers
The Spirit of Stanford, Charles Barton
Stand By All Networks, Lew Landers
Submarine Raider, Lew Landers
Sweetheart of the Fleet, Charles Barton
The Talk of the Town, George Stevens
They All Kissed the Bride, Alexander Hall
A Tornado in the Saddle, William Berke
Tramp, Tramp, Tramp, Charles Barton
Two Yanks in Trinidad, Gregory Ratoff
Underground Agent, Michael Gordon
Vengeance of the West, Lambert Hillyer
West of Tombstone, Howard Bretherton
The Wife Takes a Flyer, Richard Wallace
You Were Never Lovelier, William A. Seiter

OUTSIDE PRODUCTIONS

Larry Darmour
A Close Call for Ellery Queen, James Hogan
A Desperate Chance for Ellery Queen, James Hogan
Enemy Agents Meet Ellery Queen, James Hogan

Eden Productions
Martin Eden, Sidney Salkow

Ortus Films, Inc.
The Invaders, Michael Powell

1943

After Midnight with Boston Blackie, Lew Landers
Appointment in Berlin, Alfred E. Green
The Boy from Stalingrad, Sidney Salkow
The Chance of a Lifetime, William Castle
Cowboy in the Clouds, Benjamin Kline
Dangerous Blondes, Leigh Jason
The Desperadoes, Charles Vidor
Destroyer, William A. Seiter
Doughboys in Ireland, Lew Landers
The Fighting Buckaroo, William Berke
First Comes Courage, Dorothy Arzner
Footlight Glamour, Frank Strayer
Frontier Fury, William Berke
Good Luck, Mr. Yates, Ray Enright
Hail to the Rangers, William Berke
Is Everybody Happy?, Charles Barton
It's a Great Life, Frank Strayer
Klondike Kate, William Castle
Law of the Northwest, William Berke
Let's Have Fun, Charles Barton
The More the Merrier, George Stevens
Murder in Times Square, Lew Landers
My Kingdom for a Cook, Richard Wallace
One Dangerous Night, Michael Gordon
Passport to Suez, André De Toth
Power of the Press, Lew Landers
Redhead from Manhattan, Lew Landers
The Return of the Vampire, Lew Landers
Reveille with Beverly, Charles Barton
Riders of the Northwest Mounted, William Berke
Robin Hood of the Range, William Berke
Saddles and Sagebrush, William Berke
Sahara, Zoltan Korda
She Has What It Takes, Charles Barton
Silver City Raiders, William Berke

There's Something about a Soldier, Alfred E. Green
Two Senoritas from Chicago, Frank Woodruff
What a Woman!, Irving Cummings
What's Buzzin' Cousin?, Charles Barton

OUTSIDE PRODUCTIONS

Larry Darmour

Crime Doctor, Michael Gordon
Crime Doctor's Strangest Case, Eugene J. Forde
No Place for a Lady, James Hogan

Gregory Ratoff

Something to Shout About, Gregory Ratoff
The Heat's On, Gregory Ratoff

Lester Cowan

Commandos Strike at Dawn, John Farrow

Samuel Bronston

City without Men, Sidney Salkow

1944

Beautiful but Broke, Charles Barton
The Black Parachute, Lew Landers
Carolina Blues, Leigh Jason
Cover Girl, Charles Vidor
Cowboy Canteen, Lew Landers
Cowboy from Lonesome River, Benjamin Kline
Cry of the Werewolf, Henry Levin
Cyclone Prairie Rangers, Benjamin Kline
Dancing in Manhattan, Henry Levin
Girl in the Case, William Berke
The Ghost That Walks Alone, Lew Landers
Hey, Rookie, Charles Barton
The Impatient Years, Irving Cummings
Jam Session, Charles Barton
Kansas City Kitty, Del Lord
The Last Horseman, William Berke
Louisiana Hayride, Charles Barton
Meet Miss Bobby Socks, Glenn Tryon
The Missing Juror, Oscar (Budd) Boetticher, Jr.
Mr. Winkle Goes to War, Alfred E. Green
Nine Girls, Leigh Jason
None Shall Escape, André De Toth
Once Upon a Time, Alexander Hall
One Mysterious Night, Oscar (Budd) Boetticher, Jr.
The Racket Man, D. Ross Lederman
The Return of the Vampire, Lew Landers
Riding West, William Berke

Saddle Leather Law, Benjamin Kline
Sailor's Holiday, William Berke
Sergeant Mike, Henry Levin
She's a Soldier Too, William Castle
She's a Sweetheart, Del Lord
Soul of a Monster, Will Jason
Stars on Parade, Lew Landers
Strange Affair, Alfred E. Green
Swing in the Saddle, Lew Landers
Swing out the Blues, Malcolm St. Clair
Tahiti Nights, Will Jason
They Live in Fear, Josef Berne
Together Again, Charles Vidor
Two Man Submarine, Lew Landers
U-Boat Prisoner, Lew Landers
The Unwritten Code, Herman Rotsen
The Vigilantes Ride, William Berke
Wyoming Hurricane, William Berke

OUTSIDE PRODUCTIONS

Darmour, Inc.

Ever Since Venus, Arthur Dreifuss
The Mark of the Whistler, William Castle
Shadows in the Night, Eugene J. Forde
The Whistler, William Castle

Address Unknown, Inc.
Address Unknown, William C. Menzies

Terneen Productions, Inc.
Secret Command, Eddie Sutherland

1945

Blazing the Western Trail, Vernon Keays
Blonde from Brooklyn, Del Lord
Boston Blackie Booked on Suspicion, Arthur Dreifuss
Boston Blackie's Rendezvous, Arthur Dreifuss
Both Barrels Blazing, Derwin Abrahams
Counter-Attack, Zoltan Korda
Eadie Was a Lady, Arthur Dreifuss
Escape in the Fog, Oscar (Budd) Boetticher, Jr.
Eve Knew Her Apples, Will Jason
The Fighting Guardsman, Henry Levin
The Gay Senorita, Arthur Dreifuss
The Girl of the Limberlost, Melchor (Mel) G. Ferrer
A Guy, a Gal and a Pal, Oscar (Bud) Boetticher, Jr.
Hit the Hay, Del Lord
I Love a Bandleader, Del Lord
I Love a Mystery, Henry Levin

Lawless Empire, Vernon Keays
Leave It to Blondie, Abby Berlin
Let's Go Steady, Del Lord
Life with Blondie, Abby Berlin
My Name Is Julia Ross, Joseph H. Lewis
One Way to Love, Ray Enright
Outlaws of the Rockies, Ray Nazarro
Out of the Depths, D. Ross Lederman
Prison Ship, Arthur Dreifuss
The Return of the Durango Kid, Derwin Abrahams
Rhythm Round-Up, Vernon Keays
Rockin' in the Rockies, Vernon Keays
Rough Ridin' Justice, Derwin Abrahams
Rough, Tough and Ready, Del Lord
Rustlers of the Badlands, Derwin Abrahams
Sagebrush Heroes, Benjamin Kline
She Wouldn't Say Yes, Alexander Hall
Sing Me a Song of Texas, Vernon Keays
Song of the Prairie, Ray Nazarro
A Song to Remember, Charles Vidor
Ten Cents a Dance, Will Jason
Texas Panhandle, Ray Nazarro
A Thousand and One Nights, Alfred E. Green
Tonight and Every Night, Victor Saville
Voice of the Whistler, William Castle
Youth on Trial, Oscar (Budd) Boetticher, Jr.

OUTSIDE PRODUCTIONS

Darmour, Inc.
Adventures of Rusty, Paul Burnford
Crime Doctor's Courage, George Sherman
Crime Doctor's Warning, William Castle
The Power of the Whistler, Lew Landers
Shadows in the Night, Eugene J. Forde

Sidney Buchman Productions
Over 21, Charles Vidor

Columbia British Productions
You Can't Do without Love, Eugene J. Forde

Abbott-Herbert Corporation
Kiss and Tell, Richard Wallace

Mutual Productions
Pardon My Past, Leslie Fenton

Abbott-Solomon-Buchman, Inc.
Snafu, Jack Moss

United States Government
The Negro Sailor, Henry Levin

1946

Alias Mr. Twilight, John Sturges
The Bandit of Sherwood Forest, George Sherman and Henry Levin
Blondie Knows Best, Abby Berlin
Blondie's Lucky Day, Abby Berlin
Boston Blackie and the Law, D. Ross Lederman
À Close Call for Boston Blackie, Lew Landers
Cowboy Blues, Ray Nazarro
Crime Doctor's Man Hunt, William Castle
Dangerous Business, D. Ross Lederman
The Desert Horseman, Ray Nazarro
The Devil's Mask, Henry Levin
The Fighting Frontiersman, Derwin Abrahams
Frontier Gunlaw, Derwin Abrahams
Gallant Journey, William Wellman
Galloping Thunder, Ray Nazarro
The Gentleman Misbehaves, George Sherman
Gilda, Charles Vidor
Gunning for Vengeance, Ray Nazarro
Heading West, Ray Nazarro
It's Great to Be Young, Del Lord
The Jolson Story, Alfred E. Green
Just before Dawn, William Castle
Landrush, Vernon Keays
Lone Star Moonlight, Ray Nazarro
The Man Who Dared, John Sturges
Meet Me on Broadway, Leigh Jason
Mysterious Intruder, William Castle
Night Editor, Henry Levin
The Notorious Lone Wolf, D. Ross Lederman
Personality Kid, George Sherman
The Phantom Thief, D. Ross Lederman
Renegades, George Sherman
The Return of Rusty, William Castle
Roaring Rangers, Ray Nazarro
Secret of the Whistler, George Sherman
Sing While You Dance, D. Ross Lederman
Singing on the Trail, Ray Nazarro
Singin' in the Corn, Del Lord
Shadowed, John Sturges
So Dark the Night, Joseph H. Lewis
South of the Chisholm Trail, Derwin Abrahams
Talk about a Lady, George Sherman
Tars and Spars, Alfred E. Green
Terror Trail, Ray Nazarro
That Texas Jamboree, Ray Nazarro
Thrill of Brazil, S. Sylvan Simon
Throw a Saddle on a Star, Ray Nazarro
Two-Fisted Stranger, Ray Nazarro

The Unknown, Henry Levin
The Walls Came Tumbling Down, Lothar Mendes

OUTSIDE PRODUCTIONS

Phil L. Ryan Productions, Inc.
Perilous Holiday, Edward H. Griffith

Key Pictures, Inc.
Betty Co-Ed, Arthur Dreifuss

Edward Small Productions
The Return of Monte Cristo, Henry Levin

1947

Blind Spot, Robert Gordon
Blondie in the Dough, Abby Berlin
Blondie's Anniversary, Abby Berlin
Blondie's Big Moment, Abby Berlin
Blondie's Holiday, Abby Berlin
Buckaroo from Powder River, Ray Nazarro
Bulldog Drummond at Bay, Sidney Salkow
Bulldog Drummond Strikes Back, Frank McDonald
Cigarette Girl, Gunther V. Fritsch
Crime Doctor's Gamble, William Castle
Dead Reckoning, John Cromwell
Devil Ship, Lew Landers
Down to Earth, Alexander Hall
For the Love of Rusty, John Sturges
Framed, Richard Wallace
The Guilt of Janet Ames, Henry Levin
It Had to Be You, Don Hartman and Rudolph Maté
Keeper of the Bees, John Sturges
Key Witness, D. Ross Lederman
King of the Wild Horses, George Archainbaud
Last Days of Boot Hill, Ray Nazarro
Law of the Canyon, Ray Nazarro
Lone Hand Texan, Ray Nazarro
The Lone Wolf in London, Leslie Goodwins
The Lone Wolf in Mexico, D. Ross Lederman
The Millerson Case, George Archainbaud
Millie's Daughter, Sidney Salkow
Over the Santa Fe Trail, Ray Nazarro
Prairie Raiders, Derwin Abrahams
Riders of the Lone Star, Derwin Abrahams
Rose of Santa Rosa, Ray Nazarro
Smoky River Serenade, Derwin Abrahams
The Son of Rusty, Lew Landers
Sport of Kings, Robert Gordon

The Stranger from Ponca City, Derwin Abrahams
Swing the Western Way, Derwin Abrahams
The Thirteenth Hour, William Clemens
West of Dodge City, Ray Nazarro
When a Girl's Beautiful, Frank McDonald

OUTSIDE PRODUCTIONS

Producers Actors Corporation
Gunfighters, George Waggner

Samuel Bischoff Productions
The Corpse Came C.O.D., Henry Levin

Columbia Pictures (Australia)
Pacific Adventure, Ken G. Hall

Key Pictures
Last of the Redmen, George Sherman
Little Miss Broadway, Arthur Dreifuss
Sweet Genevieve, Arthur Dreifuss
Two Blondes and a Redhead, Arthur Dreifuss

J.E.M. Productions
Johnny O'Clock, Robert Rossen

D.A. Productions
Mr. District Attorney, Robert Sinclair

Cornell Pictures, Inc.
Her Husband's Affairs, S. Sylvan Simon

Gene Autry Productions
The Last Round-Up, John English

1948

Adventures in Silverado, Phil Karlson
The Arkansas Swing, Ray Nazarro
The Best Man Wins, John Sturges
Black Eagle, Robert Gordon
Blazing across the Pecos, Ray Nazarro
Blondie's Reward, Abby Berlin
Blondie's Secret, Edward Bernds
El Dorado Pass, Ray Nazarro
The Gallant Blade, Henry Levin
The Gentleman from Nowhere, William Castle
The Lady from Shanghai, Orson Welles
Leather Gloves, Richard Quine and William Asher
The Man from Colorado, Henry Levin
The Mating of Millie, Henry Levin
My Dog Rusty, Lew Landers

Phantom Valley, Ray Nazarro
Port Said, Reginald LeBorg
Quick on the Trigger, Ray Nazarro
The Return of October, Joseph H. Lewis
The Return of the Whistler, D. Ross Lederman
Rusty Leads the Way, Will Jason
Singin' Spurs, Ray Nazarro
Six-Gun Law, Ray Nazarro
Smoky Mountain Melody, Ray Nazarro
Song of Idaho, Ray Nazarro
The Swordsman, Joseph H. Lewis
Thunderhoof, Phil Karlson
Trapped by Boston Blackie, Seymour Friedman
Trail to Laredo, Ray Nazarro
West of Sonora, Ray Nazarro
Whirlwind Raiders, Vernon Keays
The Woman from Tangier, Harold Daniels
The Wreck of the Hesperus, John Hoffman

OUTSIDE PRODUCTIONS

Cavalier Productions
Relentless, George Sherman

Signet Productions
The Sign of the Ram, John Sturges

Producers Actors Corporation
Coroner Creek, Ray Enright

Benedict Bogeaus Productions
Lulu Belle, Leslie Fenton

Key Pictures, Inc.
Glamour Girl, Arthur Dreifuss
I Surrender Dear, Arthur Dreifuss
Mary Lou, Arthur Dreifuss
The Prince of Thieves, Howard Bretherton
Racing Luck, William Berke
Triple Threat, Jean Yarbrough

Edward Small Productions
The Black Arrow, Gordon Douglas
The Fuller Brush Man, S. Sylvan Simon
Walk a Crooked Mile, Gordon Douglas

Cornell Pictures, Inc.
I Love Trouble, S. Sylvan Simon

Gene Autry Productions
The Strawberry Roan, John English

Kennedy-Buchman Pictures
To the Ends of the Earth, Robert Stevenson

Sage Western Pictures
The Untamed Breed, Charles Lamont

The Katzman Corporation
Jungle Jim, William Berke

The Beckworth Corporation
The Loves of Carmen, Charles Vidor

1949

Air Hostess, Lew Landers
Bandits of El Dorado, Ray Nazarro
The Blazing Trail, Ray Nazarro
Blondie Hits the Jackpot, Edward Bernds
Blondie's Big Deal, Edward Bernds
Boston Blackie's Chinese Venture, Seymour Friedman
Challenge of the Range, Ray Nazarro
Crime Doctor's Diary, Seymour Friedman
The Dark Past, Rudolph Maté
Desert Vigilante, Fred F. Sears
The Devil's Henchman, Seymour Friedman
Feudin' Rhythm, Edward Bernds
Frontier Outpost, Ray Nazarro
Holiday in Havana, Jean Yarbrough
Home in San Antone, Ray Nazarro
Horsemen of the Sierras, Fred F. Sears
Johnny Allegro, Ted Tetzlaff
Kazan, Will Jason
Laramie, Ray Nazarro
Law of the Barbary Coast, Lew Landers
The Lone Wolf and His Lady, John Hoffman
Lust for Gold, S. Sylvan Simon
Make Believe Ballroom, Joseph Santley
Miss Grant Takes Richmond, Lloyd Bacon
Mr. Soft Touch, Henry Levin and Gordon Douglas
Prison Warden, Seymour Friedman
Renegades of the Sage, Ray Nazarro
Rusty Saves a Life, Seymour Friedman
Rusty's Birthday, Seymour Friedman
The Secret of St. Ives, Phil Rosen
Shockproof, Douglas Sirk
Slightly French, Douglas Sirk
South of Death Valley, Ray Nazarro
Tell It to the Judge, Norman Foster
The Walking Hills, John Sturges

OUTSIDE PRODUCTIONS

Columbia British Productions
Affairs of a Rogue, Alberto Cavalcanti

Security Pictures
Anna Lucasta, Irving Rapper

Henry A. Romm Productions
Ladies of the Chorus, Phil Karlson

Robert Rossen Productions
All the King's Men, Robert Rossen
The Undercover Man, Joseph H. Lewis

Parliament Pictures
Song of India, Albert S. Rogell

Cineopera, Inc.
Faust and the Devil, Carmine Gallone
The Lost One, Carmine Gallone
Her Wonderful Life, Carmine Gallone

Santana Pictures
And Baby Makes Three, Henry Levin
Knock on Any Door, Nicholas Ray
Tokyo Joe, Stuart Heisler

Producers Actors Corporation
The Doolins of Oklahoma, Gordon Douglas

Horizon Pictures
We Were Strangers, John Huston

Sidney Buchman Enterprises
Jolson Sings Again, Henry Levin

Key Pictures
Barbary Pirate, Lew Landers
Manhattan Angel, Arthur Dreifuss
The Mutineers, Jean Yarbrough

The Katzman Corporation
The Lost Tribe, William Berke

Gene Autry Productions
The Big Sombrero, Frank McDonald
The Cowboy and the Indians, John English
Loaded Pistols, John English
Riders in the Sky, John English
Riders of the Whistling Pines, John English
Sons of New Mexico, John English
Rim of the Canyon, John English

Walter Wanger Pictures
The Reckless Moment, Max Ophuls

1950

Across the Badlands, Fred F. Sears
Beauty on Parade, Lew Landers
Between Midnight and Dawn, Gordon Douglas
Beware of Blondie, Edward Bernds
Blondie's Hero, Edward Bernds
Bodyhold, Seymour Friedman
Born Yesterday, George Cukor
Cargo to Capetown, Earl McEvoy
Convicted, Henry Levin
Customs Agent, Seymour Friedman
David Harding, Counterspy, Ray Nazarro
Emergency Wedding, Edward Buzzell
Father Is a Bachelor, Norman Foster and Abby Berlin
Flame of Stamboul, Ray Nazarro
Fortunes of Captain Blood, Gordon Douglas
The Fuller Brush Girl, Lloyd Bacon
Girls' School, Lew Landers
The Good Humor Man, Lloyd Bacon
Harriet Craig, Vincent Sherman
He's a Cockeyed Wonder, Peter Godfrey
Hoedown, Ray Nazarro
The Killer That Stalked New York, Earl McEvoy
Kill the Umpire, Lloyd Bacon
Lightning Guns, Fred F. Sears
Mary Ryan, Detective, Abby Berlin
Military Academy, D. Ross Lederman
No Sad Songs for Me, Rudolph Maté
On the Island of Samoa, William Berke
Outcast of Black Mesa, Ray Nazarro
The Palamino, Ray Nazarro
The Petty Girl, Henry Levin
Raiders of Tomahawk Creek, Fred F. Sears
Rogues of Sherwood Forest, Gordon Douglas
Rookie Fireman, Seymour Friedman
Streets of Ghost Town, Ray Nazarro
Texas Dynamo, Ray Nazarro
The Tougher They Come, Ray Nazarro
Trail of the Rustlers, Ray Nazarro
When You're Smiling, Joseph Santley
A Woman of Distinction, Edward Buzzell

OUTSIDE PRODUCTIONS

[Outside productions began increasing steadily after World War II and soon would constitute the bulk of Columbia's releases.]

Producer Actors Corporation
The Nevadan, Gordon Douglas

Tony Owen Productions
The Travelling Saleswoman, Charles F. Reisner

Essaness Pictures
711 Ocean Drive, Joseph M. Newman

Key Pictures
Chain Gang, Lew Landers
Chinatown at Midnight, Seymour Friedman
Last of the Buccaneers, Lew Landers
State Penitentiary, Lew Landers
Tyrant of the Sea, Lew Landers

The Katzman Corporation
Captive Girl, William Berke
Mark of the Gorilla, William Berke
Pygmy Island, William Berke

Gene Autry Productions
Beyond the Purple Hills, John English
The Blazing Sun, John English
Cow Town, John English
Indian Territory, John English
Mule Train, John English

Santana Pictures
In a Lonely Place, Nicholas Ray

Screencraft Pictures
The Texan Meets Calamity Jane, Ande Lamb

1951

Al Jennings of Oklahoma, Ray Nazarro
The Barefoot Mailman, Earl McEvoy
The Big Gusher, Lew Landers
Bonanza Town, Fred F. Sears
Chain of Circumstance, Will Jason
China Corsair, Ray Nazarro
Corky of Gasoline Alley, Edward Bernds
Counterspy Meets Scotland Yard, Seymour Friedman
Criminal Lawyer, Seymour Friedman
Cyclone Fury, Ray Nazarro
The Flying Missile, Henry Levin
Fort Savage Raiders, Ray Nazarro
Gasoline Alley, Edward Bernds
Her First Romance, Seymour Friedman
The Kid from Armadillo, Ray Nazarro
The Lady and the Bandit, Ralph Murphy
Mask of the Avenger, Phil Karlson
The Mob, Robert Parrish

My True Story, Mickey Rooney
Never Trust a Gambler, Ralph Murphy
Pecos River, Fred F. Sears
Prairie Roundup, Fred F. Sears
Ridin' the Outlaw Trail, Fred F. Sears
Smuggler's Gold, William Berke
The Son of Dr. Jekyll, Seymour Friedman
Snake River Desperadoes, Fred F. Sears
Stage to Tucson, Ralph Murphy
Sunny Side of the Street, Richard Quine
Two of a Kind, Henry Levin

OUTSIDE PRODUCTIONS

Key Pictures
Hurricane Island, Lew Landers
Revenue Agent, Lew Landers
When the Redskins Rode, Lew Landers
A Yank in Korea, Lew Landers

The Katzman Corporation
Fury of the Congo, William Berke
Jungle Manhunt, Lew Landers

Gene Autry Productions
Gene Autry and the Mounties, John English
Hills of Utah, John English
Silver Canyon, John English
Texans Never Cry, Francis McDonald
Valley of Fire, John English
Whirlwind, John English

Producers Actors Corporation
Man in the Saddle, André De Toth
Santa Fe, Irving Pichel

Rossen Enterprises
The Brave Bulls, Robert Rossen

Edward Small Productions
The Texas Rangers, Phil Karlson
Valentino, Lewis Allen

Resolute Pictures
Lorna Doone, Phil Karlson

Santana Pictures
The Family Secret, Henry Levin
Sirocco, Curtis Bernhardt

RD-DR Corporation
The Whistle at Eaton Falls, Robert Siodmak

London Films
The Great Manhunt, Sidney Gilliat

Forum Productions
Pick-Up, Hugo Haas

Gregory Ratoff
Operation X, Gregory Ratoff

Superior Films
M, Joseph Losey

Esskay Pictures Company
The Magic Carpet, Lew Landers
Purple Heart Diary, Richard Quine

Sidney Buchman Enterprises
Harlem Globetrotters, Phil Brown
Saturday's Hero, David Miller

Halburt Productions
Ten Tall Men, Willis Goldbeck

Lobo Productions
Five, Arch Obler

Briskin-Smith Productions
The Magic Face, Frank Tuttle

1952

Assignment Paris, Robert Parrish
Captain Pirate, Ralph Murphy
Harem Girl, Edward Bernds
The Hawk of Wild River, Fred F. Sears
Junction City, Ray Nazarro
The Kid from Broken Gun, Fred F. Sears
Laramie Mountains, Ray Nazarro
The Marrying Kind, George Cukor
Montana Territory, Ray Nazarro
Okinawa, Leigh Jason
Paula, Rudolph Maté
Rainbow 'Round My Shoulder, Richard Quine
The Rough, Tough West, Ray Nazarro
Smoky Canyon, Fred F. Sears
Sound Off, Richard Quine

OUTSIDE PRODUCTIONS

Esskay Pictures Company
Brave Warrior, Spencer Bennet
California Conquest, Lew Landers

The Golden Hawk, Sidney Salkow
Last Train from Bombay, Fred F. Sears
Thief of Damascus, Will Jason
A Yank in Indo-China, Wallace A. Grissell

The Katzman Corporation
Jungle Jim in the Forbidden Land, Lew Landers
Voodoo Tiger, Spencer Bennet

Gene Autry Productions
Apache Country, George Archainbaud
Barbed Wire, George Archainbaud
Blue Canadian Rockies, George Archainbaud
Night Train to Galveston, George Archainbaud
The Old West, George Archainbaud
Wagon Team, George Archainbaud

Sidney Buchman Enterprises
Boots Malone, William Dieterle

Halburt Productions
The First Time, Frank Tashlin

Motion Picture Investors
Scandal Sheet, Phil Karlson

The Stanley Kramer Company
Death of a Salesman, Laslo Benedek
Eight Iron Men, Edward Dmytryk
The Happy Time, Richard Fleischer
Member of the Wedding, Fred Zinnemann
My Six Convicts, Hugo Fregonese
The Sniper, Edward Dmytryk

General Film Distributors, Ltd.
The Clouded Yellow, Ralph Thomas

Summit Productions
Storm over Tibet, Andrew Marton

RD-DR Corporation
Walk East on Beacon, Alfred Werker

Resolute Pictures
The Brigand, Phil Karlson
Cripple Creek, Ray Nazarro

Edward Small Productions
Indian Uprising, Ray Nazarro

The Beckworth Corporation
Affair in Trinidad, Vincent Sherman
Salome, William Dieterle

Producers Actors Corporation
Hangman's Knot, Roy Huggins

H-H Productions
Strange Fascination, Hugo Haas

American Pictures Corporation
Invasion U.S.A., Alfred E. Green

All American Film Corporation
Red Snow, Boris Petroff and Harry Franklin

1953

All Ashore, Richard Quine
Ambush at Tomahawk Gap, Fred F. Sears
The Big Heat, Fritz Lang
China Venture, Don Siegel
Cruisin' down the River, Richard Quine
El Alamein, Fred F. Sears
From Here to Eternity, Fred Zinnemann
Gun Fury [3-D], Raoul Walsh
Last of the Comanches, André De Toth
The Last Posse, Alfred Werker
Let's Do It Again, Alexander Hall
Man in the Dark [3-D], Lew Landers
Mission over Korea, Fred F. Sears
The Nebraskan [3-D], Fred F. Sears
Target Hong Kong, Fred F. Sears

OUTSIDE PRODUCTIONS

Esskay Pictures Company
Flame of Calcutta, Seymour Friedman
Fort Ti [3-D], William Castle
The 49th Man, Fred F. Sears
Jack McCall, Desperado, Sidney Salkow
The Pathfinder, Sidney Salkow
Prince of Pirates, Sidney Salkow
Serpent of the Nile, William Castle
Siren of Bagdad, Richard Quine

The Katzman Corporation
Killer Ape, Spencer Bennet
Savage Mutiny, Spencer Bennet
Valley of the Head Hunters, William Berke

Gene Autry Productions
Goldtown Ghost Riders, George Archainbaud
Last of the Pony Riders, George Archainbaud
On Top of Old Smoky, George Archainbaud

Pack Train, George Archainbaud
Saginaw Trail, George Archainbaud
Wagon Team, George Archainbaud
Winning of the West, George Archainbaud

The Stanley Kramer Company
The 5000 Fingers of Dr. T., Roy Rowland
The Four Poster, Irving Reis
The Juggler, Edward Dmytryk

Producers Actors Corporation
The Stranger Wore a Gun [3-D], André De Toth

H-H Productions
One Girl's Confession, Hugo Haas

General Film Distributors, Ltd.
Five Angles on Murder, Anthony Asquith

Wisberg-Pollexfen Productions
Problem Girls, E.A. Dupont

Shane-Tors Productions, Inc.
The Glass Wall, Maxwell Shane

Clover Productions, Inc.
Conquest of Cochise, William Castle
Prisoners of the Casbah, Richard Bare
Sky Commando, Fred F. Sears
Slaves of Babylon, William Castle

The Beckworth Corporation
Miss Sadie Thompson [3-D], Curtis Bernhardt

American Pictures Corporation
Paris Model, Alfred E. Green

Jack Broder Productions, Inc.
Combat Squad, Cy Roth

1954

Bad for Each Other, Irving Rapper
The Black Dakotas, Ray Nazarro
Drive a Crooked Road, Richard Quine
Human Desire, Fritz Lang
It Should Happen to You, George Cukor
Massacre Canyon Fred F. Sears
The Outlaw Stallion, Fred F. Sears
Phffft, Mark Robson
Pushover, Richard Quine
They Rode West, Phil Karlson
Three Hours to Kill, Alfred Werker

OUTSIDE PRODUCTIONS

Clover Productions, Inc.
Battle of Rogue River, William Castle
Charge of the Lancers, William Castle
Drums of Tahiti [3-D], William Castle
The Iron Glove, William Castle
Jessee James vs. the Daltons [3-D], William Castle
The Law vs. Billy the Kid, William Castle
The Miami Story, Fred F. Sears
The Saracen Blade, William Castle

Hemisphere Productions
Fire over Africa, Richard Sale

Horizon-American Corporation
On the Waterfront, Elia Kazan

Hugo Haas
Bait, Hugo Haas

The Katzman Corporation
Cannibal Attack, Lee Sholem
Jungle Maneaters, Lee Sholem

The Stanley Kramer Company
The Caine Mutiny, Edward Dmytryk
The Wild One, Laslo Benedek

Trio Films
The Mad Magician [3-D], John Brahm

Warwick Film Productions
The Black Knight, Tay Garnett
Hell below Zero, Mark Robson
Paratrooper, Terence Young

Welsch Productions
A Bullet Is Waiting, John Farrow

1955

Apache Ambush, Fred F. Sears
Bring Your Smile Along, Blake Edwards
Cell 2455, Death Row, Fred F. Sears
The Last Frontier, Anthony Mann
My Sister Eileen, Richard Quine
Picnic, Joshua Logan
The Queen Bee, Ranald MacDougall
Three for the Show, H.C. Potter
Three Stripes in the Sun, Richard Murphy
Tight Spot, Phil Karlson
The Violent Men, Rudolph Maté
Wyoming Renegades, Fred F. Sears

OUTSIDE PRODUCTIONS

Clover Productions
Chicago Syndicate, Fred F. Sears
Creature with the Atom Brain, Edward L. Cahn
The Crooked Web, Nathan Juran
Duel on the Mississippi, William Castle
The Gun That Won the West, William Castle
It Came from beneath the Sea, Robert Gordon
Masterson of Kansas, William Castle
New Orleans Uncensored, William Castle
Pirates of Tripoli, Felix Feist
Seminole Uprising, Earl Bellamy
Teenage Crime Wave, Fred F. Sears

The Katzman Corporation
Devil Goddess, Spencer Bennet
Jungle Moon Men, Charles S. Gould

Producers Actors Corporation
A Lawless Street, Joseph H. Lewis
Ten Wanted Men, Bruce Humberstone

Copa Productions, Inc.
Count Three and Pray, George Sherman

N.P. Rathvon & Company-Trans-Rhein-Filmgesellschaft m.b.h.
Special Delivery, John Brahm

Andrew L. Stone
The Night Holds Terror, Andrew Stone

Film Locations, Ltd. (Hemisphere Productions, Inc.)
Footsteps in the Fog, Arthur Lubin

Gravis Productions, Inc.
Hell's Horizon, Tom Gries

Yof Corporation
The Bamboo Prison, Lewis Seiler
Women's Prison, Lewis Seiler

William Goetz Productions, Inc.
The Man from Laramie, Anthony Mann

Warwick Film Productions, Inc.
A Prize of Gold, Mark Robson

Coronado Productions, Inc.
The End of the Affair, Edward Dmytryk

Rota Productions, Inc.
The Long Gray Line, John Ford

Facet Productions, Ltd.
The Detective, Robert Hamer

Dayle Productions, Inc.
5 Against the House, Phil Karlson

1956

[Since at this point outside productions dominate the releases, they are included in the annual listing instead of separately, as are independent productions released by Columbia.]

Autumn Leaves (William Goetz Productions), Robert Aldrich
Battle Stations (Yof Corporation), Lewis Seiler
Beyond Mombasa (Todon Productions), George Marshall
Blackjack Ketchum, Desperado (Clover), Earl Bellamy
Cha-Cha-Cha Boom! (Clover), Fred F. Sears
Cockleshell Heroes (Warwick), José Ferrer
Don't Knock the Rock (Clover), Fred F. Sears
Earth vs. the Flying Saucers (Clover), Fred F. Sears
The Eddie Duchin Story, George Sidney
Full of Life, Richard Quine
Fury at Gunsight Pass, Fred F. Sears
The Gamma People (Warwick), John Gilling
The Harder They Fall, Mark Robson
He Laughed Last, Blake Edwards
Hot Blood (Welsch Productions), Nicholas Ray
The Houston Story (Clover), William Castle
Inside Detroit (Clover), Fred F. Sears
Joe Macbeth (Hemisphere), Ken Hughes
Jubal, Delmer Daves
The Last Man to Hang (Warwick), Terence Fisher
Miami Exposé (Clover), Fred F. Sears
Nightfall (Copa), Jacques Tourneur
1984 (N.P. Rathvon), Michael Anderson
Odongo (Warwick), John Gilling
Over-Exposed, Lewis Seiler
Port Afrique (David E. Rose), Rudolph Maté
The Prisoner (London Independent Producers), Peter Glenville
Reprisal! (Lewis J. Rachmil), George Sherman
Rock around the Clock (Clover), Fred F. Sears
Rumble on the Docks (Clover), Fred F. Sears
Safari (Warwick), Terence Young
Secret of Treasure Mountain, Seymour Friedman
The Seventh Cavalry (Producers Actors), Joseph H. Lewis
Sierra Stranger (Aroma), Lee Sholem
The Solid Gold Cadillac, Richard Quine
Spin a Dark Web (Hemisphere), Vernon Sewell
Storm Center (Phoenix Productions), Daniel Taradash

Storm over the Nile (London Film Productions), Terence Young and
   Zoltan Korda
The Strange One (Horizon), Jack Garfein
Suicide Mission (Warwick), Michael Forlong
Uranium Boom (Clover), William Castle
The Werewolf (Clover), Fred F. Sears
The White Squaw (Screen Gems), Ray Nazarro
You Can't Run Away from It, Dick Powell
Zarak (Warwick), Terence Young

1957

Abandon Ship! (Copa), Richard Sale
The Bridge on the River Kwai (Horizon), David Lean
The Brothers Rico (William Goetz), Phil Karlson
The Burglar (Samson Productions), Paul Wendkos
Calypso Heat Wave (Clover), Fred F. Sears
Decision at Sundown (Producers Actors), Budd Boetticher
The Domino Kid (Calhoun-Orsatti), Ray Nazarro
Escape from San Quentin (Clover), Fred F. Sears
Fire down Below (Warwick), Robert Parrish
The Garment Jungle, Vincent Sherman
The Giant Claw (Clover), Fred F. Sears
The Guns of Fort Petticoat (Brown-Murphy Pictures), George Marshall
The Hard Man (Helen Ainsworth), George Sherman
Hellcats of the Navy (Morningside), Nathan Juran
High Flight (Warwick), John Gilling
How to Murder a Rich Uncle (Warwick), Nigel Patrick
Jeanne Eagels (George Sidney Productions), George Sidney
The Long Haul (Marksman), Ken Hughes
The Man Who Turned to Stone (Clover), Leslie Kardos
The Night the World Exploded (Clover), Fred F. Sears
No Time to Be Young (Screen Gems), David Lowell Rich
Operation Mad Ball (Jed Harris), Richard Quine
Pal Joey (George Sidney), George Sidney
The Parson and the Outlaw (R.C. Productions), Oliver Drake
The Phantom Stagecoach (Screen Gems), Ray Nazarro
Shadow on the Window, William Asher
The Story of Esther Costello (American Films Corporation), David Miller
The Tall T (Producers Actors), Budd Boetticher
3:10 to Yuma, Delmer Daves
The Tijuana Story (Clover), Leslie Kardos
Town on Trial (Marksman), John Guillerman
20 Million Miles to Earth (Charles H. Schneer), Nathan Juran
The 27th Day (Romson), William Asher
Utah Blaine (Clover), Fred F. Sears
Wicked as They Come (Hemisphere), Ken Hughes
Woman of the River (Centaur), Mario Soldati
The Young Don't Cry (Philip A. Waxman Pictures), Alfred Werker
Zombies of Mora Tau (Clover), Edward L. Cahn

1958

Apache Territory (Calhoun-Orsatti), Ray Nazarro
Bell, Book and Candle (Phoenix), Richard Quine
Bitter Victory (Transcontinental), Nicholas Ray
Bonjour Tristesse (Carlyle), Otto Preminger
Buchanan Rides Again (Producers Actors), Budd Boetticher
The Camp on Blood Island (Hammer), Val Guest
The Case against Brooklyn (Morningside), Paul Wendkos
Cowboy (Phoenix), Delmer Daves
Crash Landing (Clover), Fred F. Sears
Curse of the Demon (Chelsea), Jacques Tourneur
Ghost of the China Sea (Charles B. Griffith), Fred F. Sears
The Goddess (Carnegie Productions), John Cromwell
Going Steady (Clover), Fred F. Sears
Gunman's Walk, Phil Karlson
The Key (Highroad), Sir Carol Reed
Kill Her Gently (Fortress), Charles Saunders
The Last Hurrah (John Ford Productions), John Ford
Let's Rock!, Harry Foster
Life Begins at 17 (Clover), Arthur Dreifuss
The Lineup (Frank Cooper-Pajemar), Don Siegel
The Man Inside (Warwick), John Gilling
Me and the Colonel (Court-Goetz), Peter Glenville
Murder by Contract (Orbit), Irving Lerner
Murder Reported (Fortress), Charles Saunders
Paradise Lagoon (Modern Screen Play Productions), Lewis Gilbert
Return to Warbow (Screen Gems), Ray Nazarro
Revenge of Frankenstein (Hammer), Terence Fisher
Screaming Mimi (Harry Joe Brown), Gerd Oswald
The 7th Voyage of Sinbad (Morningside), Nathan Juran
She Played with Fire (John Harvel Productions), Sidney Gilliat
The Snorkel (Clarion), Guy Green
Tank Force (Warwick), Terence Young
Tarawa Beachhead (Morningside), Paul Wendkos
This Angry Age (Dino De Laurentiis), René Clement
The True Story of Lynn Stuart (Bryan Foy), Lewis Seiler
The Whole Truth (Valiant/American), John Guillermin
The World Was His Jury (Clover), Fred F. Sears

1959

Anatomy of a Murder (Carlyle), Otto Preminger
The Bandit of Zhobe (Warwick), John Gilling
Battle of the Coral Sea (Morningside), Paul Wendkos
City of Fear (Orbit), Irving Lerner
The Crimson Kimono (Globe Enterprises), Samuel Fuller
Edge of Eternity (Thunderbird), Don Siegel
Face of a Fugitive (Morningside), Paul Wendkos
The Flying Fontaines (Clover), George Sherman

Forbidden Island (Charles B. Griffith), Charles B. Griffith
The Gene Krupa Story (Philip A. Waxman), Don Weis
Gideon of Scotland Yard (John Ford Productions), John Ford
Gidget, Paul Wendkos
Good Day for a Hanging (Morningside), Nathan Juran
Gunmen from Laredo, Wallace MacDonald
Have Rocket, Will Travel (Harry Romm), David Lowell Rich
Hey Boy! Hey Girl! (Harry Romm), David Lowell Rich
The H-Man (Toho), Inoshiro Honda
It Happened to Jane (Arwin), Richard Quine
Juke Box Rhythm (Clover), Arthur Dreifuss
The Last Angry Man (Fred Kohlmar Productions), Daniel Mann
The Last Blitzkrieg (Clover), Arthur Dreifuss
The Legend of Tom Dooley (Shpetner Productions), Ted Post
Middle of the Night (Sudan), Delbert Mann
The Mouse That Roared (Highroad), Jack Arnold
Porgy and Bess (Samuel Goldwyn), Otto Preminger
Ride Lonesome (Ranown Pictures), Budd Boetticher
Senior Prom (Harry Romm), David Lowell Rich
They Came to Cordura (Goetz-Baroda), Robert Rossen
The 30 Foot Bride of Candy Rock (D.R.B.), Sidney Miller
The Tingler (William Castle), William Castle
The Two-Headed Spy (Chelsea), André De Toth
Verboten! (Globe), Samuel Fuller
The Warrior and the Slave Girl (Alexandra), Vittorio Cottafavi
The Woman Eater (Fortress), Charles Saunders
Yesterday's Enemy (Hammer), Val Guest
The Young Land (C.V. Whitney Pictures), Ted Tetzlaff

1960

All the Young Men (Hall Bartlett-Jaguar Productions), Hall Bartlett
Babette Goes to War (Iena Productions), Christian-Jaque
Battle in Outer Space (Toho), Inoshiro Honda
Because They're Young (Drexel Pictures), Paul Wendkos
Commanche Station (Ranown), Budd Boetticher
The Electronic Monster (Amalgamated), Montgomery Tully
The Enemy General (Clover), George Sherman
Fast and Sexy (Circeo-France Cinema), Reginald Denham
Hell Is a City (Hammer), Val Guest
I Aim at the Stars (Morningside), J. Lee Thompson
I'm All Right Jack (Charter/British Lion), John Boulting
Jazz Boat (Warwick), Ken Hughes
Killers of Kilimanjaro (Warwick), Richard Thorpe
Let No Man Write My Epitaph (Boris D. Kaplan), Philip Leacock
Man on a String (RD-DR), André De Toth
The Mountain Road (William Goetz), Daniel Mann
My Dog Buddy (McLendon Radio Pictures), Ray Kellogg
The Nights of Lucretia Borgia (Musa Cinematografica), Sergio Grieco
Once More, with Feeling (Stanley Donen), Stanley Donen

Our Man in Havana (Kingsmead), Sir Carol Reed
Pepe (George Sidney/Posa), George Sidney
Song without End (Goetz/Vidor), Charles Vidor, George Cukor
Stop! Look! and Laugh! (Harry Romm), Jules White
Strangers When We Meet (Bryna/Quine), Richard Quine
Stranglers of Bombay (Hammer), Terence Fisher
Suddenly, Last Summer (Horizon), Joseph L. Mankiewicz
Surprise Package (Stanley Donen), Stanley Donen
13 Ghosts (William Castle), William Castle
The Three Worlds of Gulliver (Morningside), Jack Sher
12 to the Moon (Luna Productions), David Bradley
Who Was That Lady? (Consark/George Sidney), George Sidney

1961

Cry for Happy (William Goetz), George Marshall
The Devil at 4 O'Clock (Fred Kohlmar), Mervyn LeRoy
Five Day Lover (Ariane Films), Philippe De Broca
Five Golden Hours (Anglofilm/Grayfilm), Mario Zampi
Gidget Goes Hawaiian (Jerry Bressler), Paul Wendkos
The Guns of Navarone (Open Road), J. Lee Thompson
Hand in Hand (Helen Winston/Associated British Pictures), Philip Leacock
Homicidal (William Castle), William Castle
Loss of Innocence (P.K.L. Pictures), Lewis Gilbert
"Mad Dog" Coll (Thalia Films), Burt Balaban
Mr. Sardonicus (William Castle), William Castle
The Most Dangerous Man Alive (Trans-Global Films), Allan Dwan
Mysterious Island (Ameran Films/Morningside), Cy Endfield
Passport to China (Hammer/Swallow), Michael Carreras
Queen of the Pirates (Max Productions/Rapid Film), Mario Costa
A Raisin in the Sun (Paman/Doris), Daniel Petrie
Scream of Fear (Hammer), Seth Holt
Stop Me before I Kill (Hammer/Falcon/Hilary), Val Guest
Sword of Sherwood Forest (Hammer/Yeoman), Terence Fisher
The Terror of the Tongs (Merlin/Hammer), Anthony Bushell
The Trunk (Donwin), Donavan Winter
Two Rode Together (John Ford/Shpetner), John Ford
Underworld, U.S.A. (Globe Enterprises), Samuel Fuller
Valley of the Dragons (Z.R.B. Productions), Edward Bernds
The Wackiest Ship in the Army (Fred Kohlmar), Richard Murphy
A Weekend with Lulu (Hammer), John Paddy Carstairs

1962

Advise and Consent (Alpha/Alpina), Otto Preminger
Barabbas (Dino De Laurentiis), Richard Fleischer
Belle Sommers (Astron), Elliot Silverstein
The Best of Enemies (Dino De Laurentiis), Guy Hamilton
Cash on Demand (Hammer/Woodpecker), Quentin Lawrence
Damn the Defiant! (G.W. Films), Lewis Gilbert

Don't Knock the Twist (Four Leaf), Oscar Rudolph
Everything's Ducky (Barbroo Enterprises), Don Taylor
Experiment in Terror (Geoffrey-Kate), Blake Edwards
Five Finger Exercise (Sonnis), Daniel Mann
The Hellions (Irving Allen), Ken Annakin
The Interns (Robert Cohn—David Swift), David Swift
Lawrence of Arabia (Horizon), David Lean
Mothra (Toho), Inoshiro Honda
The Notorious Landlady (Kohlmar-Quine), Richard Quine
Only Two Can Play (Vale), Sidney Gilliat
The Pirates of Blood River (Hammer), John Gilling
Requiem for a Heavyweight (Paman), Ralph Nelson
Ring-A-Ding Rhythm (Amicus), Richard Lester
Safe at Home! (Naud-Hamilburg), Walter Doninger
Sail a Crooked Ship (Philip Barry), Irving Brecher
13 West Street (Ladd Enterprises), Philip Leacock
The Three Stooges in Orbit (Normandy), Edward Bernds
The Three Stooges Meet Hercules (Normandy), Edward Bernds
Twist around the Clock (Four Leaf), Oscar Rudolph
Two Tickets to Paris (Harry Romm), Gregg Garrison
The Underwater City (Neptune), Frank McDonald
Walk on the Wild Side (Famous Artists), Edward Dmytryk
The War Lover (Columbia British), Philip Leacock
The Wild Westerners (Four Leaf), Oscar Rudolph
Zotz! (William Castle), William Castle

1963

Bye Bye Birdie (Kohlmar-Sidney), George Sidney
Diamond Head (Jerry Bresler), Guy Green
Fury of the Pagans (Arion), Guido Malatesta
Gidget Goes to Rome (Jerry Bresler), Paul Wendkos
In the French Style (Casanna-Orsay), Robert Parrish
Jason and the Argonauts (Morningside), Don Chaffey
Just for Fun (Amicus), Gordon Fleming
The L-Shaped Room (Romulus Films), Bryan Forbes
The Man from the Diners' Club (Dena-Ampersand), Frank Tashlin
The Maniac (Hammer), Michael Carreras
The Old Dark House (William Castle/Hammer), William Castle
Reach for Glory (Blazer), Philip Leacock
The Reluctant Saint (Dmytryk-Weiler), Edward Dmytryk
The Running Man (Peet), Sir Carol Reed
Siege of the Saxons (Ameran), Nathan Juran
13 Frightened Girls (William Castle), William Castle
The Three Stooges Go Around the World in a Daze (Normandy), Norman Mauer
Under the Yum Yum Tree (Sonnis-Swift), David Swift
The Victors (Highroad/Open Road), Carl Foreman

1964

Behold a Pale Horse (Highland-Brentwood), Fred Zinnemann
The Cardinal (Gamma), Otto Preminger

The Crimson Blade (Hammer), John Gilling
Devil-Ship Pirates (Hammer), Don Sharp
Dr. Strangelove, Or: How I Learned to Stop Worrying and Love the Bomb (Polaris), Stanley Kubrick
East of Sudan (Ameran), Nathan Juran
Fail Safe (Max E. Youngstein), Sidney Lumet
First Men "in" the Moon (Ameran), Nathan Juran
Good Neighbor Sam (David Swift), David Swift
Hey There, It's Yogi Bear (Hanna-Barbera), William Hanna and Joseph Barbera
Lilith (Centaur), Robert Rossen
The Long Ships (Warwick), Jack Cardiff
Lord Jim (Columbia-Keep Films), Richard Brooks
The New Interns (Robert Cohn), John Rich
Psyche 59 (Troy-Schenck), Alexander Singer
The Quick Gun (Admiral Pictures), Sidney Salkow
Ride the Wild Surf (Jana Film Enterprises), Don Taylor
Straight-Jacket (William Castle), William Castle
The Swingin' Maiden (G.H.W.), Gerald Thomas

1965

Arizona Raiders (Admiral), William Whitney
Baby the Rain Must Fall (Park Place/Solar), Robert Mulligan
The Bedford Incident (Bedford Productions), James Harris
Bunny Lake Is Missing (Wheel), Otto Preminger
Cat Ballou (Harold Hecht Corporation), Elliot Silverstein
Code 7, Victim 5 (Tower of London Films), Robert Lynn
The Collector (Collector Company), William Wyler
Curse of the Mummy's Tomb (Hammer/Swallow), Michael Carreras
Die! Die! My Darling! (Hammer/Seven Arts), Silvio Narizzano
The Gorgon (Hammer), Terence Fisher
The Great Sioux Massacre (F. & F.), Sidney Salkow
Harvey Middleman, Fireman (Middleman Company), Ernest Pintoff
King Rat (Coleytown), Bryan Forbes
Love Has Many Faces (Jerry Bresler), Alexander Singer
Major Dundee (Jerry Bresler), Sam Peckinpah
Mickey One (Florin-Tatira), Arthur Penn
The Outlaws Is Coming (Normandy), Norman Mauer
Ship of Fools, Stanley Kramer
Synanon (Richard Quine Productions), Richard Quine
These Are the Damned (Hammer/Swallow), Joseph Losey
The Trouble with Angels (William Frye), Ida Lupino
Winter A-Go-Go (R.C.), Richard Benedict
You Must Be Joking (Ameran), Michael Winner

1966

Alvarez Kelly (Ray David), Edward Dmytryk
Birds Do It (Ivan Tors Enterprises), Andrew Marton
Born Free (Open Road/Atlas), James Hill

The Brigand of Kandahar (Hammer), John Gilling
The Chase (Lone Star Pictures/Horizon), Arthur Penn
Dead Heat on a Merry-Go-Round (Crescent), Bernard Girard
The Desperado Trail (Rialto/Jadran), Harald Reinl
Frontier Hellcat (Rialto/Atlantis/S.N.C./Jadran), Alfred Vohrer
Georgy Girl (Everglades), Silvio Narizzano
The Heroes of Telemark (Benton), Anthony Mann
Kiss the Girls and Make Them Die (Dino De Laurentiis), Henry Levin
Life at the Top (Romulus), Ted Kotcheff
Lost Command (Red Lion), Mark Robson
The Man Called Flintstone (Hanna-Barbera), Joseph Barbera and William
   Hanna
A Man for All Seasons (Highland), Fred Zinneman
Murderers' Row (Meadway-Claude), Henry Levin
The Professionals (Pax Enterprises), Richard Brooks
Rage (Cinematografica Jalisco/Schenck), Gilberto Gazcon
Rampage at Apache Wells (Rialto/Jadran), Harald Philipp
Ride beyond Vengeance (Tiger Company/Sentinal Films/Fenady Associates),
   Bernard McEveety
Rings around the World (Caam), Gilbert Cates
The Silencers (Meadway-Claude), Phil Karlson
The Texican (M.C.R.), Leslie Selander
Three on a Couch (Jerry Lewis), Jerry Lewis
Traitor's Gate (Summit/Rialto), Freddie Francis
Walk, Don't Run (Granley Company), Charles Walters
The Wrong Box (Salamander), Bryan Forbes

1967

The Ambushers (Meadway-Claude), Henry Levin
Berserk (Herman Cohen), Jim O'Connolly
The Big Mouth (Jerry Lewis), Jerry Lewis
Casino Royale (Famous Artists), Val Guest, Ken Hughes, John Huston, Joe
   McGrath, Robert Parrish
A Dandy in Aspic (Columbia British), Anthony Mann
The Deadly Affair (Sidney Lumet), Sidney Lumet
Divorce American Style (National General/Tandem), Bud Yorkin
Dr. Faustus (Oxford University Screen Productions/Nassau Films/Venfilms),
   Richard Burton
Enter Laughing (Acre-Sajo), Carl Reiner
40 Guns to Apache Pass (Admiral), William Whitney
Good Times (Motion Pictures International), William Friedkin
Guess Who's Coming to Dinner, Stanley Kramer
The Happening (Horizon Dover), Elliot Silverstein
In Cold Blood (Pax), Richard Brooks
The Love-Ins (Four Leaf), Arthur Dreifuss
Luv (Manulis-Jalem), Clive Donner
The Night of the Generals (Horizon/Filmsonor), Anatole Litvak
The Taming of the Shrew (Royal Films/F.A.I.), Franco Zeffirelli
30 Is a Dangerous Age, Cynthia (Walter Shenson Films), Joe McGrath

The Tiger Makes Out (Elan), Arthur Hiller
A Time for Killing (Sage Western Pictures), Phil Karlson
Torture Garden (Amicus), Freddie Francis
To Sir, with Love (Columbia British), James Clavell
Where Angels Go . . . Trouble Follows (William Frye), James Neilson
Who's Minding the Mint? (Norman Mauer), Howard Morris
Young Americans (Young Americans, Inc.), Alex Grasshoff

1968

Anzio (Dino De Laurentiis), Edward Dmytryk
Assignment K (Gildor Films/Mazurka), Val Guest
Don't Raise the Bridge, Lower the River (Walter Shenson), Jerry Paris
Duffy (Columbia British), Robert Parrish
For Singles Only (Four Leaf), Arthur Dreifuss
Funny Girl (Rastar), William Wyler
Hammerhead (Irving Allen), David Miller
Head (Raybert), Bob Rafelson
Interlude (Domino), Kevin Billington
Oliver! (Warwick/Romulus), Sir Carol Reed
The Swimmer (Horizon Dover), Frank Perry

1969

Before Winter Comes (Windward), J. Lee Thompson
Bob & Carol & Ted & Alice (Frankovich/Coriander), Paul Mazursky
Cactus Flower (Frankovich), Gene Saks
Castle Keep (Filmways), Sydney Pollack
The Comic (Acre Enterprises), Carl Reiner
Corruption (Titan International/Oakshire), Robert Hartford-Davis
The Desperadoes (Meadway), Henry Levin
Easy Rider (Woodfall/Raybert/Pando), Dennis Hopper
Hamlet (Filmways), Tony Richardson
Hook, Line and Sinker (Jerry Lewis), George Marshall
Land Raiders (Morningside), Nathan Juran
Lock Up Your Daughters (Domino), Peter Coe
The Mad Room (Norman Mauer), Bernard Girard
MacKenna's Gold (Highroad), J. Lee Thompson
Marooned (Frankovich), John Sturges
Model Shop, Jacques Demy
Otley (Open Road/Bruce Cohn Curtis Films/Highroad), Dick Clement
Payment in Blood (Circus Film/Fono Roma), E.G. Rowland
Pendulum (Pendulum Productions), George Schaefer
Run Wild, Run Free (Irving Allen), Dick Sarafian
The Southern Star (Euro France/Capitole/Columbia British), Sidney Hayers
Thank You All Very Much (Palomar Pictures/Amicus), Waris Hussein
The Wrecking Crew (Meadway-Claude), Phil Karlson

1970

Age of Consent (Nautilus), Michael Powell
Cromwell (Irving Allen), Ken Hughes
The Executioner (Ameran), Sam Wanamaker
Five Easy Pieces (BBS), Bob Rafelson
Getting Straight (The Organization), Richard Rush
Husbands (Faces Music, Inc.), John Cassavetes
I Never Sang for My Father (Jamel), Gilbert Cates
Investigation of a Citizen above Suspicion (Vera), Elio Petri
I Walk the Line (John Frankenheimer/Edward Lewis/Halcyon/Atticus), John
   Frankenheimer
The Lady in the Car with Glasses and a Gun (Lira/Columbia), Anatole Litvak
The Liberation of L.B. Jones (The Liberation Company), William Wyler
The Looking Glass War (Frankovich), Frank Pierson
Loving (Columbia/Brooks Productions), Irvin Kershner
The Man with Connections (Columbia/Renn), Claude Berri
The Mind of Mr. Soames (Amicus), Alan Cooke
The Owl and the Pussycat (Rastar), Herbert Ross
Riverrun (Korty Films), John Korty
R.P.M., Stanley Kramer
There's a Girl in My Soup (Frankovich), Roy Boulting
The Things of Life (Lira/Fida Cinematografica/Sonocam), Claude Sautet
The Virgin Soldiers (Open Road/Highroad), John Dexter
A Walk in the Spring Rain (Pingree), Guy Green
Watermelon Man (Johanna), Melvin Van Peebles
You Can't Win 'Em All (S.R.O.), Peter Collinson

1971

The Alf Garnett Saga (Associated London), Bob Kellett
The Anderson Tapes (Robert M. Weitman), Sidney Lumet
Bless the Beasts and Children, Stanley Kramer
Brian's Song (Screen Gems), Buzz Kulik
The Brotherhood of Satan (First LQJ Corporation), Bernard McEveety
Brother John (E and R Productions), James Goldstone
The Buttercup Chain (Columbia British), Robert Ellis Miller
Cisco Pike (Acrobat Films), William Norton
Creatures the World Forgot (Hammer), Don Chaffey
Doctors' Wives (Frankovich), George Schaefer
$ (Frankovich-Pax), Richard Brooks
Drive, He Said (BBS), Jack Nicholson
Flight of the Doves (Rainbow), Ralph Nelson
Fools' Parade (Penbar/Stanmore), Andrew McLaglen
Fragment of Fear (Columbia British), Dick Sarafian
Glass Houses (Magellan), Alexander Singer
The Go-Between (World Film Services), Joseph Losey
Happy Birthday, Wanda June (Filmmakers–Red Lion–Sourdough), Mark
   Robson
The Horsemen (John Frankenheimer–Edward Lewis), John Frankenheimer

J.W. Coop (Robertson & Associates), Cliff Robertson
The Last Picture Show (BBS), Peter Bogdanovich
The Last Rebel (Orten Associates), Denys McCoy
The Love Machine (Frankovich), Jack Haley, Jr.
Macbeth (Caliban Films–Playboy), Roman Polanski
A Man Called Sledge (Dino De Laurentiis), Vic Morrow
Nicholas and Alexandra (Horizon), Franklin Schaffner
The Pursuit of Happiness (Paman), Robert Mulligan
The Reckoning (Columbia British), Jack Gold
A Safe Place (BBS), Henry Jaglom
Saturday Morning (Dimension Films), Kent Mackenzie
See No Evil (Genesis), Richard Fleischer
A Severed Head (Winkast), Dick Clement
Summertree (Bryna), Anthony Newley
Take a Girl Like You (Albion Films), Jonathan Miller
10 Rillington Place (Genesis), Richard Fleischer
Welcome to the Club (Walter Shenson), Walter Shenson

1972

And Now for Something Completely Different (Kettledrum Lownes), Ian
    MacNaughton
Black Gun (World), Robert Hartford-Davis
Buck and the Preacher (E & R and Belafonte Enterprises), Sidney Poitier
The Burglar (Columbia-Vides Cinematografica), Henri Verneuil
Butterflies Are Free (Frankovich), Milton Katselas
The Creeping Flesh Superstars (World), Freddie Francis
A Day in the Death of Joe Egg (Domino), Peter Medak
Dirty Little Billy (Jack Warner & WRG/Dragoti), Stan Dragoti
Fat City (Rastar), John Huston
Gumshoe (Memorial Enterprises), Stephen Frears
Images (Hemdale & Lion's Gate), Robert Altman
The King of Marvin Gardens (BBS), Bob Rafelson
Living Free (Open Road), Jack Couffer
Love and Pain and the whole damn thing (Gus Productions), Alan J. Pakula
The National Health (Virgin), Jack Gold
The New Centurions (Chartoff-Winkler), Richard Fleischer
Pope Joan (Command & Triple Eight Corporation), Michael Anderson
1776 (Jack L. Warner), Peter Hunt
Shamus (Robert M. Weitman), Buzz Kulik
Stand Up and Be Counted (Frankovich), Jackie Cooper
To Find a Man (Rastar), Buzz Kulik
The Valachi Papers (De Laurentiis), Terence Young
X, Y and Zee (Zee Films), Brian Hutton
Young Winston (Open Road), Richard Attenborough

1973

Forty Carats (Frankovich), Milton Katselas
Godspell (Lansbury/Duncan), David Greene

The Hireling (World), Alan Bridges
The Last Detail (Acrobat), Hal Ashby
Let the Good Times Roll (Metromedia Producers Corporation), Sid Levin and
  Bob Abel
Lost Horizon (Ross Hunter), Charles Jarrott
Oklahoma Crude, Stanley Kramer
A Reflection of Fear (Howard B. Jaffe), William Fraker
The Stone Killer (De Laurentiis), Michael Winner
Summer Wishes, Winter Dreams (Rastar), Gilbert Cates
Wattsax (Wolper Pictures), Mel Stuart
The Way We Were (Rastar), Sydney Pollack

1974

Buster and Billie (Ron Silverman), Daniel Petrie
California Split, Robert Altman
Chosen Survivors (Metromedia Producers/Alpine/Churubusco), Sutton Roley
Confessions of a Window Cleaner, Val Guest
Crazy Joe (Dino De Laurentiis), Carlo Lizzani
For Pete's Sake (Rastar), Peter Yates
The Golden Voyage of Sinbad (Schneer-Harryhausen), Gordon Hessler
The Gravy Train (Tomorrow Entertainment), Jack Starrett
Law and Disorder (Memorial/Leroy Street/Ugo/Fadsin), Ivan Passer
Lightning Swords of Death (Katzu), Kenji Misumi
The Lords of Flatbush, Stephen F. Verona and Martin Davidson
Lovin' Molly (Stephen Friedman), Sidney Lumet
The Mutations (Getty), Jack Cardiff
The Odessa File, Ronald Neame
Open Season (Impala/Arpa), Peter Collinson
The Take (World Film Services), Robert Hartford-Davis
Thomasine and Bushrod (Bernstein-Julien), Gordon Parks, Jr.

1975

Aaron Loves Angela, Gordon Parks, Jr.
Aloha, Bobby and Rose (Cine Artists International), Floyd Mutrux
Bite the Bullet (Persky-Bright/Vista), Richard Brooks
The Black Bird (Rastar), David Giler
Breakout (Chartoff/Winkler), Tom Gries
The Fortune, Mike Nichols
Funny Lady (Rastar), Herbert Ross
Hard Times, Walter Hill
Lies My Father Told Me (Pentimento/Pentacle VIII), Jan Kadar
Shampoo, Hal Ashby
Stardust (Nat Cohen/EMI/Good Times Enterprises), Michael Apted
The Stepford Wives (Fadsin/Cinema Associates), Bryan Forbes
Tommy (Robert Stigwood), Ken Russell
White Line Fever (International Cinemedia Center), Jonathan Kaplan

1976

Baby Blue Marine (Spelling-Goldberg), John Hancock
Countown at Kunisi (DST Telecommunications), Ossie Davis
Drive-In, Rod Armateau
The Front (Persky-Bright/Devon), Martin Ritt
Harry and Walter Go to New York, Mark Rydell
Murder by Death (Rastar), Robert Moore
Nickelodeon (Chartoff/Winkler), Peter Bogdanovich
Obsession (Litto/Blum), Brian DePalma
Robin and Marian (Ray Stark/Richard Shepherd), Richard Lester
Shadow of the Hawk (International Cinemedia Center), George McCowan
Taxi Driver (Bill/Phillips), Martin Scorsese

1977

Amsterdam Kill (Golden Harvest), Robert Clouse
Bobby Deerfield (Columbia-Warners), Sydney Pollack
Close Encounters of the Third Kind (Julia and Michael Phillips/Columbia-EMI),
    Steven Spielberg
The Deep (Columbia-EMI), Peter Yates
The Eagle Has Landed (Associated General), John Sturges
The Farmer (Milway), David Berlatsky
Fun with Dick and Jane (Bart/Palevsky), Ted Kotcheff
The Greatest (Columbia-EMI), Tom Gries
March or Die (ITC Entertainment/Associated General), Dick Richards
The Silver Bears (Winitsky-Sellers), Ivan Passer
Sinbad and the Eye of the Tiger (Schneer-Harryhausen), Sam Wanamaker
You Light Up My Life, Joseph Brooks

1978

The Boys in Company C (Golden Harvest), Sidney Furie
The Buddy Holly Story (Innovisions/ECA), Steve Rash
California Suite (Rastar), Herbert Ross
Casey's Shadow (Rastar), Martin Ritt
The Cheap Detective (Rastar), Robert Moore
The Eyes of Laura Mars (Jon Peters), Irvin Kershner
If Ever I See You Again, Joseph Brooks
Midnight Express (Casablanca Filmworks), Alan Parker
Remember My Name (Lion's Gate), Alan Rudolph
Somebody Killed Her Husband (Martin Poll/Melvin Simon), Lamont Johnson
Thank God It's Friday (Casablanca Filmworks), Robert Klane
Warlords of Atlantis (EMI), Kevin Connor

1979

All That Jazz (Columbia/Fox), Bob Fosse
The American Success Company (Scherick/Blatt), William Richert
. . . And Justice for All (Jewison/Palmer), Norman Jewison

Chapter Two (Rastar), Robert Moore
The China Syndrome (Michael Douglas/IPC), James Bridges
The Electric Horseman (Ray Stark/Wildwood), Sydney Pollack
Fast Break (Stephen Friedman/Kings Road), Jack Smight
The Fifth Musketeer (Sascha-Wien/Ted Richmond), Ken Annakin
Game of Death (Raymond Chow), Robert Clouse
Hanover Street (Lazarus/Hyams), Peter Hyams
Hardcore (A-Team), Paul Schrader
Hot Stuff (Rastar/Mort Engelberg), Dom DeLuise
Ice Castles (International Cinemedia), Donald Wrye
Just You and Me, Kid (Fein/Zeitman), Leonard Stern
Kramer vs. Kramer (Stanley R. Jaffe), Robert Benton
Lost and Found (Koppelson's Film Packages), Melvin Frank
Nightwing (Martin Ransohoff), Arthur Hiller
The Ravagers, Richard Compton
Skatetown U.S.A. (Rastar), William A. Levey
The Villain (Rastar/Engelberg), Hal Needham
When A Stranger Calls (Melvin Simon), Fred Walton
When You Comin' Back, Red Ryder? (Melvin Simon), Milton Katselas

1980

The Blue Lagoon, Randal Kleiser
The Competition (Rastar/William Sackheim), Joel Oliansky
Foolin' Around (Koppelson's Film Packages), Richard T. Heffron
Gloria, John Cassavetes
The Hollywood Knights (Polygram), Floyd Mutrux
It's My Turn (Rastar/Martin Elfand), Claudia Weill
The Mountain Men (Martin Ransohoff), Richard Lang
Night of the Juggler (Koppelson's Film Packages), Robert Butler
Seems Like Old Times (Rastar), Jay Sandrich
Stir Crazy (Hannah Weinstein), Sidney Poitier
Touched by Love (Columbia/Rastar), Gus Trikonis
Used Cars, Robert Zemeckis
Wholly Moses! (Begelman/Fields), Gary Weis

1981

Absence of Malice (Mirage), Sydney Pollack
American Pop (Martin Ransohoff), Ralph Bakshi
Cheech and Chong's Nice Dreams (C & C Brown), Thomas Chong
Das Boot (Bavaria Atelier/Radiant), Wolfgang Petersen
Happy Birthday to Me (Birthday Films/CFC/Famous Players), J. Lee Thompson
Heavy Metal (Reitman-Mogel), Gerald Potterton
Modern Romance, Albert Brooks
Neighbors (Zanuck-Brown), John G. Avildsen
Nobody's Perfekt (Rastar), Peter Bonerz
Only When I Laugh, Glenn Jordan
Stripes, Ivan Reitman
Tess (Renn/Burrill), Roman Polanski

1982

Annie (Rastar), John Huston
Gandhi (Indo-British/Goldcrest/National-India/International Film Investors),
    Richard Attenborough
Hanky Panky (Martin Ransohoff), Sidney Poitier
The Missionary (Handmade Films), Richard Loncraine
Monty Python Live at the Hollywood Bowl (Handmade), Terry Hughes
One from the Heart (Zoetrope), Francis Coppola
Richard Pryor Live on Sunset Strip (Rastar), Joe Layton
Silent Rage (Unger/Topkick), Michael Miller
Tempest, Paul Mazursky
Things Are Tough All Over (C & C Brown), Tom Avildsen
Tootsie (Mirage/Punch), Sydney Pollack
The Toy (Rastar), Richard Donner
Wrong Is Right (Rastar/Columbia), Richard Brooks

1983

The Big Chill (Carson/Columbia-Delphi*), Lawrence Kasdan
Blue Thunder (Rastar/Gordon Carroll), John Badham
Christine (Columbia-Delphi/Richard Kobritz), John Carpenter
The Dresser (Goldcrest/World Film Services), Peter Yates
Educating Rita (Acorn), Lewis Gilbert
Krull (Mann-Silverman), Peter Yates
The Man Who Loved Women (Columbia-Delphi), Blake Edwards
Richard Pryor . . . Here and Now, Richard Pryor
Spacehunter: Adventures in the Forbidden Zone (Columbia-Delphi), Lamont
    Johnson
Spring Break (Columbia/Fogbound), Sean S. Cunningham
The Survivors (Delphi/Rastar/William Sackheim), Michael Ritchie
Yor, the Hunter from the Future (Diamant), Anthony M. Dawson

1984

Against All Odds, Taylor Hackford
Body Double (Columbia-Delphi II), Brian DePalma
Ghostbusters (Black Rhino/Bernie Brillstein), Ivan Reitman
Hardbodies (Chroma III), Mark Griffith
The Karate Kid (Jerry Weintraub), John G. Avildsen
Micki and Maude (Columbia-Delphi III/B.E.E.), Blake Edwards
Moscow on the Hudson (Columbia-Delphi), Paul Mazursky
No Small Affair (William Sackheim/Columbia-Delphi II), Jerry Schatzberg
A Passage to India (Thorn/EMI/Columbia), David Lean
The Razor's Edge (Marucci-Cohn-Benn/Columbia-Delphi), John Byrum
Sheena, Queen of the Jungle (Columbia-Delphi II), John Guillerman
A Soldier's Story (Caldix Films), Norman Jewison
Starman (Columbia-Delphi II/Douglas/Franco), John Carpenter

*Delphi Film Associates was a limited partnership offering that Columbia formed in 1984
to finance and market certain films.

1985

Agnes of God (Columbia-Delphi IV), Norman Jewison
The Bride (Columbia-Delphi III), Franc Roddam
A Chorus Line (Embassy/Polygram/Columbia), Richard Attenborough
Fast Forward (Verdon-Cedric), Sidney Poitier
Fright Night (Vistar), Tom Holland
Jagged Edge (Martin Ransohoff), Richard Marquand
Just One of the Guys (Summa Entertainment Group/Triton), Lisa Gottlieb
The New Kids (Columbia/Fogbound), Sean S. Cunningham
Perfect (Columbia-Delphi III), James Bridges
St. Elmo's Fire (Columbia-Delphi IV/Channel/Shuler), Joel Schumacher
Silverado (Columbia-Delphi IV), Lawrence Kasdan
The Slugger's Wife (Columbia-Delphi II/Ray Stark), Hal Ashby
Sylvester (Rastar), Tim Hunter
White Nights (New Visions/Columbia-Delphi V), Taylor Hackford

1986

Armed and Dangerous (Grazer/Keach/Frostbacks), Mark L. Lester
The Big Easy (Kings Road), Jim McBride
Big Trouble (Columbia-Delphi III), John Cassavetes
Care Bears Movie, II: A New Generation (Nelvana), Dale Schott
Crossroads (Columbia-Delphi IV), Walter Hill
Desert Bloom (Carson/Sundance Institute/Columbia-Delphi IV), Eugene Corr
A Fine Mess (B.E.E./Columbia-Delphi V), Blake Edwards
Jo Jo Dancer, Your Life Is Calling, Richard Pryor
The Karate Kid: Part II (Jerry Weintraub), John G. Avildsen
Murphy's Romance (Fogwood), Martin Ritt
One More Saturday Night (AAR/Tova Laiter), Dennis Klein
Out of Bounds (Fries Entertainment/Columbia-Delphi V), Richard Tuggle
Quicksilver (IndieProd/Columbia-Delphi IV), Tom Donnelly
Stand by Me (Act III), Rob Reiner
That's Life (Blake Edwards Company), Blake Edwards
Violets Are Blue (Rastar/Columbia-Delphi IV), Jack Fisk

1987

The Big Town (Martin Ransohoff), Ben Bolt
84 Charing Cross Road (Brooksfilms), David Jones
Happy New Year (Jerry Weintraub), John G. Avildsen
Hope and Glory (Nelson/Goldcrest), John Boorman
Housekeeping, Bill Forsyth
Ishtar (Columbia-Delphi V), Elaine May
La Bamba (New Visions), Luis Valdez
The Last Emperor (Hemdale), Bernardo Bertolucci
Leonard Part 6 (SAH Enterprises), Paul Weiland
Roxanne (IndieProd/LA Films), Fred Schepisi
Someone to Watch over Me (Thierry de Ganay), Ridley Scott

White Water Summer (Polar Entertainment/Nippon Film Enterprises), Jeff Bleckner

1988

The Beast (A & M Films), Kevin Reynolds
The Big Blue (WEG/Gaumont), Luc Beeson
Fresh Horses (WEG), David Anspaugh
Little Nikita (Harry Gittes), Richard Benjamin
The New Adventures of Pippi Longstocking (Longstocking Productions), Ken Annakin
Pulse (Aspen Film Society), Paul Golding
Punchline (Fogwood/IndieProd), David Seltzer
Rocket Gibraltar (Ulick Mayo Weiss), Daniel Petrie
School Daze (Forty Acres and a Mule Filmworks), Spike Lee
Stars and Bars, Pat O'Connor
Things Change (Filmhaus), David Mamet
A Time of Destiny (Alive), Gregory Nava
Vibes (Imagine Entertainment), Ken Kwapis
Vice Versa (Clement/La Frenais), Brian Gilbert
White Mischief (Nelson/Goldcrest), Michael Radford
Zelly and Me (Cypress & Mark/Jett), Tina Rathborne

1989

The Adventures of Baron Munchausen (Prominent Features/Laura), Terry Gilliam
The Adventures of Milo and Otis (Fujisankei Communications), Masanori Hata
The Big Picture (Aspen Film Society), Christopher Guest
Bloodhounds of Broadway (American Playhouse Theatrical Films), Howard Brookner
Casualties of War, Brian DePalma
Eat a Bowl of Tea (American Playhouse Theatrical Films), Wayne Wang
Ghostbusters II, Ivan Reitman
Hanussen (CCC, Berlin/ZDF/Hungaro Film/Malfilm), Istvan Szabo
Immediate Family (Sanford/Pillsbury), Jonathan Kaplan
The Karate Kid: Part III (Jerry Weintraub), John G. Avildsen
Me & Him (Neue Constantin Film), Doris Dörie
Old Gringo, Luiz Puenzo
Physical Evidence (Martin Ransohoff), Michael Crichton
Revenge (Rastar), Tony Scott
She's Out of Control (WEG), Stan Dragoti
Time of the Gypsies (Forum [Sarajevo]), Emir Kusturica
To Kill a Priest (J.P. Productions/AMLF), Agnieszka Holland
True Believer (TBP Inc.), Joseph Ruben
Welcome Home (Albacore), Franklin J. Schaffner
When Harry Met Sally . . . (Castle Rock/Nelson), Rob Reiner
Winter People (Castle Rock/Nelson), Ted Kotcheff

1990

Awakenings (Lasker/Parkes), Penny Marshall
The Fifth Monkey (21st Century), Eric Rochat
Flatliners (Stonebridge), Joel Schumacher
The Forbidden Dance (21st Century), Greydon Clark
The Gods Must Be Crazy 2 (WEG), Jamie Uys
Lord of the Files (Castle Rock/Nelson), Harry Hook
Misery (Castle Rock/Nelson), Rob Reiner
Night of the Living Dead (21st Century), Tom Savini
Postcards from the Edge, Mike Nichols
Sibling Rivalry (Castle Rock/Nelson), Carl Reiner
Texasville (Nelson/Cine-Source), Peter Bogdanovich

1991

Boyz N the Hood (Indie), John Singleton
City Slickers (Castle Rock/Nelson), Ron Underwood
Double Impact (Stone Group), Sheldon Lettich
Falling from Grace (Little b Pictures), John Mellencamp
The Gladiator, Rowdy Herrington
Hard Promises (Stone Group/High Horse), Martin Davidson
The Inner Circle (Columbia-Mosfilm), Andrei Konchalovsky
Late for Dinner (Castle Rock), W.D. Richter
Men of Respect (Central City/Arthur Goldblatt), William Reilly
Mortal Thoughts (New Visions), Alan Rudolph
My Girl (Imagine), Howard Zieff
Prime Suspect (Carnival Films), Simon Moore
The Prince of Tides (Barwood/Longfellow), Barbra Streisand
Radio Flyer (Shuler-Donner/Stonebridge), Richard Donner
Return to the Blue Lagoon (Price Entertainment), William A. Graham
The Spirit of 76 (Commercial Pictures), Lucas Reiner
Stone Cold (Stone Group), Craig R. Baxley

CONTRIBUTORS

Jeanine Basinger is Corwin-Fuller Professor of Film Studies at Wesleyan University and curator of the Wesleyan Cinema Archives. Her books include *Anthony Mann*, *The* It's a Wonderful Life *Book*, and *Anatomy of a Genre: World War II Combat Films*.

Joy Gould Boyum is professor of communication arts at New York University. Her articles and reviews have appeared in the *Wall Street Journal*, *Newsday*, and *English Journal*; she is also the author of *Film as Film: Critical Approaches to Film Art* and *Double Exposure: Fiction into Film*.

Sybil DelGaudio is assistant professor of communication arts at Hofstra University and also teaches film at the New School. She has been published in *Jump Cut* and has recently completed a book on costume in the films of Josef von Sternberg.

Bernard F. Dick is professor of English and comparative literature at Fairleigh Dickinson University (Teaneck Campus). In addition to books on Billy Wilder, Lillian Hellman, and Joseph L. Mankiewicz, he has also written *The Star-Spangled Screen: The American World War II Film* and *Radical Innocence: A Critical Study of the Hollywood Ten*.

Les Keyser, professor of English at the College of Staten Island of the City University of New York, is the author of *Hollywood in the Seventies*, *Hollywood and the Catholic Church* (with Barbara Keyser), and *The Cinema of Sidney Poitier* (with André Ruszkowski).

Charles Maland is professor of English and American Studies at the University of Tennessee. He is the author of *American Visions: The Films of Chaplin, Ford, Capra, and Welles, 1936-1941*; *Frank Capra*; and *Chaplin and American Culture: The Evolution of a Star Image*, which won the 1990 Theatre Library Association Award.

Janice Mouton teaches European film in the Department of Modern Languages and Literature at Loyola Universiy of Chicago. She is currently working on a study of European women filmmakers and has published in such journals as *Jump Cut*, the *Germanic Review*, and *Literature/Film Quarterly*.

Gene D. Phillips, professor of English at Loyola University of Chicago, is the author of such books as *Graham Greene: The Films of His Fiction*; *Fiction, Film, and F. Scott Fitzgerald*; *George Cukor*; *John Schlesinger*;

Alfred Hitchcock; Fiction, Film, and Faulkner: The Art of Adaptation; and *Major Film Directors of the American and British Cinema.*

Ruth Prigozy is professor of English at Hofstra University. Currently at work on a study of Billy Wilder, she is coauthor of *Writing for Business: A Case Approach.* Her articles and reviews have appeared in *Commonweal, Twentieth Century Literature, Literature/Film Quarterly,* and the *Fitzgerald/Hemingway Annual.*

Adam J. Sorkin is associate professor of English at Penn State Delaware County Campus. He has written on American culture and the Cold War, published translations of contemporary Romanian poetry, and is the editor of *Politics and the Muse: Studies in the Politics of Recent American Literature.*

Daniel Taradash won an Oscar for his adaptation of *From Here to Eternity.* His other screenplays include *Golden Boy, Knock on any Door, Storm Center, Picnic,* and *Bell, Book and Candle.*

J.P. Telotte is professor of literature, communication, and culture at the Georgia Institute of Technology. He is the author of *Dreams of Darkness: Fantasy and the Films of Val Lewton* and *Voices in the Dark: The Narrative Patterns of Film Noir;* he is also coeditor of *Post Script.*

William Vincent is professor of film at Michigan State University, where he teaches courses in Hitchcock, Fellini, and the musical.

Jim Welsh is associate professor of English at Salisbury State University and the editor of *Literature/Film Quarterly.* His publications on film and drama have appeared in *Comparative Drama, Shakespeare Quarterly, Film Comment, Cinema Journal,* and *Film Criticism;* his books include *Abel Gance* and *Peter Watkins: A Guide to References and Resources.*

INDEX